Contending Economic Theories: Neoclassical, Keynesian, and Marxian

T0333948

Richard D. Wolff and Stephen A. Resnick

The MIT Press
Cambridge, Massachusetts
London, England

This book was set in Times Roman by Toppan Best-set Premedia Limited. Printed and bound in the United States of America.

Library of Congress Cataloging-in-Publication Data

Wolff, Richard D.
Contending economic theories : neoclassical, Keynesian, and Marxian / Richard D. Wolff and Stephen A. Resnick.
    p.   cm.
Rev. ed. of: Economics : Marxian versus neoclassical. Baltimore : Johns Hopkins University Press, c1987.
Includes bibliographical references and index.
ISBN 978-0-262-01800-5 (hbk. : alk. paper) – ISBN 978-0-262-51783-6 (pbk. : alk. paper)
1. Comparative economics. 2. Economics. 3. Marxian economics. 4. Neoclassical school of economics. 5. Keynesian economics. 6. Schools of economics. I. Resnick, Stephen A. II. Wolff, Richard D. Economics. III. Title.
HB90.W65   2012
330.15–dc23
2012004562

10   9   8

Contending Economic Theories

Contents

Detailed Table of Contents

To Our Readers

Our previous and far less ambitious version of this book, *Economics: Marxian versus Neoclassical* was well-received and quite widely used in colleges and universities since its publication in 1987. That success flowed, we believe, from that book's two broad goals and the extent of their achievement. First, we sought to produce an introduction to Marxian economics that would include and build upon several of the major analytical breakthroughs in that tradition during the last thirty-five years. Second, we wanted to formulate that introduction in a systematic relation to the neoclassical economic theory prevalent in the United States and elsewhere. Having long taught introductory economics courses, we had learned that presenting Marxian theory through a sustained and systematic comparison with neoclassical theory is an exceptionally effective method of teaching both.

Many users of our earlier book urged that we produce a new and updated version. They also offered important criticisms. One concerned Keynesian economics: it deserved to be treated alongside neoclassical and Marxian economics by means of systematic comparison. Once the long and deep economic crisis hit the world in 2007, the calls for inclusion of Keynesian economics in a new version of our book became urgent. Critiques of neoclassical economics and renewed interest in Keynesian and Marxian economics have been spreading globally now for years. Because of the rising demand for a book that presents and compares these three major paradigms and because none currently exists, we transformed, enlarged and elaborated our earlier book to meet that demand in this one.

This new book sets forth neoclassical and Keynesian economics, each developed and discussed in its own chapter, yet also differentiated from and compared to the other. To do so, we extended our humanism versus structuralism grid for differentiating economic theories to explain the tensions and oppositions between them. We connect the comparative theory analysis to the larger policy issues that divide the two camps of theorists around the central issue of the role government should play in the economy and society.

In treating Keynesian economics in a separate chapter, we emphasize Keynes's notion of radical uncertainty as it impacts the individual business investor and thereby provides an explanation for the business cycle. In showing how Keynes's structuralist economics displays an individualist (humanist) moment, we offer a new way too see the crucial similarities and differences between the Keynesian and the contending neoclassical theoretical arguments.

Readers of our earlier book also asked us to analyze recent extensions and developments of neoclassical economics (around such topics as market imperfections, information economics, new theories of equilibrium, behavioral economics, etc.). We treat these new developments in neoclassical economics in a new chapter 5. With this chapter's co-author, Yahya Madra, we raise a fundamental question: Does this body of work break from the neoclassical economic tradition? Is it a different paradigm in the sense we apply to both Keynesian economics and Marxian economics? Chapter 5 extends our comparative approach to contested economic theories to answer this question.

Based on our many years of teaching experience since the earlier book's 1987 publication and also on the changed conditions of contemporary economies (including the post 2007 global crisis), we have produced a thoroughly revised introduction chapter. It now foregrounds a central theme of this new book: that the contesting theories and their relative social prominence are both effects and causes of the social conditions in which they occur. Chapter 1 presents a sustained historical examination of how various forms and paradigms of economic thinking react back upon the society out of which they are born. We hope that this revised chapter will provide readers with a better understanding of the complex social causes of these theories and why they and their differences matter so much to the lives of citizens.

The many years of deepening hostilities between advocates of more and less government economic intervention led us to write an altogether new chapter 6. There we identify and discuss two interrelated kinds of oscillations that occur in society: (1) movements among the social predominance of one versus another economic theory, and (2) movements among alternative forms of capitalist economies themselves. We show that capitalism always varies: its shifting forms display more or less free markets; more or less private property; more or less personal freedoms. We also show why these kinds or forms of capitalism are different from socialism and communism. We hope this explanation will provide a new view of the major economic changes and conflicts across the twentieth century and why they matter to those already underway shaping the twenty-first century. Similarly we show that economic theory always varies and is always contested. It too oscillates from one to another approach and then back again. Neoclassical gives way to Keynesian economics and the latter to the neoclassical dominance again. Sometimes Marxism appears as the other in this movement between different theories. Chapter 6 explores these oscillations in society and theory and their interconnections.

This book also introduces readers to major new developments inside Marxian economics since the 1980s. These are integrated into the chapter 4's focus on what that paradigm of economics offers in comparison to the insights produced via neoclassical and Keynesian analytics. Chapter 4 assumes little or no familiarity with the subject. It proceeds from first principles through basic analytics to various applications. Since the Marxian economics tradition includes several distinct theories, we identify the particular theory that we have found most convincing and that we therefore present here. However, in this chapter and throughout the book we also try to distinguish the Marxism we present from the more traditional or orthodox Marxism that arose after Marx died and became dominant in the former USSR.

Similarly the overviews of neoclassical economics in chapter 2 and Keynesian economics in chapter 3 offer respectively a basic grounding in neoclassical micro- and Keynesian macroeconomics. We treat both as distinct and often contested theories rather than presenting "economics" as reducible to a set of neutral tools to solve economic problems in the so-called real world. Readers will see how each theory differently constructs its economic world including those problems it recognizes as such and for which it finds unique policies and solutions. These differences yield the debates over contested economics and policies (taxes, government spending, market controls, nationalizations of property, etc.) that profoundly impact our lives.

This new book is directed especially to readers interested in comparing and contrasting different ways of understanding the economy and why those differences matter so profoundly. For college and university teaching purposes, the book serves both introductory and more advanced courses. As a supplementary reading, it can usefully accompany courses at all levels (including introductory economics) where instructors wish to introduce students to alternative approaches or merely to sharpen students' grasp of neoclassical and Keynesian theories by comparing them with Marxian theory. Finally, for courses across the social sciences generally, this book introduces economics as a contested terrain struggling with its own disagreements and alternative visions as do most other self-conscious disciplines. The book clearly dissents from any notion of economics as a technical or mechanical profession.

Throughout the book, but especially in the first, fourth, and seventh chapters, important philosophical issues are addressed as they pertain to a comparison of economic theories. Recent work in epistemology is briefly and summarily raised to ground our method for comparing economic theories. We discuss verification and validity to address the important problem necessarily posed by such comparative endeavors—namely how to assess and decide among the competing claims and analyses offered by different economic theories. Consistent with the book's method throughout, we explain that theoretical differences in economics are matched by theoretical differences within philosophy, including the epistemological issue of how to decide among alternative theories.

This book's particular method of comparing and contrasting different economic theories is a useful analytical tool to compare still other forms of thinking. What we describe here as each theory's distinguishing entry-point concepts, logic, produced objects, and social consequences are generally applicable indices of difference among theories. Readers are presented with a concrete examination of particular economic theories in terms of how they differ from alternative theories.

In conclusion, this book offers two interdependent formulations that are not, to our knowledge, available elsewhere. First, it presents economics as a discipline in a format of sustained comparison of alternative theories. Modern principles of discourse analysis are applied to the confrontation among Marxian, neoclassical, and Keynesian economic theories. The distinguishing features of these theories are examined in juxtaposition as a method of teaching economics. Second, a Marxian theory is developed systematically, rigorously, and comparatively from its first principles and assumptions through its formal analytics to some of its distinctive applications to social analysis.

Stephen Resnick, my co-author, longtime colleague, and dearest friend died of cancer in January 2013, not long after this book's first printing. He too would have been pleased and gratified by its multiple printings and the contributions to teaching and research it has continued to make. Although Professor Resnick left work unfinished, his lifetime of teaching and writing lives on through his students and all those (like me) whose work benefits so much from his.

Acknowledgments

We wish to thank three individuals who helped us to prepare this revised edition. Alex Coram, a political scientist at the University of Western Australia who often writes on economics especially social choice theory and game theory, read the introductory, neoclassical, and Keynesian chapters and offered extensive comments and criticisms. David Ruccio, an economist at the University of Notre Dame who writes extensively in political economy and post-modern economics, urged us to produce a newer and better version of our earlier text. We thank both of them for their comments and support.

Special thanks go to our co-author of chapter 5. Yahya Madra is an economist at Gettysburg College and currently at Boğaziçi University, Istanbul, Turkey. Yahya helped produce what we think is a unique presentation of "late neoclassical theory" not found elsewhere. Chapter 5 systematically examines recent developments in neoclassical theory to show how they respond to criticisms of that theory and how they extend that theory to new topics in economics and beyond. Neoclassical theory's lively evolution can be read and evaluated in this chapter. We also thank Yahya for his help and guidance in preparing comments on post-Keynesian economics found in chapter 3.

We also wish to express our appreciation to the many teaching assistants who worked with us over the years and to the thousands of students in our introductory micro, macro, and Marxian economics courses. Their reactions to the ideas contained in this book helped to shape it. Finally, we are very aware of the complex overdetermination that shapes our work and want to recognize the profound influences of our spouses and children.

1 Three Different Theories

1.1 This Book and Theories of Economics

This book contrasts three very different and clashing kinds of economics. One is usually called neoclassical (or micro) economics, another Keynesian (or macro), and the third Marxism. Each is a distinct way of understanding how economies work and how they interact with the larger societies around them. In other words, these are three different *theories* about the economic part of society. This book introduces you to all three and to their differences since they compete for our attention as well as shape today's actions of governments, enterprises, unions, and others. In short, these different theories impact our lives in basic ways.

We wrote this book partly because students need to know that there is more to economics than just neoclassical and Keynesian theories. Students deserve to know not only how neoclassical and Keynesian theories differ from one another but how both differ from Marxism. We hope that learning from and about these contending theories will undermine tendencies to dismiss, repress, or even demonize whichever of them are not popular at any particular moment.

Most important, we want to show how understandings based on one theory versus the others will lead individuals, families, enterprises, governments, and societies in very different directions. Right at the start we provide an example to illustrate this important point. It responds to the question: What might be at stake in and for our lives in adopting one as opposed to another economic theory?

Consider any society whose economy is structured by private ownership of enterprises and private markets. The presence of these two institutions is usually referred to as capitalism. Whatever else can be said about capitalism, in actuality it exhibits a profound economic instability or unevenness. Times of economic expansion give way to periods of decline out of which emerge resumed intervals of expansion. Simply put: capitalism displays those ups and downs that economists, politicians, journalists, and others call its business cycles.

The three theories differ in their understandings of the causes, solutions, and the very nature of those cycles. Their differences matter in shaping our lives. We can show this by considering, first, the neoclassical and Keynesian theories and how they view capitalist economies. For both theories, capitalism is—to use a metaphor—a truly wonderful machine. For all its faults, including its uneven motion, it nonetheless remains the best of all comparable machines. Both theories affirm (and usually presume) that capitalism alone can deliver to humans the maximum wealth they are capable of producing. And it delivers this economic bounty on the basis of a profound political right: producers and consumers are free to act in their own individual economic interest. As per Adam Smith's famous "invisible hand," an economy with private property, markets, and freely acting, self-interested buyers and sellers of everything will yield the best economy delivering the most wealth possible (as if a benevolent God Himself were running everything).

From the critical perspective of these two theories, the other possible economic systems that have occurred in human history—including the feudal, slave, individual producer, socialist, and communist—just cannot deliver the same standard of living and/or political freedom. Yet alongside capitalism's wonders, both theories also recognize certain flaws.

Periodically this magical machine runs too fast, then too slow: it cycles. Consequently individuals suffer from illusions of more wealth (as prices of everything rise in periods of inflation) or the reality of less wealth (when unemployment and production cutbacks rise in a recession). Worse, prolonged inflationary or recessionary periods may pose greater risks for society: misallocated or wasted resources, social anger, personal alienation, and political unrest. Out of frustration and desperation, people may turn against capitalism and seek an alternative, noncapitalist way to organize their economy. Across the twentieth century, socialism and communism presented—usually in the terms of Marxist economics—the principle alternatives to capitalism, as solutions for its dysfunctional instability. Neoclassical and Keynesian economics responded by insisting that when compared to capitalism, socialism and communism were economic systems producing less wealth and less individual freedoms. However, both neoclassical and Keynesian economics had to deal with capitalism's instability, its recurring cycles, especially when they were deep (affected millions negatively) and lasted long times, such as the severe recessionary downturn that began in 2007.

The neoclassical and Keynesian theories disagree about how to deal with capitalist cycles. For the neoclassical view and its proponents, the proposed fix for capitalism's instabilities is very simple: leave the machine alone so that it can and will correct itself. The central idea is that the economy-as-machine contains a mechanism that, if allowed to work, will correct periods of inflation and recession. That self-correcting mechanism is the private, competitive market.

The direction in which neoclassical theory points is clear for its followers: very little or even no "outside" (meaning by the state) intervention is necessary to manage (regulate) capitalism's cycles. The market economy will best manage itself if left to its own devices. No matter how well intentioned, external (i.e., state) interventions aimed at managing the economy—for example, by regulating market transactions—will only undermine the market system's otherwise successful self-corrective properties. Believers in the neoclassical theory insist on these points: (1) deregulate markets, (2) always extend existing and create new markets to handle economic problems that arise, and (3) beware the heavy, counterproductive hand of the interventionist state (when it does anything other than to protect free markets).

In direct contrast, believers in Keynesian economics and its policy recommendations want the state to keep a watchful eye on markets, to maintain readiness to intervene to manage the inevitable market imperfections and failures that generate cycles. The Keynesians believe that if not for state intervention, market imperfections, imbalances, and the resulting business cycles could persist too long and cut too deep. For them, the neoclassicists' self-correcting mechanism just does not work as those free-marketers claim or works far too slowly to be of much practical use. Without state intervention, the Keynesians argue, the continued presence either of prolonged inflation or recession could push suffering and frightened citizens to seek the socialist or communist alternatives that both neoclassical and Keynesian theorists reject.

Notice the dramatic difference between the two understandings of the state's role in responding to economic crises and, more generally, to all economic problems. Keynesians look more to the state for the solution to the ups and down in the capitalist economy. They favor state programs to deal with persistent poverty, issues of health care, education, and retirement. In contrast, neoclassical economists prefer the private decisions of individuals and businesses reacting to and taking advantage of market incentives as better means to solve similar problems and issues.

In fact the difference between them is even more complex and interesting, for it reflects deeper oppositions between the two theories' ways of linking individuals (as component parts of society) to society as a whole. We will have more to say on this important opposition, for it will help us explain why neoclassical and Keynesian theories differ about how an economy works and what citizens should do when it doesn't work so well. Even at this point, however, we can begin to understand how these two theories might impact our lives differently, though both advocate capitalism as the preferred economic arrangement.

Different from both neoclassical and Keynesian theories, Marxian economics connects capitalism's cycles and their heavy social costs to another of the economy's components, namely its class structure. Marxian theory is profoundly critical of capitalism because of its class structure and what it sees as the effects of that class structure, including capitalist cycles. Dealing effectively with capitalism's crises, Marxists argue, requires changing its class structure. If capitalism's class structure remains unchanged, they say, then neither more government economic intervention (Keynesian) nor less (neoclassical) will overcome cycles. Marxists point out that countless political leaders influenced by those two theories over the last seventy-five years have promised that their policies will prevent future economic crises in capitalist economies, but that promise has not yet been kept.

As this book will make clear, the Marxian theory goes further in its critique of capitalism. Even in periods when capitalist economies function relatively smoothly, without inflation or recession, it finds capitalism to be neither maximally efficient nor the best available economic system. Marxian theory depicts capitalism as a destructive economic system that exploits labor and sets capitalists against workers during all phases of capitalism's cycles. That is why Marxian theory alone advocates moving beyond rather than fixing or regulating capitalism. Believers in Marxian economic theory would thus react to capitalism's cycles by proposing very different policy responses from those advocated by neoclassical or Keynesian economists.

1.1.1   Theories: Economic and Otherwise

Economic theories are attempts to understand how economies work. They exist in our minds alongside theories about how everything else that we care about in life works. Depending on our circumstances at home, in school, on the job, and elsewhere, we all become more or less aware of the particular theories we use to make sense of the world. We also become more or less aware of alternative theories that make sense of the world differently. The theories each of us uses, whether held consciously or unconsciously, play major roles in shaping all of our experiences and actions.

We just presented one illustrative example of how different economic theories shape very different responses to economic cycles. Other examples can underscore this key point. The particular theory of love and feeling that we hold will influence our intimate relationships all through life. The person whose theory of love holds it to be identical with sex will probably have very different experiences in life from those of a person who thinks that sex and love are related but distinct. Theories of spirituality and religion affect many aspects of daily living. A government founded on a theory that holds the Bible or the Koran to be the absolute source of law will often behave very differently from a government committed to a theory that necessitates the separation of religion from politics. The different theories of what is beautiful among people produce correspondingly different choices about how cities construct their streets and parks, how architects design homes and other buildings, and how individuals style their hair, clothing, personal manners, and so on.

Natural scientists debate contesting theories of biology, chemistry, and physics that also lead them to quite different research programs and discoveries. Technological change varies from community to community depending in part on which theories are believed and acted upon by community members in general and by the scientists among them in particular. Alternative theories of illness and medicine yield competing therapies and medicines.

Similarly neoclassical and Keynesian theories motivate different choices as to the role of markets and state in our society, more of one and less of the other. Marxian theory pushes us toward awareness of and choices about alternative class structures in our economy. Political leaders will prefer economic policies aimed at markets, the state, or class depending on their understandings—their preferred theories—of the economy. Embracing neoclassical theory leads politicians to a more hands-off policy in regard to the capitalist economy. Affirming Keynesian theory leads them to a more state interventionist policy in regard to regulating that same capitalism. Adopting Marxian theory will lead politicians to focus on actions to alter radically the economy's class structure, to go beyond capitalism.

Of course, individuals may hold more than one view. For example, when economic times are good, a person may affirm the neoclassical position that all is best if markets are left alone to self-correct. Then, when hard economic times arrive, the same person may switch to a more state interventionist theory and policy. And if and when hard times become very bad, the same person may adopt a more Marxist position focused on class and class change. While these twists and turns may indicate opportunism, they may also reflect the co-existence of multiple theories in one person's thought, with different theories emerging to the forefront of a person's mind depending on changing circumstances.

1.1.2 Economic Theories in Disagreement

This book might not have been necessary if everyone agreed about how economies work. If one economic theory had won universal assent, we would probably teach it in the manner that algebra, grammar, and auto mechanics are usually taught. In that case regular textbooks would suffice. However, since profound disagreement rather than agreement has always characterized economics, learning the subject requires engagement with its internal differences.

In America and around the world, the different theories produce intense debates over how economies work, how they develop, and whether and how they ought to be changed. Neoclassical, Keynesian, and Marxian economic theories contradict each other in basic ways. Their proponents contest for people's allegiance. (At the same time, to complicate matters, advocates of different versions of neoclassical, Keynesian, and Marxian theory dispute among themselves. In this book we concentrate on the three major kinds of economic theory, and only secondarily consider their differing versions.) Since we all have to live with the consequences of struggles among the three great economic theories, this book aims to help you compare and evaluate them.

Deeply felt thoughts and convictions are woven into the economic theories people believe in and use. How we think about the economy is influenced by how we think about nature, human community, politics, religion, causation, and so on. We do not easily change our allegiance to economic theories, precisely because these theories are closely connected to our understanding of the world and of ourselves. In short, different basic philosophies are involved in different economic theories. Thus much is at stake in the current debates and conflicts among economic theories. As you work out your thoughts about these theories, you will benefit from clarifying just what distinguishes one theory from another.

1.1.3 Are We All Economic Theorists?

Everyone engages in economic theorizing. We all make some sort of sense of the production and distribution of goods and services. But many individuals are unaware of the particular economic theory they use. Every time you decide to produce, buy, borrow, invest, or save, or you explain the source of profits, the business cycle, or the price of a product to another person, your mind is at work, theorizing. That is, you consider and weigh various factors in reaching your explanation and decision. Every time you listen to a politician explain his or her plans and policy aimed at social security, financial regulation, taxes and expenditures, national deficits, or a national health program, you are trying to make sense of what is said and decide whether you support, oppose, or need not care about it. Making sense of the economic realities and policies around you helps shape your likes and dislikes and the decisions you make about your schooling, employment, and voting. Whether explaining some product's price or evaluating a politician's decision about taxes or deciding whether to accept a particular job offer, you can only ever consider some of the many aspects, implications, and possible consequences of your explanation, evaluation, and decision. Which of the many factors you take into account and how you weigh them *depend on your particular theory* of how the economy works.

You cannot think about and consider everything in constructing your explanations and reaching your decisions. All anyone can do is to consider only *some* things, weigh only *some* factors, focus on only *some* aspects. Each of us selects only certain things to consider and considers them in the particular ways we think appropriate. What we select and how we consider what we select flow from the theory we use. By thus shaping how we think, the theories in our minds also influence how we act.

You may not be self-conscious about the theory you use to reach your understanding of how economies work or your economic decisions. Nevertheless, they are influenced by economic theory. Therefore, whether or not you take formal courses in economics, you necessarily use some economic theory throughout your life. Your thinking and actions will be better served if you become aware of the alternative theories available to you and which one or more you are using, than if you remain unconscious of them.

Every time a person explains why some people are wealthy and others are poor, he or she uses economic theory to produce that explanation. The same applies to explanations of why some people are employed while others go jobless, why some nations rank high or low in levels of income, and why some careers look promising while others do not. It even applies when we go to the store and speculate why the price of a new and attractive electronic device is so high. The explanations we generate with our theories then lead us to take certain actions—actions that will differ according to which theory we use.

For example, suppose that the theory we use holds that individuals' incomes are rewards for what they contribute to production. What each person gets to spend on goods and services equals what that person has contributed to producing them. Workers provide their labor, landlords their land, and capitalists their money and equipment (machines, offices, factories, etc.). In this theory, wages and salaries are labor's reward, rents compensate landlords, and interest and profit go to capitalists. From the standpoint of this theory, individuals' incomes may well seem to be fair: your earnings match your contributions. Rich people contribute much while the poor offer little or nothing. A believer in this theory might oppose government programs that shift incomes from rich to poor. Such income redistribution would seem unfair because it punishes those who contribute more to production and indulges those who contribute less. A person who theorizes in this way might also oppose redistribution because it could discourage the major contributors to production and thereby diminish the society's total output of goods and services.

Suppose we hold a different theory, one that sees various social barriers preventing some individuals from getting income they otherwise deserve, while others manipulate those barriers to their own advantage. As an example, consider when some individuals or groups enjoy more power over markets than others or have access to valuable economic information unavailable to others. A company may be a monopoly able to raise its output price higher than the competitive price, or a group of financiers may acquire knowledge about market risks that others cannot share (insider information). Another example of such social barriers occurs when some individuals are denied access to jobs or products because of their racial, gender, religious, or ethnic characteristics. These barriers may yield an unequal distribution of income favoring those wielding market powers, possessing privileged access to information, and those without those racial, gender, or ethnic characteristics subject to discrimination. People theorizing the existence and consequences of barriers like these may reach conclusions about the desirability of income redistribution very different from those who think incomes are rewards to productive contributions.

Still another theoretical approach to a capitalist economy might focus on the ever-shifting moods of passion and excitement, confidence and fears, optimism and pessimism that affect market participants. In this view, expectations about an unknowable future shape economic outcomes including income distributions. For example, if employers expect a bleak economic future, they may decide to drop plans to expand their enterprises, lay off workers, stop borrowing from banks, and so on. Those actions may propel economic contraction leading their employees and then still other employers to contract their expenditures in a downward spiral affecting the social distribution of income. Alternatively, more upbeat expectations among employers could loosen purse strings, provide jobs and growth, and affect income distribution very differently. Someone utilizing such a theory might seek ways to offset or tame pessimistic swings in employers' expectations so that citizens do not suffer lower incomes than they might otherwise receive. Such a person might want the state to regulate or manage the effects of our human passions and expectations and thereby stabilizing the economy.

Beyond these two theories—one that sees markets producing fair and appropriate income distributions, while the other sees the need for state intervention to achieve appropriate redistributions—consider a third and different theory. In this third theory, it is believed that in capitalist economies, some people receive incomes without contributing anything, while others produce more than they get back in income. A portion (often called the "surplus") of the goods and services produced by some gets transferred to others even though they did not participate in producing any of those goods and services. The rich would then be understood as those in a social position to acquire the surplus produced by others whether or not social barriers such as concentrated power, unequal information, or discrimination existed. A believer in this theory might well be outraged at what he or she sees as a kind of disguised theft in society: surpluses extracted by nonworkers from workers. Such outrage might then support a favorable attitude to income redistribution as fair and appropriate.

People thinking about the world differently by means of these three theories would likely favor correspondingly different government policies (on markets, taxes, welfare, and much else), support different political parties, and show very different attitudes toward wealth and poverty. In short, these people would act very differently just as they think very differently.

1.2 Theories and Society

So far we have been stressing how economic theories matter, how alternative theories lead people to different conclusions, different experiences, and different actions in society. However, the relation between theories and society is a two-way street. Not only do theories shape society but society shapes theories. Precisely because different theories lead individuals and communities in different directions, we have to ask the question: Why are there different theories?

This question has provoked various answers—and whole philosophic systems—across human history. We think that social conditions impact upon individuals in such a way that they come to invent or to endorse alternative theories. In different environments, people experience life differently and think about its meaning (theorize) differently as well. Sometimes the different theories are quite similar and compatible. Then people have a feeling of "being in agreement," sharing a vision of how their world works. At other times the different theories seem to contradict one another. Then people may feel a certain tension about how to understand and cope with the disagreements that keep intruding upon their conversations and interactions.

Along these lines, we suppose that people may well understand economics differently, literally "see" different things when they survey the economic scenery around them. What they see and what they think are different because their life situations and experiences have been different. We expect alternative theories of economics to arise for the same reasons that alternative theories of love, politics, or religion have emerged in history. The complex diversities of our lives provoke ways of seeing our surroundings and ways of thinking about them that add up to being alternative theories of how the economy works alongside our alternative theories about everything else.

While sometimes the different economic theories have seemed close to one another, that has not been the case since Marxism arose to challenge classical political economic theory in the nineteenth century and Keynesian economics posed its challenge to neoclassical theory in the twentieth. Today neoclassical, Marxian, and Keynesian economics not only clash as profoundly different theories, they are also linked in most people's minds to other theoretical and social conflicts that engage the passions of our time.

Each of these theories is also part of a much broader tradition of basic difference within social theory. This tradition is important to understand because it helps explain why the three economic theories differ from one another and why they have their contested impacts on society. Neoclassical economic theory is a part of *humanism*, a tradition of social theories that arose as part of the Renaissance and the transition from feudalism to capitalism in western Europe. In contrast, Keynesian theory is a part of *structuralism,* an alternative tradition of social theories that arose with humanism but especially over the last century. While both humanism and structuralism have their ancient antecedents in the history of philosophy, we are concerned here with their modern forms. Finally, Marxism—as another theoretical tradition—has always struggled with humanism and structuralism. Part of Marxism—what came to be called the "orthodox" kind basically shared the structuralist understanding of society. However, another part of Marxism—the part we will be presenting in this book—broke from both humanism and structuralism to establish a basically different way of understanding society.

1.2.1   Changes in Europe and the Humanist Tradition

The transformation of Europe from a feudal to a capitalist region of the world radically altered how life was lived there. Especially across the seventeenth and eighteenth centuries, everything changed, including how people cultivated the soil, reared their children, understood God, thought about society, and organized their economies. New theories arose, clashed with, and crossfertilized one another. Gradually a few caught the popular imagination and became the broadly accepted ways of making sense of a changed world.

Older theories, born and developed within and associated with feudal society, struck most Europeans as no longer adequate or acceptable. New social conditions not only provoked, but also required new theories to understand them. People sought some sense of control over fast-changing events that often had traumatic effects on people's lives. New theories seemed important means contributing toward such control.

The theories were expected to aid in coping with social change and even in directing the path of change. New theories were to be practical guides to social action. Once widely adopted, they exerted great influence on how capitalism actually developed. The new theoretical commitments shaped social development not only in Europe but also globally as European capitalism expanded through successive waves of colonial acquisitions.

Many theories inherited from feudalism underwent great changes during the centuries of transition to capitalism. For example, the religious theories of

God changed sufficiently to induce major conflicts, including protracted military actions, among Europeans. A whole new theory and institution arose, Protestantism, which differed from the formerly predominant Roman Catholic tradition. A key part of the new kind of Christianity emphasized the individual and his or her personal capacity to communicate directly with God without a specially appointed religious hierarchy acting as an intermediary. Nor did Roman Catholicism pass untouched through the transition to capitalism. The ability of the Roman Catholic tradition to survive into the present attests to its ability to adjust to a profoundly changed world.

Theories of natural science changed drastically too. Newton, Galileo, Copernicus, and many others invented new theories of how the universe and nature worked, rethinking the position of the earth within a larger cosmos. Scientific investigations of all sorts challenged biblical formulations, or at least modified them.

Instead of answering questions about life's mysteries by invoking God as *the* cause, science sought *the* cause elsewhere, usually in some aspect of nature and in individuals (the discovered "laws" of physics, biology, politics, economics, etc.). The results included not only new theories of how nature worked and how people might control it. New understandings of the centrality, power, possibilities, and rights of the individual also proliferated. As the poet Alexander Pope later put it, "The proper study of mankind is man."

The powerful ascent of science combined with the changes and divisions within religion to generate a broad new theoretical attitude. The mysteries of nature and society, previously ascribed to the will and workings of God, became instead riddles the human mind was thought able to solve. Science, viewed as the close investigation of how nature and society work, could and would unravel the world's mysteries. Not Divine Will but gravity, or thermodynamics, or centrifugal force, or the cellular structure of living organisms would explain events in nature. Not Divine Will but such things as markets, the accumulation of wealth, and individuals' thirst for political power would explain events in society.

The complex and interconnected changes in ways of thought that occurred amid the transition from feudalism to capitalism gave rise to some basic themes in most of the new theories. Human individuals, not God, occupied center stage. The new theories exalted the individual as the center of attention: individuals could comprehend the universe; individuals made the world go round, and were, in fact, the proper foundation for social life.

Perhaps most striking of all the changes in thought was the rediscovery and reinterpretation by Europeans of ancient Greek notions of political life. In particular, ideas of democracy attracted and inspired growing numbers. As these Europeans understood democracy, it explained the ultimate basis of society. That is, society could only exist in so far as individuals accepted limits on their freedoms. Thus the only acceptable and ultimately durable form of government in any society was one that derived its power and legitimacy from, in Thomas Jefferson's phrase, the "consent of the governed." This differed greatly from the feudal notion that government represented part of God's plan, a plan that hardly needed the consent of individuals. In feudal times, kings and nobles claimed that their power to govern derived from divine rights (granted by God). As capitalism displaced feudalism, not only divine rights but the kings and nobles themselves generally disappeared. Instead, enlightenment, society itself, and progress were seen to stem from the inherent reasoning ability (logic) of human beings, rather than from the authority and tradition of Church and King.

"Humanism" was the name often given to the broad change in theoretical attitude that accompanied the Renaissance and later the emergence of capitalism. It summarized the new focus on the individual as the ultimate source or essential cause of society and of thought. Humanism positioned the individual at the center of (and as the essence of) the universe, rather in the manner that previous religious thought had seen God in that place. In effect, a human essentialism displaced the earlier divine essentialism. As the German philosopher Ludwig Feuerbach put it, "God did not create man; it was the other way round."

1.2.2   The New Economic Theories

The transitional changes in European society stimulated not only transformations in existing theories but also altogether new theories. Economic theories were such new theories. The idea of thinking about the economy as a distinct aspect of society, of separating it out from other parts (e.g., community or family life, morality or religious practice), was new. So too was the idea that the economy was a system of particular relationships within a society. The idea that the production and distribution of goods and services constituted a special realm of society subject to its own systematic "laws," rather like nature and the universe, was an original proposition.

The growth of theories that designated "the economy" as their object had a powerful impact on Europe. As these theories elaborated their sentences— their concepts and arguments—about the economy, people came to believe the notion that there existed a special part of society called "the economy." They eventually accepted that every society as a whole depended in important ways on its internal economic system. It therefore made sense for individuals to study the economy and to design policies for governments to use when intervening to seek specific economic results (e.g., more wealth, trade, and employment). Individuals and governments used one or another of the various economic theories then available to reach decisions and pursue policies that affected the course of social developments throughout Europe.

The seventeenth and eighteenth centuries produced mostly bits and pieces of economic theory as people struggled to understand the newly emerging capitalist world. Pamphlets were written about the new systems of production that were developing in the rapidly growing towns. There, employer–employee relationships that involved wage payments were replacing the previous landlord–peasant–rent system of feudalism. The production of goods and services for sale in market exchanges instead of for use by the producers themselves (or their small, local villages) made people eager to think through how markets worked. They were most intently concerned to understand why market prices rose and fell, since their well-being increasingly depended on those prices.

Writings on that subject poured forth wherever commodity trade developed and shook societies that had not previously accomplished their production and distribution of goods and services through market transactions. These were societies, largely feudal, in which religious and customary rules governed most of the decisions about who produced what and how the products were to be divided among the population. Such societies had little need to worry about market price movements, for they did not rely so much, or at all, on market exchanges. When market transactions grew—a nearly universal accompaniment of the transition to capitalism—the worrying about the mysteries of price movements increased and turned into the formation of theories to explain what exactly determines prices.

Money, which had been present before, took on new importance as it became the nearly universal medium for buying and selling in markets. It was required to act successfully in market-oriented economies, to gain one's livelihood. Pamphleteers wrote much about the mysteries and power of money: why it was so valuable and what determined its precise value. The problems of governments too occupied their attention as well. Governments sought advice on how to design and execute policies on taxes, supply of money in circulation, regulations governing wages, prices, rents, interest rates, building canals, harbors and roads, foreign trade, and so on.

Many valuable contributions to economic analysis were made in the pamphlets, journals, and other writings that appeared in those years. Passionately committed arguments were provoked amid a growing group of active writers. This was especially true in western Europe and above all in England, where the transition from feudalism to capitalism had deepened more rapidly than elsewhere. In the late eighteenth century, general interest and an abundance of writings made it possible to organize the fragmented thinking of two centuries into a first general theory of how the new capitalist economy worked.

1.2.3 Classical Political Economy

Not surprisingly, the new general theory was deeply humanist in structure and tone. The cause and motor energy of the economy was thus assumed to be the individual. The growth of wealth depended on individual reason and laboring effort, initiative, ingenuity, and pursuit of self-interest. Problems and crises afflicting any economy were to be understood as consequences of interacting individuals' self-interested actions within the specific social conditions they faced. In short, this first modern, general economic theory also served as the foundation of the subsequently developed neoclassical theory that we treat in this book.

Adam Smith's *Wealth of Nations* (1776) introduced this first general theory. A second English writer, David Ricardo, revised, condensed, and extended Smith's somewhat rambling work into a more formal, textbook-style exposition of basic economic theory, *The Principles of Political Economy and Taxation* (1817). The general economic theory provided by Smith and Ricardo came to be known widely as "classical political economy" or just "political economy." With many additions and changes, it dominated European thought about economics from 1780 to 1880. Karl Marx read the works of Smith and Ricardo very closely and devoted voluminous critical commentaries to them. His *Capital*, volume 1 (1867), offered a basic alternative economic theory to that of Smith and Ricardo. Marx gave *Capital* the subtitle *A Critique of Political Economy*.

Over the last hundred years, both classical economics and the Marxian alternative have undergone changes and additions. Both have extended their theories to areas not included in the original formulations. Theorists in each camp have debated and argued among themselves as well as with members of the opposing camp. As a result significant changes continue to be made in both theories.

1.2.4 The History of Neoclassical Economics

In one of its biggest changes, the classical school of economics shifted its focus quite dramatically during and after the 1870s. From its concern with macroeconomic issues—the capitalist economy as a whole, and especially its growth over time—classical economics turned to detailed studies of the decision-making processes of individuals and individual enterprises—what we now call microeconomic issues. Terms like "individual preferences" and "marginal utilities," "production functions" and "marginal costs," and "general equilibrium," which had rarely figured in classical economics, now took center stage.

Not all classical economists became microeconomists. Since major macroeconomic problems (inflation, depression, stagnant growth, etc.) continued periodically to beset all the capitalist economies, some economists maintained their focus on such economywide problems. However, the broad shift was clearly toward a microeconomic theoretical foundation expressed especially in viewing all economic events strictly as results of decisions reached by self-interested individuals and firms. This shift was broad and deep enough to warrant a new name for classical economics: neoclassical economics. The period from 1870 to 1930 saw most of the basic propositions of neoclassical economics established and woven mathematically into an impressive general economic theory.

Falling within the humanist tradition, neoclassical theory starts its analysis of the economy by specifying certain mental and physical aspects of individuals. These are basically the individual's mind—the inherent ability to reason logically—and the individual's body—the natural ability to labor and to desire objects of consumption. Everything else that happens in the economy—prices, incomes, wealth, growth—is understood to derive from or to be caused by interacting individual minds and bodies. Human beings are thus taken to be the origin or essence of the economic structure their behaviors construct.

Humanism affirms that human beings can become masters of their lives on earth. Their actions alone can produce a better life for them. Neoclassical economics is the application of this humanist conception to the production and distribution of wealth. Its propositions explain how the latter result from every human being's struggles individually to use his or her personal reasoning and laboring abilities to achieve the best economic outcomes for themselves in the given circumstances. If unhampered by external, extraneous interventions, the free-market exchanges among such self-seeking individuals will yield the greatest possible wealth (equated with well-being) for everyone, given their differing contributions to production and desires for consumption.

What is remarkable in neoclassical economics is its claim that the result of individuals' self-interested buying, selling, working, saving, and so on, is, in effect, an economic utopia: a perfect economic harmony among all individuals and between them and nature. For this utopia to be achieved, according to neoclassical theory, society must (1) endow and protect each individual with the full freedom to act in his or her own self-interest and (2) establish the institutional framework (competitive markets and private property) that guarantees that freedom.

A century before Smith introduced this vision of capitalism, Thomas Hobbes, another famous British philosopher and political theorist, had argued something quite different. In his view, any society that allowed its citizens to pursue their individual self-interest without social constraints upon them would yield a nightmare. Such a society would entail endless strife and war among its citizens, rendering their lives nasty, brutish, and short. Hobbes thus called for the necessary intervention of a powerful hand—a Leviathan or, in general, a powerful state—to ensure harmony and peace within society.

Smith recognized that self-interested individuals might clash, but rejected Hobbes' powerful state (which Smith and others associated with the autocratic feudal kings of Europe's past). Instead, Smith argued that the two key institutions of capitalism—free competitive markets and private property—could and would automatically channel individual self-interest (as if "led by an invisible hand") into a societal utopia without need for state interventions or controls. Capitalism as a system, if properly organized, could transform Hobbes's nightmare into Smith's utopia. That idea grounded and inspired classical political economy. It held great appeal for the industrial revolution's capitalists. That appeal continues today.

1.2.5 The History of Keynesian Economics

However, an unexpectedly destructive and lasting depression across the 1930s shook neoclassical economics to its roots, challenging its underlying humanist tradition and utopian faith in capitalism. The "Great Depression" staggered nearly all the west European and North American capitalist economies. Massive unemployment, falling wages and prices, bankruptcies, home foreclosures, and the consequent social disruptions and clashes filled the 1930s. They forced a back-to-the-drawing-boards anxiety among neoclassical economists. Their theories, in both the original classical and the post-1870 neoclassical form, had not imagined, let alone prepared, anyone for such a depression. Most notions of an economic utopia delivered or guaranteed by capitalism faded quickly. Across Europe, only Germany and the USSR were nations with solutions for the Great Depression. There the state mandated and financed programs of full employment, but they accompanied these solutions with fascism in Germany and communism in the USSR.

Neoclassical economists had few explanations to offer for the economic crisis, and still fewer solutions that seemed adequate to the vast human tragedy and growing fears that spread everywhere in the 1930s. Most serious of all was their theory's suggestion that the state "do nothing," since they believed that the system's celebrated self-correcting mechanism would best solve the problem. A do-nothing policy struck most people then as ineffective, unworkable, and intolerably cruel in the face of so much suffering. Across the 1930s in most capitalist economies including the United States and United Kingdom, the ever worsening economy suggested to many a very broken capitalist machine.

Marxism provided a different analysis of the crisis; it was rooted in and emerging from the internal contradictions of the capitalist system. Marxism also offered a different solution; substitute social or collectively owned for private property and national planning instead of markets. To achieve such a basic social change required a mass confrontation with the entrenched powers of those occupying the top positions of wealth and power in capitalist economies. Insufficient numbers in the United States, United Kingdom, and most other countries were willing to undertake the kinds of struggles needed to overcome those positioned at the top economically and politically. This was the social climate in which the newly elected Roosevelt administration in the United States had to respond.

In England, an innovative economist cast a critical eye on neoclassical theory from the depths of the Great Depression. John Maynard Keynes published a theoretically important reaction to capitalism's great crisis in his *General Theory of Employment, Interest, and Money* (1936). The book sought to persuade neoclassical economists—Keynes's preface dubbed them "orthodox"—"to re-examine critically certain of their basic assumptions." Keynes, however, did more than merely criticize neoclassical theory's assumptions and shift the major focus of analysis back toward macroeconomics from microeconomics. He offered a radically new way to conceive of the economy and likewise a radically new policy for the state. Economics as a discipline was never the same after this.

Fearing that widespread suffering in the 1930s would eventually drive a critical mass of the population toward the national socialism of Germany or the communism of the Soviet Union, the Roosevelt administration in the United States moved implicitly toward Keynesian economics. More state intervention was the choice to save American capitalism from itself. Washington created federal programs and public works to employ many millions of unemployed workers. It passed new laws aimed to regulate what had been mostly free markets.

Dramatic as these changes were and as large the number of people directly assisted by Roosevelt's state interventions, the latter never sufficed to restore anything even near to full employment. Only World War II and its military mobilizations finally solved that problem. Nonetheless, state interventions in the 1930s, the rapid rise in state spending to finance the war, and ever more controls over private markets taught a powerful Keynesian lesson. Contrary to what neoclassical economists had long claimed, state spending, tax increases, and deficits and state regulations of production and markets were not only consistent with full employment or growth but seemed necessary to achieve them.

Other changes also occurred in American life that helped Keynesian theory to become the dominant way of thinking about economics in the thirty years after the Great Depression. One of these was a new and revolutionary textbook produced by the first American economist to win a Noble Prize: Paul Samuelson (1915–2009). Published a few years after the end of World War II, it clearly and persuasively taught basic Keynesian theory to a new generation of college and university students. Many of them became the new business and political managers and also leading academics of the era. Samuelson's textbook also presented a new "synthesis of neoclassical and Keynesian economics." It claimed not only to grasp the workings of capitalism better than either theory had done alone but also to provide a better way to achieve and sustain a humane (fully employed, equitable, and efficient) capitalism. Simply put, the state had the role of getting the economy to full employment and keeping it there (the Keynesian heritage). Once there, individuals and enterprises would respond privately to market incentives and thereby yield harmony and growth in society (the neoclassical heritage).

Another change in American life also contributed to Keynesian theory becoming dominant within and beyond the profession of economics. Attitudes toward the role of the state in individuals' lives had radically changed during the Great Depression. FDR's government had alleviated mass suffering (by hiring millions, passing social security and unemployment compensation legislation, etc.). That same government pursued and won a war that seemed just. Increasingly individuals looked primarily to the state to produce and maintain a humane and fair capitalism, one in which glaring economic inequalities would be reduced and full employment maintained.

In this way an old American debate over the social roles of the collectivity versus the individual in economic life was largely resolved for a time in favor of more rather than less state action. The state was seen as the necessary and effective instrument of that collectivity to provide a fair (reduced inequalities) and good (fully employed) society for all. The modern "welfare state" had arrived in the United States on the heels of Keynesian economic theory and the state policies that it legitimated.

1.2.6   Keynesian Theory

The shift from neoclassical to Keynesian economic theory was also a shift philosophically from humanism to structuralism. In social theory, structuralism holds that certain inner laws or rules of a society determine or cause the behaviors of individuals in that society. In the words of the famous Swiss psychologist Jean Piaget: ". . . the elements of a structure are subordinated to laws, and it is in terms of these laws that the structure qua whole or system is defined."[1]

Very different from the neoclassical economics' humanist tradition (where the individual is the essential starting point), Keynesian structuralism begins instead with the inner rules or laws of the macroeconomy's structure. The economy as a whole governs individuals' behaviors in most markets, in pricing goods and services, in determining how much they consume, and so on. As a form of structuralism, Keynesian theory analyzes and presents (1) the rules and laws that give the economy its overall structure and (2) the ways in which that structure essentially governs the activities of producers, consumers, and other individual economic actors. For example, consumers follow structural rules governing what portion of their income they devote to consumption (their "marginal propensity to consume") and what portion they save. For another example, individual entrepreneurs follow different structural rules when setting output prices (their "markups over output costs") to make profits. Individuals' spending, pricing, and other economic behaviors conform to such essential rules comprising the economy's structure. Once all the rules are specified, the theory shows how they shape and connect all the different markets into a coherent "macro model" representing the economy.

Consider for a moment the contrast between neoclassical humanism and Keynesian structuralism. The former believes that the economy is merely the aggregation (or consequence) of independently existing individuals' behavior. Simply put, individuals come first and how the economy works depends on and reflects their behaviors. Keynesians reverse the causation. For them, the economy comes first and individuals' behavior depends on and reflects its (structural) laws. Much will follow from this difference between the two.

What does this difference imply for our metaphor of capitalism as a wonderful machine? Neoclassical economists look to its essential, determining micro components, namely independently existing individuals with their intrinsic desires and wants, to figure out how it works. They logically explain how those desires and wants shape how individuals behave and thereby determine capitalism's structure and functioning. Keynesians claim instead that capitalism's inner laws govern its operation including the individual behaviors of almost all of its micro components. To understand capitalism then requires grasping the system's inner laws. We need to add "almost all," because there is a key exception (one that we think proves the rule): individuals' investment behavior reflects no inner law of the economic structure. In considering investment behavior, Keynes moves back to a kind of humanism. He introduces new assumptions about the human nature of investors, albeit ones radically different from those of neoclassical theory. Much will follow from Keynes's humanist way of treating investors and their investment.

Key results of the rise of Keynesian theory included new explanations in the 1930s for why the Great Depression had occurred and persisted until ended by massive state intervention. Those explanations—and the policies derived from them—provoked controversies then. They still do, since capitalism's continuing instability keeps generating economic crises, large and small, that keep reviving Keynesian challenges to neoclassical theory.

Keynesian theory attributed the cause of the Great Depression to a collapse in private investment. Very briefly (we examine his theory more carefully in chapter 3) Keynes believed that this collapse left an excess of private savings beyond what investors wanted to borrow: With investors borrowing less and savers hoarding the resulting excesses, total expenditures in the economy fell. That in turn reduced incomes. Those with less income could make fewer expenditures, thereby reducing the incomes of still others in the classic downward economic spiral into recession or, if bad enough, into depression.

This Keynesian theory of savings is a classic instance of structuralism. Savers are understood to follow prescribed structural rules governing the portion of their incomes that they save. The Keynesian theory of investment is quite different, rather closer to a form of humanism. No structural rules govern each individual's investment. In the Keynesian view, the investor operates in two different economic worlds. Today the investor can calculate the cost of undertaking new investment (e.g., the costs of tools, equipment, raw materials, and the interest rate paid on investment funds borrowed from a lender). But the investor cannot know and calculate now what the future market conditions will be when today's investment yields commodities for sale. Yet, to decide whether an investment is profitable and deserves to be made, the investor must imagine (or predict) and calculate a future income flow resulting from an investment now. Since the future is inherently unknowable, investment, for Keynes, necessarily depends on what investors' *expect* in that future.

Just about everything in society (political trends, climate changes, cultural shifts, economic processes, etc.) participates in shaping individuals' expectations about the future, including returns then on investments now. Investment spending thus changes, expanding or contracting, slowly or quickly, as investors shift between optimism and pessimism with their hopes and fears as to what the future will bring. Indeed investors' attitudes are not independent of one another. Good times and optimism breed worries in at least some investors that expansion cannot continue and hence they prudently reduce investment. Bad times and pessimism sometimes yield the opposite. However, it is also possible that good times provoke a kind of investor fever such as the so-called dot.com and real-estate investment booms of the later1990s and 2003 to 2007 periods, respectively. Then, to use a phrase that became popular at that time, "irrational exuberance" can seize investors producing an unsustainable "bubble" of investment that eventually bursts, often yielding another depression.

The absence of a societal structuring of individuals' private investment in Keynesian theory is what we mean by a move to humanism in what is otherwise a fully structural theory. Nonetheless, this humanist move is of great importance in Keynesian theory, for as we will see in chapter 3, investment becomes the independent variable whose fluctuations—due to human mood swings—determine what will happen to the entire economy.

If and when confident investors want to invest more than what savers save, then economic growth occurs: income levels expand. Society has then made sure that (1) all the cash that savers withheld from spending has been borrowed and spent by investors and (2) investors additionally drew and spent new money from the banking system. Those two actions by investors enable growth in income or prices or both. However, Keynesian theory was more focused on business cycle downturns such as the depression of the 1930s. Hence it focused on explaining why investors' expectations (subject in Keynes's words to "animal spirits") might sometimes be badly depressed into a deep pessimism as to future investment returns. Investments would then fall, even as savers kept following prescribed social rules about saving.

Once Keynesian theory specified the cause of economic crisis in this way—planned investments falling below savings—the policy solution followed. Another kind of spending had to be (and was) found to offset or counter individuals' reduced investments when they occurred or perhaps even anticipate them in advance so as to avoid or moderate them. The state was the institution in modern society that Keynesians identified as having the position, power, and obligation to manage (i.e., minimize, shorten, or avoid) capitalism's business cycles.

A combination of society's structure and private investors' human nature mandated the state to acquire and use its controls over money, interest rates, taxation, and government spending to prevent or compensate for the effects of socially caused declines in private investment. Keynesian economics had formulated both the structural causes of recessions/depressions (socially determined inequalities between private savings and investments) and their structural solution (state interventions to overcome such inequalities).

1.2.7 Return of Neoclassical Theory

The fifty-year dominance of Keynesian theory and economic policy ended during the 1970s. A different economic as well as political and cultural climate moved into dominance globally. Paradoxically, the partial success of state interventions that countered reoccurring capitalist cycles (and also alleviated many inequalities in national capitalisms) had contributed to this climate. The children of those who had suffered the Great Depression and World War II had enjoyed an economically more secure and more comfortable life from the 1950s through the 1970s. However, unlike their parents, they had not fought for nor did they understand the state's role in achieving it. Business and conservative leaders argued against the state's involvement in the economy by claiming it was counterproductive. For many, the need for the state to protect citizens from capitalism seemed linked to a remote and ever less relevant history.

A costly economic reality also haunted many capitalist economies during the 1970s and early 1980s: the combination of inflation and stagnation that came to be called "stagflation." That combination signaled to many that their opportunities for improved lives were fading away. It seemed that individuals no longer could or would be able to achieve economic success through their private mental and laboring efforts. Business and conservative spokespersons blamed the state's intervention and its pervasive market regulations. What Keynesians had seen as the solution for capitalism's fundamental instability was becoming viewed instead as the problem that required systematic anti-state political and economic changes.

A new claim gained traction in many capitalist economies: societies had swung too far in favor of the state and social "engineering" and away from individual initiative and responsibility. Structuralism and Keynesian economics were associated with the former and came under increasing attack from newly ascendant humanist and neoclassical critics. They insisted that a too powerful and excessively regulatory state bureaucracy was preventing capitalism from functioning properly. Markets were burdened by unnecessary state regulations, state-protected interest groups, and taxes that produced distorted prices and wages and low economic growth (stagnation). Individual freedom, responsibility, initiative—and the wealth and growth they could generate—were vanishing under the weight of overly intrusive governments. Modern societies, they demanded, should restore capitalism to those earlier and better conditions. The elections of Thatcher, Reagan, Bush I and II, Berlusconi, and others reflected and intensified such attitudes toward capitalist economies.

Alongside and complexly interwoven with these policy debates were other processes. On the practical side, many business interests had long resented and opposed the taxes and regulations that grew out of the Great Depression and impinged on their profits. They funded politicians, parties, publications, and institutions that promoted ideas and policies they preferred. In the context of the cold war, some business interests equated Keynesian with socialist economics and condemned both. In the realms of theory and academe, neoclassical economic theory revived in opposition to Keynesian theory. Nobel prize-winning economist Milton Friedman (1912–2006) and his followers led a strong critique of Keynesian that spread during the 1970s. Its defining themes became lower taxes, privatization, welfare reform, and deregulation. Keynesian theory gave way to neoclassical economic theory as changes in academic offices and government offices mutually reinforced one another.

The collapse of the USSR toward the end of the 1980s was widely interpreted as proof of the validity of the neoclassical world view. Private capitalism—often correlated with private (individual) action subject to minimal state intervention—was celebrated as superior to the contending socialist and communist alternatives—often associated with maximal state intervention.

Capitalism defined in terms of private enterprise and "free" (minimally regulated) markets had triumphed over a failed communism and, by extension, over Keynesianism too.

The return to dominance of neoclassical theory and the defeats of Keynesian-inspired state economic interventions had direct social effects. Politicians lowered taxes on corporations and individuals while also diminishing regulations on businesses and markets. Privatization—shifting from state production and distribution of goods and services into private capitalist production—swept many societies. The historical pendulum moved from collective back to private initiative.

The effects of this pendulum swing were complex and contradictory. They included spurts of economic growth and renewed price competition. However, the growth that occurred also deepened economic inequalities. Corporate profits soared as workers' real wages per hour stagnated even as their productivity kept rising. Households imploded under the stress of ever more members doing ever more hours of paid labor and the anxieties of taking on rising levels of personal debts. More labor and debt were means to offset the effect of stagnant real hourly wages, but they also carried individual, family, and social costs. Debt service diminished workers' disposable incomes, more labor time left less to sustain social, cultural, and political activities with others in communities. Even as they bemoaned the loss of "community" or "family values," individuals became more "individualistic" or "selfish" (the attitudes and even the words chosen depended on one's attitude toward the ongoing changes).

Worries mounted in the 1990s that capitalist economies were becoming dangerously dependent on debt and the rapid increases in the prices of stocks or other assets, that their income and wealth distributions were becoming too unequal, and that their relationship to their natural environment seemed unsustainable. Notwithstanding widespread feelings of impending crisis, the neoclassical answer remained true to its humanist roots: leave individuals—consumers and businesses, borrowers and lenders, investors and savers—alone freely to pursue their private, individual, self-interested actions that will best correct whatever market imbalances might temporarily occur.

1.2.8 Neoclassical and Keynesian Economics

Economic crisis hit US capitalism in 2008 and quickly spread globally. The consequent emergency government interventions—supported by almost all political parties and groups—poured state money into collapsed credit markets chiefly by reviving (bailing out) private banks and other financial businesses. Governments also enacted emergency regulations and market guarantees to try to limit the collapse. Keynesianism roared back into prominence, often led by the same business, political, and academic spokespersons who had been among its harshest critics before the economic collapse. Neoclassical economic theory retreated in the wake of severe economic decline and the new Keynesian criticisms directed against it.

While those who changed position were influenced by the theoretical arguments of neoclassical theory's critics, they also responded to the changing economic events of the day. They were caught up in the fast emerging fear that if the state did not intervene massively and take action quickly, United States and other capitalist economies faced the threat of another great depression. Moreover, as also happened in the 1930s, Marxism and socialism also returned once more as the ever dangerous alternative theory and system, the "others" always shadowing neoclassical and Keynesian theories and capitalism itself.

Keynes's writings provoked and Keynesian work still provokes the evolving tradition of neoclassical economists. It has deeply affected public discussion of economic problems and policies throughout the world since its beginnings in the 1930s. Neoclassical economists outraged by Keynes's criticisms have labored to show that he misunderstood neoclassical theory and vastly overrated some occasional, temporary "market imperfections" that can afflict capitalism. Contrary to Keynes, these neoclassical economists argue, the capitalist market itself can and will cure whatever market imperfections may temporarily occur.

Even as the capitalist crisis deepened in the years after 2007, many neoclassical economists resumed their argument that the state's interventions in and regulations of markets would stifle private enterprise and slow the return to economic growth. They pointed to the huge deficits that resulted when governments borrowed the money they use to rescue collapsed markets, arguing that state debt "crowded out" the private borrowers needed to restore economic growth. Since the Keynesians once again rejected those claims, the debate between these two theories continues.

Those who were persuaded by Keynesianism reaffirmed that the key cause of the latest crisis in capitalism was indeed, as Keynes had shown, a precipitous decline in private investment. So they once again supported government actions to offset that decline by both direct spending and the systematic overcoming of market imperfections hampering private sectors from functioning as needed to resume growth. For Keynesians, the state could and should generate full employment and economic growth.

The intense debate among economists over these different legacies of Keynes and Smith has probably been the central issue agitating economic theory. Sometimes the debate has centered on microeconomics versus macroeconomics. Sometimes the two sides have accused each other of abandoning reason. Sometimes the debaters on one side have even accused the other side of disloyalty to capitalism itself. (It is worth remembering that various socialist critiques of capitalism also participated in these decades.)

In some college and university departments of economics around the world, the two sides have coexisted (and even included a Marxist or two), but in many departments, one or the other side effectively excluded the other. The oscillations between dominant theories in academe usually reflected the parallel oscillations in the larger worlds of politics and the mass media. Politicians and political controversies also got caught up in the debate. In the United States, Republican presidents Eisenhower, Nixon, Ford, Reagan, Bush I and II, often couched their speeches in neoclassical and anti-Keynesian terms. In Europe and beyond, conservative leaders like the United Kingdom's Thatcher and others did much the same, while joining with the United States and major international organizations like the International Monetary Fund and the World Bank in promoting neoclassical economic theory and its derivative policies. On the other side, Democrats like presidents Roosevelt, Truman, Kennedy, Carter, Clinton, and Obama frequently chose Keynesian and anti-neoclassical language, as did social democrats in Europe and beyond (including many present and former socialists who sought to support Keynesians in their struggles against neoclassical economics).

Administrations influenced chiefly by Keynesian economists tended toward major economic interventions: enhanced government monitoring of the private sector, greater regulation, more economically motivated spending and tax change initiatives, and the like. Administrations that resonated more with neoclassical economics tended toward deregulation, less government monitoring of the private economy, lower spending and tax rates, and so on. Practical politics rarely permitted any administration to adhere completely to either theory; mixtures of both approaches are usual, but within contexts emphasizing one theory and its policies over the other.

Just as the dominant theoretical commitments of economists and governments have impacted societies and the people living in them, so have those societies reacted back upon the struggles among alternative theories. Society and theory continually shape each other. In the following chapters we explore and analyze both theories in the light of debates between them, their differing interpretations of how capitalist economies work, and their interactions with ever-changing governments, economies and societies. Our goal there will also be to capture those enduring, basic qualities of each theory (their humanist or structuralist assumptions) that their respective proponents have too infrequently recognized, questioned, or discussed.

1.3   The History of Marxian Economics

Karl Marx's work focused overwhelmingly on the capitalist economic system. He spent much time and effort studying the writings of Smith, Ricardo, and many others who had written on political economy before him. He often acknowledged how much he had gained from their work. However, the theory that took shape in Marx's mind broke with that classical political economy. In Marx the transition from feudalism to capitalism stimulated different ways of seeing and thinking about the modern world.

Whereas the classical political economists welcomed and celebrated capitalism's emergence from feudalism, Marx saw the transition as a very mixed blessing. His predecessors mostly justified capitalism on the grounds of its technical dynamism, productive efficiencies, and rapid rate of overall economic growth. In contrast, Marx was struck as well by the massive human costs of capitalism and their unjust distribution across populations. He reacted to workers' suffering in capitalist factories and offices, to the drudgery and powerlessness of their lives. For Marx the liberation of productive capacities accomplished in the transition from feudalism to capitalism was not accompanied by the liberation of the masses of people from oppressive living conditions. Those leading the transitions from feudalism to capitalism in Europe claimed their goal was human freedom and genuine democracy, but the resulting capitalism, in Marx's view, systematically obstructed and prevented those goals from being reached.

Marx always acknowledged what he termed the "historically positive contributions of capitalism": above all its technical and productive breakthroughs. He rather aimed to explain why, despite those breakthroughs, the transformation of feudal peasants into capitalist wage laborers occasioned so much suffering and yielded so little human liberation. In his view, the masses of people continued to be denied the qualities of work and life and consumption that their labor made possible. The freedoms that had long been limited to a tiny proportion of the people living in feudal and other pre-capitalist economic systems continued to elude the mass of people in the capitalist systems that Marx lived in as well as analyzed.

Marx's reaction to capitalism clearly differed from the reactions of the leading classical political economists. Marx's theoretical training also differed quite sharply. Whereas his greatest forebears, Adam Smith and David Ricardo, developed their thinking in the atmosphere of eighteenth-century British philosophy, Marx's heritage was the German philosophical tradition that culminated in G. W. F. Hegel. Marx's personal history likewise departed from the middle-class stability that characterized most classical political economists. While he began life in circumstances similar to theirs—Marx was the university student son of an educated state bureaucrat—his radical leanings changed his life. When political influences blocked his career as a university professor, he turned to active political involvements.

Revolutionary upheavals punctuated the transition from feudalism to capitalism in the areas that later combined into modern Germany. Those upheavals taught Marx about capitalism's darker sides and to speak out against them.

Consequently, in the 1840s, the German authorities exiled Marx, as did the authorities in France and Belgium when he sought asylum there. He finally settled in London and lived the rest of his life there under endlessly difficult and financially insecure conditions of the sort that beset most political refugees.

All of the mature works of economic analysis for which Marx is famous were written in England. Cut off from his native Germany and from the immediate scenes of social upheaval, Marx understandably shifted his emphasis from the polemics of daily activism to systematic reading, study, and theorizing (although political activism remained an important part of his life). By contrast, Adam Smith spent his life as a university professor in Glasgow, Scotland, while David Ricardo lived the life of a rich banker in London. John Maynard Keynes was a Cambridge don, successful speculator, and director of the Bank of England.

The different circumstances of their lives help explain how and why Marx produced a different understanding of capitalism from those generated by the classical, neoclassical, and Keynesian economists. The classical economists focused on the "wealth of nations" and how and why it grew and was distributed among the three great "classes" (workers, capitalists, and land-owners). The neoclassical economists focused on and began their analyses with the individual. Keynes centered his work on what he saw as the laws of the economic structure. In contrast to them, Marx began and focused his theory elsewhere: on class relationships understood very differently from what the classical economists meant by the term class.

Marx emphasized class as a common feature of both the fading feudalism and the rising capitalism. By "class" he meant one particular economic process within any and all societies in which some members of the society—the workers—perform "surplus labor." Marx defined this as labor beyond that needed to produce those goods and services that the workers themselves consumed. In both feudalism and capitalism, Marx believed, surplus labor's product—the surplus—automatically and immediately became the property of persons other than the workers who had produced that surplus. Marx defined this situation as "exploitation": production of surplus by one group and its receipt by another. When Marx spoke about classes, he mostly meant the two opposing groups defined in and by the class process: surplus producers versus surplus appropriators.

In European feudalism, individuals called "lords" appropriated this surplus in the form of regular deliveries of goods and services (or cash received from selling them) from the serfs obliged by feudal rules and customs to make such deliveries. What the European transition from feudalism to capitalism accomplished was a change in the form of this exploitative surplus labor arrangement. New people called "capitalists" replaced feudal lords, but both were receivers of other peoples' surplus. New producers of surplus called "wage laborers" or "proletarians" replaced the feudal serfs. Exploitation thus continued; only its particular form changed from feudal to capitalist. Likewise the name attached to the surplus changed from feudal "rent" to capitalist "profit."

Much of Marx's theory explored the important economic and social consequences of this historic change in the form of the class process from feudal to capitalist. His became a class theory of society. It made sense of how societies worked and changed by (1) identifying the class processes in that society—how and where surpluses were produced and appropriated and (2) showing how those class processes influenced the economy and society in which they occurred. Marx's focus on class in surplus terms sharply differentiates him from the neoclassical economists who are generally disinterested in class, deny that a surplus exists, and place their emphasis rather on individuals and their market interactions. The Keynesians also show little interest in surpluses and class processes; they focus on how economic structures shape individuals' economic behaviors.

Like neoclassical and Keynesian theory, Marxian economic theory reflects and also influences its proponents' particular agenda for social change. Marx wanted further social transitions beyond capitalism (which neither neoclassical nor Keynesian economists did or do). Marx and most subsequent Marxists were not satisfied by mere changes in the form of exploitation. They have sought the abolition of exploitation. Marx envisioned a society in which the people who produced the surplus would also receive it and decide how to utilize it: collectively, as a community. To such a society he attached the name "communism." In it people would no longer be set against one another—in the central social activity of production—pitting surplus-producers against surplus-receivers.

While neoclassical and Keynesian economists keep debating the merits of state-managed versus more private kinds of capitalism as better fulfillments of human aspirations, Marx and Marxists after him strove for transitions beyond all forms of capitalisms toward communism. Indeed they labeled such transitional periods, when capitalism would be phased out but communism not yet achieved, as "socialism." Politically they defined themselves as socialists committed to first establishing and then carrying through such transitional periods. Marx believed that his theory, with its class analysis of capitalism, contributed to the political project of establishing socialism and, beyond that, communism.

Marx reasoned that for capitalist society to be changed into communist society, it would help if people understand the class structure of capitalism. Before pursuing a new communist class structure, people would have to understand how different class processes interact with the other processes of social life. Because he found such understandings lacking in the social theories of his time, Marx developed a new theory to address class issues in ways needed by people interested in social change: to make them aware of class as an important process in their lives and in their struggles for better lives.

Marx's theory focuses on the class aspects of societies, but not because class is any more important a social force than markets, music, religion or climate, to take a few examples of other processes that likewise powerfully shape society and history. Marx developed a class theory because class in his time was—as it largely remains today—an overlooked, undertheorized, and often repressed dimension of modern capitalist society. To offset and correct that situation, Marx and Marxists focus their theoretical work on class analyses of contemporary societies.

Most Marxists agree that classical, neoclassical, and Keynesian economics together constitute an impressively complex and subtle set of theories developed over many years by many theorists. They also find those theories to be uniquely comforting to those who wish history to stop at capitalism rather than, say, continue to socialism. Marxists typically feel that their alternative theory comforts those who seek in socialism a society that can and will do better than capitalism. While intense disputes attend all their discussions about capitalism, communism, and how to accomplish the socialist transition between them, Marxists usually agree that Marx made a crucial contribution. He taught that any socialist agenda for basic changes to produce a better world must contend with the class process as an issue. Partisans of that agenda had to understand class as well as the other issues (democracy, equality, etc.) that motivated their commitments.

Marx wrote very little about the communist society he sought. He preferred to analyze the present rather than speculate on the future. His few remarks on communism reflect his life-long focus on class. The communist society he envisioned would organize the production of goods and services as follows: the working people who produced the surplus would also receive and distribute it. That is, the social division between workers and capitalists would be abolished. Everyone who labored would, by rights, also have an equal say in how much surplus was produced, who was to get it, and what was to be done with it.

Basing themselves on Marx, later Marxists went beyond his sparse suggestions. They also extended Marxian theory to topics Marx had written little or nothing about. For example, the intense European expansion into Asia, Africa, and Latin America during the nineteenth and twentieth centuries led Marxists to new theories about foreign trade, colonialism, imperialism, and international finance. Similarly the growth of large corporate enterprises (often linking manufacturers and bankers in close cooperation) generated new Marxian theories about monopoly and economic stagnation in advanced capitalist economies. Of course, when any theory is extended to new topics, it undergoes all sorts of changes that provoke debates among its practitioners. Marxian theory has been no exception. Marxists entered many new fields since Marx died in 1881 and generated Marxian approaches to such diverse topics as literary criticism, psychoanalysis, anthropology, and biology. Often Marxian theories emerged in those fields, as in economics, as the basic alternative to the prevalent theory.

The development of Marxian theory in economics, as in other disciplines, reflects differences and debates among Marxists. For example, intense passions and disagreements have swirled since 1917 around the nature and significance of the former Soviet Union. Did the economy and society created there—from the initial period associated with the revolutionary leader V. I. Lenin until its collapse in 1989—constitute a confirmation of, a challenge to, or a refutation of Marx's theories and hopes? Different answers to this question have agitated many writers in Marxian economics from 1917 to the present. A similar debate stirred Marxists after the 1949 revolutionary victory of the Chinese Communist Party in the People's Republic of China. How did the policies and evolution of that country under and after Mao Tse-tung influence Marxian theories? Different answers for both the Soviet Union and China provoked examinations of and debates over the class processes that existed in and shaped the histories of both countries (Resnick and Wolff 2002; Gabriel 2009).

Another provocative topic of debates among Marxists was the successful development of large, mass-based socialist and communist parties in many countries across the twentieth century. Marxists were influenced by, sometimes joined, and sought to inform the practical political struggles waged by these parties. For example, where such parties showed capacities to mobilize millions of voters and win elections, some Marxian theorists responded with work on socialist transitions that might be accomplished peacefully without the violence that characterized the transition from feudalism to capitalism. Some began to rethink the prospects for anticommunist violence expected if and when such parties threatened capitalist establishments. Marxists also produced new theories about ideology and mass psychology and their interactions with economic processes as large socialist parties struggled against conservative parties for the political loyalties of masses of European voters. Other Marxists argued that socialist and communist parties lost their revolutionary goals and momentum when they entered electoral arenas like the parties that effectively endorsed capitalism.

Still another major development since Marx's time that generated intense Marxist debates was the rise of powerful trade unions in most capitalist societies. As organizations committed to collective action and bargaining to improve workers' positions in conflicts with their capitalist employers, trade unions attracted Marxists' theoretical and analytical interests. For example, they sought to understand when and how capitalists utilize state power in confrontations with workers over wages, salaries, and working conditions. Similarly they offered explanations of trends in the investment plans of major corporations that related them to union organizing strategies. In yet another example, Marxian economists analyzed how and why modern, multinational corporations treated their employees inside the advanced capitalist countries differently from those inside the so-called less developed economies of Asia, Africa, and Latin America.

Since 1945 Marxian theory has experienced major challenges and changes. In the industrialized capitalist societies, it was a period of intense self-examination and reformulation. Marxists have been arguing over whether class analysis is to remain their tradition's central contribution to the complex movements toward socialism and communism. They disagree on whether to accept and absorb portions of neoclassical theory and/or Keynesian theory, and, if so, exactly which portions and with what qualifications. In many parts of Asia, Africa, and Latin America, Marxian theorists are debating the theory's applicability to the specific development problems that face these societies. In countries with Communist Party leaderships for part or all of the time since 1945, economic growth across the period and deep divisions among these countries likewise prompted much rethinking of Marxism.

We cannot here give all these developments the attention warranted by their impacts on world history. Our limited goal is to sketch the basic contours of Marxian theory as an alternative to neoclassical and Keynesian theories. However, in the case of Marxian theory, as in our discussions of neoclassical and Keynesian theories, we must take some account of the debates and rethinking that agitate and influence Marxian theory today.

Interestingly enough, the humanist/structuralist divide in non-Marxian economics reappears within Marxian economics. A structuralist view of how the economy and society functioned emerged soon after Marx's death. It eventually became the dominant interpretation in—and was distributed globally by—the former Soviet Union. Sometimes referred to as classical or orthodox Marxism, it argued that (1) inner "laws" structured each economy's foundation—its "mode of production," and (2) the structured economy ultimately determined everything else in the society. This orthodox Marxism visualized society as a building whose mode of production (economy) was the "base" that determined its "superstructure" (politics and culture). Political and cultural events, social and ideological movements, and even parts of the economy other than the production system (markets, prices, income distributions, etc.) were all reduced to effects of an underlying cause, namely the mode of production. Orthodox Marxian economists thus made production (rather than market exchanges or aggregate supply and demand) the central focus of their theory.

For them, production always presents a structure with two interactive parts or aspects. In one part, people interact with nature to transform it into humanly desired goods and services. The Marxian term "forces of production" refers to how workers transform nature, that part of production often termed "technology." The Marxian phrase "relations of production" refers to how people interact with one another in the process of producing goods and services: who decides what, how, and where to produce and what to do with the outputs. The orthodox Marxian shorthand for relations of production is *property:* the central idea is that those who own the means of production (tools, equipment, money, workplaces, etc.) therefore make the key production decisions. The mode of production—the structured interaction of technology and property—ultimately causes the kinds of goods and services produced and purchased, why unemployment rises and falls, why elections occur and have the results we observe, what kinds of music become popular, and so forth. The task and goal of Marxian analysis is to show how exactly, in each specific time and place, a society's mode of production produces its particular qualities, conflicts, and dynamics.

Such cause-and-effect thinking among orthodox Marxists parallels what we noted above about Keynesian economics. However, orthodox Marxism goes beyond Keynesian economics in its claim that the mode of production ultimately determines just about everything in society even beyond economics. Such claims won for orthodox Marxism the label of "economic determinism." Its proponents' analytical project was to show how the production system shaped the economy and how economics in turn governed the politics and culture of every possible society. To change a society (eradicate poverty, establish democracy, achieve racial or gender equality, preserve the ecosystem), the underlying structure of its forces and relations of production—its "mode of production"—had to be changed. Different forms of that structure—different modes of production—caused and sustained correspondingly different societies.

Beside such structuralist interpretations of Marxian theory, there have also been humanist interpretations. In part because the orthodox interpretation of Marxism was so structuralist, its critics inside Marxism often countered with humanist interpretations. Against the economic determinism of the structuralists, the humanist Marxists argued that politics, culture, and individuals' thoughts and actions were not mere effects of some determining economic structure. They were rather more or less autonomous causal forces in and on society. In their focus and emphasis on autonomous individual action, the humanist Marxists often approached the parallel humanism of the neoclassical economics tradition. The most influential of such Marxist humanist tendencies inside Marxian economics came to be known as "rational choice Marxism."

An important qualification needs to modify any categorization of an economic theory as structuralist or humanist: theories are rarely 100 percent one or the other. For example, despite neoclassical theory's humanism, it can and does occasionally slide into structuralism, while, as we explained above, Keynesian theory likewise slips into humanism. Orthodox Marxism remains structuralist, even though it too has its humanist moments. In the same way, humanist Marxism has its structuralist moments. These complexities and inconsistencies can become important in debates within and among alternative theories, as we shall show in this book's later chapters.

1.4   Comparing Different Economic Theories

Comparing different economic theories is tricky. Comparisons of different things always are. We can facilitate our task by making use of much recent work concerned precisely with the problem of comparing theories. In this book we compare and contrast neoclassical, Keynesian, and Marxian theories as three different kinds of something we will call "theory in general." This procedure is rather like distinguishing apples from cherries by showing how they are different kinds of fruit, or differentiating igloos from split-levels by showing how they are different kinds of housing.

1.4.1   Comparing Theories in General

A theory about something amounts to a set of sentences about it. Sometimes the words "concepts" and "ideas" are used as synonyms for what we mean by sentences. The groups of sentences, concepts, or ideas that comprise every theory display some basic similarities. The sentences of any theory focus on particular things—usually called "objects" of the theory. No one can think about everything imaginable, so all people necessarily narrow their mental energy to select and focus on some among the infinity of possible objects. Every theory is a means of making sense of some particular, selected objects. The sentences of a theory give meaning to the object of that theory. The objects we select to make sense of—to theorize about—are those that our lives provoked us to try to understand. Different societies shape in people different selections of objects and different ways of thinking about them. Even inside one society, people's different places and experiences in that society will lead them to think about different objects in different ways. In some times and conditions, the differences among people in terms of which objects are selected and how they are theorized will be large. At other times and in other conditions, those differences will be small, and people will speak of being "in agreement."

To illustrate theory in general, we may briefly compare three specific kinds of theories. Relations among moons and stars have long fascinated people and have been the major objects selected for theories that we have come to call physics and astronomy. Intimate interpersonal relations provoked interest about a hundred years ago and became the selected objects of theories that we now call psychology. In economics, the emergence of capitalism from feudalism in seventeenth- and eighteenth-century Europe provoked the selection of new objects of theorizing: the production and distribution of goods and services. The three economic theories compared in this book evolved as the major different ways of thinking about those objects.

The sentences or concepts making up any theory tell us specific things about the objects selected in and by the theory. Theories define their objects. Astronomical theories contain sentences that define what planets and stars are, what precise qualities entitle them to be understood and analyzed as such. Psychological theories define their different objects. A major originator of modern psychological theory, Sigmund Freud, wrote sentences asserting that the human mind contains something he defined as "the unconscious." He developed a large collection of other sentences (observations, analyses, and conclusions) that comprised a new theory of the unconscious that his theory defined. Psychologists since Freud dropped, changed, and added to Freud's sentences in their elaboration and development of psychological theories.

Economic theories likewise do not merely contain such objects as goods and services and production and distribution. These theories' sentences offer particular definitions of these objects and attach particular senses or meanings to them. Indeed the content of each economic theory is the set of sentences that attaches its specific meaning to the objects it selected for attention.

No theory stands still. Just as people use theories to cope with and change the world around them, the same ever-changing world also changes people and their theories. As new experiences occur, people extend their theories to try to take account of them, to construct a meaning or sense of them. Extending a theory entails selecting and defining some new objects, changing or dropping some old objects, and constructing a new linkage among all such objects. In this way theories grow and change.

When astronomers find a new body in space, they may not only extend their theory to take account of it. They may also feel the need to revise certain of their sentences about (concepts of) gravity or the trajectory of light or other specific objects of astronomy. Astronomical theories thus grow and change. Similarly psychological theories grow and change depending on how people extend the theories, where they direct their theoretical attention, and what theoretical alterations they find necessary.

The same is true of economic theories. New experiences with recession, inflation, or foreign trade problems, for example, may provoke not only extensions but also changes that economic theory appears to need. We already have seen this in economics. Adam Smith's formulation of economic theory (extending and changing concepts inherited from his predecessors) sought to explain those new economic events and processes in 1776 that later came to be called capitalism. Karl Marx extended and changed the theories of Smith and Ricardo to formulate an economic theory of surplus, class, and exploitation to inform and advance workers' struggles against capitalists in the mid-nineteenth century. Then in the 1930s John Maynard Keynes presented an economic theory that partly built on but also partly rejected and changed the previous economic theories he had learned. In reacting to a major collapse of capitalism in one of its recurring cycles, Keynes also sought to theorize a way to tame and manage those cycles. Industrial revolution, capital–labor conflict, and economic depression: each of these sets of events radically altered existing economic theories and helped bring forth new theories.

It is also common for developments inside one theory to contribute to changes in other theories. For example, new developments in theories of chemistry may lead astronomers to alter one of their theories. In the history of economics, changes in mathematics have helped transform economic theories. Debates and movements inside Marxian economics have influenced neoclassical and Keynesian economics whose changes have likewise affected Marxian economics. Each theory is always changing as the result of the many different kinds of influences shaping it. As each theory changes, so too does its impact on other theories in an endless process of mutual transformation among theories and between them and all the nontheoretical aspects of society.

1.4.2 The Logics of Different Theories

All theories establish and follow specific rules about how they connect the objects of their theorizing. There is a systematic quality—or "logic"—to the rules governing how every theory links up whatever parts of reality it seeks to understand. Theories differ according to which particular logic links their respective objects, but all theories use some logic.

A theory's logic includes its particular notion of cause and effect. Many theories assign the role of cause to some of their objects and the role of effect to others. For example, astronomers might explain the shape of one planet's orbit as the effect of a nearby star's size: the size of the star would be theorized as the cause, while the planet's orbit would be the effect of that cause. To take an example from psychology, childhood abuse might be theorized as a cause and adult neurosis as its effect. In economics, the object "recession" might be theorized as the effect of another object, "collapse in private investment." Where some objects of a theory are viewed as causes that determine other objects as their effects, we refer to the logic of the theory as "determinist."

Alternatively, theories may link their objects in a different way, exhibiting a different logic. For example, every object of a theory may be understood as always both cause and effect of every other object. An economic depression would then be approached as (1) the effect of a literally infinite number of other (economic, political, cultural, and natural) objects, and (2) as itself one among an infinity of causes of all those other objects. The objects of such a theory would be linked to one another in a logic of mutual causation that we refer to as "overdeterminist."

1.4.3 How Theoretical Differences Matter

Three basic processes comprise all theories—selecting objects to theorize about, defining those objects, and establishing logical linkages among the objects. Focusing on those three processes enables us clearly to distinguish among alternative astronomical or psychological or economic theories. Thus we can show that neoclassical, Keynesian, and Marxian theories are different collections of sentences about different objects that they link in different ways. Neoclassical, Keynesian, and Marxian theories are alternative sets of sentences with which people can and do make sense of the world. In more formal language, the three different sets of sentences constitute alternative knowledges or alternative sciences of economics.

Our comparison of these three economic theories will show how their respective objects are defined and linked differently to produce their alternative understandings of the economy. We will note that even when different theories use the same words—for example, "value," "price," "commodity," "wage," "profit," and "capitalism"—they define such objects differently. They literally mean different things by those words. The same holds in all other kinds of theory. Freudian and non-Freudian psychologists attach different meanings to words like "libido," "ego," and "unconscious." Different theories in astronomy offer different definitions for terms like "universe" and "black holes in space." Indeed, when talking with each other, two students will often use the same words—for instance, "love," "work," and "fun"—and then come to discover that they each attach quite different meanings to those words.

Finally, our comparison will lead us to ask about the consequences of different people in society using different theories to arrive at different understandings of things like the economy. What makes you theorize in one way and me in another? Can we all just compare and marvel at the different theories we each find appropriate in our daily lives? Or is this a more serious issue, since persons who think about the world in a certain way will likely also act in certain ways to cope with the world? If your economic theory leads you to strive to change the US economy in ways that my theory holds to be damaging to the nation's future, we have something beyond a disagreement in theory to deal with. Theories are one way by which people arrive at their decisions about how to act, and if such actions bother us, we will likely want to challenge the theories that lie behind them.

Thus we will end this book with an effort to come to terms with the problem of how different economic theories matter differently in and to our society. Knowing what social consequences flow from using one economic theory versus another will help you sort out your feelings about these three theories.

1.5 An Introduction to the Three Theories

Because our goal is to understand the current confrontation and debate among the world's three major economic theories, we need a systematic introduction to each theory. It must stress the contours of each theory to underscore significant points of difference among them and thus compare how they understand economics differently. This introduction will also serve as an overall guide to the detailed examination of the three theories to which chapters 2, 3, and 4 are devoted.

1.5.1 Entry Point, Objects, and Logic of Neoclassical Theory

Neoclassical economic theory directs the bulk of its attention to certain distinctive objects. Individuals, market supply and demand, prices, and quantities purchased and sold figure most prominently. In making sense of (theorizing about) these objects, neoclassical economic theory defines and connects a long list of other objects. Chief among these are individual wants (preferences), resources, and technology. These three concepts form what we will call neoclassical theory's entry or starting point. An entry point represents a theorist's choice: it is the chosen way to begin to organize theory, that is, the initial concepts a theorist focuses on so as to produce its meanings to all of its objects. Just like a carpenter uses tools to produce an object, say, a chair, one can think of an entry point as forming the (theoretical) tools of a theorist to produce a specific understanding and meaning of some object, say, market price. No object—whether a chair or price—could exist, if not for use of these tools. That is why in thinking about theory, an entry point is so important.

Neoclassical theory starts with and uses specific tools, namely the wants and productive capabilities (resources and technology) of individuals to construct a general image of how the economy works. Individuals' wants and production abilities combine to make the economy what it is. To understand an economy is then to make sense of the aggregate effects of interacting individuals' desires for material well-being and their abilities to use given resources to satisfy that desire. The key and optimal institution for these individual interactions is the market where mutually advantageous exchanges are freely negotiated between buyers and sellers. Neoclassical theory demonstrates how everyone's greatest well-being is achieved when each individual pursues his/her material self-interests by utilizing whatever productive resources each own together with the available technology to engage in production and/or market transactions. What happens in an economy is always explained as the result of individuals acting in this way (with more or less allowance being made for possible external interference with individuals' freely chosen market transactions).

In addition to an entry point of individuals' wants and productive capabilities, neoclassical economic theory also distinguishes itself by the particular cause-and-effect reasoning used to connect its entry point to all other of its objects. This reasoning forms its causal logic; it along with the entry point concept comprises the set of theoretical tools used. In neoclassical theory, the notion of causality usually has a few objects combining to cause some other object. It expresses this relationship by attaching the description "dependent variables" to objects it views as effects and "independent variables" to objects it holds to be causes.

This particular notion of causality has been called "essentialism," or sometimes "determinism," among philosophers for many years. In recent years the term "reductionism" has become popular. In this book we use these three terms as synonyms. What do they mean?

They refer to the presumption that any event can be shown to have certain causes or determinants that are essential to its occurrence. Essentialist (or determinist or reductionist) reasoning proceeds as follows: (1) when event A occurs in society, we know that an infinite number of other events are occurring simultaneously and that an infinite number of other events have occurred previously; (2) we presume that a few of this vast number of other events were the key, chief, "determinant," or "essential" causes of A; and (3) we therefore define theoretical work as separating the essential (determinant) from the inessential (nondeterminant) causes. The result is an "explanation" of A: the cause of A has been *reduced* to a few key determinants. Hence the term "reductionism" refers to theories that reduce the explanation of events in the world to showing how they are effects of a few essential causes.

For example, suppose that event A was an increase in the price of some good during August 2011. A quick survey of economic news that month would show that many other events happened then as well: interest rates rose, oil prices rose, the price of a complementary good fell, the value of the dollar rose, unemployment lessened, and so on. Further research would indicate that millions of other economic and noneconomic aspects of our world changed during and before August 2011: rainfall diminished, tax rates were cut, the President's health care plan became an issue of public concern, military conflict spread in the Middle East, and so on. Faced with this overwhelming mass of data on simultaneous and prior occurrences, all of which probably had direct and indirect impacts on the good's price, what do neoclassical economists do?

Believing that they can determine which of the many influences on the price were "the most important," they affirm the basic logic of neoclassical theory. They presume that the change in the price of the good resulted from changes in the some key causes (usually listed under the headings of supplies of and demands for the good). Neoclassical economists then investigate exactly how the independent objects (supplies and demands) determine the dependent object (price change) that they seek to explain. In other words, they explain how change in the dependent objects is (reduces to) an effect of changes in the independent objects. Thus the terms "determinism" and "reductionism" can be used interchangeably to describe this particular causal methodology.

Reductionists or determinists explain the events they deem to be important (worthy of their theoretical attention) by centering on the essential causes of those events. Their presumption—that events have some particular, fundamental causes that can be isolated—runs deep in the consciousness of many people. It appears in many theories, not only in neoclassical theory.

Neoclassical theory is reductionist across its entire range of analytical claims. In its most sweeping formulations, neoclassical theory reduces the overall levels and rhythms of economic activity—prosperity and growth or recession, unemployment and decline—to effects of its posed entry point, namely what interacting, self-interested and productive individuals do. Let us briefly outline how this theory works and then in the next chapter examine it in more detail.

Market prices are said to be essentially caused by supply and demand. In turn, supply and demand can be reduced further to their ultimately determining causes: individuals' natural desire for economic well-being, their natural endowment of resources, and their natural abilities to access and use given production knowledge (technology). Hence for neoclassical theory its entry point of human wants and productive capabilities become more than a starting point; they also serve as an ultimate cause or essence determining all other objects. Market price has been reduced to an effect of these assumed essential aspects of our human nature.

In this sense, human nature becomes the determining foundation in this theory. Questions as to the origin of human nature are not often raised or discussed in neoclassical economics texts or classes, but if they were, human nature might well be reduced further to an effect of God, evolution, or perhaps a combination as in "intelligent design" theories.

Neoclassical economists rarely question or dispute their methodological reductionism. They presume—as if it were natural or "the scientific method" or simply the only appropriate way to think—the existence of one or a few ultimately determining causes of every event. These essential causes need to be found and how they determine events needs to be shown. That is the task of explanation in neoclassical economics.

1.5.2 Entry Point, Objects, and Logic of Keynesian Theory

Keynesian theory's object is the overall, total economy—what is often called *macroeconomics* as differentiated from neoclassical theory's focus on the individual consumer, worker, and enterprise, or *microeconomics*. Thus Keynesian theory examines major aspects of the macroeconomy such as gross domestic product, national income and wealth, money supply, unemployment, consumer price index, and the economy's growth pattern. Unlike neoclassical economics, it is not especially interested in individual wants and individual market actions. Keynesian economics does *not* presume that the overall economy functions and develops as the result of individuals' wants and productive capabilities.

With one exception (the individual investor who is treated, as we will see in a later chapter, in a humanist way), Keynesian theory generally sees causality running in the opposite direction: what individuals do is determined by how the overall economy operates, by the connections or relations among the major aspects of the macroeconomy. These aspects and their relationships define the macroeconomic *structure* in and for Keynesian economic theory. It makes sense of the economy first and foremost by defining its major aspects and the structure of their interrelationships. These form its unique starting or entry point so as to understand the economy and how it works.

Individuals are presumed to be born into and shaped by that structure and to behave according to its rules. Hence Keynesian theory, just like neoclassical theory, assumes its entry point to be an ultimate cause of human behavior. However, these theories radically differ from one another in their differently chosen entry points: human nature (as ultimate cause) in one and structural rules (as ultimate cause) in the other. For Keynesian economists, the task is then to study, uncover, and show how that structure functions and evolves so that we can, individually and collectively, better fulfill our needs given that structure.

The humanist determinism of neoclassical theory confronts the structural determinism of Keynesian theory. They share in common determinist logics. However, neoclassical theory makes individual human nature the entry point and essential cause and macroeconomic outcomes the effects. In contrast, Keynesian theory makes the macroeconomic structure the entry point and essential cause and human economic behaviors the effects. Keynesian economics also entails another level of essentialism in the way it connects the major parts of the macroeconomic structure. For example, the total savings and investments of businesses and individuals determine unemployment and economic growth, recession, or prosperity. The macroeconomic structure that Keynesians analyze is filled with such cause and effect relationships among its parts as well as between that macroeconomic structure and individuals' economic acts.

1.5.3   Entry Point, Objects, and Logic of Marxian Theory

Marxian theory has its distinctive objects too, those aspects of the economy that it deems to be most worthy of attention. First among these is class: that concept forms its unique entry point. It defines class as the relationship among people in which some work for others while obtaining nothing in return. To explain class, Marxian theory requires the notion of surplus that it defines as follows: some people in society produce a quantity of goods and services that is greater than what they get to keep. This surplus is then appropriated and socially distributed by people who may or may not have participated in its production. Different class relationships among people in any society are defined by different ways of organizing how surpluses are produced, appropriated and distributed in that society. Each society's organization of the surplus positions its individuals in the roles of producers, appropriators, and distributors of the surplus. Different organizations of the surplus entail different arrangements of who produces and who appropriates and distributes surpluses: different class relations.

Beyond class and surplus, Marxian theory focuses on such objects as capital, labor, labor power, commodities, values, production and distribution, accumulation of capital, crises, and imperialism. All of these are linked to class and surplus in constructing Marxian theory's distinctive economic analyses.

Since the tradition of Marxian economic theory has evolved across the last 150 years with contributions from many different societies across the globe, it includes both determinist and nondeterminist kinds of economic logics. Until recent decades the prevailing, orthodox Marxian economic theory was determinist and also structural. Unlike Keynesian economics it was not the macroeconomic structure that determined how the economy worked and changed. It was rather the posed entry point of mode of production—the structured interaction of relations of production (property) and forces of production (technology)—that determinist Marxists argued was the ultimate cause of the economy and thereby politics and culture as well.

Determinist Marxists analytically divide societies into one group that owns the means of production (used to produce goods and services) and another group without such ownership. For them, property ownership became synonymous with class relations: the classic juxtaposition of rich and poor, propertied versus propertyless. Owners of the means of production were understood to receive the surplus produced by those without such property. Faithful to its determinist logic, orthodox Marxism explained who (which classes) produced and/or appropriated the surplus as the result of who (which classes) owned or did not own the means of production. The social organization of the surplus was the effect of (determined by, derived from) property ownership.

However, in recent decades a quite different, nondeterminist logic has become important inside Marxism (some Marxists find it already present in Marx's writings). In its view economics and politics and culture are all mutually determinant and thus interdependent. None of these components of society wields more influence than another; their qualitative differences are not reducible to a single quantitative measure. This kind of Marxist economics is thus neither humanist nor structural, since it rejects any kind of determinist logic linking its objects. It argues instead that individuals and structures are to be understood as constantly shaping and changing one another in an endless process that some call *dialectics* (linked to the ancient Greek notion of thought arising out of endless dialogs among people). Others prefer to call this pointedly antideterminist notion of mutual interaction, interdependence, and transformation *overdetermination*. This distinctive connective logic that distinguishes a major part of modern Marxian economics is discussed further below in section 1.5.5 and in chapter 4.

Marxian theory also attaches particular qualities and important qualifications to its objects. For example, it stresses the different kinds of class relationships in which surplus gets produced, appropriated, and distributed. Indeed Marxian theory uses these different kinds of class relationships to divide human history into distinct epochs: capitalist, feudal, slave, communist, and some other kinds as well. Marxian theory also very particularly qualifies certain of its objects—for example, labor and capital are each differentiated by the adjectives "productive" and "unproductive," and surplus value can be either "absolute" and "relative." These and related terms are defined and developed in chapter 4.

This partial, short list of key terms underscores two remarkable differences among neoclassical, Keynesian, and Marxian theories. First, notwithstanding that the same words and phrases appear in all three theories, they take on entirely different meanings across the three theories. For example, the basic concepts of capital and price as formulated and used in Marxian theory have completely different meanings in neoclassical and Keynesian theories. Second, central terms used in one theory may be altogether absent in another. Self-interest-maximizing individuals are as scarce in Marxian theory as surplus labor is in neoclassical and Keynesian theories. Qualifications that are central to Marxian theory—productive, unproductive, relative, and absolute—do not figure in neoclassical or Keynesian theories. Likewise the adjectives "dependent" versus "independent," which neoclassical and Keynesian theories attach to their objects, do not exist in overdeterminist Marxian theory.

1.5.4 A Digression: Theories and Their Objects

The sharp differences in the three economic theories' basic objects suggest that the objects of theories do *not* exist out there in the world just waiting for theorists to observe and theories to explain them. The world we see and the objects we find in it are shaped by the theories we use to analyze them. Here, it is important that we not get caught in a new wrinkle on that old question about which came first, the chicken or the egg. We cannot and we need not resolve the question whether the objects we find in the world came first and our theories second, or vice versa.

Rather, human beings are always observing *and* thinking at the same time. What we see is shaped *in part* by how we think just as how we think is shaped *in part* by what we see. Marxists observe class and theorize about it; their theory plays a role in influencing what they see just as their observations shape their theorizing. Neoclassicists observe individual-maximizing behavior and theorize about it; their theory plays a role in influencing what they see just as their observations shape their theorizing. Keynesians observe aggregations of individuals consuming a socially conventional portion of their income and theorize about it; their theory plays a role in helping to shape what they see in the economy just as their empirical observations shape what and how they theorize.

Of course, what each of us observes is determined by more than the theories we each find convincing. Theories we reject may also be important enough in our communities to influence us to consider their objects and find some sort of place for them in our theories. Partisans of one theory often adjust it to accommodate parts of other theories. For example, some neoclassical and Keynesian economists do admit that classes exist, but they usually define classes quite differently from Marxists. Similarly, some Marxists have come to agree that self-interest-maximizing individuals and/or aggregate propensities to consume are factors in any economy's development, although they treat them in ways most neoclassical and Keynesian economists would not accept.

Different theories not only explain the world differently but also influence us to see a different world to explain. Part of the difficulties faced by people with different theories when they try to communicate their understandings to one another is that the world each sees is not the same. For successful communication to occur, both sides need to grasp that they differ not only on how to explain the world but also on what they perceive that world to be.

This is not cause for alarm about the chances for humans to talk and interact positively. Communication among us is not made impossible because we see and think about the world differently. On the contrary, communication can be richer and more productive precisely because of our differences—so long as we are committed to honestly facing them and learning from them.

The diversity of human life that enriches and stimulates all cultures extends not only to people's different ways of dressing, praying, cooking, voting, dancing, and so on. People are also diverse in their thinking and observing—in how their minds work, how their senses interact with (see, hear, taste, touch, and smell) their environments, and how their thoughts and senses shape one another. Engaging and understanding all such differences are marks of an advanced civilization eager to learn from all the cultural diversity within it. Communication is necessary and enriching among people precisely because of their differences.

Over the centuries, civilizations learned slowly that there is no one right way to eat or dress or pray or love or vote. We need to remember also that there is no one right way to see (or otherwise sense) our surroundings nor one right way to think about them. How people theorize about their world and how they observe the world are different. Neoclassical, Keynesian, and Marxian theories thus involve more than different ways of analyzing the economy. Their objects of analysis—the "observed realities" they aim at—are also and correspondingly different. A chief purpose of this book is to confront and explore both kinds of differences.

1.5.5   The Logic of Marxian Theory

In addition to its entry point concept of class exploitation, the most striking development within the Marxian theoretical tradition in recent decades has been the concept of "overdetermination." This unique and relational notion of causality connects Marxian theory's objects to one another as always simultaneously both causes and effects. Everything in the world participates in overdetermining everything else and is itself overdetermined by everything else. As chapter 4 will explain, the Marxian economic theory presented here rejects any presumption that economic (or, for that matter, noneconomic) events have essential causes. Such presumptions can be called, as we have said, "economic determinism" when there is thought to be an essential economic determinant of the event, or "cultural" or "political" determinism when an essential cultural or political determinant is thought ultimately to cause the event. The overdeterminist Marxian theory presented here thus differs from economic and other determinisms present within the Marxian tradition.

The Marxian theory of chapter 4 will instead presume that any event occurs as the result—the effect—of *everything else* going on around that event and preceding that event. If we suppose that the world comprises an infinite number of events, then the occurrence of any one of them depends on the influence of *all* the others, not some "essential few." This means that since all events add their unique effectivity or influence to producing the occurrence of any one happening, no single event can ever be considered to occur by itself, independent of the existence of the others. Events thus always occur together, in relationships with one another. It follows that overdeterminist Marxian theory cannot use the independent-versus-dependent variable terminology or cause-and-effect terminology shared by neoclassical, Keynesian, and determinist Marxian economics. It cannot do so because each event is always understood to be simultaneously a cause (it adds its own influence to the creation of all others) *and* an effect (its own existence results from the combined influence of all others on it).

Marxian theory in its overdeterminist interpretation differs sharply from both humanist and structuralist theories in economics. It understands neither human nature nor structural laws as ultimately determining causes of economic events. Instead, it understands each person's human nature as the site of effects emanating from that person's surrounding economic, political, cultural, and natural processes. His or her human nature is both an effect and also a partial cause of all those surrounding processes. The same argument applies to any structures in society (e.g., the macroeconomy as a whole, markets, households, enterprises, the state). All such structures are likewise sites of effects emanating from the interacting processes comprising their surroundings. From the perspective of an overdeterminist theory, individuals and social structures are similarly understood: each as sites of effects. Neither can exist independently of the nexus of processes that create them and into which they are interwoven.

In the Marxian tradition, this kind of logic was historically referred to as "dialectical" reasoning, derived from Marx's way of understanding how events exist (are caused). However, despite its place within the Marxian tradition, we will not use the term "dialectics" in this book. We will use instead the newer and, we think, more exact term "overdetermination" to refer to this Marxian notion of causation. Given its long history, "dialectics" is a term overloaded with diverse meanings deriving from frequently bitter debates, especially among Marxists. One important reason for preferring "overdetermination" is to differentiate its meaning from many of the meanings attached to "dialectics." That way we can specify a unique Marxian theoretical logic not burdened with the complex intellectual history of "dialectics."

To illustrate this Marxian notion of overdetermination, consider the occurrence of an economic recession. It is *not* presumed to follow from falling investment, reduced consumer spending, falling stock prices or any limited, small group of such determinants. Rather, in this Marxian view, a recession is "caused" not only by these but also by all other factors that exist in our world. These include, among innumerable other examples, economic changes in the class structure, natural changes in climate and soil chemistry, political changes in banking regulations, voting, and legal patterns, and cultural changes in the status of consumption, taking on debt, and business confidence. All such factors—processes occurring in the surrounding world—play their distinct roles in producing and shaping the occurrence of a recession. For Marxian theory, none of these factors can be ruled out as causes—each in its particular way—of the recession. Indeed, the prefix "over-" in the term "overdetermination" is a way of signaling the reader that this event, a recession, is (over) determined by the influences emanating from *all* of these factors. If we decide to focus our attention on only some selected subset of the causes, that is no problem so long as we are aware of and explicit about the necessarily partial, incomplete, and partisan analysis that results.

Such a notion of causality sometimes startles people. They rightly wonder whether we can ever explain anything if we are required to investigate everything in order to do so. If the world is infinitely complex, if everything is caused by everything else, we can hardly examine an infinity each time we propose to understand or explain some event. How do overdeterminist Marxists respond to this dilemma?

Marxists answer that no explanation, no matter what theory is used to produce it, is ever complete, total, or finished. Human beings can no more fully explain an event than they can fully appreciate a work of art, fully understand another person, or fully control their environment. Instead, we all do these things partially, utilizing our thoughts and feelings as best we can to produce some appreciation of a painting, some understanding of a friend, and some control over our environment. So it is with any theory. It uses its particular apparatus—its objects, qualifications, and notions of causality—to produce its particular, incomplete, and inevitably partial explanation of an event.

Overdeterminist Marxists thus insist that they, like everyone else, are producing distinctively partial explanations. Their Marxian partial explanation is different from the alternative but likewise partial explanations. Each is partisan in its particular way. While overdeterminist Marxists presume that all theories and explanations are partial, their own included, nearly all neoclassical and Keynesian theorists presume that final causes of events exist. Such neoclassical economists believe their theory can and will find and disclose those final causes and thereby yield a complete explanation. Such Keynesians believe the same for their quite different theory. For both such theorists, once discovered, these final causes by definition cannot be reduced to anything else. That is why such theorists believe that they have produced (or will produce) a complete explanation.

By contrast, overdeterminist Marxists do not refer to any final causes; for them, nothing that exists is a cause without being also an effect. Each aspect of society, for them, is dependent on all the other aspects. No event or aspect of a society is independent; nothing determines other things without itself being determined by them. Marxists do not look for the ultimate causes of events because they presume that such final explanations do not exist. Most neoclassical and Keynesian theorists do look for and claim to have found such essences among the objects of their theory, although their preferred essences differ. Hence they order aspects of society into dependent and independent variables, more and less important causes differentiated from one another and from the effects they produce.

Overdeterminist Marxian theorists produce their admittedly partial explanations of economy and society and contrast them with the partial explanations produced via alternative theories. Because of its unique entry point of class, Marxian explanations focus on the class aspects of economy and society but do not claim that they do so because class is the essential, ultimate cause of social structures and changes. Such a claim would violate their commitment to overdetermination, their rejection of the presumption of and the search for essential causes of any kind. Hence class is an entry point but not an ultimate cause or essence.

If class is no more a cause of historical development than any of the other nonclass and noneconomic components of a society, then why do overdeterminist Marxist theorists focus their work on class as its entry point and present their explanations of economic and social events in class terms?

Their answer to this question has two parts: (1) class as an aspect of social life has been neglected in and by other theories and theorists, and (2) that neglect of class has prevented people from constructing the kind of societies that Marxists would like to see. A theory of social structures and historical changes that is partial to (emphasizes) class, the overdeterminist Marxists argue, can help remedy the neglect. In economics, such Marxists point out, neoclassical and Keynesian theories ignore or dismiss the existence of class, exploitation, and class conflict. Marxists want to direct attention to class because they see it as a part of social life that will have to be changed if social justice is to be achieved. Marxists clearly feel that their theory will stimulate the needed attention. Notice that their justification of the focus on class is not a claim that it is some final and ultimate determinant of historical change, but rather a judgment about how analytical thought can and should be oriented to influence and achieve social goals. That is why Marxists make class their particular starting point and conceptual tool in analytical thought.

1.5.6 Communication among Neoclassical, Keynesian, and Marxian Economists

Much separates these economists from one another. People in each camp try to make sense of the world they all live in, but they do this differently and so produce different explanations of that world. It is almost as if each kind of theorist lived in a different world. As we will see, they produce different understandings of capitalism, profits, wages, and prices. Yet they do inhabit the same world, and at times they communicate with each other. Historically they have read other's books and articles; sometimes they debate with each other at conferences. Noneconomists convinced wholly or partly by one or the other theory likewise communicate with each other in all kinds of situations inside families, workplaces, and social gatherings of all sorts.

An interesting question thus arises: What happens when people committed to different theories communicate? The answers vary. Sometimes one side gives way to the other; a "meeting of minds" occurs as people who think one way decide to change their minds and think the other way. Basic disagreement gives way to unanimity. This is one kind and result of communication among people. Sometimes, after each side has presented its conclusions (knowledge) and the theory it used to produce them (it), neither side abandons its positions. Both reflect on and react (in their own ways) to the differences between them, perhaps by adjusting their theories. This is another kind and result of communication.

Sometimes, people holding one particular theory about how the world works reach the conclusion that some other theory has dangerous social consequences in the sense that people who believe it tend to act in ways that will do harm to society. Then discussion and communication change into verbal or even physical battle as people holding these two theories seek to control, constrain, and sometimes even eliminate one another. This too is a kind of communication.

How neoclassical, Keynesian, and Marxian economists communicate—in mutually instructive exchanges of analyses, in discussions that result in a "meeting of minds," or in tense hostilities that spill over into conflict—depends on all the social conditions that overdetermine that communication. The past century has exhibited all three kinds of communication. Communications in the United States have often been laced with so much hostility and suspicion that little has been learned. Since Marxists have frequently been blocked from university or other positions that would allow their theory more exposure and general discussion, most Americans have had little opportunity to encounter Marxian theory or to communicate with Marxian theorists. This has had negative consequences for the majority neoclassicists and Keynesians and the minority Marxists. We hope that this book will improve matters by enhancing the likelihood for better, mutually instructive communication between the three theoretical traditions.

1.6 Conclusion

One major objective of this book is to acquaint readers with the central differences of the three dominant economic theories in the world today. Another equally important objective is to aid readers in reaching their own conclusions about these theories. Depending on which one (or a combination) you find convincing, your understanding of economics will be influenced in one direction or another. In turn, how you understand economics will influence how you see the world and your actions in it. In short, your theory matters tangibly in terms of your conversations and other actions day by day.

This book's concluding chapter will therefore present some of the different consequences—in terms of people's general beliefs and actions—that flow from one theory as opposed to those that emanate from the other. Our premise is that you will be concerned to know how the differences in theory explained in this book make a difference in daily life. We can assure you at this point that they make significant differences indeed.

2 Neoclassical Theory

2.1 The Neoclassical Tradition

This chapter presents the logical structure of neoclassical theory in terms of its distinctive objects, logic, and conclusions. We will do likewise for Keynesian theory in chapter 3, Marxian theory in chapter 4, and so-called late neoclassical theories in chapter 5. We begin this chapter by specifying the initial objects of neoclassical theory. These are the objects with which the theory begins to construct its analysis and around which it focuses its analysis. As explained in chapter 1, we call these the conceptual *entry points* of neoclassical theory: how it enters into its theorization of the economy. Next we discuss neoclassical theory's logic, the method it deploys to link its entry-point concepts to all the other objects contained within its theoretical structure. Finally we examine the theory's conclusions, its unique analysis of the objects with which it is concerned.

In presenting the overall structure of neoclassical theory, we have assumed that our readers are basically familiar with its specific parts, typically those covered in an introductory economics text. Our chief intention in this chapter is not to teach or even review the components of neoclassical theory—the analytics and derivation of supply and demand. Rather, it is to discuss the overall structure and logic of the theory.

This task is often neglected in introductory neoclassical textbooks. There the theory is presented and applied, but little or no attention is paid to the particular internal structure of the theory: its unique component parts and how they interact. The lack of theoretical self-consciousness reduces students' abilities to recognize and solve internal problems and inconsistencies of the theory. It hampers the creative application of the theory and also hinders neoclassical economists' ability to understand, communicate with, and learn from other theories and theorists. This and the following chapters aim to overcome these limits systematically by comparing and contrasting the different entry-point objects, logics, and conclusions of the three major, alternative economic theories.

2.1.1 Neoclassical Theory's Contributions

The originality of neoclassical theory lies in its notion that innate human nature determines economic outcomes. According to this notion, human beings naturally possess the inherent rational and productive abilities to produce the maximum wealth possible in a society. What they need and have historically sought is a kind of optimal social organization—a set of particular social institutions—that will free and enable this inner human essence to realize its potential, namely the greatest possible well-being of the greatest number. Neoclassical economic theory defines each individual's well-being in terms of his or her consumption of goods and services: maximum consumption equals maximum well-being.

Capitalism is thought to be that optimum society. Its defining institutions (individual freedom, private property, a market system of exchange, etc.) are believed to yield an economy that achieves the maximum, technically feasible output and level of consumption. Capitalist society is also harmonious: its members' different desires—for maximum enterprise profits and for maximum individual consumption—are brought into equilibrium or balance with one another.

The writings of both the early classical and the later neoclassical economists underscored these two key ideas (attaining the maximum technically feasible wealth and consumption and achieving social harmony). For the readers of Adam Smith (1723–1790), the new spokesman for and advocate of capitalism in 1776, capitalism as means to achieve any nation's maximum wealth was a revolutionary idea. Capitalism was then still struggling against feudalism, a declining but still powerful *noncapitalist* set of social institutions and ways of thinking. Smith's argument that maximum social wealth flowed from maximum individual freedom to pursue one's economic self-interest was, to say the least, startling. Indeed, over two hundred years later, it remains a remarkable claim.

Classical economists stressed the idea of maximum feasible wealth creation, while later neoclassical writers focused more on the idea that individual pursuit of economic self-interest in capitalism could and would yield a harmonious rather than a conflict-ridden society. By the end of the eighteenth century, the long transition from feudalism to capitalism in England had created new conditions that demanded a new theory to explain them. What demanded explanation was the vast new wealth pouring out of growing industrial factories. New ideas were likewise required to explain (1) the distribution of wealth among those who collaborated in its production, (2) how so productive an economic system could be reproduced and extended, and (3) how best to respond to the recurring business cycles that threatened to disrupt the new capitalist system.

The early classical writers responded to the pressures of their times: the demands for explanations of economic events and trends, but also the demands of governments for new policies to deal with new economic problems. Many focused on answering a key question: Was free trade preferable to restricted trade between nations? Others concerned themselves with debating whether monopolies granted by governments to merchant companies hindered economic growth. Still others asked whether guild restrictions on craft production should be abolished in favor of placing no restrictions on individuals' producing and selling whatever the market would bear. Economic analysis and policy prescriptions were deeply intertwined then (as they have continued to be ever since).

The classical economists' new ideas reflected their times but also reacted back upon those times. Classical economics helped shape the complex ways in which the newly emerging industrial capitalists and wage laborers understood and related to one another. Classical economics likewise influenced how the state then related to enterprises and households. In other words, these ideas of the classical writers helped create, but also changed, the very capitalist society to which they were responding.

A principal aim of first classical and then neoclassical economics was to demonstrate how capitalism could realize its potential only if all barriers and obstacles to private wealth maximization were removed. Even some of classical and neoclassical theory's severest critics, such as John Maynard Keynes (1883–1946), shared that aim. In Keynes's case the obstacle to be removed was a lack of effective demand that prevented and distorted capitalism from operating as it could and should. It took a very different kind of critic (Marx) and a very different kind of critical theory (Marxism) to challenge the classical, neoclassical and Keynesian economists' common belief that capitalism could yield the maximum well-being to the greatest number.

2.1.2 Emergence of Neoclassical Theory after Adam Smith

When Adam Smith died in 1790, no country in the world had yet become a fully capitalist society. England, however, was well on the road to capitalism and would be followed after the 1850s by the countries of western Europe, the United States, and Japan. Classical economic theory spread to and developed in all these countries, often extending its reach to issues that its two founders Adam Smith and David Ricardo (1772–1823) had barely mentioned. As capitalism spread globally, not only did classical economics move with it, but so too did the social divisions and tensions associated with capitalism. Capitalists and workers especially clashed as the new wealth production was not distributed in ways everyone approved. Socialism arose to challenge capitalism in the forms of labor unions, strikes, mass labor and socialist parties in national politics, and a new, critical economic theory articulated most influentially by Karl Marx (1818–1883) and the Marxist theoretical tradition he founded.

In response to these developments and challenges, classical economics was transformed in the 1870s. What emerged had its roots in the work of Smith and Ricardo but was different enough to merit a new name, neoclassical economics. Where classical economics had focused on national levels of wealth creation, growth, and government's economic policies, the neoclassical school concentrated more on the economic behavior of the individual elements of modern economies: enterprises, consumers, and workers. Those behaviors—based on those elements' innate desires, goals, and resulting choices—were thought to determine how economies functioned including the determination of commodity values that the old classical economists and Marx had rather attributed to labor. Neoclassical economics after the 1870s went on to produce a remarkable theoretical tradition whose central concerns grew from the analyses of consumer choice and the behavior of firms to encompass topics like income distribution, business cycles, market structures, general equilibrium, foreign trade, growth, and economic development. In the late twentieth century the traditional neoclassical theory gave way to new variations and formulations that are discussed as *late* neoclassical theories in chapter 5.

The Great Depression of the 1930s dealt a major blow to neoclassical theory. Many neoclassical economists worried that the theory that had developed over the previous sixty years was inadequate. The only solution their theory offered was to allow the workings of free markets—what neoclassical theory celebrated as the optimum economic organization—to self-correct and thereby overcome the Great Depression. Yet the suffering of so many during the 1930s was so great that the market solution, even if it worked, might come too late to save capitalism from the growing mass of its critics. The immediate danger was social revolution by the unemployed, the poverty stricken, and the many disillusioned with capitalism as an economic system. In such dangerous times for capitalism and neoclassical theory, John Maynard Keynes, an important neoclassical economist himself, engaged in a remarkable theoretical self-criticism.

Keynes attempted two things: to show why the operation of free markets alone would not necessarily end the depression and, more important, to offer another way to end the depression without destroying capitalism in the process. Keynes's explanation and new policy challenged neoclassical theory's celebration of free markets so profoundly that it effectively split modern non-Marxian economics into two, often contending schools. One retained the name neoclassical economics and has continued its focus on the micro level of economic life and its celebration of free markets. The other came to be called Keynesian economics and focused instead on the limits of markets, on the macro level of the economy, and on the market interventions needed from the state to secure maximum employment, price stability, and economic growth.

2.1.3   Which Economic Theory Will We Present?

To present all the theoretical variations within the neoclassical, Keynesian, and Marxian traditions would be an overwhelming task. Yet to present only one approach from each would be to invite the criticism that we have ignored viable alternatives.

Nonetheless, we have chosen to follow the latter course. Only one version of each of these traditions will be presented. They are the approaches with which we feel most comfortable because we have found them to be the most persuasive and coherent, especially as alternatives to one another. The neoclassical and Keynesian approaches we present are also fairly representative of those taught in most micro- and macroeconomics textbooks in the last twenty-five years or so. This last consideration is of some importance to us since we prepared the chapters on neoclassical and Keynesian theory presuming what our readers already encountered in introductory micro and macroeconomics courses.

We do make one exception to this approach. In recent years a number of economists have argued that new theoretical developments have yielded another alternative to the neoclassical, Keynesian, and Marxian theories presented here. No commonly agreed label has yet to be attached to this theoretical alternative. However, its adherents believe that it broke from prevailing economic theories and represents a new approach to the understanding of how individuals and an economy work. Because of the importance of such a claim, we will examine it in chapter 5. Doing so also will explain a number of recent theoretical developments, including game theory, and new institutional economics that have begun to appear in introductory economics textbooks. We will show why these varying developments fall within and continue the basic logical structure of neoclassical theory. Because of this continuity, we refer to these recent developments as "late neoclassical theory."

2.2   Market Values: The Analytics of Supply and Demand

We begin where most introductory economics courses start after the usual initial preparatory lectures. The set of questions—hardly minor—that neoclassical economists often ask concerns prices. First, what specifically determines the prices of goods and services produced by human beings? A similar second question asks: What determines the prices of the resources necessary to produce those goods and services? Why, for example, does an apple cost money, and why does it cost less than an automobile? Why does the performance of work command a wage, a kind of price for the laboring activity? If the wage is a reward for work, how do we account for interest as a reward for saving? What explains the origin of profit in society?

Typically the neoclassical answer to these price questions, and indeed to almost all questions about the economy entails what neoclassical economists call market analysis. Markets are considered to be locations or sites in society where prices are determined. As you likely already know from your introductory textbook, an important device of neoclassical market analysis is the graph depicting supply-and-demand schedules. These schedules are taken to reflect the behavior of individual buyers (agents of demand) and individual sellers (agents of supply) who interact with one another in and through these markets. The interactions of these buyers and sellers determine the market prices of whatever they buy and sell.

Figure 2.1 depicts the demand behavior of all buyers as Σd (where Σ signifies the summation of all the individual demands, d) and the supply behavior of all sellers as Σs (where Σ signifies the summation of all the individual sellers, s). The interaction of buyers and sellers determines the price of the commodity, $\hat{p}$. We may say, then, that $\hat{p}$ is the neoclassical economists' answer to the question of what will be the specific price for this commodity. We now

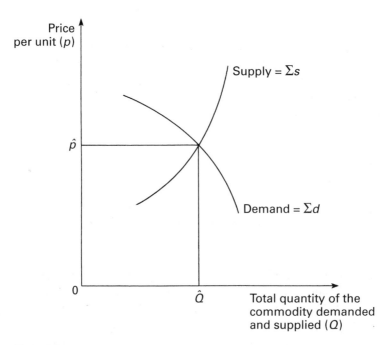

Figure 2.1
Determination of price by market actions of demanders and suppliers

know how much this commodity is worth, according to this particular theory of price.

Here we may explain our use of mathematical graphs and equations to present neoclassical theory (and other theories in this book). There is certainly no necessity to use mathematics. Everything in economics can be explained just as clearly and logically without it. However, since mathematics became the preferred language of modern neoclassical and Keynesian economics, we use some mathematical language to convey their structures.

Beginning with a few essential ideas about human nature, and on the basis of a few simple rules of mathematics, neoclassical theorists have been able to construct a deductive knowledge of some complexity and power. Their basic mathematical reasoning involves what is typically called the "constrained-maximization problem": it is assumed to be in the nature of each human being to maximize his or her well-being, subject to some societal constraint. The language of geometry is used repeatedly to express this idea throughout the different parts of the theory. Once its key location within the logic of that theory is understood, the use of math is less of a problem for students of economics, and the basic message of neoclassical theory becomes more apparent.

Neoclassical economists prefer and emphasize mathematical formulations partly because the language of mathematics, especially geometry, shares the deductive reasoning used in neoclassical arguments. Another factor is the desire of neoclassical economists to bestow on their work the aura of 'science' and 'truth' that surrounds mathematics. Many Keynesians and modern Marxists are similarly motivated to couch their arguments in as much and as advanced mathematics as possible. They have often used mathematics to suggest that their respective economic theories have the force of mathematical necessity, the absolute truth often associated with the so-called hard natural sciences, rather like the claim that $2 + 2 = 4$. Such claims of absolute truth then become the basis of declaring alternative economic theories to be matters of gross error, rather like claiming that $2 + 2 \neq 4$. In any case we use mathematics in this and the next chapters only to recognize its place in contemporary economics, not to endorse any theorist's claims that one or another economic theory has found and embodied any absolute truth.

For neoclassical economists the mathematical analysis of markets focuses on the behavior of those agents (individuals and enterprises) who relate to one another by offering to sell and/or buy privately owned goods, services, and resources. The neoclassical answers to our earlier questions now follow directly. The prices of all produced things and resources are determined in and by the interactions between agents of supply (sellers) and of demand (buyers) within a market. The prices and quantities of things exchanged in markets are the voluntary, mutually agreed outcomes of those interactions. What drives the market behaviors of buyers and sellers in reaching these agreed outcomes are their underlying desires (preferences) and productive abilities. The geometrical analytics of supply and demand is a shorthand way to depict and discuss a rather complex relationship among human beings who engage one another as potential buyers (agents of demand) or sellers (agents of supply).

Apples cost money, then, because of the peculiar interaction of the demand for and supply of apples. Automobiles cost a different amount of money than do apples because of the specifically different supply-and-demand interactions that determine their value. Laborers receive wages because of the unique demand for and supply of that which they produce and sell, their ability to work. Savers obtain interest from supplying their savings because of the unique demands for and supplies of such savings. Finally laborers receive a different amount of money than do savers because of the different supply-and-demand configurations that characterize each of these resource markets.

We now have a partial definition of the neoclassical theory of value: an object of market exchange has a value determined by the supply and demand for it. The definition is incomplete, however, because neoclassical theory then asks what exactly causes the supply and demand behaviors of the individual human agents of supply and demand.

2.2.1   The Determinants of Supply and Demand

To answer this question of what determines supply and demand, neoclassical theory takes another step: it identifies the underlying forces that ultimately shape the behavior of market agents. In perhaps its most important hypothesis, neoclassical theory argues that observed market prices result fundamentally from a basic human interaction between the wants and productive abilities of individuals. Neoclassical theory aims to show precisely how basic underlying wants and productive abilities of human beings ultimately govern, via supply and demand, the determination of market prices. Simply stated, the neoclassical hypothesis holds that the value of all goods, services, and resources is caused by the interaction between human beings' wants and productive abilities.

Put this way, the reductionist logic of neoclassical theory becomes evident in its explanation (i.e., theory) of price. In the first instance, price is caused or determined by the agents of demand and supply. The theory then "looks" behind these agents' market behaviors (buying and selling) to discover the forces that ultimately cause those behaviors. A neoclassical theory of price becomes, in the last instance, a theory of these forces: the wants and productive abilities of human beings. "Wants" are cast in a variety of terms including utilities, tastes, choices, and preferences while "productive abilities" typically refer to technologies and resource availabilities.

Is there a next step to some even more basic determinants of wants and productive abilities? The neoclassical theorists' answer is no. The wants and abilities are assumed to be the final causal determinants of supply-and-demand behavior and thus of price. One might think of them as the ultimate building blocks of economic behavior. What the neoclassical economist has discovered in these forces are essences, intrinsic components of human nature. They are the source of effects on other variables (market prices, quantities of goods produced and sold, etc.) but are not themselves affected by these other variables. Individual wants and productive abilities are the essential forces that generate all other economic events, such as demands, supplies, and prices.

Of course, the tastes and productive abilities of human beings may change. Neoclassical theory assumes, however, that such changes are caused by non-economic factors: factors exogenous to whatever economic variables neoclassical theory focuses on. So, for example, a change in prices or incomes cannot cause a change in tastes or productive abilities. Neoclassical causality runs in only one direction: from individual wants and productive abilities to the rest of the economy. This unidirectional causality is precisely what makes those wants and abilities the essences of economic life for neoclassical theory.

We are now in a position to give a preliminary description of the overall structure and logic of neoclassical theory. Its starting point involves specifying concepts of human wants and productive abilities. The notion of productive abilities is further divided into two connected concepts: the technology of production (widely referred to as *the production function*), and the available productive resources (land, labor, machinery, etc.). These three concepts taken together—individual wants (tastes, preferences, or choices), the production function, and individual's endowments of productive resources—form neoclassical theory's conceptual points of entry. However, they form more than just a way to begin theorizing about the economy. They are also understood in this theory to characterize essential attributes of human beings. The entry points of neoclassical theory are essentialized: they cause the rest of the economy to exist, but they are not also caused by the economy. In contrast, Keynesian theory offers different entry points but shares a similar essentialist logic. In stark contrast to both, Marxian theory poses not only a completely different entry point but does not essentialize it: its entry point is a cause of but also and simultaneously is caused by the larger economic system.

Neoclassical theory's essentialism means that the three concepts of human tastes, productive technology, and resource endowments generate all the other economic concepts—supply, demand, and price but also such other economic phenomena as savings, loans, and economic growth. The logic and goal of neoclassical theory is to deduce all such secondary concepts—supply, demand, price, investment, and growth, for example—from what it takes to be primary and the fundamental cause of the economy: individual human tastes and productive abilities. Deduction, or what this book calls "reductionism," is the logic of neoclassical theory.

While neoclassical theory gives a special importance to markets, it is never satisfied with merely a supply-and-demand answer to price determination. It does not understand market behavior to be the ultimate cause of price. Supply and demand are not independent and self-reproducing phenomena; they are determined by something outside of them. Neoclassical theory thus arrives at individuals' tastes and productive abilities, the theory's most basic analytical level. It does not reduce tastes and productive abilities to anything else in the economy. To construct its sense of how economies work, neo-classical theory takes those tastes and productive abilities as "givens" (what we have called "entry points") for its analytical project. By grounding its analysis at the level of individuals, it has come to be understood generally as "microeconomics."

2.2.2   Markets, Private Property, Conservatives, and Liberals

Before we explore neoclassical theory's argument that human wants and pro-ductive abilities act together to determine prices, we need to answer the fol-lowing question: Why do markets play so important a role within the theory? After all, human history displays many societies in which markets either exist marginally or not at all. In these societies, produced wealth was distributed to individuals using a variety of alternative, nonmarket mechanisms: gifts, various kinds of rules and customs governing distribution of products of labor, or planning procedures of various sorts (by chiefs, elders, local councils, priests or priestesses, etc.). Many nonmarket societies existed for a longer period than have market societies. Indeed it was because nonmarket distributive systems functioned well for long periods of time that human beings survived and eventually created market systems as well as nonmarket systems. The impor-tance of markets to neoclassical theory does not therefore reflect their quantita-tive importance in social history. Rather, the special place of markets within that theory has more to do with one of its founder's remarkable insight and its usefulness in the European transition from feudalism to capitalism in the eighteenth and nineteenth centuries.

More than two hundred years ago Adam Smith theorized that societies allowing citizens the full freedom to compete in all markets would generate more wealth for its citizens than any constriction of such freedom. If wealth measured the economic progress of any society and if maximum wealth became the social objective, then achieving that objective required establishing free, competitive markets. The idea of free competitive markets became a key concept first in Smith's classical theory of political economy and later in neoclassical economic theory.

According to neoclassical economic theory, capitalist societies are societies that establish and protect two key institutions. The first is private property: each citizen has the power freely to own, buy, or sell his or her resources and produced goods. The second is a system of fully competitive markets: no citizen has any power to control prices, and all buyers and sellers take market prices as facts on which to base their decisions. When both institutions exist, a society possesses what is typically called a "private enterprise market economy." Following Smith's insight, that society also has provided the conditions for something more: achieving maximum wealth. In other words, capitalism allows and encourages the citizens of a society to reach their maximum production and consumption potential. Thus, given these citizens' preferences and productive abilities, markets and private property offer citizens the optimum opportunity to gain the maximum wealth possible.

This conclusion of neoclassical theory has been powerful, influential and provocative. Economists have been arguing for many years about its precise meaning and consequences. We can appreciate the centrality of private property and markets for neoclassical theory by a brief look at economists who have disagreed with neoclassical theory. For example, some economists have been unhappy with certain social effects of private property. They understand this particular institution to produce unequal distributions of wealth and power among the citizenry. For that reason they sometimes advocate keeping the institution of competitive markets (they believe it permits the achievement of maximum wealth) while abolishing private property (they believe it causes the unequal distribution of that wealth). When capitalist societies have been altered in this way, they have been variously called "noncapitalist," "mixed," or "socialist" because of their loss of one definitive characteristic of capitalism, namely private property.

This kind of change that has occurred in capitalist economies is interestingly connected to an economic system often termed "market socialism" or "democratic socialism." That is a kind of economy (and politics) far more popular in Europe than in the United States. Market or democratic socialism would continue competitive markets but replace private with collectivize ownership of the means of production (factories, tools, and equipment). Collective ownership is intended to deal with the problem of too much of society's wealth going to and owned by too few of its citizens. A key goal is to prevent the social anger and alienation associated with the economic inequality believed to flow when means of production are privately owned.

Other kinds of socialists, and also many of those who call themselves communists, have advocated an economic system with neither private property nor markets. They sought to replace private with collective property in the means of production but also to replace markets with government planning as their preferred means of distributing resources to producers and products to consumers. In disagreement with them, the "market" or "democratic" social-ists have argued that competitive markets are the better distributive mechanism than planning because the power to plan concentrates too much power in the too few hands of state planners. Markets, they argue, distribute power across large numbers of individual consumers and producers free to make their eco-nomic choices (buying and selling). Market socialists, like the devotees of neoclassical theory, see markets as democratic institutions. Markets, unlike government planners, also allow choices that serve the needs and desires of all market participants (and thus the maximum wealth and consumption pos-sible) rather than primarily the needs of the government.

Market socialists believe that competitive markets also generate economic ups and down (recurring cycles of prosperity and recession, boom and bust) that can be debilitating if not dangerous to society. Thus democratic socialists follow Keynesians in advocating state controls over markets to mute and/or offset their cycles. Supporters of market socialism have thus tried to combine what they take to be the "best" aspects of the three economic theories: Marx's collective ownership of the means of production, Smith's competitive markets, and Keynes's state management of the business cycle arising from competitive markets.

Now we can clearly state the position of the vast majority of neoclassical economists. They defend and argue for both institutions, insisting that private property and competitive markets are mutually supportive of one another as well as necessary for maximum wealth. In their view, to eliminate the institu-tion of private property (hoping to achieve a more equal distribution of wealth) is to jeopardize the competitive market necessary for maximum wealth to be achieved.

Despite their differences, neoclassicists, Keynesians, and market socialists affirm the importance of markets as vehicles that allow and facilitate the citi-zens' achievement of maximum wealth. In other words, when markets perform properly, a society is efficient: it produces as much as possible with its limited resources. It follows that imperfections in markets, whatever their source, may prevent a society from achieving its maximum wealth production and con-sumption. These economists all recognize a major economic problem in the occurrence of market imperfections in modern societies.

Neoclassical theorists also propose solutions to this problem. The most conservative neoclassical economists think the best solution is to protect the institution of private property from those who would reform, regulate, or destroy it. They urge leaving competitive markets alone. They argue that most market imperfections are caused by the quite visible interference of human beings and bureaucracies in the workings of supply and demand. In their view, efforts to reform or modify private property and competitive markets are inherently wrong, since they create the very barriers to maximum wealth—

the market imperfections—that are the problem in the first place. Leave buyers and sellers alone, they insist. Let them pursue their own self-interest in free markets and work out individually their desires, wishes, and abilities to produce. Then all citizens will be better off. These economists warrant the label "conservative" because they want to conserve from change those institutions that define a society as "capitalist" and that encourage maximum wealth for its citizens. From this perspective the role of the state is quite small: basically to protect private property and competitive markets from institutions and people within and without the state who would undermine their operation.

Liberal neoclassical economists believe that the best solution to the problem of market imperfections is for some individuals and institutions to intervene in these imperfect markets to get them to work properly. Market imperfections are understood to flow partly from the very nature of buyers and sellers themselves. The only way to compensate for this imperfection in human nature is to intervene so as to get the market to work properly. In the view of liberal neoclassical theorists, to leave the market alone, as the conservatives would have it, is to allow this imperfection to continue and thus risks that society will not reach its maximum point of efficiency in generating wealth.

Keynesians economists go further than the liberal neoclassical economists. The Keynesians see more and deeper and longer lasting market imperfections that constantly threaten wealth maximization and so require constant government monitoring and intervention to overcome those imperfections and their effects. However, Keynesians rarely advocate that the state take over the enterprises from their private owners. They see no need to do that and fear its consequences for undermining the otherwise desirable workings of markets. Keynesians limit their proposals to specific state policies that can shape and regulate the economic choices of individuals and private enterprises in the interest of precluding, overcoming or offsetting market imperfections.

The market-socialists go still further than the Keynesians. They do advocate collective ownership (nationalization) of the means of production to create state-owned and managed enterprises (at least in some key industries) as the necessary way to limit or overcome business cycles and socially divisive inequalities of wealth. But like the Keynesians and the neoclassical economists, they too favor competitive markets as the best institution to manage the distribution of resources and products among individuals and state enterprises.

Most economists, at least in the United States, embrace varying combinations of these perspectives at various points in their lives. Under the pressures of changing economic and political conditions, they shift from one position to another or from one combination of perspectives to another. Likewise they may emphasize one perspective within a composite perspective more than another and then change that emphasis. The holding of multiple and shifting perspectives has stimulated other economists to search for some sort of synthesis that could command and hold the loyalty of most economists.

What is rarely challenged by these different groupings (conservative and liberal neoclassicists, Keynesians, and market socialists) is the place and importance given to markets within their theory. That is a testament to the power and persuasiveness of neoclassical theory in today's world. Irrespective of whether these economists believe that markets are working properly, their debates, teaching, and research focus on markets as the best institution so as to deliver the maximum wealth possible to society.

2.2.3   Preferences: Determining the Demand for Commodities

Neoclassical theory's conceptual entry points are human preferences (tastes, wants, or choices), human productive abilities, and the available physical resources and technology. In the following sections we intend to show how these concepts separately and together act to determine supply-and-demand behavior and thus the price of all wealth in society, including the value of its resources. We begin with human preferences.

Neoclassical theorists recognize one particular aspect of human nature as an essential determinant of economic actions. That aspect is the capacity and desire to make rational choices in regard to all economic opportunities. For our purposes here, we focus on individuals' choices concerning (1) their consumption of goods and services available for purchase in the market, and (2) their supply of the resources they own to those who buy such resources in order to carry out the process of producing goods and services. The first set of choices constitutes the demand for goods and services in the market. The second set of choices constitutes the supply of goods and services in the market. For both demand and supply, we will see the essential, determining role assigned to individual preferences as causes of their choices and thus of the supplies and demands in markets.

Given the importance of any theory's point of entry to that theory's workings and conclusions, it is not surprising that neoclassical theorists have made vast efforts over the years to refine their understanding of human preferences. We will not here attempt a full explanation of that understanding, but we will describe it in a general way. First, each and every individual in society is assumed to rank order in a consistent way his or her preferences for all conceivable goods and services that they may confront in markets now or in the future. That is, we always know and can express which of two different goods and/or services (or two differently composed bundles of them) we like more (or possibly like equally) by choosing which we want more to buy and consume. Moreover this expression of choice is further assumed to be transitive in nature, which means simply that if an individual chooses basket A over B, and B over C, then he or she will also choose A over C.

Another key component of human nature, in the neoclassical understanding of it, is that everyone always wants or prefers more rather than less of any good or service. This is sometimes referred to as the assumption of nonsatiation. Still other assumptions about human nature are perhaps less easy to understand, but they are just as crucial to neoclassical theory. One such assumption concerns how individuals can substitute one good for another to maintain the same total level of satisfaction. In other words, as an individual gives up successive units of one good, he or she must increase the quantity of another good to maintain the same total level of satisfaction from goods consumption. Neoclassical literature refers to this assumed quality of human consumption as the "diminishing marginal rate of substitution" between two goods. Humans' psychological ability or willingness to give up a unit of good A for a unit of good B falls as more units of A are given up. Since good A becomes relatively more important as a person has less of it, its continued loss can be offset only by ever-more units of B.

The characteristics of human nature discussed above comprise part of what neoclassical theorists see as its inherent "rationality." Another part of our rationality is the drive to take maximum advantage of our opportunities. Each person, regardless of circumstance, is assumed to be a rationally motivated, choice-making machine.

What determines this rationality of human nature? The neoclassical theorists seem largely to be disinterested in this question. Rationality simply is a basic component of human nature. Of course, rational preferences may change—just as human nature may change—but they do not change in response to changes in the economy. Preferences—like other parts of human nature—are understood to be the causes of economic changes, not their effects. Changes in prices or incomes are caused by human nature; they do not cause or change that nature. When preferences change, it reflects causes not found in the economy but rather, for example, in the realms of biology or culture.

From these few assumptions about human nature, neoclassical theorists construct an analytical device to examine and even to predict economic choices. This device is a set or "map" of preference or indifference curves. Each map represents for each and every individual in society how he or she assesses the desirability of all conceivable commodities. Figure 2.2 illustrates such curves. Advanced economics texts demonstrate how and why (1) this map of human rationality exists once we assume the inherent ability of all individuals to rank order all conceivable bundles of commodities; (2) movements in a northeasterly direction, to higher preference curves, represent an individual's attainment of higher levels of satisfaction (derived from the assumption of nonsatiation); (3) all curves are negatively sloped (also derived from the

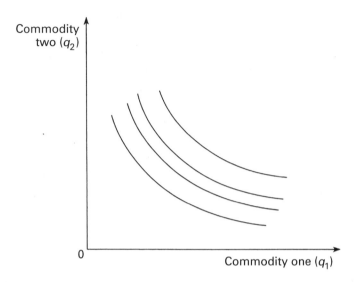

Figure 2.2
Set of preference curves depicting an individual's taste for two commodities, q_1 and q_2.

assumption of nonsatiation); (4) there are no sharp jumps or gaps in the curves (following from a technical assumption of continuity); (5) the curves do not touch or intersect (derived from the assumption of consistent behavior); and (6) all curves are convex to the point of origin (following from the assumption of a diminishing marginal rate of substitution).

Preference curves are used within neoclassical theory to help explain almost all economic choices we make as individuals, including the demand for and supply of all commodities and resources in the economy. The powerful explanatory role of these curves should not be surprising, given the essentialist logic of neoclassical theory. It is precisely the nature of a theoretical essence that it ultimately determines the actions of all other entities treated in the theory.

Neoclassical theory now adds some additional assumptions needed to construct its analysis, its picture of how the economy works. First, it assumes that the income of each individual in the economy is known. That is, each individual is assumed to own specific quantities of productive resources like land, labor, and capital that will generate rents, wages, and profits adding up to that individual's income. Second, it assumes that each individual takes the prices of commodities as given. In other words, each person has a given sum of money income to spend on desired commodities over whose prices he or she has no influence. By the way, if and when no single individual or subset of individuals has any power over price—so that all individuals are price-takers and none are price-makers—that is the definition of a perfectly competitive market. We will return to the subject of competitive markets later in this chapter.

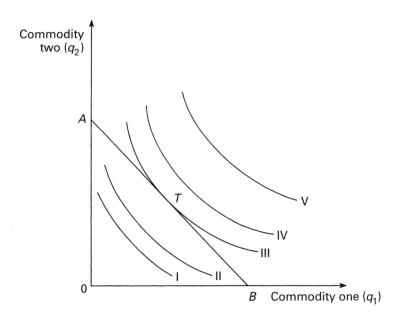

Figure 2.3
Optimal solution for the consumer is at point T, where the highest preference curve has been reached (*III*) subject to the income constraint (*AB*). The optimal point is described in the text as $mu_1/mu_2 = p_1/p_2$.

With these additional assumptions about incomes and prices, neoclassical theory constructs one of its key diagrams to explain the demand behavior of individuals. Figure 2.3 poses and answers a fundamental question: given individuals' *unlimited* wants (recall the assumption of nonsatiation and the map of each individual's infinite number of preference curves) how do they cope with *limited* money (see the only straight line, *AB*, drawn in the diagram).[1] How do individuals bring unlimited wants into harmony with the limited incomes imposed by our economic environment?

Point T in figure 2.3 represents the best point attainable by any individual. There, the individual has reached the highest preference curve achievable (thereby maximizing his or her wealth = satisfaction), given the owned resources and resulting income that constrain what that person can spend. Point T then is the outcome of each individual's struggle to make the best of his or her market opportunities in order to reach the highest possible preference (satisfaction) level. This is what neoclassical theory means with the phrase "maximizing one's opportunities." That is what the theory presumes every rational person does.

Let us examine this solution—point T in figure 2.3—more carefully. It expresses neoclassical theory's view of human beings' fundamental struggle:

to bring our *private* ability to choose rationally, given by our individual natures, into harmony with our *social* opportunities to substitute, given to us by the impersonal market. On the one hand, the social opportunity to substitute is measured by the price ratio between the two commodities, p_1/p_2, the ratio for substituting one good for the other.[2] On the other hand, the private ability to choose rationally is measured by each individual's marginal rate of substitution between the two goods derived from that individual's human nature.

We turn next to examine how neoclassical theory expresses and measures the private ability of individuals to choose rationally among commodities based on their preferences. Consider figure 2.4, where we have labeled two points A and B along the same preference curve. Relative to point A, point B indicates more q_1 and less q_2. A problem arises: How are we to compare this loss of one good with a gain in the other? Is there a unit of measure, some property common to both goods, that would allow us to compare this loss and gain?

Neoclassical theory answers yes: commodities share the property of being sources of human satisfaction, they have utility for the humans who therefore choose to acquire them. Utility, a property assumed common to all commodities, therefore serves as a standard of comparison among them in neoclassical

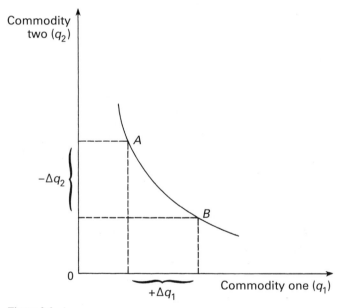

Figure 2.4
Movements along a preference curve (from A to B) can be thought of as balancing the loss in utility with the gain in utility:

$$\underbrace{-\Delta q_2 \cdot mu_{q2}}_{\text{"loss"}} = \underbrace{+\Delta q_1 \cdot mu_{q1}}_{\text{"gain"}}$$

theory's understanding of economies. As we will see in chapter 4, Marxian theory answers a parallel question quite differently. It makes "abstract labor time" rather than "utility" the common property of commodities around which Marxian theory builds its understanding of economies. Different economic theories generate different standards for comparing different commodities.

According to the definition of a preference curve, any individual will be indifferent to different bundles of commodities along his or her curve. Thus, as seen in figure 2.4, the consumer is understood to receive the same level of satisfaction or utility at point A as at point B. Therefore, if the individual in society is to remain on the same curve, we may think of the loss in satisfaction or utility incurred by giving up some q_2 to be exactly balanced by—that is, to be equal to—the gain in satisfaction or utility experienced by gaining more q_1. Figure 2.4 shows the loss in q_2 as $-\Delta q_2$, the minus sign indicating that the consumer has lost some q_2. It shows the gain as $+\Delta q_1$, the plus sign indicating the consumer's additional consumption of q_1.[3] The loss in satisfaction or utility is typically written as $-\Delta q_2 \cdot mu_2$ and the gain as $+\Delta q_1 \cdot mu_1$, where mu_1 and mu_2 represent, respectively, the per unit marginal utilities of the commodities.[4] Along the same preference curve, by definition, these two terms must always equal each other: $-\Delta q_2 \cdot mu_2 = +\Delta q_1 \cdot mu_1$.

Neoclassical theory has used what it assumes to be the common property of both commodities—that they are objects of utility—as its weighting scheme (the respective marginal utilities) to understand the substitution of one commodity for the other.

We now have an exact measure of the private ability to substitute one commodity for another along any given preference curve. Solving the equation above for $\Delta q_2/\Delta q_1$, we get

$$MRS_{12} = \frac{\Delta q_2}{\Delta q_1} = -\frac{mu_1}{mu_2},$$

where MRS_{12} stands for the marginal rate of substitution of commodity 1 for commodity 2.

Let us recast the aforementioned neoclassical solution in these new terms. The optimal point for the individual (point T in figure 2.3) can now be written as

$$\frac{mu_1}{mu_2} = \frac{p_1}{p_2}.$$

The private ability to choose rationally among commodities, as measured by this ratio of marginal utilities, is equal to the social ability to consume, as measured by the ratio of prices. In reaching this point, the individual has acted in an efficient way in regard to consumption decisions: the best possible consumption result has been achieved given the market constraint faced.

It is but a small step to derive demand curves from figure 2.3. By continually varying the price of one of the commodities, say p_1, we can predict an individual's demand behavior—that is, what amounts of commodity 1 he or she would like to buy at these different prices. Figure 2.5 illustrates this procedure. In figure 2.5a the price of commodity 1 has been decreased relative to the price of commodity 2; the new price lines, denoted in the figure as AC, AD, and AE, indicate the assumed decreases in the price of commodity 1. As the constraint faced by the individual changes with each assumed decrease in price, ever-new points of correspondence between the private and social ability to substitute are generated. The logic of the theory that asserts this essential human struggle to achieve the highest possible level of satisfaction guarantees that these new points of correspondence will be reached.

The resulting new points of balance, or what neoclassical economists often refer to as equilibrium points, are indicated in figure 2.5a by the letters U, V, and W. Obviously many such points could be produced. When all of them are connected, a price-consumption locus, denoted in figure 2.5a as TW, is constructed. Each of the equilibrium points of this locus thus represents an equality between the ratio of marginal utilities and the corresponding price ratios.

Figure 2.5b shows the derived demand curve for the commodity 1 depicted in figure 2.5a. The horizontal axes of both figures are lined up since both measure the demand for q_1. Each point on the price-consumption locus, TW, in figure 2.5a is mapped onto the demand surface in figure 2.5b. Following the dotted lines from figure 2.5a to figure 2.5b, we find the points T', U', V', and W' in figure 2.5b; these points constitute the demand curve for the commodity q_1. We know that such points must fall in a southeasterly direction because we have previously assumed a continued lower price of p_1 relative to p_2 and an increase in the demand for q_1.[5]

The well-known downward sloping demand curve for any individual is thus logically derived in figure 2.5b. Using the same procedure, we could derive an individual's demand curve for each commodity: q_1, q_2, q_3, and so forth. By adding up such demand curves across all individuals, we could derive the aggregate demand curve for each commodity in the society (as shown in figure 2.1).

Each of these curves would be constructed from individuals' preferences and incomes and from the prices these individuals faced. The logic of the diagrams illustrates this construction: figure 2.5b is derived from figure 2.5a, and figure 2.5a is derived from figure 2.3. In the interaction of preferences, incomes, and prices, we therefore have a partial answer to our initial question of what determines individuals' demand for commodities. Let us examine this conclusion more closely.

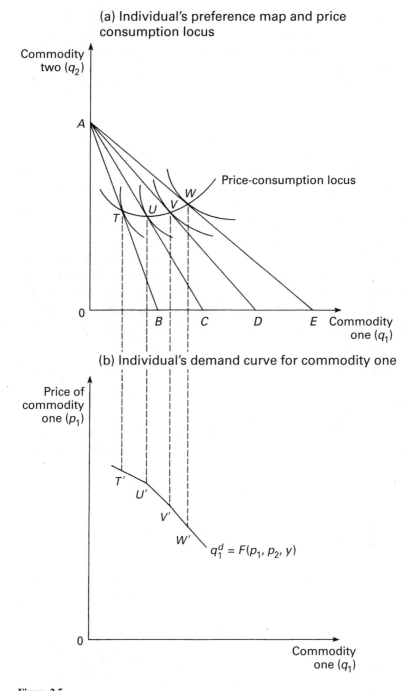

(a) Individual's preference map and price consumption locus

Commodity two (q_2)

A

Price-consumption locus

W

U V

T

0

B C D E Commodity one (q_1)

(b) Individual's demand curve for commodity one

Price of commodity one (p_1)

T'

U'

V'

W'

$q_1^d = F(p_1, p_2, y)$

0

Commodity one (q_1)

Figure 2.5
Derivation of an individual's demand curve for commodity 1 (b) from the price consumption locus of that individual (a)

For any particular individual, the prices of commodities are determined, as previously noted, by the market. Preferences are also assumed to be given, in this case by the individual's human nature. What, however, determines the individual's income?

The wage income of any one individual may be thought of as the wage rate earned per hour times the number of hours worked. If we let w stand for this wage rate and h stand for the hours worked per individual, we have $y = w \cdot h$, where y represents the income earned. The total wage income for all individuals would then be $Y = w \cdot h \cdot L$, where L stands for the given total number of workers and Y for their aggregate wage income. To keep our focus on the core of neoclassical theory, we will make the simplifying assumption throughout that the total number of laborers is fixed while the number of labor hours they offer varies.

We may now ask what determines w and hL for workers. The answer is the aggregate demand for and the aggregate supply of labor—that is, the labor market, which is depicted in figure 2.6. Figure 2.6 demonstrates that the intersection of the total demand for and supply of labor hours determines simultaneously the wage rate for each individual (w) and the total quantity of labor hours supplied and demanded (hL). Once again recalling the logic of neoclas-

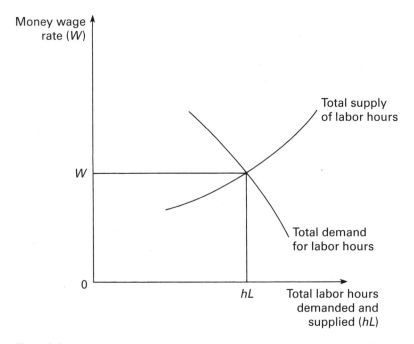

Figure 2.6
Determination of the money wage rate and the labor hours demanded and supplied in the labor market

sical theory, we may ask: What determines these particular supply-and-demand schedules and thus the wage income of individuals?

2.2.4 Preferences: Determining the Supply of Labor

According to neoclassical theory, the supply of labor hours by individuals depends on their preferences and on the given real wage rate. Neoclassicists assume that individuals spend income on commodities and that that income is derived from work—that is, from the quantity of hours allocated to work by each individual. The person who offers more hours in the labor market receives more income and can then purchase more commodities. Income provides the individual with satisfaction or utility, since it is used to purchase objects of utility—that is, commodities. However, the more hours an individual offers in the labor market, the fewer hours he or she has available for leisure. Neoclassicists assume that leisure has utility for individuals just as purchased commodities do. Therefore each individual must choose between the consumption of commodities (via offered hours of work) and the consumption of leisure.

Figure 2.7 depicts the choice between real income (the collection of commodities purchased) and leisure time. Since we are endowed with only so many hours per day, we must choose between the two items of pleasure. Parallel to our previous map of preference curves, we have drawn in this diagram a set of curves showing the trade-off between real income and leisure. It is

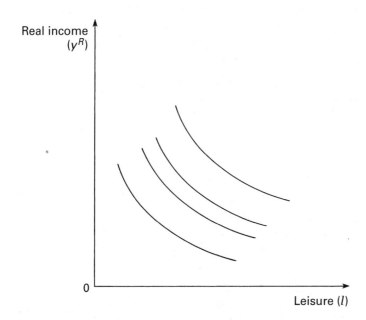

Figure 2.7
Set of preference curves depicting an individual's taste for real income (y^R) and leisure time (l)

worth underscoring the point that all of our previous statements concerning the derivation of preference curves apply here as well. They are, as always, dictated by our human nature.

Along any given preference curve, we may calculate the individual's private substitution—that is, choice between real income and leisure time. To differentiate this marginal rate of substitution from our previous one, we will use the subscripts l for leisure time and y^R for real income:

$$MRS_{ly^R} = -\frac{mu_l}{mu_{y^R}},$$

where mu_l, stands for the marginal utility of leisure time and mu_{y^R} for the marginal utility of real income.[6]

Let us now introduce the real wage rate faced by each individual. It is determined, like all prices, by the impersonal workings of the competitive market. In this case the question is: How many hours of labor will any individual offer, given this real wage rate and his or her preferences for leisure and real income? To discover the answer, we employ the same procedure that we used in the previous analysis of an individual's choice between any two commodities. The same theme repeats itself in a slightly different form: each individual struggles to achieve the highest preference curve possible, subject to whatever constraints are given. In this example, the goal of the individual is to maximize the satisfaction received from consuming real income and leisure, given the economic constraint of a real wage rate, which is the price of that leisure in terms of the real income forgone.

Figure 2.8 shows a real wage rate line, AX, which has been derived in the following way. Suppose that OX is the total quantity of hours available for both leisure and work. It may be considered the endowment of time available to any individual. Assume, for the moment, that an individual works XX' hours (measured from X) and thus chooses OX' hours of leisure time (measured from O). If the individual receives a total real income of $X'y'$ dollars, then the real hourly wage rate is

$$\frac{X'y'}{X'X} = \frac{\text{real income}}{\text{number of hours worked}} = w^R,$$

where w^R stands for the real hourly wage rate.

Introduce, now, the set of preference curves from figure 2.7 into figure 2.8. Using the logic we employed in the previous section when we discovered the most efficient consumption point for the individual (point T in figure 2.3), we can write the optimal point in figure 2.8 as T'. Here the individual laborer has once again brought into harmony the private ability to choose among objects (MRS_{ly^R}) with the social ability (w^R) to do so. We may write this new equilibrium situation as

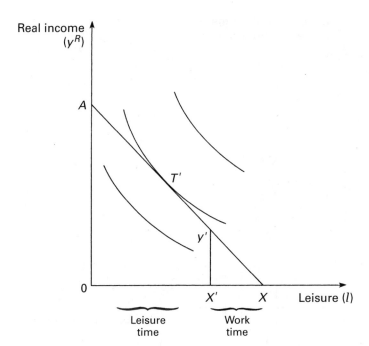

Figure 2.8
Optimal solution for a laborer. At point T' the highest preference curve has been reached subject to the real-wage constraint. The optimal point may be described as $mu_l/mu_{y^R} = w^R$.

$$\frac{mu_l}{mu_{y^R}} = w^R.$$

To derive the supply of labor hours from this preference map, let us first vary the real wage rate in figure 2.9a. Suppose that the real wage is increased, as indicated by the new lines XB, XC, and XD. New points of equilibrium are reached by the individual indicated in the diagram by the points B, C, and D, where once again the $MRS_{l_y R}$ is brought into equality with each new real wage rate. Connecting these equilibrium points, neoclassicists derive an individual's offer curve of labor hours (indicated in the diagram as $TBCD$). The supply curve is derived directly from this offer curve.

Figure 2.9b lines up its horizontal axis with that of figure 2.9a such that the hours of work offered by the individual can be measured in both diagrams (reading from right to left in both). The dotted lines drawn from the offer curve in figure 2.9a map out the points T'', B', C', and D' on the indicated supply curve of labor hours in figure 2.9b. As the real wage rate increases, the supply of labor hours rises. Simply adding up each individual's supply of labor hours at different real wage rates will generate the aggregate supply curve of labor hours in the labor market.

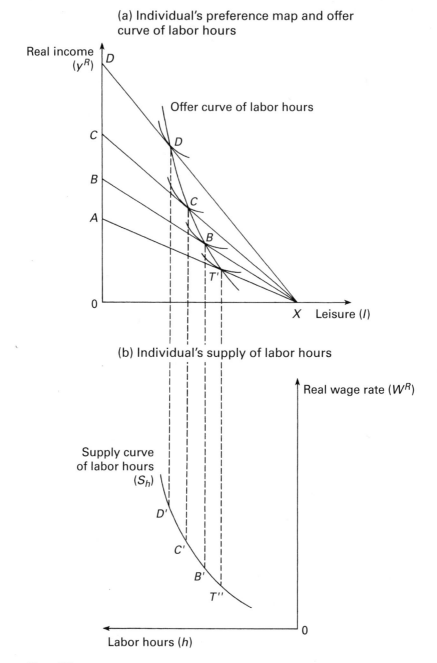

Figure 2.9
Derivation of an individual's supply of labor hours (b) from the offer curve of that individual (a)

We have then the neoclassical answer to what determines the supply of the labor resource for any individual: choice between real income and leisure, the given real wage, and the given initial endowment of hours. The individual's endowment of hours (24) is as much given by nature as is the choice between income and leisure; as before, the real wage is given by the competitive market. Thus we may conclude that for any given real wage and endowment, the supply of labor is determined by human nature—an individual's preference to acquire real income via work rather than to choose leisure and no income.

2.2.5 Preferences and Scarcity: Determining the Demand for Labor

We now turn to neoclassical theory's explanation of the demand for this labor and, therefore, to its explanation of wage determination. Any producer's decision about how much labor to hire depends on how that labor will affect the producer's profits. For example, if additional labor adds to profits, then a decision will be made to employ more. If, however, additional labor reduces profits, then the opposite decision will be made.

For any given cost of that labor—that is, wage rate—neoclassical theory recognizes two factors that affect the decision to hire and the impact of that decision on profits. Those factors are the marginal productivity of the additional hired labor (the extra commodity output it will produce), and the price of the extra commodities. If the dollar value of the marginal product is greater than its cost (in terms of the wages that have to be paid to acquire it), then the labor will be employed. If the dollar value is less, the labor will not be hired. The demand for labor then depends on the marginal productivity of labor and the price of the output produced by that labor.

We may state the same proposition in a more formal way. Let us write for a producing firm a profit equation in which we assume for the moment that the only input and thus cost of production is labor. That profit equation would read

$$\Pi = p \cdot q - w \cdot h \cdot L_i,$$

where Π stands for the firm's profits, p for the price of the commodity being produced and sold, q for the quantity of the commodity produced, w for the money wage, and where L_i stands for the workers hired by this firm and h has already been defined. The equation states simply that profits equal total revenues ($p \cdot q$) minus total wage costs ($w \cdot h \cdot L_i$).

Now let us see what would happen to this profit equation if the quantity of labor hours changed. Before we write down a new equation, however, we need to recall that each producer is assumed to have no power over commodity prices or wage rates. The competitive market gives all output and input prices to each producer. Therefore, in the profit equation above, p and w will not change when the producer produces and sells more output resulting from the assumed purchase of more labor input. Keeping this in mind, we write the new profit equation as

$$\Delta\Pi = \bar{p} \cdot \Delta q - \bar{w} \cdot \Delta h \cdot L_i,$$

where Δ indicates a change in the appropriate variable and the overbar in $\bar{p}$ and $\bar{w}$ indicates that these variables do not change because of any producer's decision to hire more labor.

To derive the final impact of the changed labor hours on the firm's profits, divide both sides of the profit equation by $\Delta h L_i$:

$$\frac{\Delta\Pi}{\Delta h L_i} = \bar{p} \cdot \frac{\Delta q}{\Delta h L_i} - \bar{w}.$$

If $\Delta\Pi/\Delta h L_i$ is positive, then clearly an increase in the demand for labor will add to profits. In this case the dollar value of the marginal product ($\bar{p} \cdot \Delta q/\Delta h L_i$) is greater than its cost ($\bar{w}$). If, however, $\Delta\Pi/\Delta h L_i$ is negative, then the additional labor will not be hired. The dollar value of the marginal product is less than the money wage. Only when the given money wage rate ($\bar{w}$) is equal to $\bar{p} \cdot \Delta q/\Delta h L_i$ will the firm neither gain nor lose profits by expanding or contracting its demand for labor. At that point, it will have maximized its assumed objective—namely its profits.

Clearly, the preceding profit equation demonstrates that the output price (p) and the marginal productivity of labor ($\Delta q/\Delta h L_i$) together determine the demand for labor. For this reason neoclassical economists often refer to the *derived* demand for labor, the demand derived from these two variables. The next logical question then becomes: What governs the price and the marginal productivity from which the labor demand is derived?

Let us begin with price. As we have already noted, price is derived from market competition and given to each producer. This means that the amount of a commodity that each producer sells depends only on the demand of consumers for that commodity. The more consumers demand, the more each producer can sell. Consequently a rise in consumer demand will have a positive effect on a producer's demand for labor.

Recall that for any given wage income and price, the preferences of each individual determine the demand for commodities. Therefore the demand for labor is, in part, ultimately derived from consumer preferences for the commodity produced by that labor. Once again, this particular neoclassical essence makes its powerful presence felt, this time in the labor market.

The number of labor hours hired also depends on the productive abilities of that labor. In turn, the latter depends on whatever skills labor is endowed with and on the availability of other resources and technologies with which that labor can be combined. Typically a greater amount of other resources per worker produces a higher marginal productivity of workers and thus a demand-for-labor curve that is further from the origin (in a northeasterly direction) shown in figure 2.6. The demand for labor is also affected by the degree to which other resources can be easily substituted for the labor resource. If, for example, other resources are a good substitute for labor, then the demand-for-labor curve in figure 2.6 will be relatively more elastic than it would be if they were not. Thus both the position and the shape of the demand-for-labor curve depend on available resource endowments, including the technology that is available to produce output, and on the given ability of these producing units to combine together the available resources to produce outputs.

The latter ability of individuals is captured in what neoclassical theorists call a "production function." For any given technology the production function is the relationship between the quantity of input resources and the maximum quantity of outputs obtainable with those inputs. Its theoretical location within neoclassical theory is as important as the already discussed preference function relating quantities of consumption inputs to the output pleasure produced. Both functions act as powerful essences within the theory and both are equally necessary to explain the ultimate determination of values in society.

The production function is sometimes referred to as a "neoclassical production function" if it satisfies certain assumed conditions. Quite parallel to the neoclassical preference function, these conditions permit this production function to exist and have certain properties that are deemed useful by neoclassical theorists. These production conditions are taken to be as natural a part of society as the conditions associated with the preference function. They are taken to be either an inherent attribute of human beings or a part of the physical nature with which we interact.

For the sake of convenience, we will assume only two inputs, labor and something called "capital." The latter will stand for the machines, tools, and other materials used in the production process. Briefly, there are several key production conditions. Both inputs, capital and labor, must be positive for output to be positive, and the more capital and labor the society has available to it, the greater the potential output will be. The marginal product of each input is positive, but this product will fall in magnitude for each input as the quantity of one increases while that of the other is held constant (texts usually refer to this property as the "natural law of diminishing marginal returns"). Thus the marginal product of capital (labor) will approach zero as the capital (labor) resource is increased while the labor (capital) resource is held constant, and the marginal product of capital (labor) will become infinitely large as the amount of labor (capital) increases while that of capital (labor) remains constant.

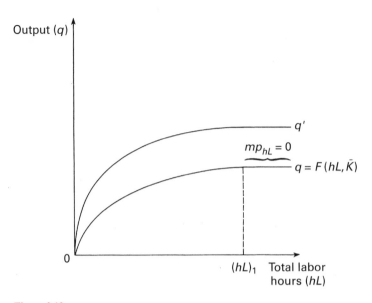

Figure 2.10
Production function showing the relationship between the maximum output (q) obtainable with the available resources: variable inputs of labor (hL) and a fixed input of capital ($\bar{K}$)

Figure 2.10 depicts such a production function. It shows the relationship between real output and a variable amount of labor input when we assume a fixed input of capital.[7] The latter is denoted by $\bar{K}$ in the equation for the production function shown in the figure. The greater the number of labor hours available to produce output, the larger that output will be. However, because of neoclassical theory's "law of diminishing marginal returns," the rate of increase of output tends to fall as more labor is used. In other words, the measure of this "law," the marginal productivity of labor, falls in magnitude when labor is increased while capital is held constant. Finally the marginal product of labor approaches zero (after point $(hL)_1$ in the figure) as we continuously expand only the labor input.

Figure 2.11 depicts the derived marginal product of the labor curve. An increase in the capital resource will now shift both the production function and its associated marginal productivity curve upward as pictured in figures 2.10 and 2.11. An improvement in the initially given technology will do the same. Therefore the marginal productivity of labor, including its shape and its distance from the origin, depends on both the underlying production function from which it is derived and the availability of the other resource—in this case, capital.

Paralleling our explanation of the origins of human preferences, neoclassical theory takes both this underlying production function (i.e., all of its properties) and the initial resource endowments as given. Once again, we encounter

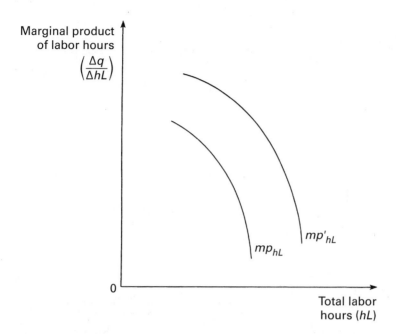

Figure 2.11
Marginal product of labor hours derived from figure 2.10. A shift in the curve is due to a change in the capital resource or a change in technology.

the assumption that human beings are endowed not only with some initial quanta of labor and capital resources but also with an inherent technological ability to be productive (expressed metaphorically as their "production function"). We may conclude, therefore, that the marginal productivity of labor (its existence, shape, and position) is governed by these two neoclassical essences: technological and resource (input) endowments.

2.2.6 Determination of Wages and Commodity Demands

The determination of wages follows logically from the supply and demand for labor. First, we add up all the demands for labor hours by each producing unit to derive the aggregate demand in the labor market. Next we consider the interaction of this aggregate demand with the aggregate supply of labor hours described in the previous section. Figure 2.12 pictures the interaction of these aggregate labor market curves. Initially it might seem that the aggregate supply of and demand for labor alone provide the ultimate explanation for what determines wage incomes. However, that would be a superficial analysis. Looking deeper (i.e., looking at the previous figures from which figure 2.12 is derived), we see that the ultimate determinants of the market supply of and demand for labor and thus of wage incomes in society are certain underlying

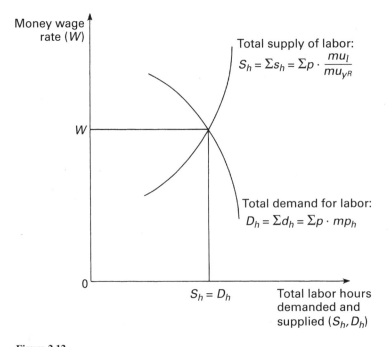

Figure 2.12
Determination of money wages and employment in the labor market as derived from the leisure–real income choice on the supply side and the marginal product of labor on the demand side

traits of human beings: their preferences, production functions, and resource endowments. This is precisely what has been shown in the last two sections. There is no need to look any further for explanations, for nothing else in neoclassical theory determines these three essences. As essences in that economic theory they cause economic events but are not caused by them.

A wage income for each consumer and wage costs for each producer in society are determined ultimately by our nature as rational consumers and productive human beings. This conclusion should not be underestimated. It means, for example (barring market imperfections), that the relatively high incomes for some individuals in society can be explained on the basis of those same individuals' preference for work rather than leisure and/or on the basis of the relatively high marginal productivity of their labor. Similarly the incomes of the poor can be explained on the basis of their choice of leisure time rather than income via work and/or on the basis of their relatively low marginal labor productivity. In either case, ruling out any market imperfections, the wage incomes of individuals in society are explained on the basis of these individuals' own human nature or the technology that is available to them. Indeed, for any given technology (i.e., for any production function and resource endowment), the relatively rich are rich because they choose to be so, while the relatively poor are poor because they choose not to be rich. Simply put, as individuals we are responsible only to ourselves for the wealth we ultimately enjoy in this world. As we will see in chapter 4, this neoclassical conclusion differs dramatically from the Marxian explanation of incomes in a society.

Now that we have considered neoclassical theory's explanation of wage determination, we may return to that theory's analysis of individual demand for different commodities. Remember that we showed how these demands were derived logically from the given preferences and wage incomes of individuals. We have just demonstrated how preferences and productive abilities determine what individuals earn as wage incomes. Therefore, adding this new information to what we already had, we may conclude that the three neoclassical essences (preferences, production functions, and endowments) govern the demand for commodities by each and every person in the society.

2.2.7 Preferences: Determining the Supply of Capital

In neoclassical theory, labor owners offer their privately owned labor resource to producers in return for a wage. In parallel fashion, owners of capital offer their privately owned resource to producers in return for a price or rental fee. This return, or as we will see, this rate of return, is the percentage return per unit of time earned by the owners of capital. For example, an individual might supply $1,000 worth of owned capital to a producing firm and be paid $100 a year for doing so. The rental price paid would then be $100 a year for the use of $1,000 of capital; alternatively, the received rate of return on the capital would be 10 percent per year (10% = $100/$1,000). Producing firms must pay this rental price of $100 per year to the owners of capital in order to acquire $1,000 worth of this resource (which is assumed to be necessary for production to take place). Thus the income of owners of capital who contribute it to production is $100 per year or a rate of 10 percent on $1,000 of invested capital.

To derive the offer curve of an individual's capital resource, we employ the procedure we used in deriving the offer curve of an individual's labor resource. Suppose that each individual in society could choose between present and future consumption of commodities. In other words, an individual might save some of his or her current income—that is, not consume all of it now—in order to make that saved income available for consumption in the future. Since we assume that both current and future consumption provide utility to individuals, each person must choose between the consumption of commodities now and consumption in the future.

Figure 2.13 depicts this choice: c_t indicates the real amount of current consumption and c_{t+1} signifies the real amount of future consumption. These preference curves satisfy all the properties previously outlined for any object

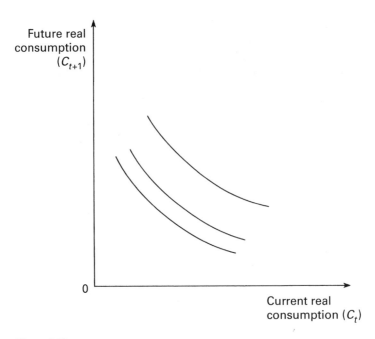

Figure 2.13
Set of preference curves depicting an individual's taste for future real consumption (c_{t+1}) and current real consumption (c_t)

of pleasure. Once again, these properties and these curves follow from neoclassical theory's conception of human nature. Along any such preference curve, we may calculate the private ability of each individual to choose between future and present consumption. To differentiate this new kind of marginal rate of substitution from previous ones, we have used the subscripts c_t and c_{t+1}. Thus we have

$$MRS_{c_t c_{t+1}} = -\frac{mu_{c_t}}{mu_{c_{t+1}}},$$

where mu_{c_t} stands for the marginal utility of present real consumption and $mu_{c_{t+1}}$ represents the marginal utility of future real consumption.[8] In the neoclassical literature this measure has sometimes been taken to represent the personal struggle we all go through in attempting to trade off present against future consumption. In a sense, it indicates the degree of our impatience about the future consumption of objects of pleasure.

Figure 2.14 introduces an individual's given current real income as measured by OA. At point A the person spends all that real income on current real consumption items: $y_t^R = c_t$. Suppose that a certain portion of that real income is saved, say, an amount of income equal to AA'. This means that only $0A'$ of

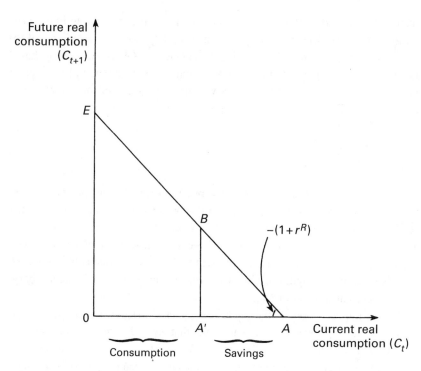

Figure 2.14
Trade-off between current and future real consumption: the real rate of return on supplied capital

that income is being consumed. Let us further assume that this savings takes the form of capital supplied to the production process. We may think of an individual as lending a portion of his or her current real income (savings) to a producing unit. This supplied capital allows the unit, or firm, to produce more goods and services and thus make possible more consumption in the future.

An alternative way to think of the same process is to recall that individuals who do not spend all of their current real income on consumption thereby make possible a diversion of resources from the production of current consumer goods to the production of new capital goods (machines, tools, materials). These new capital goods can then be used to expand consumption possibilities in the future. Therefore a decrease in current consumption (i.e., savings) makes possible an expansion in future consumption.

Returning to figure 2.14, suppose that AA' of income can be transformed via this process into, say, $A'B$ of future consumption. The slope of a line drawn from point A on the horizontal axis, passing through point B, and ending at point E on the vertical axis measures the amount of future consumption gained relative to the present income given up (i.e., the present income saved rather than consumed). If we let r^R be the real rate of return earned by an individual on the savings of AA', then this slope, measured by $A'B/AA'$, also is equal to $(1 + r^R)$. In other words, the individual's savings of AA' is assumed to have been loaned to producers in the form of capital and earns a rental of r^R percent per unit of time. The individual thus will have available in the future more consumption than is given up in the present: the earned rental income of $r^R \cdot AA'$ plus the original principal of AA'. Real consumption in the future may expand by that total amount:

$$A'B = AA'\left(1+r^R\right).\,^9$$

The borrower of this capital—that is, the producing unit—must be able to earn this real rate of return by using the capital productively in order to pay the lender for the use of this savings. In other words, the reward of r^R to the individual for not consuming now must correspond to the real rate of return earned by the borrower's productive use of this capital. The latter rate is measured by the contribution of capital to output or what is known in neoclassical theory as the marginal product of capital.

In this important sense, the lender gets back a real reward, a real rate of return on savings, exactly equal to what that loaned capital contributes to output. This distribution rule for the reward to capital owners is, of course, perfectly parallel to that used to calculate the correct real reward to the owners of the labor resource. The latter received a real wage exactly equal to what they contributed to output, no more and no less. (Recall from our previous analysis of the demand for and supply of labor that the real wage received by each laborer, w/p, is equal to the marginal product of labor.)

This neoclassical theory of the distribution of output to the owners of resources rules out the possibility that any owner might receive less or more than what his or her resources contributed to producing outputs. After each resource owner is paid its marginal product, there is, according to this logic, nothing left to distribute; the total output made possible by all the resources has been exhausted. As we will see, the Marxian theory of distribution is radically different.

Let us now bring together the set of subjective preference curves and the given rate of real return on capital supplied to producing firms. According to the usual neoclassical assumption, the latter is given to each individual by the force of market competition. Figure 2.15a demonstrates the optimal point T'' for the individual. At this point the individual has brought the private ability to choose among objects ($MRS_{c_t c_{t+1}}$) into balance with the social ability to do so $(1 + r^R)$. We may write this new equation as

$$\frac{mu_{c_t}}{mu_{c_{t+1}}} = (1+r^R).$$

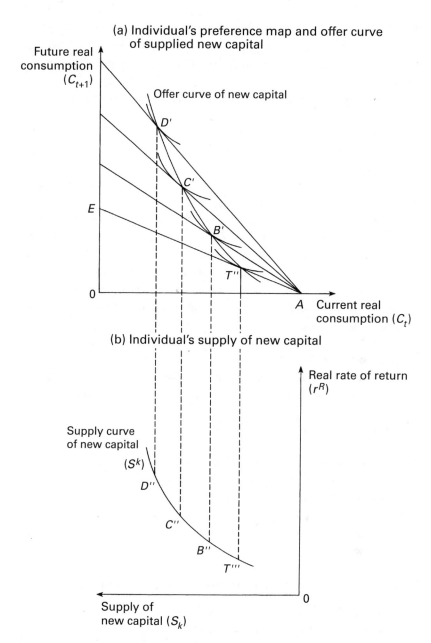

Figure 2.15
Derivation of an individual's supply of new capital (b) from the offer curve of that individual (a)

This equality signals that the individual has reached the highest possible level of satisfaction from present and future consumption, given the economic constraint faced. In that sense, the individual is maximizing his or her market opportunities.

So in all three spheres of an individual's economic life—the commodity, labor, and capital markets—the most satisfactory consumption point has been reached. Each individual acting in his or her own self-interest—that is, maximizing his or her own preferences with no regard for anyone else—has been able to achieve the maximum feasible utility in terms of specific commodities purchased, income and leisure, and present and future consumption, given the market conditions (and thus opportunities) faced.

To derive the supply of new capital from this preference map, we may vary the rate-of-return line, as shown in figure 2.15a, to derive new equilibrium points B', C', D'. Connecting them, neoclassicists derive $T''B'C'D'$ as the individual's offer curve of supplied capital. As the reward to savings rises, the individual is assumed to offer more savings (the indicated movement is from right to left along the horizontal axis: savings increase and current consumption decreases).

Figure 2.15b lines up its horizontal axis with that of figure 2.15a. We may then measure the supply of new capital offered by the individual in both diagrams. The dotted lines drawn from the offer curve in figure 2.15a map out points $T''B''C''D''$ on the curve indicating supply of capital in figure 2.15b.

We now have the neoclassical answer as to what determines the supply of capital in a society: the choice between present and future consumption, the given real rate of return, and the initial endowment of current real income. Given the last two variables, the supply of new capital is dictated by one's own human nature—the degree of impatience one has in regard to future consumption. And, once more, by adding up each individual's supply of capital, we derive the aggregate supply of capital in a society—in other words, the capital market supply curve.

2.2.8   Preferences and Scarcity: Determining the Demand for Capital

Let us now turn to what causes the demand for new capital. The logic parallels completely that used to explain the determination of the demand for labor. Once again, the production and utility functions are the essential determinants of demand.

As usual in neoclassical theory, each producing firm is assumed to attempt to maximize its profits (the difference between total revenues and the costs of production). It does this by equilibrating the dollar value of the marginal product contributed by capital and its cost. This new profit-maximizing position for each may be written as

$$\bar{r} = \frac{\Delta q}{\Delta K_i} \cdot \bar{p},$$

where $\Delta q/\Delta K_i \cdot \bar{p}$ is the dollar value of the marginal product of capital for that firm, K_i stands for the capital hired and used by the firm, $\Delta q/\Delta K_i$ is the marginal product of capital itself, and $\bar{p}$ and $\bar{r}$ stand, respectively, for the given output price and for the given money rental on capital faced by the firm. From the perspective of the firm, it must earn a money rate of return of r on this capital to pay exactly for its cost. Adding up across all producing units, we derive the aggregate demand for capital in the economy.

The price of output ($\bar{p}$) is ultimately determined by consumers' preferences for the commodity. The marginal product of capital is governed by the underlying production function and the assumed given endowment of the other resource—labor. Therefore the existence, shape, and position of the demand for capital is governed by these three essences: the predetermined preference and production functions and the given resource endowments.

2.2.9   The Determination of Returns to Capital

The rate of return (r) multiplied by the total amount of capital supplied and demanded gives us the total earnings, what is often called "capital income," going to the owners of capital. These earnings refer only to what the owners of capital, like the owners of any resource, have contributed to the production process.[10] Each resource—labor and capital—receives as income from the economy precisely what it contributes to make that income possible. Owners of the labor resource received their reward for not consuming leisure, just as owners of the capital resource received theirs for not consuming all of their current income. The private decisions to abstain from leisure time and current consumption permit these resources to flow to producing units, where they enjoy a particular (marginal) productivity.

Figure 2.16 brings together the derived aggregate supply of and demand for capital to determine simultaneously the money rate of return on capital and the amount of capital demanded and supplied in the economy. We now know, however, that both market curves are grounded in three forces that determine their very existence, shape, and position. These forces explain, therefore, the level of, and whatever change occurs in, the rate of return on capital. They are the inherent marginal productivity of the capital resource (technology), the initial endowments of labor and capital, and the degree of impatience of individuals for future consumption (preferences).

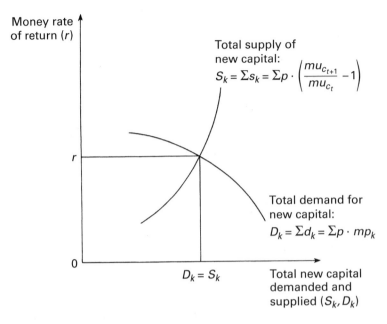

Money rate of return (r)

Total supply of new capital:
$$S_k = \Sigma s_k = \Sigma p \cdot \left(\frac{mu_{c_{t+1}}}{mu_{c_t}} - 1 \right)$$

r

Total demand for new capital:
$$D_k = \Sigma d_k = \Sigma p \cdot mp_k$$

0

$D_k = S_k$

Total new capital demanded and supplied (S_k, D_k)

Figure 2.16
Determination of the money rate of return and amount of capital supplied and demanded in the capital market as derived from current and future consumption choice on the supply side and the marginal product of capital on the demand side

2.2.10 Distribution of Income in Society: Returns to Capital and Labor

Neoclassical theory provides a unique explanation for the distribution of income, for what owners of capital and labor respectively receive from society's produced output. The specific preferences of individuals regarding the resources they may supply, the specific production functions available to producing firms, and the initial resource endowments owned by individuals combine to determine the distribution of wage and capital incomes among them. Returns to labor and capital reflect a balance between "scarcity" (captured by the given production function and resource endowments) and "tastes" (captured by the respective utility functions for income versus leisure and present versus future consumption). Each owner of a resource receives a return to that resource which is worked out by this balance.

It follows that the neoclassical explanation for what ultimately determines income and its distribution in society is remarkable both for what it claims and for what it rules out as a possibility. The claim is that each individual gets back from society a quantum of wealth exactly proportional to what each has contributed to society. This theory of distribution is remarkable for its inherent fairness. It is also remarkable for what it rules out: exploitation. Exploitation, in the sense of some individual or set of individuals receiving some produced wealth from society without giving any in return to it, is clearly not possible. Yet exploitation is precisely what Marxian theory claims does exist in society. What neoclassical theory logically rules out as a possibility is, in fact, the entry point of Marxism. This paradox has both fascinated and provoked economists for the last hundred years.

We want to make one final comment on income distribution. The question of whether an individual is a receiver of returns either to capital or labor (or possibly both) can be answered only by examining that individual's preferences. Some may prefer, for example, to offer labor hours and consume all their income now. Such individuals would receive only wage incomes. Others may prefer to do the opposite; they would receive only capital incomes. Still others may prefer to do both, thereby receiving both wage and capital incomes. The key point is that their decision to occupy one or more of these positions is a function only of their personal preferences, which are grounded in their human nature. The decision of one individual to be a receiver of income from capital has absolutely nothing to do with the decision of another individual not to be one. This is guaranteed by the initial assumption that the preferences that produce such decisions are essential parts of each person as a unique individual.

How, then, could one fault an individual for receiving, say, a relatively large capital income, since for any given technology, that income is caused by that same individual's decision to be thrifty, to abstain from being a spendthrift? According to neoclassical theory, capital income is due partly to an individual's personal actions in regard to saving and partly to the productivity of a thing called capital. This explains the source of capital incomes in an economy. Therefore to criticize an individual for receiving a relatively high capital income is virtually absurd. Are we to cast blame on the inherent productivity of a nonliving thing, capital—which makes about as much sense as criticizing a flower for being too beautiful? Or are we to damn an individual's preferences for savings and future consumption—which makes hardly any more sense?

2.2.11   Preferences and Scarcity: Determining the Supply of Commodities

We now have sufficient background to discuss the neoclassical determination of the supply of commodities. Recall, first, that each resource was paid the dollar value of its marginal product (mp). This result was derived from the condition that each producing unit maximizes its profits. For the resources of labor and capital, we have the respective input demands from each producer:

$$w = mp_{hL} \cdot p$$

and

$$r = mp_K \cdot p.$$

Let us solve each equation for the price variable faced by each producer:

$$p = \frac{w}{mp_{hL}},$$

$$p = \frac{r}{mp_K}.$$

It follows, then, that for each producer

$$\frac{w}{mp_{hL}} = \frac{r}{mp_K}.$$

Profit maximization implies equality between the extra cost (w) incurred by a producer per extra output added by labor (mp_{hL}) and the extra cost (r) paid per extra output produced by capital (mp_K). To maximize profits, each producer equates the extra cost per extra output received from each resource input.

Each of these ratios is nothing more than the extra dollar costs incurred by a firm per unit of extra output produced. This expression is what neoclassicists call the "marginal cost" of a producing unit. Therefore we may rewrite the equation above for each producer as follows:

$$\frac{w}{mp_{hL}} = \frac{r}{mp_K} = mc_q,$$

where mc_q stands for the marginal cost of a firm, or the extra total costs incurred per unit of extra output produced.

Now let us recall that each producing unit in the economy is assumed to maximize its profits. Let these profits be equal to the difference between total revenue and total costs:

$$\Pi = \bar{p} \cdot q - c,$$

where $\bar{p}$ is given by the competitive market to each producer and c now stands for that producer's total costs, the sum of wages ($w \cdot h \cdot L_i$) and capital ($r \cdot K_i$) costs. Consider the change in a producer's profits when both revenues and costs change:

$$\Delta \Pi = \bar{p} \cdot \Delta q - \Delta c,$$

where $\bar{p}$ is a constant because each producer is assumed to be a price-taker.

To consider the impact on profits of a change in the quantity supplied by the producer, divide both sides of the equation by Δq to derive

$$\frac{\Delta \Pi}{\Delta q} = \bar{p} - \frac{\Delta c}{\Delta q},$$

where $\Delta c / \Delta q$ stands for the marginal cost of output that we just derived from a firm's input costs and production function (the profit-maximizing equality between w/mp_{hL} and r/mp_K).

If $\bar{p} > mc_q$, the extra dollar profit received by the producer from supplying more output is greater than the extra dollar cost to do so. Clearly, the firm will want to supply more since that particular action raises the level of its profits. If, however, $\bar{p} < mc_q$, then the firm will have absolutely no desire to supply more output. Indeed, it will want to produce less because the extra dollar cost of producing more would be greater than the extra benefit the firm would receive by doing so. Producing more in such a situation would only lower the firm's level of profits. It is only when $\bar{p} = mc_q$ that the producer has maximized profits. At that point marginal profits are neither rising nor failing.

This equation and the resulting dynamic of a producer are illustrated in figure 2.17a, where dd' represents the demand curve facing a producer, and ss' indicates the firm's marginal cost. For the different levels of prices faced by this firm, different quantities will be produced according to the firm's given marginal-cost condition. For example, it could maximize its profits only at the point where the given demand price intersects the firm's marginal cost curve (point U in the diagram). Any point to the left of U would mean that profits could be expanded if the firm supplied more ($\bar{p} > mc_q$ in the equation above). That would be the firm's signal to expand. Any point to the right of U would mean that profits could be expanded if the firm supplied less ($\bar{p} < mc_q$ in the equation above). That would be the firm's signal to contract. Neoclassicists conclude that this marginal-cost curve is the competitive firm's supply curve. By adding up all such curves across all producing units, they derive the aggregate industry supply curve for each commodity in the economy. This is shown in figure 2.17b.[11]

In neoclassical theory the supply curve of any commodity is a function of its input costs and the marginal productivities of those inputs. However, as shown in previous sections, those input costs and productivities are derived, in turn, from individuals' preferences, ability to produce, and resource endowments. We may conclude, therefore, that the supply of commodities in a society is also derived ultimately from these same three essences, which form, of course, the entry point of neoclassical theory.

According to this account, firms supplying commodity outputs are purely passive entities. Their producing behavior merely reflects more basic underlying behaviors: those that flow from the preferences of suppliers of resources to firms and from the preferences of consumers of the products produced by them. The producers' behavior likewise reflects the relative scarcity of

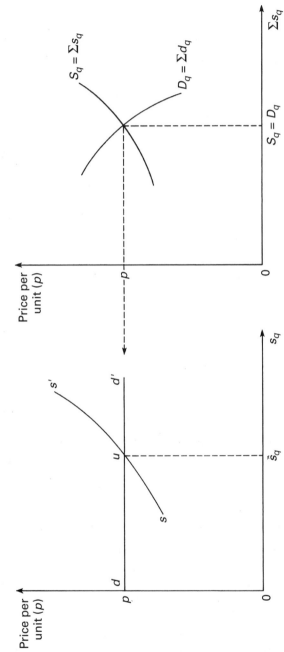

Figure 2.17
Derivation of the aggregate supply curve of a commodity from the supplies of individual producers. The aggregate supply curve of an industry (b) is the sum of the supplies of the industry's individual producers, one of which is represented in (a).

resources shaped by the available production function (technology) and by the resource endowments given naturally. Given the technology, any firm's behavior reduces to and is therefore explained in terms of the will of those who own and supply its capital and its labor as well as the will of those who demand its commodities in the market. It has no autonomous will of its own.

2.2.12 Demand and Supply Again: Determination of Prices

We have now assembled all the parts needed to complete the explanation of the neoclassical theory of value. Figure 2.18, which summarizes the overall structure and logic of the theory, combines the different pieces of the argument presented in the previous sections. Reading from left to right, we first encounter the theory's three governing essences—preferences, production function, and endowments—in the entry-point column. Following the arrows emanating from this column, we see the influence of preferences on the demand for commodities (along the bottom of the diagram), and the influence of preferences, the production function, and endowments on the supply of commodities (upper part of the diagram). Other arrows trace how preferences and productive abilities determine the different demands for and supplies of the two resources in what are called factor-of-production markets. In turn, the arrows emanating from these competitive resource markets show the influence of incomes on the demand for commodities and of costs on the supply of commodities. The resulting demand for and supply of commodities act together to cause price, as shown in the last column at the right of the diagram.

In neoclassical theory the value of things, after all is said and done, depends on our tastes and productive abilities as human beings. The value of our wealth and well-being may rise or fall depending on what we ourselves want and what we ourselves are capable of producing. The mystery of value dissolves into the mystery of our own human nature.

One may start anywhere in figure 2.18 and by following the arrows eventually retrace the ultimately determinant influence of human preferences and productive abilities. That is precisely why they are considered to be essences: in one way or another, all other conceived objects owe their existence to them. Whatever the economic objects of neoclassical theory—incomes, prices, supply, or demand—they ultimately rest on the fundamental building blocks of human tastes, technology, and endowments. There is nothing to the left of the entry-point column in figure 2.18 that might explain what caused those fundamental building blocks. If one supposed that tastes and technology were caused by human genes, then a theory of biology would be required to help explain economic behavior. And indeed that is the direction in which some economists would take neoclassical theory.

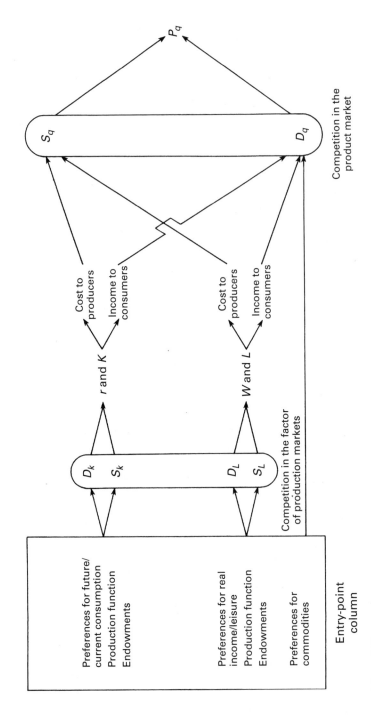

Figure 2.18
Structure and logic of the neoclassical theory of value

As we claimed initially in this chapter, figure 2.18 demonstrates that reductionism is the overall logic of neoclassical economic theory. Reductionism is likewise the geometric method used in all of the previous diagrams elaborating the theory. The meaning of each diagram ultimately rests on the same three essences. The power of those essences is that they ultimately determine what will be.

2.3 Efficiency and Markets

2.3.1 Adam Smith's "Invisible Hand"

If each and every individual in a fully competitive society acts rationally in his or her own self-interest—consumers maximizing utility and producers maximizing profits—the result will be an efficient allocation of both consumption outputs and resource inputs. In neoclassical theory the term "efficient" when applied to a society means that that society has attained the greatest wealth possible given the constraints it faces. An extraordinary conclusion on the part of neoclassicists is that if each citizen in a society acts in a selfish manner, maximizing individual self-interest, then with supply equal to demand in all markets, that society will have the maximum possible wealth available to it. It will have fully realized its potential output.

Of course, the availability of more goods and services to a society does not say anything about how they will be distributed among its citizens. Indeed, assuming different individual resource endowments and tastes, it would not be surprising to discover that some individuals receive more produced wealth than others. Neoclassical theorists have always recognized that possibility. They have also recognized that the produced inequality of rewards could become a political issue that would require some economic action. Consequently over the years they have devised various schemes to, in effect, redistribute some income from certain citizens to others. However, these redistribution schemes have been designed to disrupt the efficiency of a market economy only minimally.

There is a close connection between this efficient or optimal consumption and production result and the role of competitive markets. To see this connection, first recall that competitive markets require that each individual in the society be a price-taker. Each is assumed to have no power over the determination of price. Also recall that each is assumed to own privately all commodities and resources. Hence, while each individual has no power over price, each has complete power over the disposal and acquisition of privately held wealth.

This asymmetry of individual power, on the one hand, bestows complete freedom to the market to determine prices of commodities and resources and, on the other hand, provides each person with the complete freedom to decide what wealth and how much of it he or she will supply to and demand from others. The specific decision taken by each in regard to this demand for and supply of privately owned wealth depends, as we have seen, on that person's unique maximizing behavior. In a sense, the condition of private property permits this selfish behavior to take place. Individuals may offer and demand as much as they please of what they privately own and desire whether it be labor, capital, or commodities. Their offers and demands depend on their own personal likes and dislikes. The competitive fact of the market, however, forces them all to be price-takers and thus constrains their offers and demands. We recognized this each time we presented a diagram showing the interaction between an individual's private utility maximization and various socially determined price constraints.

In neoclassical theory, markets are sites of social interaction between existing owners and prospective buyers of wealth. Markets offer each group an opportunity to gain wealth. Individuals may do so by offering to either supply or demand some good or resource. The common goal of each individual is to reach his or her highest possible preference curve. Achieving that goal defines the neoclassical notion of maximizing social wealth. Efficient or competitive markets allow the maximum social wealth to be achieved by private wealth-seeking sellers and buyers. Neoclassicists often say the same thing in slightly different terms—that is, an efficient market is in equilibrium for it cannot offer opportunities to one person to improve his or her wealth position without also making someone else worse off. In contrast, inefficient markets are not in equilibrium for they offer opportunities for gain that individual buyers and/ or sellers may take advantage of without making anyone else worse off.

Neoclassical theory combines the private decisions of all pleasure-maximizing individuals to derive the market demands and supplies for all commodities and resources. Thus the power of each individual to make decisions in his or her own self-interest is competitively aggregated into the markets, which then act to negate any individual's desire for power over prices. The tyranny of the market as a ruler of price is a product of the very freedom individuals have to own and dispose of their privately held wealth as they see fit.

In neoclassical theory, there is a precise and necessary correspondence between a fully competitive private-property economy and an optimally efficient one. The insight of Adam Smith is retained in neoclassical economics: each individual having the power (freedom) to act in his or her own self-interest will be led as if by an "invisible hand" (the fully competitive market) to actions that produce the maximum wealth (efficiency) for a society of individuals.

Recall that when individuals maximize utility subject to given market prices and income, the private marginal rate of substitution between any two consumption goods is brought into equality with the ratio between their market prices. Let us write such an equilibrium equation for each of the many different individuals in a society:

$$MRS_{12}^A = \frac{p_1}{p_2},$$

$$MRS_{12}^B = \frac{p_1}{p_2},$$

$$MRS_{12}^C = \frac{p_1}{p_2},$$

$$\vdots \qquad \vdots$$

$$MRS_{12}^N = \frac{p_1}{p_2},$$

where MRS_{12}^A, MRS_{12}^B, MRS_{12}^C, and so forth, stand for the different marginal rates of substitution between commodities 1 and 2 for individuals A, B, C, and so on. Since each one of these individuals is, of course, unique, the marginal rate of substitution between any two commodities is unique to each as well.

Yet these equations point to a striking fact: all of the private, unique marginal rates of substitution are brought into equality with a common price ratio. Utility-maximizing buyers all face the same price ratio when confronting that market. It follows that their private rates of substitution must then be set equal to market price ratios and thus to one another. The competitive market has forced this equality, which may be formulated as follows:

$$MRS_{12}^A = MRS_{12}^B = MRS_{12}^C = \ldots = MRS_{12}^N.$$

Let us then summarize this key neoclassical conclusion. As each individual (A, B, C, . . ., N) maximizes his or her own selfish interest, there results, as if by some mysterious force, an equality among the private abilities of individuals to substitute one good for another. What is this mysterious force? The answer is clear: it is nothing other than the competitive market. First the competitive market permits each person to make exchanges for the maximum gain possible. Then it brings those gains into balance or harmony with one another. The resulting equality of marginal rates of substitution is neoclassical theory's precise definition of an efficient distribution of consumption commodities among individuals in a society.

This distribution of commodities is considered to be an efficient one, first, because each and every individual has reached his or her highest feasible preference curve; each has therefore made the most of the market opportunities faced, and in that sense each is best-off. Second, the resulting equality of individuals' different marginal rates of substitution means that it is not possible to improve the welfare position (the consumption gain) of any one individual without simultaneously damaging some other individual's position. Therefore neoclassical theory has shown that no other possible result could improve upon this particular competitive market solution. In that sense, the achieved distribution of commodities among individuals is optimal.

Let us now turn to the production side of the economy. Recall that each producing unit is also assumed to act in producer's own self-interest by maximizing profits. Each unit has the complete freedom to produce any quantity the producer desires. As a result the quantity chosen by each producer indicates that this is the point at which its marginal cost of production equals the given market price.

What then determines this market price, if individual producers have no power over its determination? The summation of all firms' individual supply curves produces the aggregate supply in the industry producing that commodity. Firms' individual supply curves result from their respective profit-maximizing behavior, namely from before $\bar{p} = mc_q$. The summation of individual demands from all the utility-maximizing consumers produces the aggregate demand for the commodity produced in that industry. Together, the two aggregates determine the price that confronts each individual producer and consumer in an economy as a given (figure 2.17a and b).

Let us write the equilibrium conditions for the production of commodities one and two by each of the many—that is, n producers in that economy:[12]

$$p_1 = mc_1^a, \quad p_2 = mc_2^a,$$

$$p_1 = mc_1^b, \quad p_2 = mc_2^b,$$

$$\vdots \quad \vdots \quad \vdots \quad \vdots$$

$$p_1 = mc_1^n, \quad p_2 = mc_2^n.$$

We may now bring together the two sides of the story told so far. By maximizing his or her own interest (consumption), each consumer produces an efficient consumption result:

$$MRS_{12}^j = \frac{p_1}{p_2},$$

where $j = A, \ldots, N$ individuals (consumers). By maximizing its own interest (profits), each producer in the two industries produces an efficient production result. For the two commodities produced in the economy, we may write this result as an equality between the ratio of marginal costs for producers and the market price ratio:

$$\frac{mc_1^i}{mc_2^i} = \frac{p_1}{p_2},$$

where $i = a, \ldots, n$ producers.

The marginal rate of substitution for individuals and the ratio of marginal costs for producers are both equated to the same market price ratio. Therefore they are also equal to each other. Rewriting the marginal rate of substitution in terms of marginal utilities, we have as the optimal result in a competitive economy

$$\frac{mu_1}{mu_2} = \frac{mc_1}{mc_2}.$$

Neoclassical theorists call this equality of "consumption" and "production" a "Pareto optimal point," after the theorist who first discovered it, Wilfredo Pareto (1848–1923). It indicates that the demand (ratio of marginal utilities) and supply (ratio of marginal costs) sides of an economy are in balance with each other.

2.3.2 Pareto Optimality

The Pareto point is optimal in the sense that it signifies that a society has fully realized its potential output. It is operating at the outer limit of its productive capability, given the technology and resource endowments available to it. To see this, first consider the concept of a society's potential output. This refers to the total quantity of goods it could potentially produce with its given production function and its initial resource endowments. Neoclassical theory uses a geometric diagram to illustrate this concept. As shown in figure 2.19, this diagram is called a "production possibilities curve."

The diagram indicates that a society produces its maximum output potential, q_1 and q_2, if it operates at any point along its frontier, PP', but not below it. This frontier is delineated by the PP' curve in figure 2.19. The curve itself is derived from the production functions of the two commodities and their given labor and capital resource endowments. In other words, these two neoclassical essences govern the shape and position of the curve. We may conclude, therefore, that the relative scarcity of commodities in a society follows from the relative scarcity of its resources and from the productive abilities of its producers.

The trade-off between the two commodities along the production possibilities curve is known in neoclassical theory as the "marginal rate of transformation." It shows the decreased production of commodity 2 that would be needed to increase the production of commodity 1. Any point along the curve measures the quantity of commodity 2 that would have to be decreased in order to release sufficient resources of labor and capital to produce an additional unit of commodity 1. Recall that the marginal cost of producing commodity 1 measured how much an extra unit of that commodity would cost in terms of

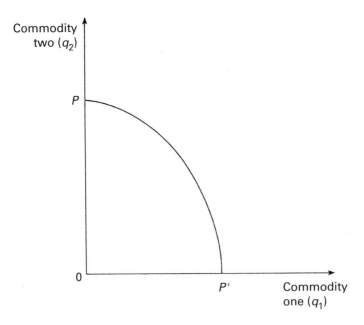

Figure 2.19
A society's production possibilities curve

resources. If the production of commodity 1 were expanded by a unit, this cost would be MC_1. By the same logic, if the production of commodity 2 contracted, the marginal cost of resources saved would be MC_2. The ratio of MC_1 to MC_2 relates the extra cost of resources required to produce one more unit of commodity 1 to the resources released by reducing the total production of commodity 2 by one unit. This ratio of marginal costs is therefore the same as the marginal rate of transformation, for they both measure the opportunities and costs that a society confronts when it considers producing more of some and less of other commodities—that is, moving along its production possibilities frontier.

We may substitute the marginal rate of transformation for the ratio of marginal costs and write the Pareto optimal point simply as $MRT_{12} = MRS_{12}$. In a competitive economy where each individual maximizes his or her own utility and his or her own profits, an equality between this utility-maximizing (MRS) and this profit-maximizing (MRT) behavior will result. At this point the citizens of the society, the various utility- and profit-seekers, will have available to them the maximum wealth possible.

The fact that $MRS_{12} = MRT_{12}$ means that the allocation of resources throughout the economy is Pareto optimal. However, if these marginal rates were not equal, then it would be possible to increase the welfare possibilities of consumption by means of a reallocation of resources. In other words, an inequality between these two marginal rates would indicate that consumers preferred a different output mix in the economy than the one produced.

For example, suppose that the equated marginal rates of substitution of consumers equal one-fifth. This means that individuals in the society are willing to give up five units of commodity 1 for each unit of commodity 2 gained. Suppose that the marginal rate of transformation at a point on the PP' curve in figure 2.19 is one-third. This means that three units of commodity 1 must be given up to produce an additional unit of commodity 2 in the society. In this situation the producers are making commodity 1 in excess of what consumers would like. Producers are making an additional unit of commodity 2 at a marginal cost of three units of commodity 1 given up, while consumers are willing to give up five units of commodity 1 to gain an additional unit of commodity 2.

Consumers therefore can be made better off by a reallocation of resources in which more of commodity 2 and less of commodity 1 is produced. Suppose this happens. The society produces three fewer units of commodity 1 and gains one unit of commodity 2. Suppose that individual A's real consumption falls as a result of these three units of commodity 1 being given up. More than enough units of commodity 2 have been produced to compensate individual A for this loss in consumption and still have units of output left over to raise the welfare position of other individuals (B, C, etc.) in society.

To see this, recall that the MRS_{12} of each and every individual, including A, was one-fifth. It follows that reducing A's consumption by the assumed three units of commodity 1 requires a three-fifth increase of commodity 2 to maintain A's same level of satisfaction (utility). Since society gained one unit of commodity 2 by moving along its PP' curve, three-fifths of this gain may be given to A, with the result that there is no change in A's welfare position. The remaining two-fifths of commodity 2 may then be divided in a number of different ways among all the other individuals in society (B, C, ..., N), thereby raising their welfare. This example illustrates that the output mix of an economy in which $MRS_{12} \neq MRT_{12}$ is nonoptimal, since by reallocating resources to alter this mix it is possible to raise the welfare position of at least one individual without hurting the welfare position of anyone else.

In neoclassical theory the achievement of a correspondence between producers' selfish maximization of their own profits and consumers' selfish maximization of their own preferences is also the achievement of a perfect harmony between physical and human nature, between scarcity and choice. The two parts of our human nature—unlimited wants and the ability to produce and satisfy them—are in balance. At this point the maximization of profits for each and every private producer is the same as the maximization of consumption—economic well-being—for each and every consumer.

The demonstration that maximum profits are consistent with and indeed necessary for the maximum well-being of individual consumers is surely a radical conclusion for neoclassical theory. It underlies dramatic policy proposals and consequences. Neoclassicists can, and many times do, endorse government policies to enhance profits on the grounds that such policies would thereby benefit everyone. Similarly they often oppose policies that would reduce profits, claiming that reduced profits would necessarily reduce the well-being of individuals.

For neoclassicists the equation of profit maximization with the maximization of consumer satisfaction seems to be in complete conformity with our nature as human beings. Yet, as will be shown in chapters 4 and 7, this conclusion is radically different from the one arrived at by Marxists, who argue that the maximization of profits corresponds to the maximization of exploitation, and thus discord, in society. The social implications of the two theories could not be more different.

3 Keynesian Theory

3.1 The Challenge of Keynes

Ever since 1936, when John Maynard Keynes (1883–1946) published *The General Theory of Employment, Interest, and Money*, there has been controversy over its meaning and its specific implications for neoclassical theory. To date, it has more or less split non-Marxian economic theory into two branches: microeconomics and macroeconomics. The former deals with the formal structure of neoclassical theory; the latter typically deals with the Keynesian contribution, although this has been changing as we will see in this chapter when we discuss post-Keynesian and new-Keynesian economics. Despite the latter developments, non-Marxian economic theory is generally taught today in terms of this split, which began with a text written over seventy-five years ago.

As might be expected, many economists are extremely uncomfortable with this dichotomy. They have labored over the years to synthesize the two parts, an effort sometimes referred to as the "neoclassical-Keynesian synthesis." Indeed, for some, the very term "neoclassical" means an attempt to shape the traditional classical and the Keynesian contributions into a new form of economic reasoning. This effort began almost as soon as the ink was dry on Keynes's book. In 1937 John Hicks (1904–1989) produced a famous article that offered an explanation of the relationship between Keynes's contribution and the then dominant economic theory: "Mr. Keynes and the 'Classics': A Suggested Interpretation."[1] Since then economists of every political persuasion have offered their explanations.

Over the years some economists have argued that the Keynesian theory provides a devastating critique of neoclassical theory. For them, it is as basic an alternative to neoclassical theory as we argue that Marxian theory is. In contrast, other economists insist that the Keynesian contribution is at best overblown and at worst logically flawed. For them, it merely suggests some important but overall minor changes needed by the basic and still quite adequate neoclassical theory. Between these two extremes a middle position has emerged: it is possible to integrate Keynesian and neoclassical theories, thereby modifying both somewhat but yielding an enriched and strengthened economics.

This middle position has dominated the thinking of most economists since World War II. However, starting in the late 1970s and early 1980s a sharp defense of the integrity of neoclassical theory against the influence of Keynesian thinking re-emerged in the writings of many leading economists. They attacked Keynesian theory and reaffirmed, with some secondary changes, the neoclassical body of thought, more or less as presented in the previous chapter. Here we will examine the content and implications of the Keynesian critique. First, Keynes introduced into economic theory not only new concepts but also an entirely new and different entry point than we found in neoclassical theory. That, we believe, has been a source of major problems for neoclassical economists these last seventy-five years. An additional and distinct source of controversy has been Keynes's rejection of a significant portion of neoclassical theory's traditional entry-point concepts. Adding some new entry-point concepts and rejecting some old neoclassical entry-point concepts produced difficulties for and controversies with neoclassical theorists.

On the one hand, Keynes accepted the essentialized entry-point concepts of given initial endowments of resources and their inherent marginal productivity that were affirmed by traditional neoclassical theory. On the other hand, Keynes profoundly questioned, if he did not reject outright, the usefulness of given human preferences for explaining economic behavior, especially in regard to the supply of savings and labor. Here he seemed to reject the utility side of the neoclassical theory of value. In place of individual utility maximization, he offered a new concept of savings based instead on mass psychology and habit, and he used it to explain the supply of savings. Likewise Keynes offered a new concept of money wages as based on institutional power and mass psychology, and he used that to determine the supply of labor hours.

He also introduced a new idea about what determines the level of investment—the demand for new capital in the form of investment goods. The individual investor and his/her goals and desires explained the level of investment. Yet this was not a return to the individualist maximization framework of neoclassical economics because Keynes introduced the factor of uncertainty. Investors' attitudes and responses to uncertainty shaped their decisions about the level of their investments and introduced a crucial volatility to that level that had broad economic implications of instability to capitalist economies.

Keynes's criticisms of neoclassical theory and the changes he introduced led logically to different explanations of prices, incomes, and employment. Furthermore, save for the individual investor, Keynes also shifted the overall focus of economic thinking by emphasizing mass psychology, habit, and institutional power rather than individual decision-makers maximizing their individual utilities. In other words, Keynes's focus of analysis became the economy as a totality—a structure of relationships—that shaped individuals' behaviors. In contrast, neoclassical theory stresses the roles of the individual producers and consumers as shapers of the larger economic structure. This shift in focus contributed to the very different view of the state and its proper relationship to the economy that distinguishes Keynes from neoclassical economists.

Why did Keynes challenge and break from neoclassical theory in these ways? Why did he question the utility-based determination of the supply of labor hours, wages, and employment? Why did he question the utility-based determination of the supply of savings, interest rates, and investment? Why did he accept neoclassical theory's assumption of given resources and a given production constraint on the economy? Given Keynes's structuralist approach generally, why did he revert to a humanism only when discussing the individual investor's behavior? Our answers to these questions and the presentation of Keynesian economics they produce begin with some attention to the times in which Keynes taught and wrote.

After World War I in Europe, the world economy experienced generally some twelve years of uneven but nonetheless continuous expansion. This growth ended dramatically with the depression of the 1930s, which ushered in a period of economic decline. The capitalist economies experienced falling prices, incomes, and wealth and rising unemployment. The resulting suffering provoked many to question the existing economic institutions or even the entire system—capitalism—that delivered so much misery. The times imperiled the continuation of capitalism also because of the challenge of the contending Marxian theory, which was advocated by many around the world. Marxism not only explained capitalism as the source of the 1930s economic crisis and its social costs; it also offered an alternative set of social institutions that promised to abolish capitalist crises permanently.

Like economists throughout history, Keynes and his writings were provoked in part by the events of the day ("in part" because some of Keynes's theory was developed before the Great Depression). Nonetheless, Keynes's theory and criticism of neoclassical theory responded to the threat that the depression presented to capitalism. Broadly, his goal was to save capitalist society from the dangers posed by rising unemployment and falling wealth. He thus offered explanations for developments in the labor and savings and investment markets that differed from those presented by both neoclassical and Marxist theorists. Likewise his disinterest in questions of scarcity of resources and products likely followed from the fact that huge quantities of productive resources were then sitting idle and not generating outputs. Perhaps most important of all, Keynes's work offered policies to end the depression and preclude future depressions that would reform but not destroy the crucial institutions of capitalist systems, especially private property and enterprises and only partly regulated markets. This Keynesian contribution is of no minor importance: Keynesian theory and most Keynesians recognize the severe social damage to workers unemployed in and by recessions and depressions. In a sense their focus on effective demand in their approach reflects not only their object of analysis and policy but also their concern for workers. Unemployed labor is the deep problem of capitalism; its solution lies in boosting effective demand via state action.

3.2   The Neoclassical Answer to Capitalist Recessions

To better understand the Keynesian alternative and solution, we return briefly to the neoclassical explanation for possible economic downturns. Their causes could include (1) changes in nature, such as a poor harvest due to lack of rain, (2) changes in resources, such as a growth in labor supply due to newly arrived immigrants or reduced oil reserves, (3) changes in technology altering commodity-production functions, and (4) changes in institutions, such as individuals acquiring monopoly power in markets or a change in the state's supply of money. Note that neoclassical economics explains economic decline in terms of exogenous events impacting the economic system from outside. For example, a temporary imbalance between the demand for and supply of labor may result from some change in nature: for example, improved rainfall produces an increase in the food supply that lowers the death rate and thereby increases the supply of labor, putting downward pressure on wages. To take another example, wages may fall when legal and illegal immigration increases because of problems in other countries. The existence of a temporary disequilibrium in any market is thus always a distinct possibility.

Neoclassical theory treats changes in technology much as it treats changes in physical nature: as exogenous to human beings. For example, newly discovered ways of combining capital and labor to produce output would be treated like "improved rainfall," as the gift of a changed nature. The result of an exogenous technical change might be a change in the shape of the demand curve for labor (which becomes more inelastic as capital and labor become poorer substitutes for each other) or a leftward shift of the labor-demand curve because of the introduction of a labor-saving innovation in society. In these two cases employment will grow less rapidly than it would otherwise.

Imperfections in markets can arise due to our human nature, and they can produce temporary disequilibrium situations. For example, unemployment may arise because workers' union enforces a wage that is higher than the market equilibrium. The source of this market imperfection and the market disequilibrium it entails is found in individuals' will for power. Thus unionized workers may attempt to control markets in order to gain special advantages for themselves at the expense of others.

All such neoclassical explanations for deviations in the wage rate from the full employment wage find their causes in either human or physical nature. This is hardly surprising since, as we have already noted, these are the essences to which neoclassical theory reduces all its arguments. It follows that these deviations are not endogenous to the capitalist system, not intrinsic aspects of how they function. Rather, the causes of deviations from equilibrium are found outside of that system—in the essential determinants of economic life.

The neoclassical solution to these deviations from full employment equilibrium holds that individuals need and should do nothing other than make their usual market transactions. That is because the market, if allowed to work free of external interference, is a perfect self-healing entity when troubled by exogenous disturbances of the sort mentioned above. There is one exception to this neoclassical solution: the case of market imperfections caused by individuals who have gained control over prices. The latter problem is special; it requires state intervention to rid the society of such barriers to the market's achievement of both full employment and maximum wealth for its citizens. It follows that the state, in one way or another, must tame the individual will for power over markets. It must do this to enable genuinely competitive markets to fulfill their destined role in capitalist society. Indeed, if the state intervened more than to maintain competitive markets (and private property), its interventions might well contribute to economic depressions.

In and for neoclassical theory, given private property and human nature, competitive markets inherently tend to equilibrate when each and every individual is left alone to maximize his or her own interest. That equilibrium is defined as one in which supply equals demand in all markets. In a word, society has achieved its Pareto optimal point. Assuming that the state performs its properly minimal role of securing the existence of private property and competitive markets, those markets will permit and encourage the society of private-property owners and maximizers to achieve and reproduce the full employment and maximum output equilibrium.

Consider, for example, the previously discussed aggregate labor market, depicted once again in figure 3.1a. Suppose that there is significant unemployment there, as indicated by AB in the diagram. According to neoclassical theory, the proper solution is for money wages to fall from w_0 until that excess labor supply of AB becomes zero at the equilibrium wage, w_1, in the diagram.

Whatever so-called unemployment remains at that equilibrium wage may be thought of either as transitional in nature or as strictly voluntary. The former idea indicates the possibility of temporary unemployment due to an individual's being in transition from one job to another. The latter idea refers to individuals who have decided of their own free will to choose leisure rather than

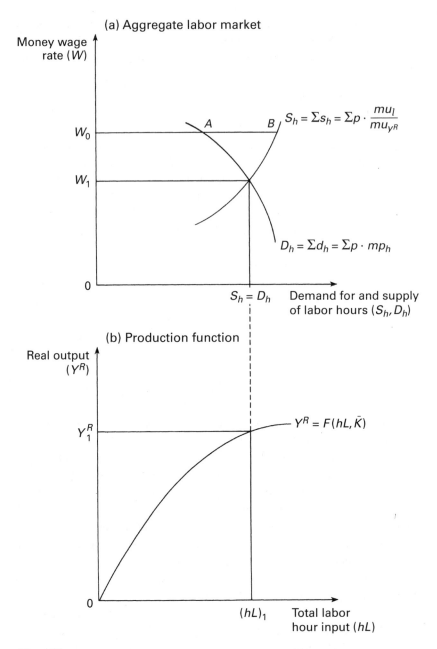

Figure 3.1
Derivation of employment and real output from the labor market

income from working at the wage w_1. Clearly, this "unemployment" is quite voluntary; it is not a social problem and warrants no governmental action because it is freely chosen by individuals who thereby maximize their well-being given the utility they derive from income and from leisure.

This full employment level in the labor market also tells us what will be the corresponding level of full employment output in the society. To see this clearly, consider figure 3.1b, which presents our previously specified neoclassical production function. We have lined up employment in the two diagrams so that by reading off the full employment point at which the aggregate demand for and supply of labor hours equal one another in figure 3.1a, we can derive as well the full employment output level of Y_1^R in figure 3.1b. The logic of this determination means that the neoclassical essences—preferences (the choice of individuals between real income and leisure) and scarcity (the marginal product of labor)—govern the final equilibrium output in the economy.

The stark implication of this reductionism is that the aggregate supply of goods and services, and by logical extension the full employment level to which it corresponds, are completely unaffected by changes in the aggregate demand for those goods and services. For example, suppose that the demand for all goods and services increases because the state increases the money supply. Since, as shown, the supply of goods and services must be fixed by these essences (which by assumption have not changed), the only effect of such a change by the state will be for prices to rise as individuals try to purchase more of a given supply.

Now, consider the labor market again. An increase of prices will only act to shift both the aggregate supply and the aggregate demand for labor hours so that there is no net effect on the full employment level, $(hL)_1$, and therefore none on the implied full employment output level, Y_1^R. To see this, consider that the rise in prices, because of an increased money supply, shifts the aggregate demand for labor hours upward and to the right. The reason for this demand shift in the labor market is that for any given money wage, producers will demand more labor at the higher prices because that given money wage corresponds to a lower real wage. In addition the same rise in prices acts to shift the aggregate supply of labor hours upward and to the left. The reason for this supply shift in the labor market is that for any given money wage, laborers will supply fewer labor hours at the higher prices because that given money wage corresponds to a lower real wage. We show these respective demand-and-supply shifts in figure 3.2 from D_h^1 to D_h^2 and from S_h^1 to S_h^2. At the original money wage, w_1, there will now be an excess demand for labor hours, as measured by xy in figure 3.2. Money wages will therefore rise to w_2 in the figure at the point at which the excess demand for labor hours becomes zero.

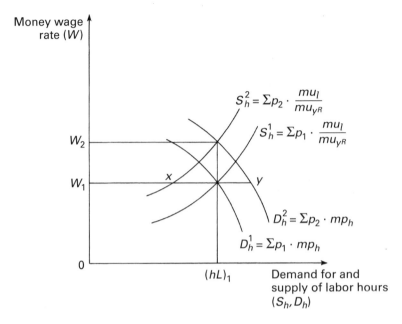

Figure 3.2
Shift in both supply of and demand for labor hours as a result of price change. Both curves shift upward by the same proportion so that total hours of employment, on the horizontal axis, remain the same

Thus an increased money supply produces an increase in the money wage, but the increase in prices exactly offsets it so that the real wage remains at its equilibrium level. Since the real wage remains unchanged, so must employment and real output. In other words, higher prices caused by an expansion in the money supply would induce an increase in real output only if producers' money–wage costs did not rise proportionately. Since they did, however, real output, Y_1^R, remains unchanged.

Let us summarize this neoclassical logic by considering the aggregate supply of and demand for commodities as shown in figure 3.3. There the supply is drawn as a perfectly inelastic line. The reason for this is that only so-called real factors—that is, labor-versus-leisure choices and marginal productivity of labor—govern it. The aggregate supply of commodities is given, as it were, by the play of these forces or, as we have been calling them in this book, these essences. It is thus unaffected by changes in aggregate demand.

Of course, this still leaves open the question of what determines the price level in a society. Stated differently, the question is, What determines the position of the aggregate-demand curve in figure 3.3? The neoclassicists answer this question by specifying a new equation in which price level is related to the money supply.

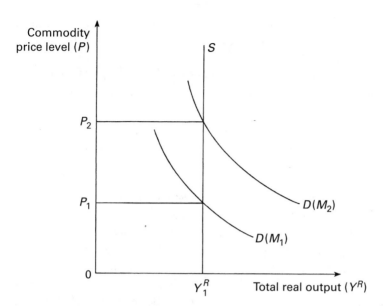

Figure 3.3
Neoclassical aggregate-supply and aggregate-demand curves

The Fisher, or Cambridge, equation thus completes our explanation of the neoclassical system. In its Cambridge version, we may write the equation as

$$P = \frac{M}{kY^R},$$

where P represents the absolute price level; M, the demand for money to finance market purchases of commodities; k, the proportion of real income individuals want to hold for these transaction purposes; and Y^R, real income. Since Y^R is given by the so-called real side of the economy (i.e., by the labor market and the production function), and k is assumed to be given by mass human psychology, we have a simple relationship between prices and the demand for money in a society.

To see this clearly, suppose that the citizens of a state empower it to supply money to them. Consider now a given state-supplied stock of money, $\bar{M}$. To derive the aggregate neoclassical demand curve, let us rewrite the Cambridge equation in the form

$$\bar{M} = kPY^R.$$

Suppose that real income rises in the society. A rise in real income means, according to this equation, that the demand for money will rise to finance these increased real transaction needs (assuming that here no change in k). If, however, the state does not alter the money supply ($\bar{M}$), there will be an excess demand for money in the society. An excess demand for money is equivalent to saying that there will be an excess supply of commodities as individuals try to build up their cash balances.

This excess supply of commodities will tend to depress prices (P in the above equation). Prices will fall until the real cash balances individuals desire to hold are equal to k times the new Y^R. (Note that here the only change in the fraction $\bar{M}/P$ occurs in the denominator.) Consequently we have a negative relationship between the price level and real income as shown by the negative slope of the aggregate-demand curve in figure 3.3.

The aggregate-demand curve, however, will shift if the state decides to increase the supply of money. Suppose, for example, that the state decides to increase the supply of money even though there has been no change in real income or in k. In this case there will be an excess supply of money at the current level of real income and prices. This means that individuals will begin to spend their excess holdings of money on the given supply of commodities ($\bar{Y}_1^R$), thereby bidding up their prices. This process will continue until the real cash balances are once again in line with the unchanged k times the unchanged $\bar{Y}_1^R$. (Note that in contrast to the previous example, both numerator and denominator change in the fraction M/P.) This shift in aggregate demand as a result of an expansion of the money supply is shown in figure 3.3. Prices will thus rise from P_1 to P_2.

Let us now see exactly why in neoclassical theory an expansion of state expenditures can affect only the composition but *not* the level of aggregate demand. Suppose the state expands its purchase of commodities in the society by selling government bonds to citizens. This will have absolutely no effect in the just described aggregate demand-and-supply market. Since the money supply has not changed, the aggregate-demand curve does not shift. Since there is no change in the real side of the economy (i.e., in the productivity of labor or in labor-versus-leisure decisions), there can be no change in the aggregate-supply curve.

It follows that change occurs only in the capital market. To the private demand for savings, we may now add this new public demand. These demands compete with each other, thereby driving up the rental rate on capital. This increased rate, in turn, acts to decrease the real demand for new capital. And this induced decrease in private investment allows resources to be shifted from the production of commodities for the private sector to the production of goods for the state.

According to neoclassical theory, the expansion of state expenditures has a purely redistributive effect on the economy; it does not alter the existing level of real output, demand, or employment in the society. Neoclassicists thus conclude that there is no role for the state to play in determining employment and real output, for these are *already* determined within the society's competitive markets and ultimately by the real forces (essences) that govern those markets. If left alone, competitive markets will correct whatever temporary disequilibria may occur in the society.

3.3 The Keynesian Answer to Capitalist Recessions

Keynesian economists criticize this neoclassical view and the implied policy of no state intervention. They argue that markets can and often do not adjust in the way that neoclassical economists wrongly presume or they adjust too slowly with the result that involuntary unemployment persists. In those situations the state's economic interventions can correct or offset market failures or inadequacies. In effect Keynes challenged neoclassical theory's explanation of what determined society's output and employment. He criticized and rejected the role of markets as automatic stabilizers by questioning their underlying determinants, especially the role of individual utility.

Consider first Keynes's position on the supply of labor hours. His notion is that workers' attitude toward wages reflects a given psychological propensity, namely to resist declines in their money wages. This propensity or rule of behavior belongs to the structure of societal customs. Workers' unions do likewise, and their behavior belongs to the institutional structure of society. Presuming the structures of social customs and institutions, Keynesian theory produces a perfectly elastic supply of labor hours at a psychologically and union-determined money wage. In figure 3.4a this supply is indicated by the horizontal line drawn from the fixed money wage, $\bar{w}$, to the point of intersection of that line with the demand curve $D_h^C(\bar{P})$. In sharp contrast to the previous neoclassical concepts, Keynes has now created the possibility of involuntary unemployment of an amount CZ at the money wage $\bar{w}$.

Two observations are in order. First, this involuntary unemployment results from Keynes's new assumption about how structural customs and institutions reveal themselves in this market. The neoclassical utility calculus of the individual's choice between real income and leisure no longer governs the supply behavior of laborers. Keynes replaced that with a new kind of human rationality derived from what he took to be given rules of human psychology and institutional power. The latter are as presumed to be rooted in the structure of our economy just as the neoclassical economists presume that their axioms about nonsatiation, consistency, and so forth, are rooted in our genes. Keynesian and neoclassical economists are both causal essentialists, although they prefer different essences: for Keynes, structuralism, and for neoclassicists, humanism. (Of course, from the perspective of the neoclassical economist as humanist, the "Keynesian human" may appear to act in a quite irrational way. The reason is that individuals in the neoclassical world are assumed to calculate decisions in terms of real wages and not this Keynesian money wage.

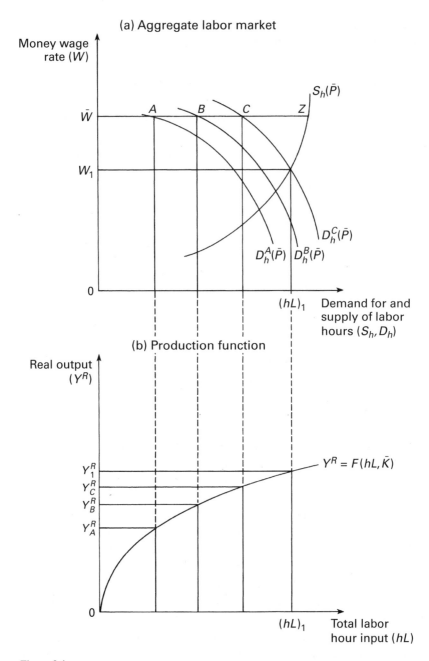

Figure 3.4
Involuntary unemployment in the labor market and less than full employment output in the economy, with money wages and prices assumed to be constant

Indeed the Keynesian human is often asserted to suffer from "money illusion," which represents a way to describe this assumed irrationality.)

Second, this perfectly elastic supply of labor at the fixed money wage amounts to a kind of market imperfection such as those discussed earlier in this chapter. Keynes has found a barrier that prevents the labor market from self-correcting. An excess supply of labor is not competed away by having money wages fall; it is a market imperfection introduced into the labor market.

We will now examine carefully what happens in the labor market when the demand for labor falls. We will also assume for the moment that prices remain constant. The reasons for the latter assumption will be given after we explore the effects produced by a fall in the demand for labor.

Given the assumption of constant prices, suppose that a fall in the demand for labor is caused by a decrease in investment (perhaps resulting from rising business uncertainty about future prospects for profitable sales). Shifts in the demand for labor to the left will trace out a series of different employment points along the given money wage line $\bar{w}$. These points are shown in figure 3.4a as C, B, and A. Each of these employment points will be below that of full employment at $(hL)_1$.

At each point along the line CBA, there is involuntary unemployment. Individuals are willing to work additional hours at the wage $\bar{w}$, but they are prevented from doing so by the very customary and institutional forces that set the money wage at that level. Clearly, market competition is not working properly in this labor market. Consequently the equilibrium employment that results with any given demand-for-labor curve is not that of the full employment curve at $(hL)_1$.

If we now take into account the production function as shown in figure 3.4b, we can derive the real output in this economy for each of these less than full employment points. This is shown in figure 3.4b, where Y_1^R indicates the full employment output.

Given these less than full employment real outputs, the aggregate-supply curve is easily derived. Since prices have been assumed to be constant, the supply of real output must be perfectly elastic at whatever the given price level is assumed to be. The different employment levels in figure 3.4a produce different real outputs in figure 3.4b. Each of these employment levels, however, corresponds to the same given price level ($\bar{P}$ in figure 3.4a). Since these different outputs are also related to the same price level, the aggregate-supply curve must be a horizontal line. Such a Keynesian supply curve is shown in figure 3.5. We have also noted there the previously derived neoclassical, perfectly inelastic supply at the full employment income Y_1^R.

It is worth noting that this neoclassical, perfectly inelastic supply curve is based on two key assumptions: (1) that all markets, including the labor one, are assumed to be completely flexible, and (2) that all agents of supply and

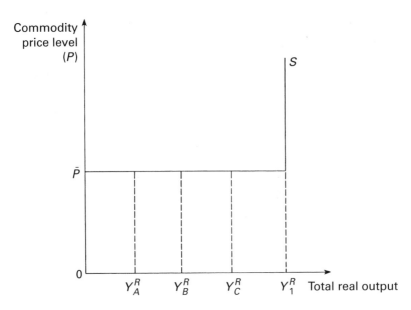

Figure 3.5
Keynesian and neoclassical aggregate-supply curve

demand are assumed to be perfectly informed about price and wage movements. In fact we have assumed implicitly that all laborers in the labor market
are perfectly informed about price and wage movements and that the operation of this market is not hindered in any way by market barriers. In stark
contrast to these neoclassical assumptions, Keynes's way of looking at the
labor market produces a constant money wage there and a perfectly elastic
aggregate-supply curve. This constancy of money wages persists in the face
of significant involuntary unemployment, the possibility of which neoclassical
theory rules out.[2]

There is another reason for this Keynesian, perfectly elastic aggregate-
supply curve. It too is based partly on the previous assumption that changes
in the demand for firms' output do not produce changes in their prices. One
might think of this assumption in terms of a given and constant marginal cost
of output whenever firms operate significantly below their potential capacity.
Over that relevant range of their supply curve, the marginal product of labor
may be assumed to remain more or less constant when additional labor is hired.
This constancy of the marginal product, along with the unchanged money
wage, produces a constant marginal cost and thus a constant output price.
(Recall that $mc_q = w/mp_{hL}$, and that for profit maximization $P = mc_q$; if both
numerator and denominator in this mc_q fraction are constant, then prices also
will be constant.) In a sense the recession could be a cause of this situation
for producing units because it creates so much excess capacity in the economy.

Let us now turn to the demand side of the Keynesian theory. With his new assumptions about supply conditions, Keynes produced the theory that demand is the essential determinant of aggregate output and employment. Instead of the neoclassical essentialization of supply, Keynes substituted an essentialization of demand. According to neoclassical theory, changes in demand have absolutely no effect on real output or employment. The supply or real output and the level of employment are essentially effects of utility and scarcity. Changes in demand do not touch those essences. In contrast, Keynes stressed that these neoclassical essences do not matter at all in situations of less than full employment. Their irrelevance is expressed geometrically by the Keynesian, perfectly elastic supply curve.

Thus space was created for Keynes's new theory of aggregate-demand behavior. There are basically two parts to this demand theory. One deals with the savings-versus-consumption behavior of individuals, and the other concerns the demand of individuals for money. We will begin with the savings-versus-consumption decision.

Keynes rejected the role assigned by neoclassical economics to individual preferences as the key determinants of the supply of new capital or savings. For him savings responded less to the rental rate on capital than to the real incomes earned by potential savers. Given any rental rate on capital, all individuals will save money because they all have a psychological propensity (habit or custom) to put aside some of their income for the future. This propensity, taken to be more or less constant, is called the "marginal propensity to save" (MPS), a savings coefficient that reveals how much of any additional income will be saved. Like Keynes's other psychological propensities, the MPS is also grounded in a kind of mass psychology.

The other side of this psychological law of savings is the parallel law that determines real consumption: whatever individuals do not save out of their incomes, they consume. Thus the total consumption by individuals is also a function of their real income. This dependence has been called the Keynesian consumption function. It specifies a more or less fixed relationship between added consumption and added income. That relationship has been called the "marginal propensity to consume" (MPC).

To better appreciate the Keynesian theoretical alternative, consider the neoclassical analysis of the capital market. For the neoclassical economists, what produces equilibrium in the capital market is the movement of the rental rate for capital. The capital market works as follows: if investment increases, an excess demand for new capital will develop that will bid up the rental rate of capital and produce additional savings until a new equilibrium between investments and savings is established at a higher rental rate. Consumption will fall by just enough to release the necessary additional savings to fuel the increased investment goods desired by society. We may thus conclude that increased investment creates its own increased savings by changing the rental rate of capital (the price of future relative to current consumption).

Keynes's consumption function injects a new and important change into the neoclassical idea that adjustment inside the capital market alone produces equality between savings and investment. If savings are a function of income, then in a situation of less than full employment an increase in investment spending will raise incomes and thereby also savings. There is no necessary change in the rental rate of capital. It is quite possible that the new equilibrium rental rate will remain the same as before rather than necessarily rise (as in the neoclassical theory). Keynes emphasized the impact that rising investment would have on income and employment in a less than fully employed society.

Keynes next expanded his theory for determining the rental rate on capital in the so-called money market. He introduced still another new psychological determinant that also belongs to the economic structure: all individuals have a propensity to hold money not only for the traditional reason, to make transactions, but for liquidity or speculative purposes as well. Consequently, he theorized, in a money market the demand for money becomes a function not only of real income (as in the previously specified Cambridge equation) but of the rental rate as well, because of speculative or liquidity needs. Formally, the total demand for money in the economy became a function of both real income and the rental rate on capital. Parallel to other functional forms, this one too is expressed typically in an equation in which coefficients reflect the two rules of money behavior, transactions and liquidity or speculative needs.

Keynes's theory of liquidity preference suggests that as the rental rate rises, an individual's demand for money will decrease. This is because holding cash balances becomes less attractive when higher yielding assets (bonds) can be purchased. In addition, as rates rise, expectations tend to build that they will eventually fall. Given that expectation, it makes sense for an individual to try to buy higher yielding assets now because their prices will rise (yielding capital gains) when rental rates on capital do drop.

In Keynes's theory, choices about savings, investments, buying bonds, and holding cash decisions came to depend on both the rental rate on capital and on real income. This differed from the neoclassical dichotomy, in which savings-and-investment decisions depended only on the rental rate, and the demand for money depended only on real income. By thinking and linking the capital and money markets differently, Keynes was able to determine simultaneously the equilibrium real income and the equilibrium rental rate on capital. These equilibrium levels were determined by the given marginal propensity to save, the inherent marginal product of capital, the propensity to demand money for both transaction and speculative needs, and the state-given supply of money. These determinants became the new essences—the given structural rules (coefficients)—within the Keynesian theory.

Given the resulting determination of the equilibrium real income in terms of these essences, we can find the corresponding employment level by examining the production function (the number of workers needed to produce the equilibrium level of income). There is no necessity for this equilibrium level of income to be at or even near the full employment level of income. Modern capitalist economic systems do not, in Keynes's view, have any inherent tendency to produce or to sustain full employment.

In the neoclassical view, employment (determined by preferences between income and leisure) determines society's real output and its members incomes. In the Keynesian view, spending (effective demand) determines society's real output and thus its equilibrium level of employment. For neoclassical economists the rental rate of capital is determined without regard to what happens in the money market, while aggregate demand is determined in the money market without regard to what happens in the capital market. In sharp contrast, for Keynesian economists the rental rate *and* real income are determined simultaneously by the interaction of forces emanating from both of these markets.

In figure 3.6 we consider once again the Keynesian and neoclassical supply segments of the aggregate-supply curve. To these we add the Keynesian aggregate-demand curve. A change in spending by either or both consumers and investors will shift the aggregate-demand curve to the right, thereby increasing real income in the society from Y_A^R to Y_B^R, as shown in the diagram. This result is exactly what Keynes set out to show; it presumes the Keynesian supply curve in figure 3.5.

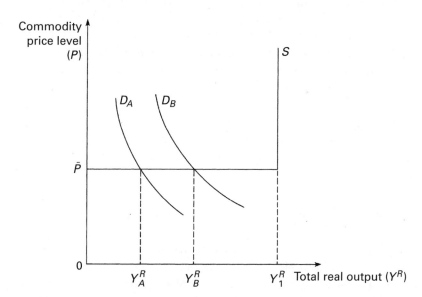

Figure 3.6
Keynesian and neoclassical aggregate-supply curve and the Keynesian aggregate-demand curve

The precise quantitative impact of this change in spending on real income and thus employment depends on the size of the marginal propensity to save; that is, the proportion of income saved determines the magnitude of the Keynesian multiplier. Its impact depends partly on the existence of unemployed resources so that a change in spending will not merely bid up prices and wages (that is why the perfectly elastic supply curve becomes so important). Its impact also depends on the effect of increased spending on the rental rate of capital. Increased incomes generated by an increase in spending produce a rise in the transaction demand for money. With an unchanged supply of money, this rise in the transaction demand for money creates an excess demand for money, and rental rates are bid up. To the extent that investment is sensitive to such an increase in this rate, then the multiplier impact of increased spending on real income will be smaller. Yet if prices and wages are more or less constant or are slow to change, and if changes in investment spending are not that sensitive to changes in the rental rate, then a change in aggregate spending in society will have a significant impact on the level of real incomes.

A problem arises: in depressed economic conditions there may well be little reason to expect investment demand to increase. Indeed, as explained in the next section, poor business expectations help cause a lack of effective demand. In addition, since consumption spending is tied to real income, when incomes stay depressed, there is not much hope that consumption will rise. Therefore, since increased spending is the essential Keynesian solution to the depression, that spending becomes the state's task. It must increase its spending and the supply of money in order to shift the aggregate-demand curve to the right and thereby secure full employment equilibrium.

However, suppose that in times of depression the propensity of individuals to hold their wealth in the form of cash balances is high. Then any increase in the money supply will largely be held as cash balances, not used to purchase bonds, and thus have only a minimal impact on lowering the rental rate (the so-called Keynesian liquidity trap). In this case the ultimate determinant of real output and employment becomes state spending. The key to achieving full employment is for the state to run deficits (increased spending whose impact is not offset by increased taxes) sufficient to push the otherwise inert economy to full employment.[3]

3.4 Investment Behavior

In the Keynesian system we have seen how structural rules govern what occurs to most economic variables such as consumption, money holdings, pricing, and the labor market. However, Keynes abandons his structuralism on one point, when he considers the demands of investors' for investment goods.

Attributes of individual human nature determine investment spending. In this sense Keynesian macroeconomics remains a mostly structural approach, save for this one remarkable and consequential shift into humanism.

For Keynes, uncertainty is key. Investors suffer from the human imperfection of not being able to know now what will occur in the future. Uncertainty haunts them when they try to calculate the expected profitability of new investments. Their calculations today are affected by everything happening around them and its possible impacts on the future. Business investment is therefore highly unstable, expanding or contracting because of how almost any societal change today affects investors' minds and moods and their resulting profit calculations. Most important, their erratic behavior can propel the entire economy into expansion or contraction. Keynes made the instability of capitalism an effect of its capitalists' unstable individual investment behavior grounded in their imperfect natures: a philosophical humanism.

Consider how an economic downturn or contraction might occur. Investors' confidence in the future profitability of planned investments might be undermined suddenly because of a unanticipated fall in common stock prices, a government announcement of a rise in housing foreclosures over the previous quarter year, or some international political crisis, even though these events need have little direct bearing upon the profitability of those proposed investments. What matters is that today's business climate or mood darkened because of these events. For a different example, investors may begin to worry that an expanding economy cannot be sustained. After all, they like everyone else have memories of booms too often and too quickly turning into busts. Acting cautiously and prudently, they postpone new investment spending. They begin instead to hedge their bets: to reduce future risk, more of their net profits are used to purchase relatively safer financial assets (e.g., US treasury notes) than perceived risky investment goods.

In these examples, the mind and mood of investors have turned pessimistic, resulting in their demand curve for investment goods to shift downward and leftward. This reduces effective demand and hence overall income in the economy. Because much of investment is concentrated in the hands of a few hundred corporations and their boards of directors, the changed investment decisions of these few can have a major impact on the many. Of course, the curve could alternatively shift up and to the right because of different circumstances. Optimism might rise because of a rising stock market, rumors of a technological breakthrough, election of politicians thought favorable to business, a newly signed peace treaty, discovery of vast reserves of crude oil, and so on. In these cases the minds and mood of investors exude confidence that good times will continue or soon will arrive.

Whether the response of investors to their imagined future environment is to contract or expand spending on additional capital goods, two key questions need to be asked (to which Keynes provided answers). The first is: what will be the impacts of more or less investment on the overall level of income in society? The second is: why might other markets not correct/offset downward or upward spirals resulting from changes in investment spending and their impacts on income? Answers to both questions are based on Keynes's assumed structuralism.

We can calculate precisely the quantitative impact of, say, a fall in investment (I) on society's income (Y) by calculating the system's multiplier. That multiplier merely reflects the quantitative combination of the presumed structural rules. Calculated in note 3, it is $1/(1 - c)$ times whatever the change in investment is, where c is the rule (the structural coefficient) that determines how much consumption changes when income changes. The more rules introduced into the macro economy, the more coefficients appear in the associated multiplier calculation. Based on the resulting multiplier, Keynes is able to provide a quantitative answer to the first question: $\Delta Y = 1/(1 - c) \times \Delta I$. Clearly, his answer to the overall impact of a collapse in investment spending, due to the ever-changing moods of the investor, is based on the underlying and powerful assumption of theoretical structuralism.

Turning to an answer to the second question, we see again how the assumed structural rules governing the labor market prevent any corrective mechanism from occurring. If the economy is at full employment, then a fall in investment shifts the demand for labor to the left, resulting in unemployed labor. However, money wages do not fall to clear what is now an excess supply of laborers at the full employment wage. The reasons are two: as we explained, a psychological rule governs the minds of all workers, and it combined with the power wielded by workers' unions serve together to fix wages at $\bar{W}$ in figure 3.4a. Consistent with structural reasoning, the relationship between buyers and sellers in the labor market are governed by particular institutional and customary rules (workers' money illusion and power) belonging to the economic structure. Hence no market correction arises to eliminate unemployed labor. In fact, if market prices on goods sold by business fall to any degree in a recession, then real wage costs to business even could rise.

The individual investor's human nature in the Keynesian world is far different from what it is in the neoclassicist's world. For Keynes, human nature in an inherently uncertain world generates a moody and erratic investor who oscillates between periods of business euphoria and those of depression. Clearly, this is a very different nature than that posed by the neoclassicists with their carefully crafted assumptions of human rationality enabling all agents, including investors, to operate under conditions of full knowledge of the present and future.[4]

Perhaps it should come as no great surprise then that the unintended harm done to the economy by the always potentially unstable business investor requires social intervention. State controls are deemed necessary to minimize the potential damage that can be done to the societal body by these out-of-control private agents who, through no fault of their own, nonetheless can throw the economy into recession. On the other hand, despite being unstable in this way, these business investors are nonetheless necessary to the functioning of privately owned, market capitalism.

Still another important implication of Keynes's theory of investment and investors is to underscore the powerful impact of investors' ideas on the economy. In effect Keynes made investors' ideas, their guesses about future business profitability, shape their investment behavior and thus the economy too. Indeed, because of the presence of the multiplier, investors' conception of the future can significantly impact the lives of everyone in society. But, as we just saw, causation goes the other way too: investors' ideas were shaped by changes in the economy, some of which result from the very change in investment that occurred. Here we have still another example of what we discussed in chapter 1: the interaction between theory (investors' ideas) and society (the economy) or, using the language developed there, the overdetermination of one by the other. But why stop only with investors? Why can't this kind of causal interaction apply to all economic behavior in addition to business investment? Recently some economists argue precisely for this kind of extension at least in regard to changes in personal consumption (Akerlof and Shiller 2009, ch. 10).

After Keynes, a number of his followers tried to explain variations in investment by reducing them to effects of structural rules governing investors' behavior. They were trying to change Keynes's "humanist moment" back into an extended structuralism. For example, not too long after publication of Keynes's *General Theory*, structural explanations arose that reduced investment to an effect of a change in consumption spending (Samuelson 1939). In this case, changes in consumption would induce—"accelerate"—new investment spending in some proportionate relationship. This move allowed a calculated quantitative impact of investment on the economy by combining both the multiplier (the measured impact of changed investment on income and consumption) and a newly defined "accelerator" (the measured impact of changed income and consumption on investment). Thereafter still new investment equations were introduced that set forth new structural rules of business behavior as macroeconomics tried to explain private investment's changes.

3.5   Post-Keynesian Economics and Other Reactions to Keynes

Perhaps because Keynesian theory speaks to abiding problems presented by capitalist economies, the reactions it has provoked among economists and those who think about economics have kept it a very lively and enduring tradition of thought and policy. Despite rises and falls in its popularity among economists, policy makers, and the general public, and from country to country, there has been a remarkable continued presence of Keynesian theory over the last half century. For those who rejected the neoclassical tradition and likewise Marxism and Marxian economics, Keynesian theory always offered an attractive alternative. However, it is also true that two more partisan responses have also been prominent among the reactions to Keynesian theory.

The first of these partisan reactions was very defensive. Those economists who wished to maintain neoclassical theory's two essential organizing ideas—scarcity and preferences—viewed the Keynesian contribution mostly as an attack. For them, Keynesian theory subtracts what they deem essential (preferences and scarcity) and substitutes structural laws and unexplained new essential determinants of economic events (e.g., workers' and investors' psychology, power, and societal institutions). Such economists responded to the rise of Keynesianism by constructing arguments to show that what Keynes substituted—structural laws and new essences—were themselves effects of (reducible to) human preferences and/or scarcity. They thereby reaffirmed basic neoclassical theory and dismissed the Keynesian critique as rather trivial, one of the many "critiques" that neoclassical theory has encountered and overcome.

Certain new ideas or emphases introduced by Keynes have remained. Neoclassical economists accepted them, but only as secondary complications easily accommodated within the neoclassical tradition of self-adjusting markets based on the rational behavior of suppliers and demanders. For instance, Keynes's uncertainty principle is treated as a problem of choice. Rational economic agents readily solve the problem of uncertainty by shifting from choice among known or certain alternatives to choice instead among alternatives that have been assigned the probabilities of their occurring. This admission and accommodation of uncertainty by an otherwise unchanged neoclassical theory satisfied the preponderance of the neoclassical tradition.

However, it did not satisfy those who read in Keynes's work a more radical critique of the neoclassical tradition and a more radical notion of uncertainty as a kind of irreducible incapacity to know the future. That uncertainty precluded knowing and thus assigning a probability to alternative outcomes. Such economists reacted to Keynes's new entry-point concepts of structural rules, human psychology, power, and institutions by developing and refining new concepts, or "macro-models." They extended Keynes's contributions and deepened his challenge to neoclassical theory. One increasingly influential group, calling themselves post-Keynesian, emerged as a new and somewhat heterogeneous school of thought. Post-Keynesian economics enriches the Keynesian tradition as another heterodox alternative to the neoclassical tradition that is also very different from Marxian economic theory.

Using Keynes's notion of 'fundamental uncertainty' (as distinct from probabilistic uncertainty) as one of its privileged entry points, post-Keynesian economics posits investors' desire for capital accumulation as the driving force of capitalism (a humanist assumption). The especially important figures that have contributed to this tradition include G. L. S. Shackle (1903–1992), Hyman Minsky (1919–1996) and Paul Davidson. In their best-known formulations, the moody and erratic behaviors of financial market investors lead capitalist economies through periods of expansion followed by recessions.[5] Following the broader Keynesian tradition, post-Keynesian economics emphasizes, on the demand side of the economy, the importance of social structures as well as expectations in aggregate consumer behavior. On the economy's production or supply side, however, post-Keynesian economists tend to draw upon other non-neoclassical economists such as Karl Marx, Michal Kalecki, Piero Sraffa, and Joan Robinson. The post-Keynesian school thus theorizes both product and factor markets as characterized by imperfect forms of competition (monopolies and oligopolies). Firms with various degrees of market power determine prices. As we explain in chapter 5, market power is typically theorized in terms of these firms being able to mark up their average costs to yield a selling price. The resulting "markup equation" introduces still another structural rule, this time on the economy's supply side, namely the given markup coefficient associated with costs.

There have also been some economists who seem to advocate something of a middle position between neoclassical and Keynesian economics that attempts to synthesize the two. Some of them swing from one to the other, depending on the times. The global crisis in capitalism since 2007 generated such swings. Before then, it seemed that they basically subscribed to neoclassical economic theory; since then, they sound rather more Keynesian in their analyses and policy prescriptions.

Yet another kind of middle position finds economists with basically neoclassical commitments who also hold certain Keynesian views. They have sometimes seemed concerned especially about neoclassical theory's explanations of unemployment and poverty as voluntary and that theory's insistence that markets self-correct. For instance, a school called new-Keynesian economics evolved that differs from both the traditional Keynesian and post-Keynesian approaches. New-Keynesian economics provides an explanation for involuntary unemployment without relinquishing the neoclassical entry point of fully rational economic actors. Using recent neoclassical theories of "information failures" (that relax the assumption of perfect information), new-Keynesian economists have developed new theories of labor and credit markets. The new-Keynesians fault traditional Keynesian macroeconomics for lacking the sort of methodological individualist (or humanist) foundations that distinguish neoclassical economics. So they seek to furnish Keynesian insights

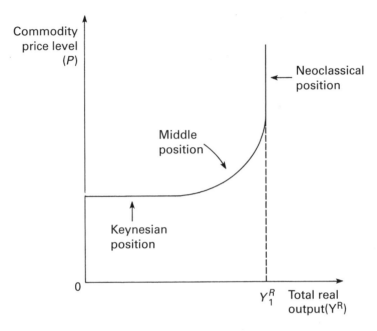

Figure 3.7
Different segments of the aggregate-supply curve offered by the three different positions provoked by Keynes's theory

pertaining to nonclearing market outcomes with microfoundations of individual preferences. We treat new-Keynesian theories further in chapter 5's section on information failures and missing markets, since they are basically late neoclassical theories exhibiting the influence of some Keynesian themes.

Another popular reaction to Keynes relaxes the Keynesian assumption of fixed prices, but leaves money wages fixed, as before, by the psychology and power of laborers. The result of this somewhat ad hoc approach has been the creation of an aggregate-supply curve that is neither perfectly elastic nor inelastic. Such a curve is shown in figure 3.7.

A rightward shift in aggregate demand will still cause an increase in real income and employment, but the multiplier's size will be smaller to the extent that the demand shift drives up prices. In the economy described by figure 3.7, there is room for the concerns of both neoclassical and Keynesian economists: state spending, changes in the money supply, and market adjustments can all have their respective effects on the level of real income and employment in the society. For example, if the demand curve shifts leftward (demand falls) from its full employment level, it sets into motion an automatic offsetting tendency. The fall in prices will create an increase in individuals' real cash balances. This increase in the supply of loanable funds will depress interest rates (assuming that no liquidity trap is operating there) and thereby stimulate investment spending. Rising real cash balances may well stimulate consumption spending too. The upshot of these two effects is that real income will not fall as much as it might otherwise.

However, with money wages still rigid, the economy can remain locked in a new less than full employment equilibrium. Thus there is room for increased state spending and/or an increased money supply to shift the aggregate-demand curve back to its former full employment level. The need for state intervention is reduced the more important these automatic market adjustments become. In other words, a kind of variable mixing of neoclassical and Keynesian elements is at work.

Interestingly, such mixings can veer to either extreme. For example, why not theorize the possibility that wages are as flexible as prices? That is precisely what happened in the years before the crisis hit in 2007 in the development of what some called a new macroeconomics. If wages and prices are theorized as freely adjusting to whatever changes occur in demand and supply, we return to a perfectly inelastic aggregate-supply curve. In other words, we have rediscovered the neoclassical theory in which there is no way for the state to influence aggregate real income or employment. Once again, preference calculations and scarcity determine the value of all commodities, the level of employment, and the aggregate real incomes of all individuals.

This last approach has been called "new classical theory." It is an appropriate name, for the content of that new theory is precisely what has been presented in the previous chapter. And what becomes of the Keynesian criticisms of and alternatives to neoclassical theory? Basically, by reaffirming the inherent market rationality of all individuals, new classical theory reacts to Keynes by making Keynesian economics disappear.[6]

3.6   Role of the State in Capitalist Society

Keynesian theory divides total private spending in an economy into two parts—consumption and investment—and claims that consumption spending is the more stable. The theory then infers that an economy operating at less than full employment has likely suffered a fall in investment spending (mostly by private businesses). As we noted above, consumption spending follows prescribed structural rules in Keynesian theory whereas investment does not. Confronting uncertainty, business investors must make investment decisions that are unavoidably dependent on predictions and expectations about an inherently unknowable future.

Keynesian theory thus uses its structural rule operating on the side of consumption to show that savings (the residual of income left after consumption) remains more or less stable in society, a relatively fixed portion of aggregate income. On the other hand, business investment is dependent on relatively unstable predictions and expectations about an uncertain and unknowable future, and it is therefore unstable. The result is always the possibility and usually the likelihood of disruptions between savings and investments. In this sense, declines in investment spending are nobody's fault; the cause is ultimately reduced to our imperfect human nature. When investments drop relative to savings, declines in production, employment, and income result.

Because of market imperfections, such as Keynes's liquidity trap and his wage and price rigidities, the economy is not able to correct itself and restore the full employment equilibrium. Therefore the state must enter the picture. The state's visible hand, equipped with Keynesian insights, guides the economy back to that full employment, Pareto optimum point where individuals finally have the freedom to choose whether or not they want to be unemployed and whether or not they want to be rich or poor. Instead of laissez faire capitalism, Keynesian economics sees crucial roles for the state in anticipating, preventing, and/or offsetting recurring imbalances between savings and investments.

The state must play such roles when a less than full employment economy generates less wealth than that economy could produce. One cause for state intervention is then a limitation on our intrinsic human nature, a limit on what we can know. We need to plan and carry out investments now whose success depends on future conditions that are uncertain, volatile, and that we cannot know now. Our consequently unavoidable guesswork can and often does prevent achieving an economy's potential output. Other causes of the state's necessary economic interventions—other market imperfections—can be traced to the nature of the macroeconomy: given psychological propensities or rules of aggregate behavior, institutional power, and societal customs.

The Keynesian understanding of the economy is very different from the neoclassical view. The Keynesian view is strongly structuralist (save for the investor). The neoclassical view is strongly humanist or individualist. Even when Keynesians break with structuralism and borrow a humanist perspective in their theory of investor behavior, theirs is a very different human nature. It is far from the neoclassical economists' notions of human natures that make continuous utility calculations with perfect foresight and full knowledge of all their options.

Neoclassical and Keynesian economists do share something in common. Neither theory has any place for the alternative Marxian view that explains how the functioning and contradictions of a society's class structure can, in a wide variety of circumstances and for quite heterogeneous reasons, generate a crisis, in the sense of a decline in investment spending. Some post-Keynesian economists would disagree with our characterization. While not fully embracing the Marxian class approach and analysis, they have grave doubts about the capacity of the capitalist institutions of private property and markets to achieve a fully employed society. The combination of an institutional structure (a societal distribution of power) and uncertainty promises continually to plunge capitalist societies into deep and recurrent crises.

In conclusion, the state, for the Keynesians, and the market, for the neoclassicists, generate social effects that are similar to those often attributed to religion. Each reforms whatever evil is given to society by our natures and limits as human beings. However, both Keynesians and neoclassicists share the view that capitalist economies—with the relation of employer and employee at the productive core—represent the optimum social arrangement for generating and distributing wealth, the fruits of labor. Marxists do not share that view. Nor do they believe in the theoretical systems of the neoclassicists and the Keynesians. Their different theory offers an altogether different interpretation of the structure and problems of capitalist economies.

Appendix: Rational Expectations

One might expect neoclassical economists to worry about the assumption that human beings somehow possess perfect information about price and wage movements. Consequently, for this reason alone, deviations from the full-employment equilibrium are always a possibility since individuals will make mistakes in foreseeing future prices and wage changes. In recent years the issue of imperfect individual forecasts has occupied a number of neoclassical economists.

A so-called rational expectations school has developed to deal with the problem. Neoclassical economists working on this new approach have modified the basic neoclassical theory presented so far in this chapter by introducing new concepts into the theory in regard to how individuals form expectations of future price and wage movements. As might be expected in logically extending the concepts informing neoclassical theory, individual expectations or forecasts are made in a rational way. This extension amounts to a new attack on the Keynesian approach. In particular, it is an attack on the Keynesian assumption that at least in the short run, with money wages fixed, a shift in the demand for labor to the right (caused by a change in the money supply) will increase the level of employment in the economy.

Suppose, for example, that individuals expect the supply of money to increase. The expected rise in the money supply will shift the aggregate-demand curve to the right, and prices will then be expected to increase. In turn this rise in prices will shift the demand curve for labor hours to the right in the labor market. In the Keynesian world, in response to this rise in prices, the supply curve of labor hours will *not* shift upward and to the left, at least not in the short run. Thus a rightward shift in the labor-demand curve, combined with an unchanged supply-of-labor curve, indicates that employment and real output are on the rise in the economy.

However, the assumed world of rational expectations modifies the movements of these curves to obtain a very different analysis and outcome. With rational expectations, the supply curve of labor hours will shift upward and to the left in the short run because workers rationally expect that a rise in the money supply will increase prices in the economy. Therefore, being rational, these labor suppliers demand higher money wages per hour of their work, unlike their irrational Keynesian counterparts. The labor market reaches a new equilibrium at a higher money wage and price level, but no change takes place in the real wage. The result pictured in figure 3.2 is reproduced here. Thus the labor market returns to its initial full employment level, and consequently real output in the economy does not change.

Comparing the two approaches, we can see how in the Keynesian world, laborers are "fooled" by or react slowly to price increases induced by changes in the money supply, whereas in the rational-expectations world, laborers are never systematically fooled by policy changes. The rational reaction to an expected increase in the money supply is to demand higher money wages to offset higher expected prices. It follows that the rational-expectations school has in effect returned us to the neoclassical world. Once again, the state cannot, even in the short run, affect any real part of the economy— for instance, its level of employment or its real output.

4 Marxian Theory

4.1 The Marxian Tradition and Its Theories

Marxian theory is a class theory. Its originality lies not in claiming that classes exist; people have said that for thousands of years and used class to understand their societies. Marx's originality lies in how he understands and defines class, then derives his notion of exploitation, and finally shows how class and exploitation influence people's conceptions, perceptions, and actions. Marxian theory concludes that class exploitation occurs at multiple sites in modern society and that our politics, literature, family structures, sports, television programing, religions, and incomes are all complexly shaped by exploitation. Of particular relevance to this chapter, we will explain how prices, incomes, wealth, and so on, are shaped by class exploitation.

These may be bothersome conclusions. They force us to contemplate a relationship, a connection, between social institutions we may hold dear—political freedom, the family, private enterprise and markets, baseball, religion, and the like—and a social relationship we typically find bad—namely exploitation. Marxian theory also suggests the likelihood of tensions and struggles and even revolution in our society: exploiters versus exploited. While perhaps unsettling, such an understanding can be liberating, in the Marxian view, because the capacity to see exploitation in our society and its damaging effects may well be a necessary step toward achieving the social changes needed to eliminate it and its effects.

Parallel to neoclassical and Keynesian theories, Marxian theory too conveys its particular ethical messages. They concern its chief object, the class process in which the society's laborers who produce its goods and services typically produce more than what portion of them they received for their own reproduction. The excess of output over what its producers consume—that *surplus* so central to Marxian theory—is not only its entry point but also forms its ethical message. Marxists want and strive for a social change that will place laborers in the social position to receive and distribute the surpluses they produce. They believe that when laborers are not in that position—when people other than themselves receive and distribute the surpluses they produce—a kind of social theft occurs. For Marxists, the term "social theft" is appropriate because the thieves (the receivers of surplus) *take* what others (the performers of surplus labor) have produced; they give no output of their own in return. Marxists label the two sides "exploiters" and "exploited."

Just as we become upset and angry when personal theft strikes us, our families, and our communities, Marxism encourages parallel emotions in response to the existence of exploitation, the social theft of one group's surplus labor by another. Just as society has established laws, morals, teachings, and customs that oppose and condemn personal theft, so Marxism calls for society to do likewise in regard to social theft. It analyzes class to draw people's awareness and attention toward ending exploitation. In the Marxist view, neoclassical and Keynesian economic theories celebrate modern capitalism (while differing over the appropriate interventions of the state in capitalist economies). In contrast, Marxian economic theory takes a critical position toward the exploitation that it shows to be central to capitalist economies, and it seeks social change beyond capitalism in favor of a nonexploitative economy and society.

Marxian theory also underscores how capitalist society has produced ideas, politics, and economic structures that not only repress knowledge of exploitation as social theft but also encourage the growth and spread of capitalism as "economic progress" without recognition that this entails more exploitation. Indeed classical, neoclassical, and Keynesian economics are themselves idea systems that, in the Marxian view, help make exploitation possible in society chiefly by making it invisible. This situation provoked Marx and Marxists after him to direct their work toward a criticism both of capitalist society and those theories that support it by denying or ignoring the existence and social consequences of class exploitation. The Marxian tradition has developed around these twin critical objectives.

The Marxian economics presented in this chapter is part of the larger Marxian tradition of thought and action that treats far more than just economics. That tradition is the context of Marxian economics much as the broader philosophical, political, and cultural tradition of Europe (that emerged in its transition out of feudalism) has provided the context for classical, neoclassical and Keynesian economics. We need briefly to sketch the history of the Marxian tradition precisely because it is not familiar. Otherwise, students would understandably confuse matters by attempting to cram Marxian economics into the non-Marxian tradition with which they are familiar. To grasp the distance separating Marxian from neoclassical and Keynesian economic theories, we need to know what that distance is. Placing Marxian theory within its broader tradition will help us do that.

Karl Marx (1818–1883) did both theoretical and practical political work throughout his adult life. The child of "comfortable" parents (his father was a middle-level German state bureaucrat, and his mother was from an educated Dutch family), he became radicalized as a university student. He responded to, and joined movements for basic social changes: for democracy against the despotic aristocracies and monarchies of Europe, for free thought instead of religious dogmatisms, and for economic well-being distributed to all rather than reserved for rich minorities. The legacy of his lifetime of analytical writing and active political organizing has been a growing Marxian tradition, including both theoretical output and practical political organizations.

The tradition that Marx's work inaugurated has since extended into many areas not touched by Marx himself. Marx did not theorize much about how parents interact with children or about the way artists' works impact on society or about the economic problems of lawyers and doctors. Indeed he said little about how future socialist or communist economies might operate (there had been no national experiments with such economic systems during his lifetime) or what problems they might face. However, in the over 125 years since he died, thinkers influenced by Marx have contributed their thoughts on these and many other topics. Similarly the revolutionary movements for basic social justice in Europe that drew Marx's enthusiasm have since grown and changed partly under the influence of Marx and Marxists since. Such movements exist on every continent, more or less in every country, and Marx's name and writings play some role in nearly all of them.

4.1.1 Marx's Contributions

After his days as a German university student, Marx matured into a full-time activist in the ongoing European movements for social change. He shared their excitement at the possibilities for democratizing societies opened and promised by the French Revolution. The shifts from concern with God and piety to concern with the social and economic conditions for human happiness attracted his enthusiasm. Like many others, he traced many of the miseries of his time to the great inequalities of wealth and power everywhere around him. He saw those inequalities rooted in the institution of private property, which he therefore opposed. He joined organizations that sought to transform capitalist Europe into a cooperative commonwealth of freethinkers, often called "socialism" or "communism." The 1840s meant to Marx something like what the 1960s meant to many young Americans.

But the revolutions of 1848 across Europe, which had inspired Marx to imagine the imminent possibility of social transformation, were not enough to usher in socialism or communism. The shock waves of 1848 did alter Europe fundamentally. Feudalism never recovered, and capitalism exploded across the continent at an accelerating pace. Capitalism, not socialism, established itself as the dominant system after 1848. That reality forced Marx to rethink his understanding of European society, to analyze why revolutionary movements in 1848 had been unable to realize a socialist transformation. It also forced Marx into exile when the local authorities determined that his ideas were too attractive to revolutionaries to allow him to stay in his native Germany.

His exile took place in London where he remained for the rest of his life. Able only occasionally to engage in practical revolutionary work, Marx therefore threw himself into the work of the social analysis for which he became increasingly famous and influential. He decided to criticize and re-evaluate the theories used by the movements in which he had participated and whose thinking he had absorbed. With his close colleague Friedrich Engels he aimed to reformulate revolutionary theory. They would learn from and build on what went before but also radically alter basic concepts to fashion an understanding of capitalism capable of guiding a more successful revolutionary movement when capitalism was again convulsed by its recurring crises. During the last two decades of his life, Marx published the results of his prodigious studies and reflections, above all in his masterwork, *Capital*, his new and original analysis of capitalism as an economic system.

Marx's originality was and remains his lasting contribution to social theory and to modern revolutionary movements for social justice. Marx believed that he had found an important flaw in the way revolutionaries had previously understood European society. They had underestimated the significance of economics in shaping societies and their histories. More precisely, the revolutionaries of 1848 had neglected the role of class, by which Marx meant the performance of surplus labor and the distribution of its products within capitalist economies. That neglect blinded them to the class aspects of European society. That blindness weakened their analyses of capitalism and contributed to the failure of their revolutionary projects.

Marx's writings were aimed directly to correct this flaw. He analyzed capitalism around a focus on class. *Capital* focused attention on the complex interdependence between the production and distribution of the surplus (the class structure) and every other aspect of modern capitalist societies. He made class his entry point into the analysis of society to overcome the neglect of class among his fellow revolutionaries.

Not only did Marx write theory after he began his exile in London, but he also later resumed his political activism. He used his new class theory to help define new strategies and tactics for revolutionary movements in Europe and America. The passions of his youth resurfaced in the writings of his maturity and his intense participation in revolutionary politics (e.g., including his antislavery articles and agitation around the Civil War in the United States). He ridiculed the idea of "dispassionate analysis," suspecting it was the disguise of analysts who preferred to excuse rather than expose social injustices. Every analyst, Marx believed, makes a particular commitment to social values and to a particular kind of future society. Marxists, neoclassicists, and Keynesians have their particular values, passions, and visions of a better society. One dimension of their theoretical differences is the different set of social values, commitments, and passions that animate the typical representatives of the three economic schools of thought.

For Marx, capitalism was a mass of contradictions: mixtures of good and bad, tensions between pressures for growth and for decline, struggles between advocates and critics. For example, on the one hand, he praised capitalism for its technological dynamism that promised an output of wealth on a scale unimaginable to prior generations. On the other, he criticized capitalism for simultaneously tearing peasants from the land, working them ruthlessly in factories, and generating needless suffering on an equally massive scale world-wide. The promise of plenty contradicted the reality of degradation as chronicled by such novelists of nineteenth-century capitalism as Dickens, Zola, Dostoevsky, and Balzac. On the one hand, capitalism celebrated human relationships based on free, voluntary contracts between adults. On the other, it put people into such unequal situations that the poor and oppressed entered "voluntarily" into exploitative relationships with employers since their alternatives were even worse. On the one hand, Marx readily acknowledged, capitalism stimulated vast new developments in human knowledge and cultural creativity. On the other, most people were reduced to performing routine, menial production tasks that earned relatively little, exhausted them physically and mentally, and thereby precluded them from engaging and enjoying much of the culture that capitalism stimulated.

Marx's theory, like the Marxian tradition it engendered, understood itself to be one particular product of capitalism that was not only critical of capitalism but was also an attempt to save and enhance its positive contributions while overcoming its negative qualities. The point was to analyze capitalism in order to transform it, to liberate its potential by removing its oppressive components. In Marx's view, to liberate the possibilities created by capitalism required a social transformation to a different system, a kind of collective, community of workers whose productive enterprises would not be internally split into exploiters and exploited. Capitalism was too hopelessly mired in contradictions that condemned the vast majority of people to needless and unjustifiable denial and suffering. Marx applied a particular name to the community of "associated workers" that he viewed as the preferable future to capitalism. That name was "communism"—a term he borrowed from past social critics who had long opposed divisions within their societies (unequal wealth distributions and undemocratic power distributions) that had set citizens against one another. Marx shared the idea that such divisions—which capitalism entrenched inside each enterprise—were the enemies of peace, prosperity, and social solidarity. The community/communism of workers who overcame such divisions (by themselves collectively running enterprises as well as working within them) could liberate the fruits of technology and cultural creativity so that they could benefit everyone equally.

Marx did not spend time or effort analyzing communism; he rarely and only briefly sketched its broadest contours since he seems to have frowned on speculation about a future no one could know in advance. His work concentrated on understanding capitalism. His analysis focused on class. Marx believed that without a full appreciation of class, society could not be liberated from the negative consequences of capitalism (with its divisions, struggles, and destructive social consequences). Class had to be added to people's understanding of capitalism and class changes had to be added to political agendas if the projects for social transformation aimed at community and solidarity (i.e., "communism" in those senses of the term) were to succeed.

This liberation inspiration of Marx's theories parallels that of another similarly original theorist whose work came a few years later. Sigmund Freud began as a physician seeking to free certain patients from intense pain and suffering. When he and other doctors failed to find physical causes for some patients' suffering—and also failed to relieve it—Freud decided to reexamine critically theories of the relation between mind and body used by his profession. In that way Freud arrived at his new theory of "the unconscious."

As a part of the human mind overlooked by his fellow doctors, this unconscious, Freud showed, played an important role in the life and suffering of patients. He developed a psychology to analyze the unconscious and techniques—psychoanalysis, psychotherapy—that could treat patients for their psychological problems. Psychologically trained doctors engaged in sustained conversations with patients could produce shared insights into their patients' unconsciousness, identifying contributors to their suffering of which they had previously been unaware. Freud's new theory of the individual mind and body enabled people to see individual suffering in a new light as shaped in part by the individual's unconscious. His goal was thereby to help liberate individuals from their suffering by alerting them to their unconscious and its effects upon their lives. In parallel fashion, Marx sought to liberate people from the effects of class and exploitation by making them aware of those dimensions of capitalist societies.

4.1.2 Marxism since Marx

When Marx died in 1883, no country was yet governed by a state calling itself socialist or communist. The workers' state established by the Paris Commune of 1871, which deeply impressed Marx and Engels, had lasted only a few months. Marx's theory remained chiefly a framework for analyzing capitalism and determining revolutionary strategies to go beyond it. Marx's work gradually attracted adherents among radicals in Europe and America, but this was a slow process that depended on individual contacts and the spread of small editions of the works of Marx and then those of his followers.

Marxism grew in Europe and most markedly in Germany. Political parties based primarily on workers in capitalist enterprises increasingly absorbed and applied Marx's theories. In the years before World War I, the German Social Democratic Party became a major political force in Germany. This situation brought new and different pressures and influences to bear on Marxian theory. No longer was it developed chiefly by small groups of revolutionaries. A large, established political party with elected officials to protect and an electoral image to maintain left its imprint on Marxian theory.

The German Marxists extended the theory to groups and issues Marx had barely touched. Marxian analyses of the legal system, of the social role of women, of foreign trade, of international rivalries among capitalist nations, and of the possible role of parliamentary democracy in a transition from capitalism to communism drew animated debates. Extending in these ways, the theory attracted many new adherents, but it also changed. Ambiguities in Marx's writings were found and resolved in different ways by the different sides in the debates. Marxian theory (singular) gave way to Marxian theories (plural).

World War I (1914–1918) deepened differences and splits within anticapitalist movements and parties. Some supported their countries in the war while others denounced the war as a profit-driven struggle among competing capitalists that workers should neither fight in nor die for. Then the Russian revolution of 1917 shocked Marxian theory again. For the first time, men and women inspired by Marxian theory seized state power and aimed for a massive social revolution. Their leaders, especially V. I. Lenin (1870–1924), adapted Marxian theories to the urgencies they faced. The Russian civil wars of 1918 to 1922, the attempt to reorganize the shattered Russian economy, the campaign to collectivize the country's agriculture, and the launch of massive industrialization were officially analyzed using Marxian terminology and concepts. Putting Marxian theory to such tests altered it further in yet new ways. Moreover Marxists around the world disagreed about the significance of the newly named Union of Soviet Socialist Republics (USSR). For some, it represented the fulfillment of Marx's ideas and of the Marxian tradition. Others evaluated the USSR's development negatively, as a perversion of Marxism clothed deceptively in Marxian language.

Both sides of this sometimes bitter debate changed how Marxian theory was understood and extended. Some Marxists elaborated the theory into an official explanation and justification for the USSR's policies at home and abroad. Others developed it to criticize and attack those policies. Both sides pushed Marxian theory into such new areas as analyses of socialist economic development, analyses of the conflicts between capitalist and communist economic systems, and debates over the definitions and relations between socialism and communism. All this added yet more and different Marxian theories to the tradition.

World War II, the subsequent growth of the USSR to superpower status opposite the United States, its split with former ally China, the growth in political and economic importance of Asian, African, and Latin American societies, and the emergence of more or less independent communist political parties in countries around the world—all these developments induced still more theoretical variations comprising the Marxian tradition. Recently broad movements to alter the oppressive social conditions of women and various racial and ethnic groups have stimulated other theoretical innovations. Marxism has become a rich tradition of diverse theorizations and accumulated practical experiences critical of capitalism and advocating various kinds of socialism or communism.

It is thus unacceptable, inaccurate, and misleading to treat any one theory within the tradition as if it were the whole tradition. To take a parallel case, one kind of Christian theory endorsed the Inquisition in Spain and another kind endorsed South Africa's apartheid regime. However, those facts do not warrant equating Christianity with either institution. One kind of neoclassical theory was used to support repressive governments in Chile and South Korea, yet that does not warrant equating neoclassical theory with right-wing dictatorships and torture. Some Marxists in power politically repressed their political opponents, yet once again that does not warrant equating Marxism with dictatorship, and so on. The Marxian tradition like any other is a complex diversity of theories and practices.

4.1.3   Which Marxian Theory Will We Present?

How then will we proceed in this chapter? To attempt somehow to encompass everything in the tradition would produce a long, tedious survey. To present one theory within the tradition, even one growing in importance, would invite criticism that we left out alternative Marxian theories.

Nevertheless, we have chosen the second path. We do present one particular Marxian theory. It is the one we have found to be the most coherent, systematic, and persuasive, especially as a clear alternative to neoclassical and Keynesian theories. Since it is one Marxian theory and we do not pretend that it is Marxism in general, we are obliged to explain and justify its place at the center of our attention.

Over the last thirty years, the Marxian tradition has changed radically. There are many reasons for this. The pro- versus anti-Soviet pole around which many Marxian debates swirled after 1917 largely dissolved in the aftermath of the

USSR's disappearance. Movements for social transformation arising in advanced, industrial capitalist societies (feminism, environmentalism, antiracism, etc.) added new concerns and dimensions and thereby changed Marxism. Globalization—capitalism's ever-deeper penetration and integration of evermore parts of the world—provoked new currents of resistance to capitalism that contributed their experiences to Marxism. Since 2007, capitalism's worst economic crisis since the Great Depression of the 1930s has brought many to engage or re-engage Marx and Marxism. The promise that modern capitalism's various twentieth-century reforms and "stabilizers" would prevent deep and long-lasting economic downturns had been broken. The high unemployment, home foreclosures, loss of job benefits, and precariousness of employment prompted many new critics of capitalism. They not only found their way to the Marxian tradition's accumulated analyses and experiences with capitalist crises, they also added new insights to the tradition. Marxism in the twenty-first century is already significantly different from what it was across the first century after Marx's death.

We have chosen to present here a Marxian theory that responds to all of these developments. It begins on the solid and systematic logical foundation set by Marx. It builds on the achievements and strengths of Marxism in the twentieth century while avoiding and rejecting its weaknesses and mistakes. A basic virtue of this Marxian theory lies in its focus on the interdependency between the class and nonclass, economic and noneconomic, aspects of society. Finally, this Marxian theory emphasizes class as Marx did. It aims to teach the existence and implications of class in modern capitalism, especially to those motivated and open to understand from a critical standpoint.

What follows is a particular Marxian theory drawn from Marx as well as many Marxists since. It benefits from those who work with this Marxian theory and also from those who work with different Marxian theories. The Marxian theory stressed in this book incorporates important non-Marxian insights (e.g., those of Freud mentioned above) that, appropriately questioned and adjusted, can and do contribute much to Marxian theory. Finally, this Marxian theory helps to clarify differences among Marxian, Keynesian, and neoclassical economics.

Helping readers distinguish among alternative economic theories is, of course, a basic goal and purpose of this book. We seek to sharpen the intelligence that readers bring to differentiating, assessing, and utilizing the arguments and claims made by neoclassical, Keynesian, and Marxian theories. We hope readers will learn to go beyond the simplistic notion that there is a right and a wrong economics. After all, the study of economics is like the study of any other group of theories. It requires attention to the differences among them rather than presuming and then searching for some finally and absolutely correct one.

4.2   The Logical Structure of Marxian Theory

Marxian theory helps to produce a distinctive understanding or knowledge of how economies work and change. That understanding or knowledge depends in part on the concrete facts presented to Marxists by the world they wish to understand and in part on the particular theory used to gain that understanding. So we begin with an examination of that theory's logical structure.

4.2.1   The Basic Concepts of Marxian Economics

Marxian theory approaches economics with a major concern for the relationship between the economy and the society as a whole. Thus "economics" refers to all those processes in any society that involve the production of goods and services and their distribution among producers and consumers. The term "noneconomic" then refers to all the other kinds of processes that, together with the economic processes, form the totality called "society." There are three different kinds of those noneconomic processes: the natural, the cultural, and the political.

Natural processes are those involving the transformation (biological, chemical, etc.) of physical properties of matter. Political processes are those involving the control (legislative, judicial, administrative, etc.) of individual and group behavior within society. Finally, cultural processes are those involved in the construction and dissemination of meaning (speaking, writing, making music, praying, studying, etc.).

To get at an important specific difference between the Marxian theory we develop here and many alternative theories, it is useful to consider how different theories understand the relationship between economic and noneconomic aspects or processes of society. Alternative theories typically make one the cause and the other the effect. In some of these, economics is thought to make the world move. Phrases appear such as "money talks" or "the business of society is business" or "money makes the world go round" to express the idea that economic aspects of life determine everything else. How often have you heard someone insist that "it was not love nor politics nor religion nor nature" that caused some event, "it was economics?" How often have politicians chided one another by explaining political outcomes as follows: "it was the economy, stupid."

Such thinking is called "economic determinism." Determinist reasoning is what we also encountered in neoclassical and Keynesian theories: some basic causes determine the workings and history of society. Economic determinists generally locate the final or essential causes of social events in its economy. Marxism is often equated with economic determinism. Yet that kind of reasoning is just as frequently found among non- and anti-Marxists. For example, a former president of General Motors, Charles E. Wilson, famously said, "What's good for GM is good for America."

Although many Marxists and non-Marxists theorize in economic determinist ways, there are those on both sides who do not. The Marxian economic theory analyzed in this book rejects economic (or any other kind of) determinism. Instead of a determinist linkage between economy and society, Marxian theory here is committed to a linkage called "overdetermination." As noted in chapter 1, we will use this term rather than the traditional term "dialectics" to describe the existence of and interaction among all aspects of society, economic and noneconomic alike.

4.2.2 Overdetermination and Process

From the standpoint of an overdeterminist theory, the economic and noneconomic aspects of society influence—indeed, as explained below, create—each other. Determination flows in both directions, not only in one. For example, economic considerations certainly influence decisions about marriage and family life, but the latter likewise influence the economic decisions people make. Economic calculations affect US foreign policies, and foreign policy decisions make their marks on our economy as well. In short, the Marxian theory presented here assigns no determining priority to economic over noneconomic aspects of society. *All the different aspects shape and are shaped by all the others.* No one part of a society, neither the economy nor any other part, determines the whole society. Every aspect of society, including the economic, is overdetermined by all the others. Economic or any other kind of determinism is rejected here in favor of overdetermination.

The unique overdeterminist way of understanding causation clashes with the reductionisms presented as the basic logics of neoclassical and Keynesian theories. Marxian theory, as presented here, explains the causes and thus the existences of individuals, institutions, and indeed everything in society in radically different ways. Each aspect or component part of society is approached as the combined effect of all the other aspects or parts of that society. This idea is best described by the word "constitutivity." Each aspect or part of society is constituted—literally created—as the combined effect of all the other aspects or parts. Nothing can exist independently of everything else, or as the ultimate cause of everything else, since it is everything else that constitutes whatever exists.

It follows that each aspect of society owes its existence to the other aspects. Each is constituted by the interactions among all the other aspects of society. Overdetermination means that every aspect of society is always a cause *and* an effect. Each aspect plays its particular role in constituting—that is, in causing the existence of—every other. In contrast to overdetermination, neoclassical theory assumes that some aspects (scarcity and preferences) are causes but are *not* also effects. These causal aspects have a prior existence; they occur first and serve as the ultimate determinants/causes of other aspects of society. Much the same applies to the economic structure in and for Keynesian economic theory. Neoclassical and Keynesian theories do not assume that causes constitute their effects *while being simultaneously constituted by them,* but that is precisely what an overdeterminist theory does assume.

In overdeterminist Marxian theory, because the economy is determined by all the other natural, political, and cultural aspects of society, it is literally pushed and pulled in all directions by all those diverse overdeterminants. This in turn implies that the economy is always in a state of tension and change. A change in climate will favor some kinds of production and distribution and inhibit others. Changing political trends will favor and inhibit certain kinds of production and distribution. Changing cultural patterns too will stimulate some kinds of production and distribution and stifle others.

There is no reason to expect all of those changes to impact on the economy in the same way, pushing it in the same direction at the same pace. Rather, the economy is full of contradictory impulses, tensions, and uncertainties. These reflect the many different influences that overdetermine any economy.

An example can suggest the rich play of diverse overdeterminations constituting any one aspect of the society, in this case a personal decision. Suppose that you are considering what courses to take to prepare for a career. Your feelings and emotions propel you toward the arts. Your parents favor law or medicine for you. Changing university priorities discourage you from considering certain majors that may be phased out soon. Your sense of the political future suggests not preparing for a government job. Mounting student loans pressure you toward a career that will earn money and quickly. Your process of deciding is overdetermined, pushed and pulled in conflicting directions, by all of these (and many more) diverse influences.

Your final course choice will be the complicated product of all the diverse influences overdetermining it. Your choice is in part an economic event, part of the overdetermination of the supply of various kinds of labor in the economy. If many are overdetermined to choose computer or health sciences, that may depress wages and salaries in those fields, and that will affect the investment decisions of companies who hire people trained in those fields. That in turn will affect the pattern of exports and imports of computer components, and so on. The economy is simply the total of all such overdetermined events of production and distribution.

A similar argument applies to individuals' choices over anything and everything from choosing whether to purchase more apples or oranges to the choice of supplying more or less labor when the wage changes to the decision of whom to date Saturday night. All choices are a complex effect of interacting social (economic and noneconomic) and natural forces. This is a very different perspective than that of the contrasting neoclassical approach in which individual choice is immune from either direct or indirect economic influences. In this Marxian approach, choice not only is overdetermined but one of the economic overdeterminants is that of class.

In the Marxian view, the economy is ceaselessly changing *because* it is overdetermined. A change in any noneconomic aspect of society will necessarily impose a change upon the economy. For example, when the US presidency passed from Carter to Reagan, priorities inside universities changed. Some academic departments obtained more money to hire faculty, expand course offerings, and the like, while other departments withered. This change affected students' course and career choices and so changed the economy. To take another example, changes in the science of birth control and cultural changes in attitudes toward family planning continue to have momentous economic effects. Couples with fewer children are changing their demands for housing, entertainment, and automobiles, to name just a few commodities. Declining population growth induces further changes in all kinds of economic supplies and demands, and so on.

Each change in a noneconomic aspect of society exerts its particular effects upon the economy. Since the many noneconomic aspects of society are themselves always changing in different ways (after all, they too are overdetermined), their changes impact and change the economy. Changes in the economy in turn generate changes in the noneconomic aspects of society and so on *ad infinitum*. The changes in any one part of society are simultaneously the causes *and* effects of changes in every other part.

Marxian theory's commitment to overdetermination thus leads directly to the view that everything in society is forever changing. Change is the mode of existence of everything. Nothing is fixed. Every event, person, institution, and relationship exists in change. Theories, governments, economies, nature, and music, all are in the ceaseless movement of coming into being, changing, and passing out of existence. These changes are sometimes barely perceptible and sometimes dramatically revolutionary.

To underscore the endless change it sees in every aspect of every society, Marxian theory conceives of them all as forever in movement, as "processes." Processes are thus the basic elements of Marxian theory's analysis of society. Individuals, relationships, activities, institutions, and organizations are just particular groupings of processes (of the four basic types: economic, political, cultural, and natural). Each society is thus conceived to be a mass of different processes, each and every one constituted by all the others.

For example, economic processes do more than merely influence cultural processes. They help "constitute" cultural processes—literally bring them into existence. Thus corporate expenditures on advertising not only shape the cultural creations on television; they literally make their existence possible. The climate of North America (a natural process) does not merely influence crop yields; it makes them possible, it helps create them. Political processes of lawmaking not only influence economies, their effects help bring into being the specific economic processes (buying, selling, importing, lending, producing, etc.) that will exist.

To take another example, consider people engaging in the economic process of saving money. They do so because of (as the complex effect of) all the other processes in society. The cultural processes that help constitute savings include ideas about frugal living, expectations about the future, religious convictions, articles in newspapers, and the like. Political processes play their role: for instance, laws are passed that establish our right to own and control what we save, judicial decisions deter others from taking such savings, administrative procedures govern inheritance, and so on. Natural processes also participate in overdetermining the process of saving: fears and uncertainties of climate and health provoke savings, deteriorating tools necessitate saving to pay for their replacement, and so on. Finally, other economic processes also overdetermine savings: paying interest induces savings, price fluctuations sometimes provoke savings as insurance against market downturns while in times of inflation they discourage savings, central bank management of supplies of money influences savings decisions, and so on.

All the other processes in society have effects that together bring into existence the one particular process of saving. They give it whatever particular features it displays in a particular society at a particular time. Change or remove any one of those other processes or introduce a new one, and the consequence will be to change or remove the saving process. It only exists because they do. No one of them causes saving; they all do. Saving is not merely the effect of any one or a subset of the other processes in society; it is rather the overdetermined effect of them all as they interact with one another. And the same is true of every other process.

Overdetermination functions within the Marxian theory presented here as the logical connection among the processes that together form any society. It is the glue that links the parts into the social whole. Its centrality has two profound consequences for the theory. We have already noted the first one: a change in any one process leads to changes in all the other processes, which then impact back on the first process to change it, and so on. Marxian theory summarizes this implication of its commitment to overdetermination by stressing the ceaseless change that characterizes every process in society and hence the society as a whole.

4.2.3 Contradictions

A second consequence of the Marxian idea of overdetermination is the parallel centrality of contradictions. Since every process exists as the effect of all other processes, each process is consequently a bundle of contradictions. That is, each social process contains within itself the pushes and pulls emanating from all the other processes that make it what it is. As all those other processes change, so do the pushes and pulls they exert, and that gives movement to the process they overdetermine.

For example, the process of loving another person is overdetermined and hence contradictory. It contains within itself the different effects of the need for companionship, sexual desire, ego gratification, financial considerations, religious taboos, parental preferences, peer-group pressures, fears of loneliness, and so on. All of the other processes surrounding both people that overdetermine the process of love between them likewise push and pull that love in conflicting directions. The process of loving is thus contradictory with the lovers caught up in what a vast literature describes as complex, shifting combinations of attraction, repulsion, indifference, resentment, elation, passion, and so on. Moreover, as all those other processes change, they thereby differently overdetermine the process of loving as well as each of the lovers, and that changes all of them.

Change in each process alters how it determines all other processes and also the contradictions within them. These new contradictions impart new kinds of change in those processes, which thereby change the ways in which they influence other processes. Contradiction is, for Marxian theory, the consequence of overdetermination, the mechanism whereby change becomes the universal mode of existence of society and of all its parts.

Marxian theory generally proceeds in its analysis of any society by (1) identifying the processes in it, (2) examining the overdetermination among them, and (3) then demonstrating the resulting contradictions in those processes. The point is to understand the social changes emerging from the contradictions in the society. More specifically, Marxian economic theory focuses on the economic processes within the society and their contradictions. The theory aims to identify how those contradictions generate both economic and other changes in each society that is an object of the theory. Marxist political practice aims to use the theory to inform its interventions to transform that society.

By comparison, neoclassical and Keynesian theories are not committed to overdetermination. Rather, they are determinist or essentialist in nature, as discussed earlier. According to the neoclassicists, social changes are usually reduced to being effects of economic changes. Economic changes are in turn reduced to being determined by a very few essential causes, such as individuals' preferences, their productive capabilities, and their privately owned resource endowments.

The geometric diagrams used by neoclassical economists to portray economic relationships typically make some economic phenomena causes and others effects, an essentialist idea. Other neoclassical models, whether simple linkages of effects to causes or more complex systems of simultaneous equations, also cannot represent overdetermination because overdetermination means that all economic aspects are simultaneously causes *and* effects, in the sense of constituents, of one another and of all the noneconomic aspects of society too. The conventional mathematical models of neoclassical economics do not express relationships of overdetermination because that theory does not connect the different aspects of the economy and the society in that way.

Much the same applies to Keynesian economics. It theorizes the micro-behavior of firms and individuals as the effect of macro-level social structures. This reproduces the determinism of neoclassical economic theories but reverses its direction. The micro-level nature of individual persons and firms is determined by (rather than determines) the larger economic and social structures. In this book's final chapter, we will focus on the difference between the determinisms (essentialisms) of neoclassical and Keynesian theories and Marxian theory's overdeterminism (antiessentialism) to show its major consequences in shaping the very different conclusions and policy recommendations reached by the different theories.

4.2.4 Processes, Activities, and Relationships

In the Marxian theory we develop here, processes never occur by themselves in society. They always occur in groups. For example, a person who reads (cultural process) also breathes (natural process). Someone who orders another person to follow a rule (political process) also thinks (cultural process) and digests (natural process). An employer hiring workers (economic process) talks to them (cultural process) and directs workers' behavior during the working day (political process). Such groupings, often of many processes, are what Marxian theory defines as "relationships" or "activities" or "practices."

An activity or practice by any person can always be broken down analytically into the basic processes that composed it. For example, when a person runs down the street, he or she may also be perspiring, thinking, earning interest on investments, and obeying someone's order to run, all at the same time. Those processes together constitute a particular activity of running. Indeed it is not quite accurate to call this activity merely "running," since that one-word label does not take into account the many different processes simultaneously involved. Similarly the practice of organizing a trade union is a composite of processes: talking to people, thinking through strategies, perhaps changing laws, buying paper for leaflets, and so on.

As with activities and practices, relationships among people are decomposable into their constituent processes. When you and I talk, we also look at each other, possibly touch each other, and possibly transact some economic business with each other, and so on. Each particular relationship is a complex grouping of specific processes. As with activities and practices, it is never quite accurate to give relationships a single name or qualifying adjective, such as a "business" relationship, a "love" relationship, or any other. Relationships are always complex groupings of specific processes. You can avoid grief in your relationships if you remember not to interpret them unidimensionally.

The complete sets of activities of a group of people and their relationships form a society (which Marxists often call a "social formation"). Marxian social analysis aims to specify which processes are grouped in what ways into the particular activities and relationships that distinguish each social formation. For example, in some societies, buying and selling processes never occur. Instead, goods and services pass from their producers to their consumers by means of religious processes of distribution following sacred rules. In another society, processes of praying accompany every economic process according to elaborate rituals. In still another society, sexual processes never occur without rigid political controls by parents over children throughout life.

From the standpoint of Marxian theory, to understand any society requires systematic attention to the particular processes that occur within it and how they are grouped into the activities and relationships that compose it. The objective is to grasp and express the contradictions that give that society its particular qualities, tensions, and changes. Since Marxists usually favor certain kinds of social change, they seek an understanding that will guide their personal and organizational decisions about how to act politically to facilitate those social changes.

4.2.5   A Theoretical Dilemma

An analytical problem is posed immediately by Marxian theory's view that societies are immense collections of diverse processes, activities, and relationships intertwined in complex contradictions. To fully unravel them all is likely impossible and any systematic exposition would take huge numbers of Marxian theorists vast amounts of time. Moreover, by the time the task would be done, all the theorized processes, activities, and relationships would have changed. The analyzed society would have become an historical relic superseded by the new, current society in which the Marxists lived and which they presumably wanted to change. They would have to start all over, but the same dilemma would confront them.

This dilemma is still more troubling given the idea of overdetermination. If any one social process exists and has its specific qualities and contradictions by virtue of the effects of all the other social processes, a theorist would have to study them all to ever completely understand that one social process. Such completeness is not practically possible.

From the Marxian standpoint, the task of a comprehensive social analysis is, in principle, not achievable, neither for Marxian nor for any other kind of theory. It is rather like people achieving birdlike flight (without mechanical help) or avoiding death or eliminating all loneliness from a lifetime. Like those impossibilities, the human incapacity to produce complete social analyses need not and should not bother us very much. To deny or dwell morosely upon our limitations promises little beyond bitter disappointments or bouts of depression or both. The point is rather to recognize that the limitations influence but do not prevent our efforts to build productive personal and social situations.

In this spirit Marxists recognize that all social analyses, no matter which theoretical frameworks are used to produce them, are partial and never complete or finished. No one can fully understand or write the whole story about how a society is structured and how it is changing. No one ever has done that. Every theory involves an inevitably partial stab at social analysis. Marxists reject as vain any hope that one analysis will be complete while others remain partial. Nor should anyone credit the claims of those who, frightened by the limits of our theoretical capacities, imagine and insist that they have found some miraculous way to completeness, the truth, the final explanation.

This recognition of the partiality of all theories and the social analyses they can produce is controversial among both Marxists and non-Marxists. Some Marxists find it unacceptable; they remain committed to the idea that somehow, someday, a complete analysis will be accomplished and that they are working toward that end. However, the kind of Marxian theory being discussed in this book, based as it is on overdetermination, contradiction, and process, logically arrives at a direct affirmation of its own partiality as well as that of all other social theories.

Is this admission of partiality debilitating? Does it mean that there is no point in trying to explain anything since we can explain nothing fully? Does Marxian theory's insistence on its partiality invite us to ignore its arguments and conclusions?

4.2.6   Marxian Theory and Its Entry Point

The answer to all of these questions is no. Marxists committed to overdetermination do not hesitate to generate their analyses by using their theory. They accept partiality as a quality common to all theories and social analyses. What distinguishes one theory from another is precisely that they are partial in different ways. Different theories produce different partial analyses as is exemplified by Marxian and non-Marxian economic theories.

That no theory can produce a complete analysis does not bother the Marxists. They argue that all theories, notwithstanding their partiality, exert specific effects on the societies in which they occur. The economic analyses produced with neoclassical and Keynesian economic theories are socially influential. They participate in overdetermining everything else in the society where and when they occur. The different partial analyses produced by those using Marxian theories likewise participate in overdetermining everything else in society. The point is that the three kinds of theory influence, push, shape, the society in different ways and different directions.

How is one theory partial in a different way from another theory? As we have seen, the answer lies partly in the important notion of entry points. All theories of society confront a complex social totality: a multidimensional mass of diversity. Every theory has to begin somewhere with some selected aspects or part of society (starting everywhere is not possible and would, in any case, entail incoherence). Every theory makes its particular sense (knowledge, understanding, truth) of society from (and partly depending on) the perspective of its particular entry point. Social theories are always partial because of the impossibility of theorizing from or about every aspect of the social totality.

Neoclassical theory's partiality is identifiable by its three broad entry-point concepts: individual preferences, technology, and initial endowments. Neoclassical theory builds up its particular analysis or knowledge of modern economies by entering into that analysis from these distinctive entry points. The same applies to Keynesian theory in relation to its entry-point concepts of specific social structures, mass psychological tendencies, and uncertainty. Marxian economic theory has a very different entry point—class—and builds its distinctively partial analysis by entering into the study of the economy via its particular concept of class process.

Our analysis of Marxian theory thus requires that we examine carefully what is meant by the Marxian entry-point concept of class. Doing so will enable us to clarify this basic difference between Marxian and both neoclassical and Keynesian economic theories. Then we can proceed to clarify their other differences by tracing how their different entry points lead them to sharply divergent understandings of economics. The final chapter of this book explores the social significance of these theoretical differences—how our lives depend on the struggles among the differently partial theories and among those committed to them.

4.2.7 The Class Process

Marxian theory generally begins its study of any society by first inquiring into its class processes (aspects) that together comprise the class structure of that society. It then proceeds to examine how the society's class structure is overdetermined by all of the nonclass processes that are its social context or framework. Finally, Marxian theory aims to show how, in turn, its class processes participate in overdetermining all of the nonclass aspects of the society.

Class is thus the entry-point concept of Marxian theory. It is that particular aspect of society which this theory aims to highlight, focus upon, and understand. Class operates in Marxian theory rather like the concept of individual human nature operates in neoclassical theory and the concepts of social structures and psychological propensities function in Keynesian theory. Each theory begins with definitions of its respective entry point(s) and elaborates from there its complex understanding of how any economy works and interacts with the rest of society.

The Marxian economic theory developed in this book defines class in a very particular way that it takes from Marx's work. Class refers to a particular social process—namely the production of *surplus labor* (defined in the next paragraph) by some members of any society. Every society is assumed to require that at least some of its members interact with nature and one another to produce goods and services consumed by all members of the society. This interaction is called *the labor process*: the expenditure of human muscles, nerves, and brain power to transform objects found in nature into goods and services satisfying human needs and wants. Those members of society who do this labor are called *direct laborers*.

What then is surplus labor? All labor takes time. Part of the direct laborers' work time produces the goods and services that they themselves consume in order to reproduce their capacity to work. That part of their work time is *necessary labor*. It is necessary in the precise sense of being required to meet the direct laborers' consumption-focused demands for goods and services. However, direct laborers always perform more labor than the necessary labor; they work for a longer period of time than needed to supply their own needs and wants. That extra labor time is what Marx called surplus labor.

Direct laborers thus participate in two different processes: the labor process of transforming nature, and the class process of performing surplus labor. It is one thing to transform nature through human labor; it is another and different thing to be involved in the production of surplus labor. The class and labor processes have existed in all societies, from the earliest known to the contemporary, but recognizing and analyzing class processes as different from labor processes is a very new phenomenon dating from Marx's work.

If the class process entails performing surplus labor, that immediately entails two extensions of the concept. The first concerns what we call the product of the surplus labor, the output of goods and services not consumed by the direct laborers themselves: this will be henceforth referred to as the surplus product or simply the surplus. The second immediate extension of the concept of surplus labor refers to what happens to the surplus after its production by the direct laborers. Marx handles this in a straightforward way as a matter of the *distribution of the surplus.*

We may now summarize the concept of class that functions as Marxist economic theory's entry point: the economic processes of producing and distributing surplus labor. Notice that class as a singular process has morphed into class as a plural process. Class refers not only to the production of surplus, but also to its distribution. We will return to this complexity below.

Class processes coexist and interact with the entire natural, political, cultural, and other economic processes—nonclass processes—that constitute any society. Class processes are overdetermined by all those other, nonclass processes. Like any other processes, class processes are contradictory and constantly changing. Similarly they participate in overdetermining all the nonclass processes and hence in shaping the contradictions and changes of the entire society.

Notice that Marxian theory, by making class its entry point, arranges the complexity of the society it seeks to understand into two contrasting parts or aspects: class and nonclass. The theory thereby organizes the topics it will treat around the task of thinking through the relationships in any society between its class and nonclass aspects. The analyses generated by Marxian theory focus upon the interdependence between the class and nonclass parts of the social whole.

4.3 The Marxian Concept of Class Elaborated

The Marxian concept of class that we have defined in terms of surplus labor is only one of many different concepts of class used for centuries before Marx and also used since. It is important therefore to separate the concept of class developed in this chapter and book from the many—and very different—other concepts of class that have appeared and continue to appear in the works of some Marxists and most non-Marxists. For example, since ancient Greece, class has been used for groups of people according to the wealth or property they own. The class of haves confronts the class of have-nots. The rich classes confront the poor, and the high-income class confronts the lower classes. These are variations of a definition of class in terms of property ownership. A second and very different definition of class, as old as the first, refers not to ownership of wealth or income but to power. This concept of class groups people according to whether they wield power over others (give orders, have authority, etc.) or have power wielded over them. Variations on this definition of class speak of the ruling class or the power elite or the class of the powerless.

These property and power concepts of class are probably still the most widespread understandings of the term. They differ from our surplus labor concept of class. We, like many others, are interested in how wealth and power are distributed in societies past and present. We, like many others, have learned from social analyses that have focused on wealth and power distributions. We too have wondered why societies have found it so difficult to construct more egalitarian distributions of wealth and power than have so far been achieved (despite revolutions like the American, French, and Russian that moved in those directions). Marx responded to such wondering when he argued that earlier revolutionary efforts failed because their proponents had not understood the importance of the organization of surplus labor in reinforcing their societies' inequalities. They had likewise failed to understand the need to transform the organization of the surplus if sustained movement toward egalitarian wealth and power distributions was to succeed.

So Marx aimed to refocus class analysis and social movements for equality onto what they had earlier overlooked: the social organization of the surplus. To drive home his basic point, Marx used class to refer not to wealth and power distributions but rather to processes of producing and distributing surpluses in society. Marx himself was not 100 percent consistent in his new usage of class in terms of surplus. He sometimes slipped back into using the concepts of class developed before him—those that referred to rich and poor, rulers and ruled. After all, he was very enthusiastic for the egalitarian goals of the French and American revolutionaries who often used class defined in terms of wealth and especially power. However, Marx's unique and lasting contribution was to invent and develop a new concept of class and class analysis. He aimed thereby to provide an understanding of how each society's organization of the production and distribution of surpluses shaped its operations, its history, and the opportunities and obstacles for those seeking to establish more egalitarian distributions of wealth and power.

4.3.1   The Fundamental Class Process and Exploitation

In his writings Marx sometimes attached the adjective "fundamental" to the class process. This followed from his theoretical strategy of focusing readers' attention on the process of producing surplus labor. However, he seems to have wanted the adjective also to distinguish one kind of class process from another. Indeed, as we have already noted, Marx's economic theory does present two kinds of class process.

We will use "fundamental class process" to refer to the process whereby the direct laborers perform not only necessary but also surplus labor. Their necessary labor results in the produced goods and services they consume. Their surplus labor results in a further quantity of goods and services that we will call surplus product or just surplus. One question arises immediately: Who gets that surplus? In Marx's language, who *appropriates* that surplus (receives it directly into his or her hands)?

The answer is: It depends. One possibility is that the direct laborers may themselves collectively appropriate their own surplus product. For example, a community of agricultural or industrial laborers might periodically stop their collective work activities to collectively gather into their hands the surplus those work activities produced. An alternative would have individuals working by themselves such that each individually appropriates the surplus he or she produces. For example, consider an individual producer of computer software programs. She produces a quantity of these programs, sells them, and uses the money to purchase the goods and services she consumes to maintain her standard of living. This quantity represents her necessary labor. However, she normally produces more than this quantity of programs. This extra quantity is hers to sell and reap the rewards from. She divides the rewards into two parts: one part is used to replenish the materials used up in producing her output, while the other part is the surplus generated by her labor. She is the individual appropriator of her own surplus labor.

These are not the only possible answers to the question of who gets the surplus. The direct laborers who perform the surplus labor may not appropriate their own surplus product, neither collectively or individually. Consider, for example, a society in which the direct laborers are also slaves. When the slaves perform labor for their masters, all the products of that labor belong immediately and automatically to the masters. Usually they return a portion of the slaves' output to the slaves for their consumption, thereby to maintain the slave system of that society. That portion would comprise the necessary labor of the slave class structure. Another portion goes to replenish the materials used up in the slaves' production of the total output. A final portion, what the masters keep (appropriate), is the slave surplus. In general, masters are nonslaves and do not participate in the production of output.

Precisely this situation, when the direct laborers do not appropriate their own surplus labor, is what Marx called "exploitation." One person exploits another, in Marxian theory, if and only if he or she appropriates the surplus labor of that other. Exploitation is a basic concept in Marxian economics.

Marxian theory's basic range of alternative social organizations of the surplus includes more possibilities. If the direct laborer is not a slave, is rather legally free (cannot be owned by another), and is the hired employee working in a factory or office, the system is called capitalist. In this case the direct laborer—usually a wage or salary earner—helps produce goods and/or services for sale. Called commodities, these goods and services, once produced, are automatically and immediately the property of the employer. The direct laborers who produced them have no ownership of them. The employer normally sells them for money—revenues—and uses part of that money to pay the direct laborer's wage or salary. That part represents the laborer's necessary labor. The employer usually uses another part of revenues to replenish the tools, equipment, and raw materials used up in producing the commodities. Finally, the employer appropriates the remaining part, the surplus.

This system is called *capitalist* for historical reasons. Capital was a concept that referred to the use of wealth to beget more wealth. For example, money functions as capital when it is lent at interest. A certain sum of wealth, say 100, is lent for a period of time; at the end of that time that sum must be returned to the lender plus an interest payment of, say, 5. The lender is a capitalist because he or she has used wealth to beget more wealth. The same applies to a person who buys a commodity in order to sell it at a higher price. Such a person, historically called a *merchant*, is also a capitalist because he or she is using wealth to beget more wealth through commerce. Moneylending and merchant capitalists have existed for a very long time in human history.

A modern employer—a more recent historical phenomenon, especially as a general way to organize production in an economy—is someone who buys (hires) the capacity to work of direct laborers and also buys the tools, equipment and raw materials for them to work with and on. The employer sets what he has purchased to work, to produce specific goods and services. The employer is also the owner and seller of the commodities that result from production. When the resulting revenues exceed the costs of hiring the direct laborers and buying the materials used up in production, the excess represents the surplus produced by the direct laborers and appropriated by the employer. The employer has thus expanded his or her wealth through the production process (which is a different way from how the moneylender or the merchant expands wealth). The employer is thus a capitalist like them, but this is an industrial capitalist rather than a moneylending or merchant capitalist. An industrial capitalist is one who expands wealth by means of production.

Note that the industrial capitalist, like the slave master, appropriates the surplus product of his or her direct laborers. The slave master returns a portion of the slaves' total output to them for their reproduction. The industrial capitalist returns to direct laborers (as their wages or salaries) a portion of the revenues received from selling what they produced. That is the necessary labor portion of their work. The industrial capitalist uses the other portions of those revenues to replenish used-up inputs and to increase the capitalist's capital. That increase retained by the capitalist is the portion of the capitalist's revenues that represents the surplus labor of the direct laborers.

Marx and Marxists refer to the organization of production in this way as industrial capitalism (or often just capitalism, for short). Industrial capitalism is an exploitative class structure because the direct producers of the surplus are not also its appropriators. Other people, namely those capitalists who employ the direct laborers, appropriate the surpluses. That is what defines such an economic system as capitalist exploitation.

Marxian economic theory recognizes still other kinds of exploitative class structures. They will be further discussed below in section 4.3.3 on the different forms of the fundamental class process. Marxists often divide the histories of societies they analyze into periods according to which forms of the fundamental class process coexisted in what sorts of relationships. This approach to understanding societies is part of what Marxists mean when they describe their theoretical work as "class analysis."

4.3.2 The Subsumed Class Process

The logic of the fundamental class process led to the question of who appropriates the surplus. The answer provided above then generates the next question: What do the appropriators of surplus product do with it? Do they consume it? Do they hoard it to save for a future use? Do they invest it in the sense of using it to hire more direct laborers, buy more material inputs, and expand production? Do the appropriators distribute the surplus to the masses in periodic festivals and carnivals? Do they use it to feed and arm special groups that do no productive work but rather engage in wars?

Actually those are just some of the many possible ways for surplus appropriators to distribute it across their societies. The distribution of the surplus by its appropriators will be called the *subsumed class process*. It is thus different from the production and appropriation of the surplus that we call the fundamental class process. In the rest of this chapter and book, the combination of a fundamental class process and a subsumed class process comprise a class structure.

Any society's actual subsumed class processes—its actual ways of distributing the surpluses it generates—influence how life is lived by its people. How the appropriators divide up the surplus and to whom they distribute the portions will help shape the structure, contradictions, and changes characterizing that society. Marxian theory therefore analyzes the complex causes that together overdetermine the subsumed class processes as well as fundamental class processes in any society chosen for examination. It likewise analyzes the consequences of both class processes for the structure and changes in that society.

In articulating his theory of the fundamental and subsumed class processes, Marx stressed the contradictory position of the appropriators. On the one hand, they receive into their hands the surplus, the fruits of human labor above and beyond what is needed to produce the generally accepted standard of living of the direct laborers and replenish means of production. On the other hand, the appropriators of the surplus dispose of what is basically the discretionary fund of the society. On the one hand, this positions surplus appropriators in a heady position of power. On the other hand, it ties their hands. As Marxian theory shows, appropriators are always under multiple, complex pressures to distribute the surpluses to others.

The basic pressure to distribute the surplus comes from the fact that failing to do so risks their position as surplus appropriators and the very production of surplus itself. On the one hand, it is obvious that without a fundamental class process that generates a surplus and delivers it into the hands of appropriators, there could not be a subsumed class process (surplus distribution). On the other hand, as Marx stresses, the reverse holds as well: unless the surplus is distributed in certain ways, the fundamental class process will not survive. Fundamental and subsumed class processes depend on and shape one another within the context of all the nonclass processes that overdetermine the two class processes and their interaction.

We can illustrate this basic theoretical point in Marxian economics by considering a slave master who exploits some slave direct laborers. They do necessary labor, the product of which the slave master allows them to keep enabling them to continue working. They also do surplus labor, the product of which the slave master appropriates. However, the slave master's happiness at being the recipient of this surplus is quickly overshadowed by anxiety. He or she worries about many possibilities. For example, the slaves may rebel against constantly delivering their surplus product to the slave master and refuse to do so. The slave master would then lose the surplus and the position of surplus appropriator. To prevent this, the slave master must consider the subsumed class process (the distribution of the appropriated slave surplus).

One way to seek to prevent slave revolts would be to maintain a police force. The slave master would have to make a subsumed class payment (distribute a portion of the appropriated slave surplus) to hire, train, and equip such a force. Thus, once the master appropriated the surplus, a portion of it would have to be distributed to maintain the police. Not only would the hired police personnel produce no surplus for the slave master, they would drain away a portion of the appropriated surplus.

Another way to prevent slave rebellions would be to educate slaves along particular lines. Secular or religious schools could be established to administer classes, rituals, and ceremonies designed to convince slaves that rebellions are futile or blasphemous or both. The costs of hiring and equipping schools would have to be defrayed by the slave masters' subsumed class outlays.

Many other nonclass processes—beyond policing and educating—may be required for the slave fundamental class process to continue providing surplus to slave masters. Slaves who die must be replaced. If that necessitates ship expeditions (hired crews, etc.) to secure new slaves, those expeditions' costs are claims upon the slave surplus. The ship crews do not produce any surplus (like the slave direct laborers), but their maintenance and equipment costs drain a portion of the slave surplus. Slaves may require supervisors to ensure efficiency and hard work. Such supervisors are not direct laborers; they produce nothing. However, they may be indispensable—rather like the police, educators, and hired ship crews above—for the slave direct laborers to continue to generate surpluses for the masters. The costs of hiring and equipping supervisors are covered by subsumed class payments from the masters' appropriated surpluses.

Our examples from a slave form of the fundamental class process have perfect parallels within a capitalist form of the fundamental class process. Indeed we will be using such examples throughout the rest of the chapter. However, the slave example suffices to permit us to draw some initial conclusions here about the distribution of surplus by appropriators.

The distribution of the surplus by appropriators is called "the subsumed class process." It is a class process because it directly concerns surplus labor and its fruits. It is called "subsumed" because it seems logical that we consider the distribution of the surplus after we consider its production, which is the fundamental class process.

The subsumed class process occurs after the fundamental class process. It is motivated by the appropriators' aim to continue the fundamental class process and their position in it. The subsumed class process is the way appropriators pay for the performance of certain nonclass processes without which the fundamental class process could not exist. In our example of the slave fundamental class process, the police and military processes, the educational and religious processes, the shipping and supervisory processes, were all precisely nonclass processes. The people who performed these nonclass processes did not themselves produce or appropriate surplus labor. Instead, they provided certain of its conditions of existence. For doing so, they received distributed shares of the slave surplus from its appropriators. They therefore participated in a subsumed class process. They were subsumed classes because they obtained a distribution of the surplus for providing conditions of existence for the reproduction of that surplus.

In all societies, according to Marxian theory, fundamental and subsumed class processes occur. They coexist with the vast array of nonclass processes in constituting any society. Given the logic of overdetermination, Marxists argue that in any society, the various forms of the fundamental and subsumed class processes that coexist there help shape one another and all of that society's nonclass processes. They also argue that simultaneously the nonclass processes together overdetermine the class processes, fundamental and subsumed.

We may now formulate a brief summary of the goals and structure of a Marxian theory of society. The theory aims to identify and analyze the fundamental and subsumed class processes that coexist in any society chosen for examination. It seeks further to understand the overdetermined interactions among coexisting class processes and between them and their environment of nonclass process. On that basis the theory aims to show how class influences the social structure, its contradictions, and social change.

4.3.3 Different Forms of the Fundamental Class Process

Marxian theory recognizes that societies differ from one another in their class structures. While all societies exhibit some coexisting class processes, fundamental and subsumed, they differ in the mix of the particular forms they contain. The rich diversity of human communities has produced a wide variety of arrangements whereby men and women perform surplus labor and distribute its fruits. Marxian theorists have constructed sketches of some historically important forms of the fundamental class process, but have examined most exhaustively the modern capitalist form.

One form is commonly called "the primitive communist" class process, after Marx's initial usage of the phrase. While he used "primitive" because his particular examples had occurred long ago or in much less economically developed parts of the world in Marx's time, we will drop the primitive since we now know that this kind of class process has existed and exists now in many different societies. In the communist form of the fundamental class process, *the direct laborers themselves collectively appropriate the surplus they have produced*. Those direct laborers produce the goods and services that they themselves consume (the fruit of their necessary labor), but they also produce more goods and services (the fruit of their surplus labor). The communist subsumed class process occurs when such direct laborers distribute portions of the communist surplus to others (for performing various nonclass processes that provide conditions of existence for the communist fundamental class process). Those others—recipients of distributed shares of the communist surplus—constitute communist subsumed classes.

A second form of the fundamental class process is that which Marx called "ancient." He used that term because his examples of that particular form of the fundamental class process were drawn initially from ancient Rome's individual peasant farms. In an ancient fundamental class process, direct laborers individually produce a quantity of output equal to what they themselves individually consume, but then they also produce more than that: the ancient surplus. They individually appropriate that surplus as when, for example, an individual farmer produces and sells enough wheat not only to secure his standard of consumption but also more than that to obtain a surplus. Such ancient surplus producers-cum-appropriators then distribute shares of their surpluses to various persons who perform nonclass processes that provide conditions of existence of the ancient fundamental class process, namely of its reproduction over time. Individual producer/sellers of computer software programs, craft products, medical care, and plumbing repair, and so on, are examples of the ancient fundamental class process.

Earlier we discussed the slave form of the fundamental class process, but we have not yet described the feudal form. It most typically involves possessors of land, called "lords," and direct laborers on that land, often called "feudal peasants or serfs." The direct laborers, who are not slaves, work the land part of the time for themselves. They keep the fruits of this labor; it is their necessary labor. The rest of the time they work for the lord, performing surplus labor; the lord appropriates the fruits of that work, the feudal surplus. A complex personal relationship involving loyalties and obligations enables and enforces the feudal fundamental class process that connects lords and serfs. The lords distribute portions of the feudal surplus to the feudal subsumed classes.

Capitalism differs from all other forms of the fundamental class process. The direct laborers do not also appropriate the surplus they produce, neither collectively (as in the communist form) nor individually (as in the ancient form). The direct laborers are not connected to the other people who appropriate the surplus as slaves (as in the slave form) nor as serfs with personal ties of loyalty (as in the feudal form). Instead, the capitalist form of the fundamental class process inserts the institution of the market between direct laborers and the other people who appropriate the surplus.

Direct laborers sell their capacity to work—their "labor power" in Marx's words—to a set of buyers called capitalists. The latter pay the direct laborers for their labor power. The buyers then "consume" that labor power by setting it to work together with the tools, equipment, and raw materials ("means of production") also purchased by the buyers of labor power. The buyers have the right, in this system, to keep and sell the products of the direct laborers' work.

In calculating how the capitalist fundamental class process works, Marx proceeds by assuming that the value of the tools, equipment, and raw materials used up in production is automatically transferred to the final products. For example, the chair has in it the value of the wood, glue, saws, hammers, and so on, used up in producing it. However, the chair's value also reflects the "value added" by the human labor done on the raw materials (wood, glue, etc.)

with the tools and equipment (saws, hammers, etc.). The value of the chair is greater than the value of the raw materials, tools, and equipment in it. The value of the chair includes the value of the used-up means of production *plus the value added by the direct laborers.*

The final step of Marx's calculation reveals where and how the surplus arises in a capitalist fundamental class process. The capitalist buyer of the labor power only pays the direct laborers in wages a portion of the value added by their work. The capitalist retains the other portion. That's what the capitalist gets out of the production process. In effect, during part of the time that direct laborers work—the working day—they add value equal to what they get back in wages. The rest of their working day is time during which the direct laborers also add value, but that value accrues to the capitalist employer, not to the direct laborers. It is value added over and above what is paid in wages.

The labor time of workers that adds value used to pay their wages is their necessary labor. The time of workers that adds value going to be retained by capitalists constitutes the capitalists' surplus and Marx calls that *surplus value.* If workers received in wages the full value added by their labor, nothing would remain for the capitalist who would therefore gain nothing from the production process. Capitalists appropriate the surpluses of direct laborers by hiring them in the market, setting them to work with purchased means of production, and taking exclusive ownership of the products of that work.

Another way to grasp Marx's point is to consider what capitalists do with the revenues they receive from selling the products of capitalist production. They divide those revenues into three parts. The first part goes to the direct laborers as their wages (payment for their labor power). The second part goes to purchase replacements for the raw materials, tools, and equipment ("means of production") used up during production. The third part is the surplus appropriated by the buyers of labor power.

There are key differences separating the five basic forms of the fundamental class process that Marx and Marxists have identified and elaborated: communist, ancient, slave, feudal, and capitalist. Each form differs in the ways that the surplus is produced and appropriated (by whom and how) and distributed (to whom, how, and to secure what conditions of existence). Each form reflects and embodies its distinctive overdetermination by its social context (the totality of nonclass processes as well as all other coexisting forms of the class processes).

Production and appropriation of the surplus by the same people defines a nonexploitative fundamental class process. The production and appropriation of surpluses—when performed collectively by the same people—define what Marxist economic theory means by the communist fundamental class process. The ancient fundamental class process is like the communist in terms of being nonexploitative but differs from the communist because the production and appropriation of the surplus is individual, not collective. Very different from both of them is the slave fundamental class process. It is exploitative—the producers of the surplus are not identical to its appropriators. Indeed the producers are the private property of other persons.

Finally, there are two other forms of exploitative fundamental class processes. First, the feudal differs from the slave because it does not entail human beings owning other human beings. Instead of slaves and masters, feudal fundamental class processes have people connected by relationships of loyalty, personal obligations, and religious sanction. Those relationships condition and impel one group of people to produce a surplus appropriated by another group: for example, serfs and landlords in classical European feudalism. The last of Marxism's five basic forms of the class processes is the capitalist. There, the mass of direct laborers is free (not slaves). There, free laborers are not bound by loyalty, personal obligations, and religion to others who appropriate the surpluses they produce (they are not serfs). Instead, they enter into market relationships of employer/employee such that the latter produce a surplus appropriated by the former. The capitalist fundamental class process is exploitative like the slave and the feudal, but in a systematically different way centered on markets and the transformation of productive resources (especially labor power) as well as products into commodities, objects produced primarily for sale.

Last, Marxian theorists have a long-standing interest in establishing modern forms of the communist class process. They prefer that nonexploitative fundamental class process to the exploitative capitalist form now globally prevalent. They also prefer the influence of communist over against capitalist class processes on the rest of society. Most Marxists have recognized that the transition they seek from a predominantly capitalist to a communist class system would likely take time. There would likely be varying kinds and durations of transitional societies seeking to move toward the eventual dismantling of their capitalist class processes in favor of establishing communist class processes in their place.

Marxists took the name "socialist" to refer to such transitional periods. They likewise labeled as socialist those societies, movements, and political parties committed to carrying through such transitions. Sometimes, in moments of speculation about socialist transitions to possible future communisms, their advocates have spoken about "classless societies." Presumably these would mean societies in which the distinctions between necessary and surplus labor would have disappeared as would the surplus itself. In glimpsing this possible future, Marxian theory and theorists envision the conditions for their own passing, the end of their own history. No comparable theoretical self-consciousness of its own limits is found in either neoclassical or Keynesian economics. We do not examine the futuristic possibility of classlessness in this book.

4.3.4   Social Formations and Social Transitions

Marxian theory approaches society as a complex bundle of interacting class (fundamental and subsumed) and nonclass processes. Considering the class processes first, it seeks to determine precisely which forms of the fundamental class process coexist in any society it chooses to analyze. Do people there perform and appropriate surplus labor within the capitalist and/or feudal and/ or ancient forms, and so on? How are the forms that coexist in the society changing? Are some disappearing while others expand? Are new forms coming into existence and possibly into prominence? As noted earlier, Marxists prefer the term "social formation" to "society" because it underscores their particular way of approaching society as a set of several forms—a formation—of the class processes.

Within any social formation, some of the forms of the fundamental class process will be more socially prominent than others. More goods and services emerge from some forms than from others. For example, the United States today is a capitalist social formation. This means that the capitalist form of the fundamental class process overshadows the other forms in generating total output and in shaping the nonclass processes of the society. However, noncapitalist forms of the fundamental class process also exist in the United States. Millions of individual, self-employed persons perform and appropriate their own surplus labor within the ancient form of the fundamental class process. Some Americans today live and/or work in religious or secular "communes" that exhibit sometimes the primitive communist and sometimes the feudal form of the fundamental class process. However, when looking at the United States as a whole—its complex of cultural, political, and economic processes—most Marxists agree that the capitalist form of the class process is the most prominent.

For this reason Marxian theorists refer to the United States as a "capitalist social formation." The label attached to the social formation names the particular form of the fundamental class process most prominent in that social formation. After identifying the most prominent and the other coexisting forms of the fundamental class process in the United States, Marxian theory undertakes the equally important task of assessing the changes or transitions occurring among and within those forms.

We will use the word "change" to describe the constant alterations occurring within and among the various forms of the class processes coexisting within a social formation. We will reserve the word "transition" to describe a situation in which a formerly prominent form of the fundamental class process in a society is giving way to another form that is becoming prominent. Changes, from the standpoint of Marxian theory, are always occurring in and among all of the forms of the fundamental class process in every society. However, transition is different and happens relatively rarely.

In the United States today, changes in all of its nonclass processes are overdetermining changes in and among all its coexisting forms of the fundamental class process. And those class changes are reacting back upon the nonclass processes of the United States in a constant back-and-forth dialectic of mutual transformation. While the predominant capitalist class structure in the United States and beyond has been in a major crisis since 2007 and subject to growing criticism, it is an open question whether a class transition may be underway.

During the early part and middle of the twentieth century, communist political parties leading several countries (Soviet Union, People's Republic of China, several eastern European countries, Cuba, etc.) undertook transitions from societies in which the capitalist form of the fundamental class process was predominant toward societies in which the communist class process would become predominant. Marxists debated then (and still do) what those countries' efforts at socialist transition achieved, how far their transitions progressed, and whether and why they set in motion reverse transitions to a renewed prominence of capitalist class processes. The early twenty-first century certainly displays far less socialist transition than typified the twentieth century. At the same time the capitalist crisis that exploded in 2008 and shook the world economy renewed interest everywhere in the Marxian critiques of capitalism and in rethinking new projects of socialist transition.

4.4 The Capitalist Fundamental Class Process and Commodities

Marx's three-volume work, *Capital*, provides the foundation and the broad logical structure of Marxian economics. In Vol. 1, Marx concentrated on the capitalist fundamental class process. In Vol. 2, he stressed the uniqueness of his theoretical approach to economics by differentiating it from others. He did this by concentrating on a class analysis of the market circulation of commodities and money. In Vol. 3, he focused chiefly on the capitalist subsumed class process. There he showed how the interdependence of these fundamental and subsumed class processes constituted the specifically capitalist class structure of the west European social formations he aimed to analyze.

While we will explore how Marxian economic theory has evolved since Marx's beginnings, we start as *Capital,* Vol. 1, does, by describing the capitalist fundamental class process. Like Marx, we will begin by defining and discussing commodities. That provides a basis for contrasting Marxian economic theory with neoclassical and Keynesian theories. Where they focus on commodities and markets (exchange and distribution), Marx and Marxian economics discuss them as secondary aspects of their analysis of capitalism. For Marxian economic theory, the primary focus is on (1) the production and appropriation of a surplus and (2) on the subsequent distribution of that surplus to secure the continued production and appropriation of surplus.

4.4.1   Products, Markets, and Commodities

In all human societies, people take objects given in nature (land, water, plants, animals, etc.) and transform them to meet human needs and wants: the labor process. Its results are produced goods and services: products. Usually some members of society produce them while all members get distributions of them, since survival is rarely possible without access to at least a minimum of such products. The products are not necessarily "commodities." For a product also to be a commodity, it must not only be useful; it must also be exchanged (for money or for another commodity) on some market.

In modern societies, products usually pass through a market in their journey from producers to consumers. For most of human history, products made that journey without going through markets (and thus without having prices attached to them). After production, most societies arranged for the distribution of the products by means of customary rules. Elders, chiefs, clerics, or variously constituted councils of the community often decided who was to get what share of community output. Sometimes religious or customary rules guided the social distribution of products.

In short, most historical societies distributed products much as most families today distribute products they make or buy with their incomes. The parent who cooks dinner does not usually charge children a price to buy it. One spouse does not charge the other for taking out the garbage. Instead, complex rules of family interaction govern decisions about who does what labor tasks and products get distributed among family according to prevailing notions of appropriate family behavior that usually exclude market exchange.

True, markets as means of product distribution have existed at various times and places in history, but most products did not go through them. Only very recently, in terms of historical time, have *most* products in any society gone through markets and thereby acquired prices. This remarkable new feature of modern society struck all early economists as especially significant. They addressed the historically new problem of explaining why one product fetched a high price on the market while another did not, or why the price of a product was high now but low earlier or high here but low in a market some distance away. Of course, it was not only economists who wondered about prices; the rest of modern society wondered and worried too.

When markets were inserted among and between producers and consumers, everyone had to be concerned about prices. Making or doing something well to meet community needs no longer sufficed to assure a person a comfortable place in the community. Now another test had to be passed. Could that individual's product be sold in the market, and would the price it fetched allow him or her in turn to buy enough of the products of others to lead the sort of life he or she desired? Market conditions became central to everyone's life, yet no one had any clear ideas about what determined those conditions. What caused prices to be high or low, to rise or fall?

4.4.2 Commodity Values

Most early economists attempted to unravel the mystery of markets. They invented theories of value to explain commodity prices and price movements. In the sixteenth and seventeenth centuries, Europeans wrote many articles, pamphlets, and books proclaiming their various value theories. Toward the end of the eighteenth century, two writers sifted critically through that literature and arrived at a general theory that has been part of economics ever since. Adam Smith (1723–1790) wrote first, and then David Ricardo (1772–1823) corrected and condensed this general theory. It explained the price of a commodity as chiefly reflecting the labor embodied in it (later named "the labor theory of value"). That particular theory was their centerpiece of what we now refer to as "classical economics."

Their basic idea was relatively simple. The price of a good or service in the market was determined by the amount of labor ("toil and trouble") devoted to its production. If a pair of shoes required an average of two hours of labor to produce, it would be priced an average of twice as high as a vase that took only one hour. In the market one pair of shoes would be exchanged for two vases. If shoes cost $10 per pair, then vases would cost $5 each, and so on. A century later, neoclassical economics would reaffirm the classical economists' focus on markets and prices as the core concern of economic analysis, but would reject the labor theory of value in favor of a utility theory of value.

In contrast, Marx had responded to Smith and Ricardo differently. His theory did not focus on markets and prices. His entry point was class, understood as the production, appropriation, and distribution of the surplus. For just that reason Marx applauded the labor theory of value presented by Smith and Ricardo. By linking market prices to labor, they had—in Marx's view—gone half-way the distance to seeing and theorizing his central concern, namely surplus labor. So Marx structured his *Capital,* Vol. 1, to begin with a brief discussion of commodities, values, and markets (because that is what his contemporary readers understood economics to be about). He there stresses his own different and developed version of the labor theory of value. After and based upon a few initial chapters on those topics, Marx takes his readers the rest of the distance to a discussion focused on surplus value, surplus labor, and exploitation in production. The remainder of Vol. 1, and also Vols. 2 and 3, of *Capital* then elaborate this class analysis of capitalism to constitute the core of Marxian economic theory. It stands as a systematic alternative to the market-focused, utility-based analysis of neoclassical economics. The two represent very different and opposed interpretations and developments of the foundation of modern economics established by Smith and Ricardo.

4.4.3 Commodities and Fundamental Class Processes

In Marxian theory commodities in modern capitalist social formations are the fruits not only of the processes of labor and exchange but, in addition, of the capitalist fundamental class process. Direct laborers not only produce goods and services and thereby endow them with value later realized in commodity exchange (when those goods and services are sold). Those direct laborers also participate in the capitalist fundamental class process. They perform necessary and surplus labor. The product of their surplus labor—the surplus—is appropriated by other people, namely the capitalists who hired them. However, before we examine the capitalist class process and capitalist commodities in some detail, an important point needs to be clarified.

Commodities—products produced for sale in markets—need not be and have not historically been produced only in and by capitalist class structures. Consider, for example, direct laborers who are slaves. The surplus they produce is appropriated by slave masters when they sell those slaves' products in markets. Marxian theory would describe them as slave commodities. The adjective "slave" would designate the particular fundamental class process from which those commodities emerged. If, instead, feudal peasants and lords were the performers and appropriators of surplus labor involved in producing some goods sold in markets, those goods would be feudal commodities. If capitalists and wage workers were respectively the appropriators and performers of surplus labor, the resulting products would be capitalist commodities. The presence of commodities and markets is not the same as the presence of the capitalist class structure.

A market is one among a variety of past and present social mechanisms for distributing resources and products. A class structure is an organization of the production, appropriation, and distribution of surpluses. Markets can coexist with any or all of the different kinds of class structures (feudal, slave, communist, ancient, and capitalist). Likewise any or all of those class structures can utilize alternative, nonmarket mechanisms for distributing resources and products. There is no need or warrant in Marxian theory for confusing or conflating markets and capitalist class structures.

Marx and Marxian theory often begin with discussions of commodities for two main reasons. First, most modern societies contain capitalist class structures that happen, for historical reasons, to coexist with markets as their major mechanisms of distributing resources and products. Second, the major alternative economic theories—classical and neoclassical economics and also Keynesian economics—focus almost exclusively on commodities and markets to the point of defining economics per se as the study of those objects. Thus Marx and many Marxists after him have thought it wise to begin their works by discussing initially what readers expect as objects of texts on economics: commodities and markets. However, they quickly lead readers from those objects to the distinctively different entry point of Marxian economic theory: class processes in general and the capitalist form of fundamental and subsumed class processes in particular.

4.4.4 Marx's Labor Theory of Capitalist Commodity Values

When direct laborers sell their ability to work (labor power), as a commodity, they exchange it for money. Buyers of labor power set it to work with purchased equipment and raw materials to produce salable goods and services. Those products are exchanged for money in the market. There are then three distinct commodity values to compare: the value of the labor power, the value of the other inputs to production (the equipment and raw materials), and the value of the products finally sold.

The values of used-up equipment and raw materials and of the commodities sold are clearly understood in terms of the labor theory of value: the values of commodity inputs and outputs are determined by the amount of labor embodied in them. The meaning of "labor" here is the average amount of work needed to produce each commodity. The different skill levels of individual workers are averaged to determine what Marx called "the socially necessary" labor needed to produce each commodity. That average, not each individual worker's productivity, is what determines each commodity's value.

Theorizing about the value of labor power is somewhat more complicated. The value of labor power is understood to be equal to the value of the goods and services that laborers require to keep selling their labor power day after day. In other words, the value of the commodities that direct laborers consume equals the value of the labor power reproduced by that consumption. The buyer of labor power has to pay for it what it costs the direct laborer to produce that labor power, day after day.

To illustrate Marx's theory, consider a simple example of the value of a commodity—say, a chair. Suppose that it takes an average of eight hours of labor *now* to produce a chair in an assembly line factory. Suppose further that it takes an average of six hours of other workers' *past* labor to produce the tools, equipment, and raw materials (glue, hammer, nails, wood, etc.) used up now in producing a chair. The value of those used-up inputs passes into the value of the final product. In Marx's theory, then, the value of the chair is 14, the sum of living labor expended now (8) added to the past labor embodied in the tools, equipment and raw materials (6) used up in the chair's production and thereby transferred to its value. Living labor done now (8) adds value (8) to the tools, equipment and raw materials used up in production (6) to compose the value of the chair (14). To keep our example simple, we assume an average eight-hour working day; thus eight hours of daily labor produce a chair worth 14.

We look next at the value of the direct laborer's daily labor power—his or her capacity to work. That value is what the buyer of labor power—the employer—must pay as a wage if the direct labor power is to reproduce and sell his or her labor power each day. Suppose that the bundle of goods and services purchased and consumed each day by a wage-earning direct laborer embodies an average of six hours of labor. In other words, it takes six hours of socially necessary labor to produce the wage commodities (food, clothing, shelter, entertainment, travel, etc.) required by workers to reproduce and keep selling their labor power. Thus the buyer of labor power must pay the direct laborers the value of their labor power (6) as their daily wage.

Now all is in place to make a key point in Marxian economics. Eight hours' worth of *living labor* is embodied in the daily commodity output of one chair. We will label this living labor *LL*. Additionally six hours' worth of previously *embodied labor* is used up and thereby transferred into the finished chair's value. We will label this embodied labor *EL*. Finally, Marxists use the letter *W* to designate the value of commodity output; in this example that is the value (14) of the chair.

The relationship between values going in and values coming out of the commodity production process can then be written as

$$EL + LL = W,$$

where embodied labor, *EL* (6 hours), plus living labor added, *LL* (8 hours), equals the total value of commodities produced, *W* (14 hours).

This apparently simple summary of the labor theory of value in capitalist commodity production allows Marxian theory to pose and answer key questions. First, how are we to understand the difference between the daily value added by the living laborers (8) and the value of their labor power paid to them in their daily wage (6)? One way in which Marx answered this question looked at it as a capitalist employer might. The employer would likely need to have money available to go out and buy tools, equipment, and raw materials and to hire workers. In our simple example, that would mean a capital of 6 to be spent on the former plus 6 to be spent on the latter, for a total of 12. The incentive or inducement for the capitalist to undertake chair production now becomes clear: the cost to the buyer is 12 while the value of the end product, the chair, is 14. And it is the buyer of the labor power, in a capitalist system, who owns that product, sells it, and keeps the revenue gotten from that sale.

This buyer has thus gotten more value out of entering into chair production that he had before doing so. Marx's German language term for that more (*mehr*) value (*wert*) was *mehrwert*; it became translated into English as *surplus value*. Because the buyer used money to make *more* money—to generate and capture a surplus value—Marx defined that buyer as a capitalist. (In contrast, anyone using money for another purpose—e.g., to buy an apple and consume it—is not using money as capital, is not a capitalist.)

Surplus value is a central part of Marxian theory. It emerges in and from production as follows: the direct laborer adds 8 hours worth of value during the production day, but is paid a wage (equal to the value of labor power) that is less than that (6 in our example). The value added by the direct laborer exceeds the value paid to the direct laborer: the difference is the surplus value. The values of capitalist commodities (those that emerge from the capitalist form of the fundamental class process) include that surplus value. Marxian theory analyzes (decodes) commodity exchange values to reveal the class process from which they emerge.

4.4.5 Surplus Value of Capitalist Commodities

In our chair example, the eight hours of living labor performed daily by hired laborers, LL, can be broken down into two parts. During the first part, the laborers add a value (6) equal to what their employer must pay them for purchasing their labor power. During the second part, the laborers add a value (2) that is extra, more, or surplus to the value paid to them for their labor power. In the terms of Marxian economics, part of living labor is paid for and part is not. The unpaid labor yields the surplus value.

We can now rewrite our earlier equation to take account of the division of living labor (LL) into its two parts, the paid (LL_p) and the unpaid (LL_u):

$$EL + LL_p + LL_u = W,$$

where $LL = LL_p + LL_u$.

With this equation Marxian theory can draw a conclusion intended to take readers over the theoretical bridge from commodity analysis to class analysis. Surplus value arises and accrues to a capitalist because (1) he or she can buy labor power from a direct laborer, and (2) the value—wage—paid for that labor power is less than the value added by the direct laborer. Capitalism, as a system of production, only survives where and when the conditions exist to enable (1) and (2) above. Surplus value represents the unpaid portion of the direct laborer's living labor, the portion of the total output that is appropriated by persons other than the direct laborers who produced it. Surplus value is the form taken by surplus labor in the capitalist fundamental class process.

This fundamental class process occurs together with the labor process in production and the commodity exchange process in markets. One of the aims of Marxian theory is to unravel the complex interconnection of all three processes—class, exchange, and labor—in order to highlight the fundamental and subsumed class processes. In contrast, neoclassical and Keynesian economic theories focus primarily on the exchange process and markets and only very secondarily on the labor process. They deny the existence of the fundamental and subsumed class processes that Marxian theory makes its entry points. It is then not surprising that these different economic theories reach different conclusions and interpret economic events in divergent ways.

4.4.6   A Summary of Marxian Value Theory

Marxian theory explains the value of a capitalist commodity in terms of the embodied and living labor materialized in it. Living labor is further divided into paid and unpaid labor. That unpaid labor is shown to be the capitalist form of the surplus labor appropriated by the capitalist employer as surplus value. Thus the capitalist commodity is analyzed in terms of the conceptual focus of the theory, class processes, on which the rest of the theory also focuses.

The overdeterminist logic of Marxian theory is also at work in its explanation of commodity values. The amounts of labor socially necessary to produce capitalist commodities are overdetermined by all the other processes existing in society. Economic processes of exchange, competition, and lending, for example, will influence how much labor will be required to produce chairs. So too will political and cultural processes ranging from legal factory regulations to technological inventions affect labor requirements. In their unique ways each will participate in overdetermining how much labor will be socially necessary to produce chairs. Throughout *Capital*, Marx showed how various economic, political, and cultural processes exercised their influence on commodity values.

The role of overdetermination can be further illustrated in terms of the basic equation connecting embodied and living labor to the value of commodity outputs. This is meant to be a two-directional relationship:

$$EL + LL_p + LL_u \leftrightarrow W.$$

It is *not* Marxian theory's idea to reason that value inputs determine value outputs in a unidirectional way. That would be a kind of essentialism; it would reduce the determination of commodity values to socially necessary labor inputs. Instead, Marxian theory insists that outputs also participate in overdetermining inputs.

For example, production of a new commodity output might induce laborers to demand such commodities and the higher wages to pay for them. This, then, would be an output (W) that influences inputs (LL_p). Another example would be the output of a new piece of machinery for making chairs. Suppose that this machine altered the efficiency of both lumber utilization (fewer board-feet needed per chair) and labor utilization (fewer workers needed per machine and so per chair as well). In that case an output (W) would again exercise its influence on various inputs (EL and LL_p). To take a different example, a change in some commodity output's value could well provoke changes in buyer's attitudes toward this and related commodities. Buyers' reactions to a changed value of outputs (W) could and would likely alter the quantities and values of the inputs (EL and LL) used in production. Here commodity output values influence inputs. Such examples could be multiplied endlessly: every output exercises its unique effects on everything in its environment, including, of course, inputs to commodity production.

Marxian theory's overdeterminist arguments and explanations contrast with the reductionisms of neoclassical and Keynesian theories. The former utilize a unidirectional explanation of values, reducing them to a predetermined human nature and its three governing essences. Keynesian theory deploys a similar unidirectional explanation reducing values to a predetermined structure and its governing rules. In contrast, the Marxian theory we present here makes its causes and effects mutually interdependent: outputs, inputs, and their values are interdependent; no aspect of an individual or society is predetermined. In striking contrast to this Marxian theory, traditional Marxism displays an essentialism quite parallel to that found in these non-Marxian theories. Despite this similarity, traditional Marxism offers an essence different from human nature or structural rules by reducing values ultimately to given (predetermined) technical and physical labor requirements ("forces of production").

Traditional Marxism's essentialist reasoning also yields its logical inconsistencies that have provided its critics with ammunition to refute and reject its value and surplus value theories. Given many critics' ideological goals, they then proceeded to reject all of Marxism based on the logical inconsistencies of one of its multiple interpretations and theorizations. We devote this chapter's appendix B to a brief overview of this controversy and to explain why and how an overdeterminist perspective to understanding values resolves the issue of logical inconsistency. Consequently it enables Marxian theory to continue as a viable and contending way to understand how the economy works.

4.5 Capitalists and Laborers

The Marxian theory discussed in this book discards simple dichotomies between good and bad, strong and weak, rich and poor, or powerful and powerless. Rather, capitalists and laborers are shown to be of diverse kinds and to be involved in many different sorts of relationships to one another. Marxian theory's analysis of capitalists and laborers is unique among modern social theories.

4.5.1   What Are Capitalists?

Marxian theory focuses on "capitalists" as appropriators of surplus labor in the form of surplus value. It emphasizes the kind of capitalist who buys and combines labor power and other means of production and who owns and sells the commodities produced thereby. Yet the theory also recognizes other kinds of capitalists who do not appropriate surplus labor. We can introduce Marx's own notation to clarify the different kinds of capitalists.

All capitalists start with a sum of values, usually in the form of money, M. Their goal is to use their money to "make money"—to secure an increment, ΔM, as an addition to their original M. Mathematically this can be stated as $M \to M + \Delta M$. Capitalists of the sort we have been discussing convert their original M, via market purchases, into labor power, equipment, and raw materials. Marx calls the expenditure on labor power "variable capital," or V; his choice of term expresses the idea that this component of the capitalist's capital will grow or vary. Marx calls the expenditure on equipment and raw materials "constant capital," or C, and his choice of term reflects the idea that the value of these commodities passes unchanged (unvaried) into the final commodities produced from them. Thus the purchase of EL and its utilization in production added precisely EL and no more to the value of the produced commodity output. The following incomplete expression summarizes this Marxian approach:

$$M = C + V \to W = M + \Delta M.$$

This equation begins with a sum of value, M, and ends with a larger sum of value, $M + \Delta M$. ΔM refers to the growth accomplished by the capital as it engages the fundamental class process. ΔM is the surplus value that attaches itself to money in the course of capitalist production. Marx defines this variation as the "self-expansion of capital." He then completes the equation of capitalist commodity production as follows:

$$C + V + S = W.$$

This equation precisely parallels our earlier equation, because $C = EL$, $V = LL_p$, and $S = LL_u$. Capitalists achieve the expansion of their capital, from $C + V$ to W, by appropriating the surplus labor embedded in the commodities they sell. The initial capital, $C + V$, grows to W because of the addition of S during production and because the capitalists appropriate that S. A measure of the rate at which capital self-expands would be

$$\frac{\Delta M}{M} = \frac{S}{(C+V)}.$$

If this rate rises, capital is relatively successful in expanding; if it falls, it is having problems.

Marxian theory attaches the label "productive" to such capitalists to distinguish them from other kinds of capitalists. All capitalists appropriate surplus value, but only productive capitalists do so by appropriating the surplus labor of direct laborers. This raises two closely connected questions. What other kinds of capitalists exist? How can a person appropriate surplus value without at the same time appropriating surplus labor?

Marxian theory defines "capital" as a sum of money that expands itself by going through some social process: literally, as "self-expanding value." The fundamental class process is one way for a sum of values, M, to expand itself into $M + \Delta M$. However, the fundamental class process is not the only way that values expand themselves.

Lending money at interest is another way. If M is lent to a person and then eventually repaid plus an interest, $M + \Delta M$, that interest, ΔM, is surplus value for the lender, the amount of self-expansion for the lender's capital. Another example is the process of renting out land. A sum of values, M, is spent to buy a piece of land. Usage of this is then granted to another person for some agreed time in return for a rental payment, ΔM. At the end of this time, the landowner retains the land and its value plus the rental received: the landowner's capital as expanded to $M + \Delta M$. The rent is surplus value for the landowner. A third example is merchant capital. Merchants typically begin with an amount of money, M, spent to buy commodities for resale at a price higher than their purchase price. The revenues from the resale, $M + \Delta M$, include a surplus value for the merchant, ΔM. The merchant's money becomes capital—self-expanding value—by means of engaging the purchase-for-resale sequence of market exchanges.

Moneylending, landlord, and merchant capital are called "unproductive" capital, because no surplus labor is involved in them. Their self-expansions do not occur in production. When I lend money to you at interest, I am not employing you or obtaining any commodities from your labor. You must return to me more money than I lent to you. My gain is your loss. In the borrower–lender relationship, no new value is produced, no labor or surplus labor is done, no new commodities are created. The same applies to surplus value obtained through renting out land or merchant transactions.

In contrast, "productive" capital is defined as self-expanding money engaged in production and more precisely in the capitalist fundamental class process. There, hired direct laborers perform surplus labor whose fruits are appropriated by employers. The surplus value thereby accruing to employers measures the self-expansion of productive capital. Unproductive capitalists have existed, more or less generally, for thousands of years. Ancient social records demonstrate the existence of moneylenders, merchants, land renters, and the like. Productive capitalists may have existed marginally and sporadically before the seventeenth century, but only since then have they become the powerful, socially prominent group typical of modern history.

Marxian theory, given its entry point of class, stresses the differences among capitalists. It does this to pinpoint the specific social role and importance of productive capitalists since it is chiefly they who appropriate surplus labor in modern society. For Marxian theory, productive capitalists represent the individuals who sit atop the fundamental class process. They are therefore key objects of a class analysis of modern capitalist social formations.

4.5.2   What Are Laborers?

Like capitalists, laborers may be either productive or unproductive. Productive laborers are those who sell their labor power to a productive capitalist and also perform surplus labor appropriated by that capitalist. The direct laborers that we have been discussing in this chapter are productive laborers. However, there are also unproductive laborers who perform vital functions in capitalist class structures. Unproductive laborers also sell their labor power to capitalists, *but they do not perform surplus labor*. Marxian theory not only stresses the difference between productive and unproductive capitalists; it similarly distinguishes unproductive from productive laborers.

The following is an example of unproductive labor. Suppose that I sell you my ability to do work in your garden for two hours next Saturday. You agree to pay me $30 for my time and effort. When I get there, you direct me to help you clear brush from your garden. I am a laborer; I sell my labor power. I also participate in a labor process and may also use implements to aid my labor. However, I produce no commodity for my employer, you, to sell. I perform no surplus labor; you realize no surplus value; you appropriate no surplus from me. In this relationship between us, my labor is unproductive; the labor power I sell is unproductive. (Were the relationship to alter, e.g., by having my two hours of gardening become part of your commercial production and sale of vegetables, then my labor power would be productive. In other words, by adding the fundamental class process to the relationship, the same labor becomes productive.)

Consider a second example. I sell my labor power to a productive capitalist, perhaps the one in our earlier example of the enterprise making and selling chairs. This productive capitalist does not, however, combine my labor power with equipment and raw materials to produce chairs. Rather, the productive capitalist directs me to provide certain conditions that enable productive laborers to perform their surplus labor. One such condition is disciplinary supervision. The productive capitalist directs me to supervise productive laborers, to make sure that they perform the maximum possible surplus labor and that they do not arrive late, take breaks or talk with coworkers. In this case I do unproductive labor since my labor power is not a direct part of producing the commodities sold by the capitalist. The same unproductive label would apply to all other employees of a productive capitalist who (1) do not perform surplus labor embodied in the commodities sold by the capitalist and (2) instead provide conditions for the productive laborers to produce surplus for the capitalist employer.

Another kind of unproductive labor is that performed by the employees of unproductive capitalists. For example, the clerk in a merchant, moneylending, or land-renting enterprise is hired, paid a wage, and required to do work. But that work is not directly involved in producing commodities that embody surplus labor. It is rather involved in helping unproductive capitalists (merchants, bankers, and landlords) expand their capital in the unproductive ways discussed above.

To understand Marxian theory it is vital to note that the difference between productive and unproductive laborers is *not* a matter of their importance to the survival and reproduction of the capitalist structure. Both kinds are indispensable, although in different ways. The productive laborer produces the surplus that the productive capitalist appropriates. The unproductive laborer provides the conditions without which the productive laborers could not or would not produce that surplus.

The adjectives "productive" and "unproductive" are Marxian theory's way of differentiating wage-workers who participate in the fundamental class process from those who do not. The two kinds of laborers are subject to different pressures and play different roles in capitalist economies. This distinction parallels the role played by these words in differentiating among capitalists. In both cases the purpose is to highlight the existence and uniqueness of the fundamental class process and its overdetermined connections to the many different nonclass processes occurring in modern capitalism.

4.5.3 Exploitation

People have used the word "exploitation" in many ways for many years. Positively, the word sometimes means "to make good use of some resource," as in "the pioneers who exploited the opportunities of virgin forests and streams." More often it carries a negative connotation, meaning "to take advantage of or abuse some person or resource." Phrases such as "those parents exploit their children" or "that government exploited its minority citizens" illustrate this negative usage. Marxian theory attaches an altogether different definition to "exploitation."

"Exploitation" describes—in Marxian theory—any fundamental class process in which the person who performs surplus labor is not also the person who appropriates it. The appropriator(s) is (are) then understood to exploit the producer(s) of the surplus. It follows that communist and ancient forms of the fundamental class process are not exploitative, since performers collectively or individually appropriate their own surplus labor. The slave, feudal, and capitalist forms are exploitative.

The capitalist fundamental class process involves the exploitation of productive laborers by productive capitalists. Marxian theory is concerned with both the quality of exploitation (is it feudal, capitalist, etc.?) and its quantitative dimensions (the value of the surplus and its relation to the values of capital invested and total output). In terms of our earlier notation, the size of the surplus value, S, depends on the difference between the value added during the work time of productive laborers and the value of their labor power. To see the significance of exploitation in Marxian theory, we look more closely at the relationship among these values.

In general, the value of labor power, V, depends on two social circumstances. First, how many of which commodities do laborers require to be able and willing to keep on selling their labor power? Second, how much labor is socially necessary to produce those required commodities? Both circumstances vary from one economy to the next and from time to time within any economy. At any time the value of labor power, V, is the product of the list of required commodities multiplied by the amount of socially necessary labor necessary to produce each one.

The higher the standard of living to which laborers become accustomed (sometimes called "the real wage"), the more commodities they will require and thus the higher the value of their labor power will be. Yet, as commodity production becomes more efficient, it requires fewer hours, on average, to produce each commodity. This means that each commodity will have less value (will require less socially necessary labor to produce it). This in turn will lower the value of labor power since the individual commodities consumed by laborers will contain less value.

A simple equation can make this point clear:

$$V = e \cdot q.$$

Here $e \cdot q$ *is* the total of all the quantities (q) of wage commodities required multiplied by the value of each per unit (e). If e should fall (because of a drop in the per-unit value of wage commodities) more than q rises (owing to an increase in workers' real wages), then the value of labor power would fall despite the increase in the standard of living of those workers. Such a circumstance may well have characterized capitalist economies since Marx's death. This would mean that increased exploitation *and* increased real wages have been the experience of productive workers over the past hundred years. This remarkable insight and lesson is unique to Marxian theory; it is not possible in alternative theories.

Since "value," in Marxian theory, is another word for "socially necessary embodied labor time," the value of anything depends on the time over which labor was expended to produce it, on how long the work of producing it took. The more hours per day performed by the average worker, the greater the value he/she added; the fewer the hours they work, the less value they add. Given some particular value of labor power, V, the size of the surplus value, S, will depend on how much value laborers add on average during the time of the labor process. The surplus value produced by workers will be as large or as small as the difference between the value added and the value of labor power:

$$S = [S + V] - V.$$

Another way to state this is to focus attention on the value added during the length of the working day. That length is represented by the following line, AB:

$$A _____ B$$

The distance AB represents all of the value added in one day by a productive laborer—say, eight hours' worth. Now we can divide this line into two parts:

$$A _____ X \_\_\_\_\_ B$$

The length AX represents an amount of value added that exactly equals the value of labor power in this particular economy at this time, $AX = V$. Assuming that the laborer is paid for his/her labor power an amount $AX = V$, it follows that this portion of the working day's labor is called "paid labor." XB must then represent the surplus labor performed and the surplus value appropriated, S. Indeed XB is that portion of the day during which the laborer adds value that he/she is not paid for.

The ratio between the two parts of the day, S and V, is Marx's "rate of exploitation":

$$\frac{XB}{AX} = \frac{S}{V} = \text{rate of exploitation.}$$

The rate of exploitation shows the ratio of the surplus to the necessary labor performed by productive laborers. It offers a quantitative measure of the capitalist fundamental class process: just how effectively productive capitalists are appropriating surplus value from productive laborers.

Using the numbers from our original chair example, where paid labor was six hours and unpaid labor was two hours, we can calculate the rate of exploitation in the chair enterprise: $LL_u/LL_p = 2/6$. If the length of the working day, LL, were to be increased, say, to nine hours, while the value of labor power (LL_u) remained unchanged, the surplus value (LL_u) would rise to three hours. In this case the rate of exploitation would rise to 3/6.

Marx used his theory to interpret the contemporaneous social conflicts over the lengths of the working day and week. In the eighteenth and nineteenth centuries in Europe, as capitalism spread there, productive laborers were often required to work twelve-, fourteen-, and sixteen-hour days as a matter of course. The novels of Charles Dickens in Britain and Émile Zola in France offer detailed descriptions of workers' living conditions under such circumstances. These long days served productive capitalists by increasing the ratio XB/AX. For the same wage, workers were pressured to work longer hours, with the fruit of those longer hours accruing to the capitalist employers. In Marxian terminology, productive capitalists lengthened the working day to increase the rate of exploitation of labor. Not surprisingly, productive laborers eventually began to fight back, organizing trade unions to fight for laws that restricted the length of the working day. Major social movements and struggles evolved that achieved laws limiting the length of the working day to eight hours and the work week to forty. That has remained the basic law in the United States to the present.

However, the logic of the capitalist fundamental class process has worked to drive capitalists constantly to reopen the question of the length of the working day or week. Thus, in the United States today, employers seek and often get "voluntary or compulsory overtime," as lengthened working days or weeks are now called. Capitalists do this not because they are insensitive or obsessed by greed, but because their survival depends in part on how effectively they exploit productive laborers. Lengthening work times is one way to enhance exploitation.

The pressure on productive capitalists to increase rates of exploitation is nothing other than capitalist competition. As each capitalist acts to secure his or her own position as a surplus labor appropriator, their actions threaten the abilities of other capitalists to secure their positions. For example, one capitalist innovates with a new technology that cheapens the value and hence per-unit price of that capitalist's output. As explained below, this action threatens the survival of all capitalists producing that same kind of output. The result is a constant state of tension among them. Each fears the consequences of the others' attempts to innovate, grow, or survive. Each struggles to offset those consequences by taking private steps that only provoke new dangers for and reactions on the part of other capitalists, and so on. In Marxian theory, competition is understood to be this interdependent network of risks and dangers imposing all kinds of actions upon productive capitalists. However, before turning to a discussion of capitalist competition, we need to consider the effects on productive laborers when capitalists seek to enhance their rates of exploitation.

4.5.4   Class Struggles

How do productive laborers react to capitalists seeking to increase their rate of exploitation? Depending on the complex circumstances they face, such workers may simply accept doing more unpaid labor. On the one hand, they may even accept ideas and arguments that disguise or deny their growing exploitation. On the other hand, they may decide not to accept this situation. They may act by themselves or with all kinds of allies—spouses, the unproductive employees of the capitalist, professionals involved in the ancient class process, elected state officials, and so on. They may limit their efforts to specific employers. Alternatively, they may help organize a social movement demanding changes in the quantitative dimensions of the capitalist fundamental class process: for example, a new law shortening the length of the working day or week.

A struggle ensues over the capitalist fundamental class process, in this case over the ratio between XB and AX, the rate of exploitation. All kinds of people involved in all manner of different class and nonclass processes take sides in this struggle. One side fights for a higher S/V; the other for a lower S/V. Because this is a struggle over the class process, Marxian theory refers to it as a "class struggle."

A union of productive laborers that presses for higher wages is a class struggle. Management pressing productive laborers to accept compulsory overtime is a class struggle. The fight between two groups of representatives in Congress over a law that would raise the legal minimum wage is a class struggle. Each of these instances is a class struggle because of what the struggle is about. The groups struggling include persons involved in all manner of class and nonclass processes, but theirs is a class struggle because class is the object of their struggle.

When complex groupings of people fight over nonclass processes such as school curricula or medical ethics or criminal justice procedures or equal political rights, we refer to these as nonclass struggles. Any society involves an ever-changing mix of both class and nonclass struggles. Because of Marxian theory's focus on class, it has always been most concerned to locate, identify, and connect class struggles to the other processes and struggles occurring in any society under scrutiny.

Class struggles concern not only the quantitative dimensions of the fundamental class process, such as the rate of exploitation in capitalism. Groups of people also struggle over the qualitative dimensions of class processes. For example, the issue may be alternative forms of the fundamental class process rather than the ratio of paid to unpaid labor time within a fundamental class process. One side may want to preserve the capitalist form of surplus labor production. The other side may want to change to another form of the fundamental class process—say, a communist form. This too is a class struggle because the object of the struggling is the class process. This time the struggle is over the qualitative form of the fundamental class process rather than its quantitative dimensions. Of course, people may struggle simultaneously over the quantity and quality of the fundamental class process.

The class struggles discussed so far have concerned fundamental class processes, but social groups fight over subsumed class processes as well. Subsumed class struggles concern the size, form, and recipients of the distributions of surplus by its appropriators. For example, section 4.7 below shows how capitalism includes subsumed class struggles over the interest payments productive capitalists make to bankers to secure their access to credit. Section 4.7 also details subsumed class struggles over the tax payments productive capitalists make to the state and over the salaries they pay to the unproductive laborers they hire as managers and over dividends they pay to owners of the means of production.

Marxian theory generally sees an array of different class struggles (fundamental and subsumed) that occur in, influence, and change any society. Those struggles concern either the quantitative or the qualitative dimensions of either class process or both. In Marxian theory, class struggles are like class processes: both are overdetermined by all the other processes and struggles occurring in a society.

Traditionally Marxists distinguish their perspective from that of other social reformers by stressing the need for a qualitative change in the fundamental class process (sometimes referred to as a "revolutionary" perspective). Marxists see the capitalist fundamental class process as a major barrier to the construction of a just, peaceful, and democratic society. They declare to others seeking to construct such a society: *Unless you take into account the capitalist fundamental and subsumed class processes and understand how they interact with the rest of modern society, you will not successfully transform society in the directions we all want.* Marxian theory takes class into account systematically because it aims for more than social analysis; it also seeks to inform movements for social transformation and to add class change to their agendas. Of course other economic theories, as we have seen so far, take other, nonclass aspects into their different agendas.

4.5.5 The Complexity of Industrial Capitalist Firms

The productive capitalist who appropriates surplus value from his productive laborers may be an individual or a group (collective) of individuals (the typical modern corporate board of directors). In either case the appropriation of surplus value occurs quite literally at those places in society usually called commodity-producing "enterprises" or "firms." Those places are likewise the sites of surplus value distribution, the capitalist subsumed class process. We will henceforth refer to productive capitalists as "industrial capitalists" to distinguish them from the unproductive capitalists (e.g., merchant, moneylending, and land-renting capitalists).

Many nonclass processes occur together with the capitalist class processes (appropriating and distributing surplus value) inside industrial capitalist enterprises. Cultural processes there include speech among persons, the writing of all sorts of business histories, reports and forecasts, the design of products, ideas aimed at developing new products, and so on. Political processes include the giving and taking of orders among the persons working in this firm, the writing of behavioral rules for employees, and the adjudication of disputes among people present inside the firm. Natural processes include the physical transformation of inputs during the production of commodity outputs, climatic changes occurring where the firm is located, pollution occurring inside the firm, and so on. Other economic processes occurring at the site of the firm, besides the capitalist class processes, include buying inputs and selling outputs, borrowing and lending, and saving and investing.

Over time, the diverse class and nonclass processes that comprise an industrial capitalist enterprise change (as all processes do). Thus all such enterprises are likewise always changing. If the changes are extreme, the industrial capitalist enterprise may collapse, dissolve, or otherwise cease to exist. For example, if natural processes changed to drop average temperatures to -100 degrees Fahrenheit, the firm would expire. If a virus deprived employees of their ability to work, the firm might disappear. Lesser changes in natural processes would alter but not destroy the industrial capitalist enterprise (provided that it can and does take steps to adjust to the changed natural processes).

The continuation of the industrial capitalist firm also depends on the ever-changing cultural processes that overdetermine it and whether the firm accommodates to those cultural changes. If its employees changed religions and embraced a deity who counseled a rejection of work for the firm's employers because of their different religious commitments, the firm's existence would be jeopardized. The firm might respond by expending funds to counteract that religion, or its employers might convert, or some compromise might be achieved to enable the industrial capitalist firm to survive although changed in perhaps significant ways.

Political processes inside the firm—for instance, employees following the orders of their supervisors—are usually crucial conditions of existence of the production and appropriation of surplus value there. If, for example, resentments over wages and working conditions or other concerns lead workers to refuse supervisors' orders, either the firm will collapse or some accommodation that changes the firm must be found so that the changed industrial capitalist enterprise will continue.

The firm likewise needs the many economic processes that provide the conditions of its existence. For example, the firm would be at risk if the conditions for it to buy and sell its inputs and outputs were changed or threatened. A war or a disastrous climate change could disrupt market exchanges, for example. Then the industrial capitalist firm could try to use its own resources to revive the old and/or organize new exchange processes necessary for its survival although in a changed form. It might or might not succeed.

If the nonclass processes inside and outside the firm change—but not in ways that undermine the industrial capitalist firm—then it survives. Whether it grows or shrinks and how it changes depends on how the various nonclass changes combined to overdetermine changes in the capitalist class processes and thus the enterprise as a whole. However, it is always possible that changes in the nonclass processes will threaten to destroy the capitalist class processes in the firm. If, for example, nonclass changes led productive laborers to insist on much higher wages, industrial capitalists might decide to end production and close the enterprise. It might then cease to exist unless a different class process, not capitalist, might be established in its place. To continue the example, workers who demanded the higher wages that destroyed the capitalist industrial enterprise might then take over after the capitalists had closed the enterprise. They might reopen it as a communist enterprise where the workers collectively functioned as their own board of directors. This is what happened in Argentina early in the opening years of the twenty-first century.

While change is continual and even disappearance always possible for industrial capitalist enterprises, we focus here on analyzing firms that are able to adjust and thereby perpetuate themselves. For each of them, actual or potential changes in all the nonclass processes on which their firm's survival depends are continuing issues of intense concern. When changes in those processes appear to threaten the firm's capitalist class processes, the industrial capitalist must act to deflect the threat by adding to, removing, or differently changing nonclass processes. Moreover industrial capitalists quickly figure out that at times the best defense is a good offense. Part of their adjustment is to actively alter various nonclass processes not only aimed at ensuring the enterprise's survival and growth but also forestalling and discouraging potentially threatening actions on the part of other industrial capitalists.

To undertake these actions, any industrial capitalist needs a regular flow of resources to be able to adjust to threatening changes in nonclass processes and to mount offensive changes. Such a flow of resources is the surplus value appropriated from productive laborers. The industrial capitalist appropriator then distributes it in ways intended to secure and expand the firm's capitalist class processes.

The capitalist fundamental class process provides the surplus that enables the subsumed class process. The latter distributes the surplus with the aim of thereby reproducing the capitalist fundamental class process. The two kinds of capitalist class processes—fundamental and subsumed—depend on and enable one another. They are conditions of each other's existence.

4.5.6 Competition

Competition arises among industrial capitalist firms because one firm's actions to secure its own survival often jeopardize other firms' reproduction. This need not necessarily reflect the intentions of any capitalist. Rather, the structure of class and nonclass processes within which all capitalists function make certain efforts at self-reproduction by one capitalist threaten the survival of others. The resulting struggles among industrial capitalists, as each seeks to survive the consequences of others' efforts to survive, are collectively labeled "competition."

Marxian theory attaches great significance to industrial capitalist competition for several reasons. First, these competitive struggles continue to exert deep and lasting impacts on all modern societies. Second, competitive struggles contribute to business cycles. Third, neoclassical theory claims that competition is a purely positive force that generates optimum economic efficiency—a claim that Marxists refute. Fourth, competition among industrial capitalists often provokes various sorts of class struggles. Marxists seek to understand and transform such class struggles into movements for social justice and democracy built upon nonexploitative fundamental class processes.

Industrial capitalist competition takes many forms. Because of its importance to the Marxian analysis of capitalism, we add appendix C to this chapter explaining, based on a few simple numbers, how competition works and its many consequences. Here we present another (nonnumerical) explanation. Consider, again, our chair example. Suppose that several capitalist firms produce identical chairs; they form a competitive chair industry.

Suppose that the board of directors of one of these firms, wanting more productivity from its hired productive laborers, decides to distribute more surplus to hire and equip more supervisors of those laborers. The strategy works to increase output per productive laborer. That is, the same amount of productive labor is now embodied in more chairs. This means that each chair marketed by this industrial capitalist firm has a lower value than before. But that's only the beginning of the competitive story.

In a competitive market, the unit value of a chair—its market value—is the average of the different labor times required by each industrial capitalist to produce its chairs. Like any average, some capitalist firms produce below that average, some above, and some may even produce at the average. In other words, productive efficiencies as measured by these respective labor times differ across enterprises within the chair industry. The socially necessary labor attached to a chair is in fact precisely the computed average of all these individual enterprises' labor times. In our example the average (socially necessary labor) falls because one chair producer has reduced its amount of labor time to produce each chair: hence the average of them, namely the market value of a chair, falls (see also the first part of appendix C).

A competitive market for chairs means that all industrial capitalists have no choice but to sell their enterprise's produced chairs at the newly established lower market value. Trying to sell them at a higher value ensures that they sell none, since customers can purchase identical chairs from those capitalist firms selling at the lower, average value. Choosing to lower their value below the average makes no economic sense because they can sell as many chairs as they can produce at that higher average value. In other words, competition means that each capitalist faces a perfectly elastic demand at the market determined value for produced chairs.

Capitalists competing inside the chair industry with this productivity-raising firm now face a potential economic disaster that may drive them out of business. The reason for this existential threat is the difference between their newly changed revenue position—each must sell its chairs at the new, lowered average value per chair while their unchanged productivity means that their costs have remained the same. Hence their profits are reduced. That constrains their subsumed class distributions, thereby threatening their survival as industrial capitalists in the chair industry. Meanwhile the firm that raised its productivity earns higher profits. Like its competitors, it too must sell its chairs at the same lowered market price; but unlike them, its productivity increase reduced its cost of producing each chair. While its production costs of C+V have not changed, it found a way to produce more chairs with the same amount of living labor (increased productivity). By reducing its costs per chair produced, this firm became the least cost producer of chairs in its industry. Its higher profits enable its board of directors to expand subsumed class distributions to grow the firm.

The result of such productivity improvement is stark. The competitive markets literally redistribute surplus value from the least to the more efficient capitalist firms within industries (appendix C). Marx calls the extra profits earned by the latter a "super profit." It represents an extra value earned (at the expense of other firms) because some firm's capitalists raised production efficiency. It is important not to conflate these two very different sources of value:

super profit arises from an industrial firm's board of directors deploying strategies to become the least cost producer in a competitive market; surplus value arises from that same board exploiting its own workers. The former is a non-class (market) source of revenue; the later a class source.

The competitive lesson is quickly learned by all capitalists: reduce your enterprise's costs of production or risk decline and even bankruptcy. Of course, like everything else in life, learning a lesson is one thing and doing something about it is something else. For example, relatively inefficient firms may well understand that competition causes their profits to fall, but they may still not implement a counterstrategy of reducing costs fast enough to withstand the relentless competitive pressure on price. They face business failure. Should that happen, the innovative capitalist might not only capture their former customers but also buy up their machinery, raw material inventories, and so on, at depressed prices. Competition may drive so many relatively inefficient firms out of business that the surviving industrial capitalists are large and few enough to control the market price for chairs. In other words, competitive capitalism can dissolve itself into its opposites: oligopoly (a few large firms) or even monopoly capitalism. Capitalist competition within any industry thus provides great incentives (profits and growth) for each capitalist enterprise to improve its productive laborers' efficiency while it simultaneously threatens every enterprises that does not do so as fast as its competitors.

Suppose that those other industrial capitalists do try and reproduce the strategy of the innovative capitalist who hired the extra supervisors or else pursue other parallel strategies. One capitalist might invent a new piece of machinery or buy a newly invented piece of machinery to enhance efficiency (lower production cost per unit of output). Another capitalist might discover a new, cheaper source of lumber, an input to chair production, which would lower the unit cost of producing a chair. The survival of each industrial capitalist in the chair industry depends on how quickly they match its competitors' cost reductions. Each industrial capitalists' success over time depends on innovating first—utilizing some new machine, new process of supervision, new style of management, or new source of cheaper inputs—to lower its per-unit costs.

Industrial capitalists strive for value-reducing innovations both to defend against their competitors' possible innovations and as an offensive strategy for growth and prosperity. The capitalist class structure of enterprises interacts with their competitive coexistence inside each industry to make the cost reductions of any one threaten all the others. Their competitive relation is structural and imposed on all capitalists within each industry. Some individual capitalists internalize this requirement and adjust their personalities, consciously or unconsciously. Capitalist competition does not result from particular human traits, it is more the reverse.

4.5.7   Competition and the Accumulation of Capital

Perhaps the most famous example of capitalist competition concerns the decision by one capitalist to "accumulate capital." This decision deserves careful examination. Consider, again, the basic equation for a capitalist firm producing a given commodity:

$$C + V + S = W.$$

The capitalist sells the chairs produced by productive laborers for revenue equal to W. Presumably this capitalist uses a portion of the W to replace the tools and raw materials used up in producing the chairs. This equals the C in the equation. Likewise the capitalist uses another portion of the W to pay for the productive labor power purchased from the laborers. This equals the V. That leaves the capitalist with an appropriated surplus value, S, which must be distributed to secure the various conditions that are necessary if he or she is to continue to appropriate S.

Now suppose that this capitalist decides to use part of the S to buy extra tools and raw materials and to hire additional productive laborers. This process is called "accumulating capital." The extra C and V purchased out of S will generate extra S for the capitalist. We can show this in terms of two consecutive time periods for this capitalist:

Period 1: $C + V + S = W,$

where S is used to buy additional C and V (denoted as ΔC and ΔV, respectively).

Period 2: $C + V + \Delta C + \Delta V + S + \Delta S = W + \Delta W.$

This second equation shows the capitalist using up and replacing more tools and raw materials $(C + \Delta C)$ and hiring more labor power $(V + \Delta V)$. These expanded input costs represent capital accumulation. However, since more productive laborers generate correspondingly more value, the capitalist also appropriates additional surplus value (ΔS). Thus the accumulation of capital augments the mass of appropriated surplus value from S to $(S + \Delta S)$.

The capitalist's goal in accumulating capital is clear: the more surplus the capitalist appropriates over time $(S + \Delta S)$, the more to distribute in subsumed class payments to secure the conditions of the firm's survival. And, again, the reaction of competing capitalists is to see danger immediately. The accumulating capitalist may use the additional surplus to buy an expensive new machine or hire more supervisory personnel that nonaccumulating capitalists might not be able to afford. Their increased productivity (lowered average cost of production) will set off new competitive pressures on all competing firms who cannot afford to replicate them.

It does not matter that the capitalist who first adds supervisors, or buys new machines, or accumulates capital does not intend to trouble the existence of competing capitalists and simply acts to secure the enterprise's survival and growth. Whatever the intention, each capitalist's private action impacts all other competing capitalists. Hence competing capitalists are and feel threatened by the dangerous possibilities occasioned by the first capitalist's accumulation of capital.

Moreover competing capitalists will then likely take comparable steps. They too will hire more supervisors, and/or buy new machines, and/or accumulate capital. They may take still other steps to enhance their security, find new ways to distribute their surplus value to subsumed classes. Those steps will, for all the same reasons, threaten the first capitalist, who in turn will take more steps. Competition is this never-ending, mutually threatening struggle among capitalists in each industry to survive.

One of the most interesting results of this competition among capitalists within each industry is that it drives down the value per unit of that industry's output. As competitors replicate or outdo one another, they reduce the average amount of socially necessary labor required to produce a unit of the industry's output. The process is visible in the history of commodity values wherever capitalism takes hold (in recent times, consider the tendency for market prices of computers, cellphones, electronic games, high definition TV sets, etc., to fall). As we will see below, the fall in unit output values has its economic consequences for capitalist competition, the flow of capital among industries, and other aspects of the entire capitalist system including the business cycle.

4.6 Capitalist Economies and Social Development

In the Marxian theory elaborated here, the interaction of the capitalist fundamental class process and the commodity exchange process (markets) not only generates competition but also plays an important, broader role in shaping modern history. Marx began the analysis of that role and it was developed much further by later Marxists. They sought to demonstrate the analytical reach and power of Marx's class theory by using it to construct explanations of the growth of the modern international economy, the distribution of income in capitalist societies, and the boom–bust cycles that afflict capitalist economies. Briefly considering their arguments here can provide an introduction to the broader structure and implications of Marxian theory.

4.6.1 Growth of a Capitalist World Economy

As competition among industrial capitalists drives down the per-unit prices of commodities, the social consequences are very significant. Ever-cheapening commodities present ever-widening opportunities for selling these commodities. Marx attached great importance to this remarkable feature of capitalism. Wherever it took hold, the productive capitalists eventually realized that falling commodity values opened new marketing possibilities where such cheaper commodities might be sold. In the eighteenth and nineteenth centuries, for example, the falling values of their textile commodities led British capitalists to seek and find worldwide markets for them. Locally produced textiles in continental Europe, Asia, Africa, and the Americas had to compete with ever cheaper British textiles. If their local producers could not keep up, they (very much like our relatively inefficient chair producers) would disappear from the industry. In fact many did, since they were unable to compete with British textiles.

Capitalist competition helps secure the continuation and growth of the capitalist fundamental class process by cheapening its commodity outputs and thereby winning more markets for their sale. Capitalism's relatively early arrival in the nations of western Europe, in North America, and in Japan enabled them to grow and become powerful in part because competition drove down their industrial output prices. Expanding exports profited those nations' capitalists, while those exports' falling prices outcompeted the more costly local products they encountered around the world. The consequently disrupted local systems of production around the world (often noncapitalist in their class structures) typically sank into social disorganization and vulnerability.

Displaced local producers now looked for other kinds of gainful work to survive. Many flowed into the production of food or various raw materials destined to be exported to the capitalist nations. Some looked for work in the growing port areas stimulated by expanding international commerce. In this way, expanding exports from capitalists helped to create a ready labor supply for the expansion of local capitalist and noncapitalist class structures and their produced commodities. Some of the latter were exported, that is, became the imports of industrial capitalists located in western Europe, North America, and Japan.

The nations where capitalist competition took hold earliest eventually carved up the rest of the world into colonial properties. They then subordinated and economically reorganized their colonies still further to enhance the colonizers' wealth. For example, the colonies were made to produce food and raw materials to be sent to the colonizers' capitalist enterprises as cheap inputs. In short, the competition that emerged from the interaction of the capitalist fundamental class process and the exchange process contributed significantly to the extremely unequal division of wealth and income that has characterized the world economy increasingly over the last three centuries.

The last two centuries might well be called the era of capitalist growth toward world dominance: a global capitalist market and economy. The disruption and destruction of many noncapitalist class structures in Europe's colonies was a continuation of what had occurred earlier inside Europe during the long transition from feudalism to capitalism. Then new capitalist industries in urban centers had sold their commodities to mostly feudal agricultural hinterlands disrupting their traditional production systems. Waves of unemployed and displaced rural people moved to the cities and, to survive there, sold their labor power to industrial capitalists.

As capitalist competition spurred further growth seeking foreign as well as domestic market expansion, such domestic migrations evolved into vast international migrations. The economic histories of the United States and the United Kingdom, for example, are inseparable from this combination of internal and international migration. Drawn from dissolving old and often noncapitalist class structures, the migrations continue to this day. They are now both international and domestic (e.g., as in the mass internal migrations characterizing contemporary China).

The disruption of societies based on noncapitalist class structures became still more intense in the later nineteenth and in the twentieth century. Then capitalist commodity exports were joined by exports of capital itself. Driven as always by the competition their class structure compels, industrial capitalists in western Europe, North America, and Japan established investments in the rest of the world. Beyond shipping food and raw materials back to their capitalist centers, they erected factories in Asia, Africa, and Latin America to exploit lower wage levels there. Colonial governments dutifully obliged by establishing and maintaining profitable conditions for such investments. Even after colonial power had given way to local, nominally independent regimes, the desperate economic circumstances of these governments (legacies of colonialism) led most of them to continue to invite, subsidize, and protect foreign industrial capitalist investments.

In some of the colonial and postcolonial societies, social crises prompted by capitalist commodity exports and later by capital exports generated a different response. Their link to European capitalism was itself identified as the problem, the source of their crisis. Their solution would be to break away from the capitalist world market. The Soviet Union, China, Cuba, and many other countries pursued this alternative for at least the early phases of their modern histories. They aimed to create the space for rapid internal economic development by largely cutting themselves off from world capitalism, at least initially. They did this by replacing privately owned factories, land, and equipment (often owned by foreign capitalist enterprises) with collectivized, publicly owned property. They likewise minimized or strictly controlled trade with capitalist countries and rejected foreign private-capitalist investment in their countries. Later, if and when they had achieved the scale and wealth to profit from a return to participation in the world market, they might do so, although often with many controls still in place.

For many decades such countries closed themselves off, more or less, from global markets. Capitalist competition and accumulation thereby produced their own limitations and obstacles via the reactions they provoked. Even where socialism and communism did not literally close parts of the world to capitalist enterprise, many so-called third world countries, especially after 1960, demanded better returns from participating in the world market. Some tried to do that by controlling their export prices through cartels like OPEC for petroleum or the International Coffee Agreement. Or they threatened to discontinue paying off the massive debts incurred as part of their economic dilemmas before 1970. In the last twenty years there have been widening discussions about reorganizing the world economy to alleviate the disruptive, accumulated inequalities and tensions attending the evolution of the capitalist world market.

The capitalist fundamental class process, interacting with markets and competition, contributed much to the formation of a truly world or global economy for the first time in human history. In addition to the growth already discussed, capitalist competition also provoked major technical innovations in metal manufacture, engines, shipping, and weaponry. These made possible the transportation, trade, and warfare that accompanied the foreign economic activities of industrial capitalist firms. Indeed rapidly rising surplus value appropriated by European industrial capitalists enabled their rising tax payments to European governments. In return they demanded and received military supports and protections for capitalists' growing overseas ventures.

In Marxian theory there is the most intimate connection between the capitalist fundamental class process and the histories of colonialism, imperialism, and the contemporary world economy. In elaborating that connection, Marxian theory produces insights into the contradictions and dynamics of the world economy that are different from the analyses constructed by all other theories.

4.6.2   Capitalism and Real Incomes

As capitalist expansions (chiefly from Europe) disrupted societies elsewhere, real incomes—actual goods and services consumed—dropped drastically for most of the people in those societies. Usually only a relatively few local appropriators of surplus labor and some subsumed classes found ways to accommodate capitalist expansion and thereby secure or even enhance their incomes. These included local feudal lords, some ancient classes, and some native small industrial capitalists among the fundamental classes. Local subsumed classes typically included merchants, landlords, moneylenders, and various levels of bureaucrats.

In the centers of capitalist industrialization, the movements in real incomes were uneven. In the early stages of capitalist enterprise in western Europe,

North America, and Japan, laborers usually drawn from rural areas to industrial centers experienced extreme privation. However, as generation after generation of productive and unproductive laborers worked in capitalist enterprises, their real incomes rose.

Yet, as suggested earlier, for Marxian economic theory, rising real incomes can be consistent with a simultaneously rising rate of exploitation. And this has important implications for the structure of modern capitalist economies, especially those in western Europe, North America, and Japan. Did those economies achieve relative social stability because they provided industrial capitalists with rising rates of exploitation and simultaneously provided workers with rising real incomes? How was this possible? Can it last? In its answers to these questions, Marxian theory explains how higher real incomes did indeed coexist with rising rates of exploitation.

Recall the division in Marxian theory between V and S in the $C + V + S = W$ equation for all industrial capitalist enterprises. V is the value of labor power, say, per day. It is the value of the goods and services that productive laborers require per day in order to be able and willing to keep on working for their capitalist employers. The latter pay their laborers a money sum of value—the wage—used by them to purchase commodities for their daily consumption. That sum, V, when subtracted from the total value added by the laborers per day, yields S, the daily surplus value appropriated by the industrial capitalist.

Suppose that for some time the following two dimensions of production do not change: (1) the value of labor power, V, and (2) the length of the working day during which productive laborers add value, $V + S$. It follows then that the surplus value, S, is also fixed as is the rate of exploitation, S/V. Now, finally, consider what might happen if competition among capitalists who produce the wage goods (food, clothing, housing, TV sets, etc.) drives down the per-unit values of those wage goods (see appendix B to this chapter). Workers could then buy more of such cheapened wage goods with their unchanged wages (value of labor power). Their "real wage" or standard of consumption would have risen, while their rate of exploitation by capitalist employers would have remained unchanged. *Real wages are one thing, but in Marxian theory exploitation is something else.*

It is a simple next step to see how a rising rate of exploitation can also coexist with rising real incomes. Suppose that a capitalist was able to cut productive workers' wages by 10 percent (lower V). Assuming that the length of the working day remains the same, those workers' value added would likewise remain the same each day. If the value they add remains the same but the value paid to them falls by 10 percent, then the surplus, S, appropriated by capitalists would rise. Moreover a higher S in relation to a lower V would mean that the rate of exploitation, S/V, had risen. Now, finally, add again the likelihood that competition among capitalists producing wage goods had driven down their per-unit values by, say, 15 percent. The workers who had 10 percent less value as their wages—and were thus more exploited than before—would still have a higher level of consumption because the values of the wage goods they purchase has fallen further, namely by 15 percent (see appendix D to this chapter).

From the standpoint of Marxian theory, this last situation has existed in the centers of capitalist enterprise for the last hundred years. The value of labor power fell faster than the length of the working day was shortened, so that the surplus portion of the day's labor rose relatively. The S/V ratio—exploitation—therefore also rose. Productive laborers delivered an ever-growing surplus to industrial capitalists, thereby enabling them to secure their conditions of existence and of rapid growth. At the same time the unit values of commodities purchased by workers fell even faster than the value of their labor power. This was partly the result of the capitalist competition we noted above. It was also partly the result of capitalist expansion to the rest of the world where new, cheaper sources of food and raw materials were colonized, exploited, and brought back home to permit cheaper commodities to be produced. *The last hundred years thus brought rising real incomes for most workers in the capitalist centers even as their exploitation intensified and workers' real incomes in the rest of the world declined.*

By these means, capitalist class relations were reproduced and extended where they had first arrived. Especially western Europe, North America, and Japan adjusted politically, culturally, and psychologically to a prosperity that coupled rising exploitation and rising real incomes. On the one hand, this yielded unprecedented wealth, power, and global predominance for the industrial capitalists and governments of these societies. On the other hand, these societies became dependent on being able to continue to combine rising real incomes with rising rates of exploitation. When threats arose to such societies' ability to enjoy rising real incomes and rising rates of exploitation, extreme reactions occurred.

Thus, when productive workers organized labor unions to demand changes in wages and working conditions that would have lowered the S/V ratio, their organizations were usually repressed politically, ideologically, and even physically. Socialist and communist organizations and revolutions—who usually made their anticapitalism explicit—suffered harsher repressions. When movements for political independence as a means to economic modernization in Asia, Africa, and Latin America threatened to challenge their colonial roles as providers of cheap inputs into capitalist commodity production in the capitalist centers, they too were suppressed.

The responses of nations in these capitalist centers to all such possible threats to the prosperity of their class structures contributed to local, national and international social tensions, disruptions and—twice in the twentieth century—the cataclysms of world war. These in turn generated new and formidable obstacles to the continuation of those societies' capitalist structures. Thus, the two world wars played major roles first in forming (1917 and thereafter) and then in expanding (1945 and thereafter) the communist group of nations who were critical of and opposed to capitalism. The world wars also destroyed vast numbers of workers as well as capital equipment and infrastructure in the warring capitalist center countries, weakening their capacity to hold on to their colonial empires. Meanwhile, the repression of independence movements in Asia, Africa, and Latin America before the 1960s and 1970s provoked the determination in many countries there to fight for independence and to improve their economic conditions if necessary at the expense of advanced capitalist economies.

The arresting irony in this class-focused history of capitalism is that the strivings of industrial capitalists to secure their conditions of existence undermined as much as they reproduced them. These are some of the specific internal contradictions of capitalism. Another set of capitalist contradictions, to which Marx devoted considerable attention in *Capital*, generate the periodic disruptive cycles or crises that result from capitalist competition. Marxian theory's treatment of these cycles demonstrates further insights such class analysis makes possible.

4.6.3   Cycles or Crises of Capitalist Economies

Marx was not the first observer to note capitalist economies' cyclical ups and downs, what economists call "recessions" and "recoveries" and most people call "booms" and "busts." However, Marxian theory offers a distinctive explanation for their occurrence. We can sketch the complex overdetermination of cycles, building upon preliminary notions first presented by Marx in *Capital* and further developed earlier in this chapter.

Cycles are periods of time in which capitalist economies undergo a phased shift from one set of conditions to a roughly opposite set. In the boom, prosperity, or upswing phase, the distinguishing economic phenomena include falling unemployment, rising quantities of output, capital accumulation, growing commodity sales, and rising incomes. In the bust, recessionary, or downswing phase, the distinguishing signs include rising layoffs, falling output, dis-accumulation, shrinking sales, and diminishing incomes. Over the history of capitalist economies both phases show varying durations and degrees of movement. Upswings can be larger and last longer than downswings (capitalists speak of such periods as long-run booms), or, alternatively, the opposite can occur (in which case the word "depression" is often heard). The cycles of capitalist economies have persisted despite the varied policies invented to eliminate them. They have provoked many economists to interpret and explain their recurrence.

Nor are capitalist cycles merely matters for economists' special interests. Urgent practical concerns motivate efforts at explanation. Economic downswings (rising unemployment, company bankruptcies, falling incomes, etc.) reduce tax revenues to governments who often respond by cutting public services. Competitors in economies not experiencing such downturns often gain crucial advantages. Unemployed workers can become angry and may eventually question the desirability of a capitalist system that subjects them to the privations of recurring unemployment. Unemployed workers sometimes emigrate and do not return even when the next upswing occurs. The personal damages suffered by unemployed workers, bankrupt entrepreneurs, and their families may have lasting and costly social effects long after the downturn has passed over into the next upturn. Economists and many others have therefore long searched for government policies that might minimize the social costs of capitalist cycles or, if possible, eliminate them altogether.

A capitalist downturn might trigger a social movement aimed not merely to hasten an upturn but also to radically alter the existing economic system, including its class structure. As suggested in previous chapters, the fears of capitalists and their allies during the depression of the 1930s focused on its social costs. The risk then was a possible movement toward criticizing and targeting capitalism, and such a movement did grow then in the United States and in other countries as well. Similarly the Great Recession—a popular name in the United States for the global crisis that began in 2007—raised a similar risk. Once again, unemployed workers, foreclosed former homeowners, bankrupt entrepreneurs, students unable to afford education, overstressed family budgets and households, and others feeling the impacts of economic crisis might develop preferences for different, noncapitalist economic systems.

If the victims of capitalist cycles believed that noncapitalist systems could be free from cycles and their social costs, they might organize themselves politically. Swelled in number at the bottom of a downturn, they might move radically to transform the economic class structure. The preferred transformations range from kinds of feudalism or fascism, on the political right, to kinds of socialism and communism, on the left.

How to prevent such transformations has motivated many neoclassical and Keynesian studies of cycles and their causes, consequences, and possible remedies. We noted earlier that an explicit goal of many Keynesian policy proposals was to lessen the duration and intensity of capitalist cycles (and partly also to counter Marxian analyses of and proposals for dealing with cycles). Marxists have studied cycles as well, but with different motivations. They demonstrated that cycles have proved historically to be intrinsic, unavoidable aspects of capitalism, a conclusion likewise reached theoretically in

Marxian economics. They also argued that overcoming cycles and their huge social costs required transition from the capitalism that repeatedly reproduced those cycles. In short, Marxian treatments of cycles form one part of the Marxian critique of capitalism and argument for socialism. Partly for that reason cycles are often referred to in Marxian literature as "crises" of capitalism.

Using the term "crisis" supports the Marxian notion that cycles are, or at least can be critical moments in the life of capitalist economies. Economic downturns may lead people to question capitalism and sometimes to consider radical critiques of its class structure. Some Marxists have argued that cyclical downturns worsen over time, eventuating in economic collapse. This became a theory of capitalism's inevitable collapse under the weight of its own internal economic contradictions.

The Marxian theory at work in this chapter interprets cycles differently. Whether and when a particular cyclical downswing might eventuate in a transition beyond the class structure of capitalism depends on all the class and nonclass processes of the society experiencing the downswing. Just as cycles are overdetermined as to their occurrence, duration, and intensity, so too are any possible transitions from cycles to social revolutions.

Cycles do not result from some essential cause or causes. The Marxian theory at work here does not reduce cycles to mere effects of one or another quality of capitalism. Nor does it reduce them—in the manner of the neoclassicists and Keynesians—to such factors as state economic interventions or behavioral conventions in the face of uncertainty. Rather, the task of Marxian analysis is to explore some of the myriad social processes that together overdetermine cycles with special emphasis on why and how capitalist class processes contribute to their recurring pattern. Marx began to work on that task in *Capital* and later Marxists took it further. Continuing their work, we sketch here the crisis argument we find persuasive in Marxian theory.

One mechanism that contributes to the generation of cycles is capitalist accumulation. As we noted earlier, industrial capitalists typically utilize a portion of their appropriated surplus value to secure their conditions of existence by accumulating capital. This means that they increase their purchases of physical means of production (C) and hire more labor power (V). Such capital accumulation encounters no problem so long as additional labor power is available to hire. However, such ready-to-be-employed reserves of labor power need not always exist. When demand for additional labor power outpaces supply, economic cycles may emerge.

Excess demand will normally drive up the market price of labor power (increase money wages). This tends to happen toward the end of periods when capitalists have been successfully appropriating surpluses, experiencing an economic upswing, and thus confident in accumulating capital. When reserves

of unemployed laborers ready and willing to be hired are exhausted, capitalists seeking to accumulate may be able to secure additional labor power only by hiring away productive laborers already employed by other capitalists. They do this by offering higher wages that other capitalists have to match or risk losing their employees; thus wages start a general rise.

Given the length of the working day (and thus the total value added by productive laborers), generally rising wages diminish the surpluses left for capitalist employers. They experience this as declining profits, and that means both declining resources and declining incentives to accumulate capital. Not all capitalists are equally hurt by rising wages; the greatest losses happen to those who rely most heavily on labor (vs. machines) in production. But many capitalists will likely feel constrained to respond to reduced profits from rising wages by reducing their accumulation of capital and reducing some of their production activities. They will close operations, lay off workers, and cut back orders to their suppliers of equipment and raw materials. Laid-off workers will in turn cut back purchases since their wages have disappeared. Their suppliers will lay off workers since they have lost sales. Thus the growing ranks of unemployed reduce their purchases alongside the reduced purchases of inputs by employers. The result will in effect be a downward economic spiral characterized by falling incomes, employment levels, output, sales, and accumulation.

The key internal contradiction of capitalism here is this: a period of successful surplus production and appropriation as well as capital accumulation sets in motion its own opposite, an economic downswing of classic dimensions. Capitalist accumulation negates itself. The first half of the capitalist cycle is this self-transformation of economic upswing into economic downswing. Moreover the same mechanisms that transform an upswing into a downswing generate the reverse movement and thus the second half of the cycle.

When a downswing deepens unemployment and constricts production enough, desperate unemployed workers begin to accept lower wages, and bankrupt firms begin to offer their equipment and supplies at cheaper prices. As wages and physical input prices keep falling, eventually some capitalists begin to anticipate profits if they resume production and if other capitalists do likewise. So they begin to rehire and buy means of production and raw materials. This stimulates demand for the output of other capitalists setting off a spiral upward of mutually reinforcing capitalist activities. An upswing of rising surplus production and appropriation and capital accumulation recommences. The class structure of capitalist production and its interaction with the markets for its inputs and outputs thus generates a cyclical pattern of activity.

This Marxian explanation that connects cycles to capitalism's contradictions does not imply that cycles result necessarily from accumulation. Whether accumulation has such results depends on everything else that is occurring simultaneously—that is, on all the conditions of the existence of a particular phase of accumulation. For example, if accumulation began to outrun available national supplies of labor power, rising wages might not occur for years if rising immigration were to sustain the accumulation. Alternatively, changes in family life might propel formerly home-bound wives and children out to seek jobs in growing numbers that would sustain accumulation without raising wages. Or reduced pension benefits might propel retired persons to return to the job market. A combination of such developments might make possible an indefinitely extended period of accumulation without labor shortages or rising wages.

Another possibility is that even if wages were driven up, capitalists might respond not by cutting back production or accumulation but rather by automating their production lines. If labor-saving machines were available, capitalists might buy them to reduce the impact of higher wages. Some of the workers laid off by automation might find work in the factories producing those machines. In this case accumulation might lead to rising wages and squeezed profits, but these would not last long nor provoke a serious cycle, since automation might limit the unemployment and economic downturn that might otherwise have occurred.

However, accumulation can generate a cycle in which the cyclical downswing is deeply disruptive of the capitalist society in question. In such a case accumulation can set in motion dis-accumulation (when capitalists do not even fully replace the C and V used up in production) and thereby reduce the scale of production. Entire national economies may then contract, perhaps for several quarter-years, as in the Great Recession that began in 2007, or for many years, as in the depression of the 1930s. In such an environment, movements for radical social change could grow and perhaps win power. The political turbulence of the 1930s across western Europe and North America offers examples of this possibility. Again, the political upheavals across the world erupting in recent years often have roots in the global capitalist crisis that began in 2007.

When they speak of cycles as crises, Marxists mean that downswings may threaten capitalism. Whether or not they do depends in part on how the people who suffer their consequences (unemployment, business bankruptcies, home foreclosures, reduced job and social benefits, state austerity regimes, etc.) understand the cycles and their consequences. If they don't see cycles as linked closely to the capitalist class structure of production, then they will not likely see changing that class structure as a way to overcome cycles. They will not then likely join political movements aimed at transitions beyond capitalism.

This leads us back to the neoclassical and Keynesian economic theories that have very different analyses of and solutions for economic downturns and cycles. Neither of them connects these economic "problems" to the class structure of capitalist production as we have argued Marxian theory does. Neoclassical economics argues for letting the capitalist market self-correct as the best solution for whatever imbalances and downturns emerge from exogenous shocks to the system or from unwarranted state or other institutions' interferences in the workings of private property and free markets. Keynesian theory links crises to market imperfections and human decisions in the face of those imperfections and ineradicable uncertainties about the future. Hence it focuses on state economic interventions such as monetary and fiscal policies that can "solve" the cycle problems of an otherwise desirable capitalist system. State interventions, if properly advised and executed, can thereby offset the impacts of market imperfections and uncertainties. Keynesian theory, like its neoclassical counterpart, sees no need to question, let alone transition beyond the capitalist class structure of production since those theories do not link that structure to cycles as Marxian theory does.

Thus Marxian economic theory shares neither the neoclassical confidence in capitalism's self-healing properties nor the Keynesian confidence in state intervention. It is not particularly interested in the endless debate across most capitalist societies between those two theories and their proponents' respective solutions for cycles. In the Marxian view, the huge social costs of the recurring cycles undermine the neoclassical approach, while the failure of Keynesian interventions to prevent the cycles' recurrence undermine the Keynesian approach. After the Great Depression of the 1930s, cycles seemed, for a while, to have been relatively less severe (except for the downturn of the mid-1970s). The Marxian perspective on cycles lost adherents. However, in the wake of the major global capitalist crisis that began in 2007, interest in the Marxian analyses and solutions was renewed.

4.6.4   Cycles and Policy "Solutions"

A final brief discussion of cycles needs to question, from a Marxist standpoint, the whole idea of a policy that will solve crises. Each crisis is the overdetermined result of an infinity of social processes that all interact to cause it and all its particular qualities. Likewise the overcoming of crises depends on that same infinity of social processes having changed in such a way as to make a particular downturn become an upturn. What a particular society chooses as a policy or set of policies to respond to a crisis can only ever be a tiny subset of the overdeterminants that either will or will not together bring an economic downturn to an end. To imagine that economics can or should seek to determine the right, key, or best policy is to engage in a determinist theoretical project. If one assumes that there are key causes of economic cycles, then it makes sense to find the policies that will change those key causes and thereby reverse a downturn. If one does not assume that there are key causes, say because one assumes overdetermination instead, then no policy focused on one or a few causes is ever sufficient to "solve" the cyclical problem.

A Marxian overdeterminist perspective sees the policies advocated and debated by alternative theoretical schools as attempts to use the real social costs and problems of capitalism's recurring cycles to advance the debaters' alternative theories and social agendas. Each theory's policy prescriptions cannot be solutions—since a small number of policy tools are always inade-, quate to such a task from the overdeterminist perspective. Rather, the respective policies that each theory proposes are means to draw the attention of those concerned about cycles to what each theoretical school already believes are the key dimensions of contemporary economies that everyone ought to focus upon.

The importance of this overdeterminist perspective in Marxian economics can be further demonstrated by exploring Marxian theory's recognition of a vast multiplicity of possible causes of capitalist cycles beyond the accumulation cause discussed above. For example, Marx originally (and famously) pointed also to competition among capitalists that might well foster technological improvements that required capitalists to purchase ever more expensive pieces of machinery. The constant capital (C) portion of total capital would rise in relation to both V and S. As a result the ratio of S to ($C + V$)—one measure of capitalists' rate of profit—would fall. Capitalists confronting such falling profit rates might then hold back production, thereby setting in motion the cyclical pattern discussed earlier (for further discussion, along with an illustrative numerical example, see part 2 of appendix C).

Still another potential cyclical mechanism, often mentioned by Marx, is the problem he called "realization." Industrial capitalists must find buyers for the commodities produced by their productive laborers. Only then will they realize, in money form, the surplus value appropriated from those workers. This money enables them to at least replace used-up raw materials, equipment, and labor power and thereby maintain the production process. Should any social development prevent capitalists from finding the necessary buyers, this too might set off production cutbacks, layoffs, and the cyclical downswing. Beyond climate, political upheavals, and other factors that might prevent capitalists from realizing their surplus value, Marxists also seek to show how such a crisis mechanism might also emerge out of the internal contradictions of the capitalist system.

In this case a realization problem can be shown to be an ever-present possibility in capitalism. The reason for this is a contradiction within the relation between industrial capitalists and their employees. To survive competitively, each capitalist strives to keep expenditures on wages and salaries as low as possible. Yet capitalists collectively rely heavily on the same employees to purchase, out of their incomes, the consumer commodities that capitalists sell in the market. The more successfully they restrict their employees' incomes, the more likely they are to face a realization problem when it comes time to sell the commodities those employees produce. If they cannot sell them, they may set in motion the cyclical pattern again. Then again, if foreign buyers can be found to offset constricted domestic demand due to lower wages and salaries, realization problems may be postponed for a long time. Or perhaps a government spending program might intervene to absorb otherwise unsold commodities, and so on.

Cycles can thus emerge out of any of the myriad particular contradictions of the capitalist class structure and also out of an infinity of possible combinations of the (political, natural, cultural and economics) conditions of existence of that class structure. Capitalism is hardly the smoothly functioning, unambiguous engine of growth and prosperity its enthusiasts keep suggesting—at least not in and for the Marxian theoretical perspective developed in this chapter.

Other social processes may alter or offset a particular set of capitalist contradictions so that the potential for a cyclical downswing does not become actual. Likewise a downswing can under certain historical circumstances function as the prelude to long and intense cyclical upswings. However, Marxian theory's class analysis of capitalism by means of its value equations explains why cycles tend to recur periodically, although each cycle has its unique, overdetermined dimensions. Various internal contradictions (of which a few examples were presented above) tend toward cyclical movement. While, that movement may be delayed or modified in this or that specific historical instance, Marxian theory and the empirical record support the notion that capitalism's structure engenders cycles. The endless (and unresolved) debates between neoclassical and Keynesian economists over explaining and managing the recurring cycles support that notion as well.

Marxian theory's distinctive interpretation of cycles does not seek a "solution" in the manner of neoclassical and Keynesian theories. Rather, Marxian theory's treatment of crisis is part of the theory's larger project of a critique of capitalism. Thus Marxian theory aims to show how capitalism is vulnerable to a literally endless list of possible crisis causes stemming from all its various conditions of existence. More particularly, its class structure interacts with markets to contribute systematically to recurring, periodic crises/cycles. Marxian theory's approach to crisis is part of its project of criticizing capitalism in favor of a transition to a different class structure of production as discussed earlier in this chapter. In contrast, neoclassical and Keynesian theories approach crises as part of projects celebrating capitalism and precluding the sorts of class changes favored by Marxism.

It is worth concluding this discussion of crises by noting that a transition of the sort Marxists seek would remove the capitalist class contributors to the system's cycles. It would hardly exempt a postcapitalist class structure from instabilities unique to its different, noncapitalist class structure. But a noncapitalist class structure would generate different patterns of instability and likewise organize different social responses to and programs for such instability. And presumably theorists within such a postcapitalist society and economy would commence debating the causes and appropriate responses to its instabilities. Their debates too would likely emerge from and reinforce their broader attitudes toward their society.

4.7   Capitalist Subsumed Classes

To this point, our discussion has emphasized mainly the capitalist fundamental class process. Our major protagonists have been productive laborers and industrial capitalists, the performers and appropriators of surplus value respectively. However, as we have noted, a capitalist class structure includes both the subsumed class process (distributing appropriated surplus value) and the fundamental class process (producing and appropriating the surplus value). The fundamental classes include the producers and the appropriators of the surplus value. The subsumed classes include the distributors and the recipients of distributed portions of the already appropriated surplus. We can show the subtlety and complexity of Marxian economics by examining some representative examples of capitalist subsumed classes and how they interact with capitalist fundamental classes to shape the function and dynamic of capitalist economic systems.

4.7.1   Moneylenders and Subsumed Classes

The competitive struggles among industrial capitalists often compel them to borrow from moneylenders for various purposes. For example, one industrial capitalist needs a loan to purchase some inputs that are temporarily cheaper than usual, lest a competitor do so. Another industrial capitalist needs a loan to install an expensive new technology before a competitor does. Yet another borrows because temporary delays in selling commodity outputs interrupt cash flow needed to maintain production (i.e., to pay employees or raw material suppliers, who might then orient their business elsewhere). A loan to cover the time in which buyers are found will allow workers and suppliers to be paid.

In each case borrowing money enhances the industrial capitalist's competitive survival, secures conditions of existence. From the standpoint of the moneylender, the ultimate use of the loan is of little or no concern. The lender's goal is to recover not only the money loaned but also a fee for lending: interest. Interest is the moneylender's income. The industrial capitalist repays the loan plus the interest. The industrial capitalist distributes a portion of appropriated surplus value as that interest payment to the moneylender. As a recipient of a distributed share of surplus value, the moneylender occupies a capitalist subsumed class position.

We can sketch the economic relationships involved here by slightly expanding our original value equation for capitalist commodity production. Thus we would rewrite our $C + V + S = W$ equation as

$$C + V + S_1 + S_r = W.$$

In this equation S_1 is the portion of appropriated surplus distributed to moneylenders as interest payments while S_r is the rest of the appropriated surplus value.

The relationship between industrial capitalist and moneylender includes, among the many other processes involved in any relationship among persons, two processes of special concern here. First, there is the nonclass process of borrowing and lending. It is a nonclass process because it is precisely (and nothing more than) the act of temporarily passing funds from one person to another. Second, there is the subsumed class process of distributing a portion of appropriated surplus value as the interest payment accompanying the return of the borrowed funds. The S_1 term in the equation locates the subsumed class process and the two subsumed class positions it defines: distributor of appropriated surplus value (the industrial capitalist) and its recipient (the moneylender).

For the moneylender S_1 is the interest income earned from lending, the subsumed class payment received from the industrial capitalist. We can represent the transaction from the moneylender's perspective as

$$M \rightarrow M + S_1.$$

The moneylender is another kind of capitalist, since the lending process accomplishes the self-expansion of the lender's money. As noted earlier, the moneylender is not an industrial capitalist because the self-expansion of value is not accomplished by the direct appropriation of surplus value from any productive laborers. For that reason we call such moneylenders "nonproductive capitalists."

The moneylending process can occur in various modern institutional settings. Banks, insurance companies, industrial corporations, individuals, governments, and others can and do lend money. Moneylenders do not lend money only to industrial capitalists. Money lent to persons other than industrial capitalists generate interest payments that are not distributions of appropriated surplus value. Only industrial capitalists appropriate surplus value in capitalist class structures, so only they can distribute it in subsumed class processes. Only when loans go to industrial capitalists does the relationship between lender and borrower include the subsumed class process as well as the moneylending process. Marxian theory is concerned with distinguishing lending that does from lending that does not directly engage class processes, since those class processes are its chief object and focus.

Loans to persons other than industrial capitalists typically carry interest charges. For example, one worker can lend money at interest to another worker. The interest payment involved is not a subsumed class payment, since the interest-paying worker does not appropriate surplus value. The interest payment is a nonclass payment precisely because no distribution of appropriated surplus is involved.

A capitalist economy's supply of and demand for loans as well as money-lenders' evaluations of the relative risks of lending to different borrowers will determine interest rates. One overdeterminant of interest rates in a capitalist society is the class structure. That is, the specific conditions of the production, appropriation, and distribution of surplus value will influence interest rates, and vice versa. The Marxian approach to analyzing interest rates will stress (1) their overdetermination by class as well as nonclass processes and (2) how interest rates participate in overdetermining class processes. That is, Marxian theory presents a class analysis of interest rates.

4.7.2 Managers and Subsumed Classes

Just as industrial capitalists often depend on the nonclass process of lending to secure some conditions of their existence as appropriators of surplus value, they likewise depend on many other nonclass processes. One of these is the process of managing enterprises involving planning, organizing, and directing their business activity. Managers write histories of the corporation explaining why some product lines were successful and why some were not, devise various competitive strategies, help design and invent new commodities, control certain behaviors of subordinate managers, and supervise the productive laborers they employ. For one example, consider more fully their supervisory work.

Management is required to make sure that purchased labor power is fully devoted to producing commodity outputs. After industrial capitalists purchase their labor power from productive laborers, they set them to work with purchased tools, equipment, and raw materials. While working, the laborers may produce more or fewer commodities. Having sold their labor power for a wage payment, they may or may not work hard to produce commodities for the industrial capitalists to sell.

If they do, well and good: industrial capitalist can then distribute surplus value elsewhere to survive competitively. However, suppose that workers cannot or do not work hard. This worries the industrial capitalist, who must fear the competition from industrial capitalists who do have hard-working laborers and so obtain more output per worker from them. As discussed previously and also in appendix C of this chapter, lowered labor productivity can threaten the continued operation of the enterprise. Managers may solve the problem by supervising laborers to ensure their maximum effort. The managing process is then a condition of existence of surplus labor appropriation. To secure that management process, the industrial capitalist has to distribute a portion of the appropriated surplus value to cover the wages or salaries of managerial personnel and purchase the means for them to perform management. Managers sell their labor power to industrial capitalists and do work, but they produce no commodity sold by their employer. They perform no surplus labor nor generate any surplus value. They are unproductive laborers receiving subsumed class distributions.

Of course, were the management process accomplished without requiring any distribution of appropriated surplus, then no subsumed class process would be involved. For example, if workers' beliefs committed them to intense labor for employers without any supervision, then no subsumed class payments would be required for managers. Indeed, if managers could instill in workers those beliefs, then industrial capitalists would then have more appropriated surplus value left to distribute to secure other conditions of existence. One example of this might be workers' self-management programs.

Finally, we can show how the Marxian theorization of the subsumed class of managers parallels that of the subsumed class of moneylenders. We can rewrite an expanded value equation to include a subsumed class distribution to managers for their salaries plus means of managing:

$$C + V + S_1 + S_2 + S_r = W.$$

The surplus distribution, S_2, is the subsumed class distribution to managers from the industrial capitalists who employ them.

The process of managing people, including workers, need not and often does not occur together with the capitalist subsumed class process. The two processes occur together only when the people being managed are productive laborers and when management costs are defrayed out of surplus value distributed by an industrial capitalist appropriator. For example, if a worker hires a group of fellow-workers on a Sunday to paint the worker's home, and if a manager of those workers is hired as well, no subsumed class process is involved. The salary paid to this manager cannot come from surplus, since the worker doing the hiring does not appropriate any surplus. No subsumed class process is involved, although the managing process certainly is.

4.7.3   Merchants and Subsumed Classes

Another potential competitive problem may and often does require industrial capitalists to solve it by distributing a portion of appropriated surplus. This problem is the time it takes industrial capitalists to find buyers for produced capitalist commodities. The faster industrial capitalists can exchange finished commodities for money, the sooner that money can in turn be exchanged for labor power and raw materials. The faster an industrial capitalist literally turns over his/her capital from money to commodities and back to money, the more surplus value that industrial capitalist appropriates per year. Turnover time can be as crucial to the outcome of competition among industrial capitalists as are technical efficiency, access to credit, and quality management.

For example, consider two industrial capitalists starting with equal initial capitals, technologies, and rates of exploitation. The only difference between them is turnover time. Thus each capitalist takes, say, one month to go from the purchase of labor power and commodity inputs to acquiring finished commodity outputs ready for sale. However, one capitalist takes one month from end of production to sale of commodities, while the other takes two months.

The first capitalist will sell commodities produced in January by the end of February. The revenues realized from that sale can then be spent on labor power and commodity inputs to renew the production cycle again in March. The next sale will occur at the end of April, and so on. The second capitalist will not sell January output until the end of March. Thus this capitalist's production cycle can recommence only in April, and the products of that cycle can be sold only by the end of June. Over a year's time the first capitalist will turn over capital six times, while the second will turn it over only four times. The first capitalist's capital will produce and realize surplus value six times per year, while the second capitalist's capital will realize surplus value only four times. Thus, despite their identical technologies and rates of exploitation, the first capitalist will have more surplus to distribute by year's end than the second, and may thereby secure the conditions of his or her existence more successfully than the second.

It thus becomes quite literally a condition of the second industrial capitalist's survival to secure reduced turnover time. Enter the merchant. The merchant has a stock of money, rather like a moneylender. However, unlike moneylenders, merchants do not make loans. They use stocks of money to buy commodities and thereafter to sell them. Merchants engage in the nonclass economic process of exchanging commodities and money. The exchange process is different from the class processes of producing, appropriating, or distributing surplus value. However, suppose that our second industrial capitalist, worried about competitive survival, offers a merchant a deal. The merchant agrees to buy the industrial capitalist's commodity outputs as fast as they emerge from the production line. In return the second capitalist pays the merchant a fee. This deal will greatly speed up the second industrial capitalist's turnover time, perhaps thereby even outcompeting the first capitalist. The merchant's performance of a nonclass process—timely commodity exchange—secures a condition of the existence of the second industrial capitalist's continued appropriation of surplus value.

Merchants will not agree to this proposed deal unless they make money from doing so. Marx calls them merchant capitalists precisely because their merchanting activities (buying in order to resell) yield them more value at the end of their activity than they began with. If they buy an industrial capitalist's commodity outputs at their values and then resell them at their values, they would obtain no gain from these transactions, no merchant income. Therefore, to secure a merchant's performance of timely commodity exchange, an industrial capitalist must distribute to the merchants a fee (of mutually agreed size) for doing so. If the industrial capitalist distributes a portion of appropriated surplus value to a merchant as such a fee, then we can speak of commodity exchange and the subsumed class process occurring together. Such merchants would thus constitute another capitalist subsumed class. We may then add this subsumed class process, the fee to merchants, as S_3 in our expanded enterprise equation:

$$C + V + S_1 + S_2 + S_3 + S_r = W.$$

In practice, industrial capitalists and subsumed merchants *net* the two opposite flows of money: (1) payment by merchant to industrial capitalist for purchase of commodity outputs (2) payment by industrial capitalist of fee to merchant for timely purchase of outputs. The industrial capitalist does not both sell the merchant commodities at full value and then send merchant a check for the fee. Instead, industrial capitalists typically subtract the fee to the merchant from what they charge the merchant for the commodity outputs they sell. Only one combined transaction occurs. The merchant acquires the industrial capitalist's commodities *at a discount from their value*, a merchant's discount equal to the agreed fee. When the merchant then sells those commodities at their values, the merchant's income is precisely the difference between the merchant capital expended to buy the commodities and the larger revenue the merchant receives when those commodities are resold.

From the perspective of the merchant, the transaction is

$$M \rightarrow C \rightarrow M + \Delta M.$$

Here ΔM represents the difference between what the merchant paid for the commodities and the revenues received from their sale. Marxian theory offers a distinctive interpretation of the economics of merchants by focusing on the relation of merchants to the production, appropriation, and distribution of surplus value. In our example ΔM is a subsumed class payment by an industrial capitalist to secure the condition of existence known as minimization of turnover time: $\Delta M = S_3$.

Merchants are thus another kind of capitalist, although different from both industrial and moneylending capitalists. Merchants are capitalists because their buying and selling typically accomplishes the self-expansion of the value they deploy (self-expanding value is the definition of capital). However, they are unlike industrial capitalists because they neither appropriate surplus value nor produce commodities. They expand their capital through buying and selling, not through exploitation in production. Merchant capitalists are unlike moneylending capitalists because their self-expansion does not involve the nonclass process of lending; it rather involves the nonclass process of commodity exchange.

Merchant capitalists invest their capital in buying commodities to be resold for more than they cost; their goal is to increase their capital by ΔM. Moneylending capitalists invest their capital in making loans; their goal is to increase their capital by interest payments. Industrial capitalists invest their capital in producing commodities; their goal is to increase their capital by appropriating surplus labor as surplus value, S. Presumably there is some mobility of capital between these different kinds of investment. An industrial capitalist who could obtain greater expansion of his or her capital in merchanting or moneylending might shift out of industrial capitalist investment into one of those processes, and vice versa. Marxian theory thus expects a tendency toward converging rates of return on capital among all three kinds of investment, unless counteracting tendencies intervene.

As noted above in the cases of the nonclass processes of moneylending and managing, the nonclass process of merchanting may but need not occur together with the subsumed class process. Whenever a merchant buys commodities from someone who does not appropriate a surplus during their production, no subsumed class distribution of surplus occurs together with the commodity exchange process. For example, if a manager sells a used car to a merchant who resells it for more, the merchant capitalist has indeed expanded his or her capital. However, the source of the expansion, ΔM in the merchant equation above, is *not* then surplus value appropriated by such a manager. Managers do not appropriate surplus value; only industrial capitalists do that.

Marxian theory, as a class analytical project, seeks to explore the connections and interactions between class and nonclass processes. It seeks to clarify when and how class processes shape and are shaped by such nonclass processes as moneylending, managing, and commodity exchange. Neoclassical and Keynesian economics also treat lending, managing and commodity exchange, but they do not explore their interactions with class processes.

4.7.4   Other Capitalist Subsumed Classes

Moneylending, managing, and merchanting are only three of the many kinds of nonclass processes that may or may not occur together with the capitalist subsumed class process. In other nonclass processes performers also receive distributed shares of surplus value from industrial capitalist appropriators. A brief discussion of some other nonclass processes will further clarify the notion of subsumed classes, illustrating how Marxian theory extends to encompass ever more specific features of capitalist economies.

Landowners may occupy subsumed class positions. They grant access to portions of the earth's surface that they own to industrial capitalists. Seeking to appropriate surplus value, the latter must obtain access to some land for that appropriation to occur. Industrial capitalists secure this particular condition of existence by distributing a share of appropriated surplus value to the landowners. For historical reasons, payments for access to privately owned land are called rents. When rent is paid by a surplus appropriator to secure a condition of existence for the production of that surplus, it is a subsumed class distribution.

Other kinds of rent payments do not occur together with the subsumed class process; they are thus not subsumed class payments. For example, providing access to privately owned land to anyone who is not a surplus appropriator (a laborer, a manager, etc.) will typically fetch a rent payment in return. However, that rent is clearly not a subsumed class payment since it is not a distributed share of surplus appropriated by the rent-payer.

Rent payments may disappear. For example, if private property in land were abolished in a capitalist society and if instead the government allocated land to capitalist producers according to some ethical or political rules, no rental payments would occur. In this case access to the earth's surface—which remains, of course, a condition of existence of the capitalist fundamental class process—would not require any distribution of surplus value. Hence, in this case, the nonclass process of providing access to the earth's surface would occur without being combined either with the rent payment process or the capitalist subsumed class process.

In most capitalist societies the state provides certain conditions of existence for industrial capitalists and typically receives taxes in return; those taxes are subsumed class payments. For example, high-tech industrial capitalists may require highly skilled productive laborers. Those skills constitute conditions of existence for the appropriation of surplus value in those high-tech enterprises. The state may build and operate schools that teach those skills. The state thereby performs a nonclass process, teaching, that secures a condition of existence for industrial capitalists. If the state obtains in return a distributed share of the surplus appropriated by industrial capitalists as their tax payments, then the state officials who receive tax payments would occupy a subsumed class position. In this example, the nonclass process of public school teaching occurs together in society with the subsumed class process. Once again, tax payments and subsumed class payments need not occur together. Taxes paid by anyone other than surplus appropriators are not subsumed class payments, since they are not distributed portions of appropriated surplus value. The Internal Revenue Service of the United States differentiates corporate from individual income taxes; a rough parallel to the difference between taxes that are, and those that are not, subsumed class payments.

A state might alternatively provide industrial capitalists with public schools without demanding or receiving any tax payments from them. This could be accomplished if surplus appropriators were exempted from paying taxes. Then no subsumed class payment would be required from them to secure the public school teaching of skills. Marxian theory expects industrial capitalists to seek to shift the burden of taxation onto others while also seeking to secure the state's provision of their conditions of existence. It would also expect those others to resist, especially if they became aware, via Marxian theory, of how capitalist class structures influence the social distribution of tax burdens.

The military forces organized, maintained and deployed by a state—another nonclass process—may protect the existing class structure from its opponents (foreign and/or domestic). Security is another condition of existence of industrial capitalists. Its costs of providing security may lead the state to tax industrial capitalists. Then the state's provision of military security would occur together with the capitalist subsumed class process. Alternatively, the taxes that pay for the military might fall entirely upon non–surplus-appropriating individuals and thus, to that extent, make capitalist subsumed class tax payments unnecessary.

Owners of industrial enterprises (as differentiated from corporate boards of directors: see below) occupy subsumed class positions. Share-holders legally own an incorporated enterprise's assets: its buildings, tools, equipment, and raw materials, or, in general, its means of production. They grant access to these assets to the enterprise's industrial capitalists—typically its board of directors—in return for the power to select who will sit on an enterprise's board of directors and sometimes also in return for regular payments. For historical reasons, such payments are called dividends. They represent subsumed class distributions of the enterprise's appropriated surplus value undertaken to secure the enterprise's access to means of production. Under some conditions distributed dividends can be reduced or even not paid at all and yet industrial capitalists can nonetheless secure access to the means of production they need.

Tax laws may exist that apply lower rates on owners' realized capital gains on shares of stock they sell than on dividends they receive. Owners might well then prefer industrial capitalists to redirect surplus from the payment of dividends to them and instead expand capital accumulation, grow the enterprise, increase its productivity and its profits, and thereby push up its share price. This higher share price enables the owners not only to enjoy expanded wealth, but also to realize capital gains if and when they decide to sell some or all such shares. Under the assumed tax laws, their realized gain is taxed at a lower (capital gain) rate than dividends would have been taxed. Hence owners may well prefer distribution of surplus to foster growing profits rather than dividends. Many capitalist corporations today, large and small, pay no dividends to their shareholders.

Typically corporate boards reward their managers with stock options in addition to or as a partial substitute for salaries (again, because the former are taxed at lower rates than the latter). As a partial substitute for salary payments, stock options allow these boards to free up portions of the surplus no longer needed for salaries to instead enable other subsumed class distributions. Stock options also can provide incentives to managers to help secure their various nonclass processes as well as continued loyalty to the corporation while getting paid the same or even lower salaries.

What merits special attention here is the difference between those who own the means of production and those who appropriate surplus. These different positions are too often conflated or confused within the Marxian tradition. Granting access to privately owned means of production and appropriating surplus are different processes, although connected to one another in the way we have described. Too often socialists have claimed that by replacing private with collective ownership of the means of production they either will have eliminated class exploitation itself or placed the society on an inevitable journey to its elimination. The first argument conflates the two positions and the second falls into determinist reasoning.

Specifying distinct processes in the way we have argues against conflating the two; affirming overdetermination as a causal logic rejects determinist logic. No doubt a change in who owns the means of production can radically alter capitalist society. Often a huge proportion of a capitalist society's means of production is owned by a relatively small segment of its population. That concentration can enable that segment to reap economic gain as well as wield political power over the many. Moreover laws and legal maneuvers often allow such concentrations of wealth (and income and power) to continue across generations. Changing all of this, say, by equalizing the distribution of property across the population or by replacing private with collective ownership of the means of production, can be revolutionary both economically and politically. However, a change in *who* owns what is *not* the same as *nor* does it necessarily correspond to a change in how the surplus is organized (produced, appropriated, and distributed). For example, even if the means of production were changed from privately to collectively owned, the organization of production might nonetheless entail productive laborers producing surpluses appropriated and distributed by a different group of people. In that case collectivized property could coexist with an exploitative (and perhaps a capitalist) class structure. We will explore this important point again in chapter 6 when discussing the history of the former USSR. For now, the lesson is not to confuse or conflate a change in a nonclass (political) process such as ownership with a change in a class process.

Monopoly is still another nonclass process that can occur together with the capitalist subsumed class process. Monopoly entails a seller's control of buyers' access to the market for a commodity. Monopoly control requires that alternative markets or other sources of the commodity be unavailable to buyers. The monopolist's control of access to a market enables the demand for a fee if buyers seek access to that market. Note the parallel between monopoly and private property in land, between the rental fee and the monopoly fee.

Consider, for example, an industrial capitalist who occupies a monopoly position as the seller of the commodity produced in his enterprise: a unique kind of computer game. If copyright laws permit no other firm to copy and sell the same kind of game, the industrial capitalist producer has a monopoly. The producer can charge a fee to any buyer who wishes to enter the market for that kind of game: a monopoly fee in addition to the value of the commodity. In effect the monopolist-producer combines both the value and the monopoly fee to gain a total sale price for the commodity that is higher than its value.

From the standpoint of the game-producing industrial capitalist, the surplus appropriated from hired productive laborers is supplemented by the charge to the firm's customers for access to the monopolized market. The monopoly revenue over and above the commodity's value accrues to that industrial capitalist no matter who buys the game: laborers, other industrial capitalists, merchant capitalists, and so on. Of course, the monopoly revenue will only accrue so long as buyers demand the game and lack alternative sources for buying it.

From the standpoint of Marxian class analysis, we look more closely at who pays the monopoly fee for access to the market for that computer game. Suppose that one buyer is an industrial capitalist who purchases the game to make it part of the services provided to patrons of the hotel operated by that industrial capitalist. The game is then an input (C in the usual $C + V + S = W$ equation for capitalist commodity production) into the industrial capitalist's production and sale of hotel services. The industrial capitalist pays for the game not only its value but in addition the monopoly fee. That fee is paid out of the hotel capitalist's appropriated surplus. It is a subsumed class payment because access to the market for that game is a condition of that hotel's continued ability to appropriate surplus value from its productive employees. In this case, because the nonclass process of controlling access occurs together with the capitalist subsumed class process, the monopolists exercising that control constitute a capitalist subsumed class. Likewise, when those monopolists sell games to buyers who are not industrial capitalists, their monopoly revenues are not subsumed class payments, and such monopolists do not then constitute a capitalist subsumed class.

In all of the examples above, the subsumed class process differs from nonclass processes such as moneylending, managing, merchanting, landowning, teaching, owning, and monopolizing. Only the processes of surplus labor appropriation and distribution refer to class, while "nonclass," by definition, encompasses all of the other processes of social life. Marxian theory inquires whether, when, and how these nonclass processes provide conditions of existence for the capitalist fundamental class process, for exploitation. It inquires further whether industrial capitalists distribute portions of the surplus value they appropriate to secure these nonclass processes. One key goal of Marxian analysis is to examine and assess how well a capitalist class structure is securing its various conditions of existence (how sufficient is its appropriated surplus, how effectively distributed, etc.). Another is to identify which of its conditions of existence may be in jeopardy and how that may affect the reproduction of the class structure.

4.8 Class Positions and Individuals' Incomes

In Marxian theory, with its concern to show how class processes matter in modern societies, considerable attention is directed to individuals' incomes. Neoclassical theory is mostly interested in the connection between individual income and the marginal productivity of the resources (labor and/or capital) that each individual contributes to production and the decisions of that individual to supply labor and/or capital. Keynesian theory is mostly interested in how individuals divide their incomes between consumption and saving and the impacts of that division on employment and income. By contrast, the aim of Marxian theory is to show the role of class in overdetermining the distribution of incomes among individuals in any society, to explore the interrelation between class processes and income distributions.

4.8.1 Class Processes and the Distribution of Income

In terms of Marxian class analysis, an individual in a capitalist society can obtain income in three ways. By "income" we mean a flow of values that can be exchanged for commodities. First, a person may obtain income by appropriating surplus value in the capitalist fundamental class process. Such a person would be an industrial capitalist. Second, a person may occupy a subsumed class position receiving a distributed share of appropriated surplus value. Moneylenders (bankers), managers hired by industrial capitalists, landlords, monopolists, and merchants, and owners exemplify recipients of subsumed class payments. Third, a person may obtain income by participating in nonclass processes that generate inflows of value. For example, one laborer sells an inherited antique watch to another laborer. This is an income-generating, nonclass process of commodity exchange. No fundamental class process is involved; no surplus value is produced or appropriated by either individual in the exchange of antique watch for money. Nor is any subsumed class process involved, since neither laborer appropriates any surplus nor therefore can either distribute any. Selling the antique watch is simply a nonclass process that generates income without either the fundamental or the subsumed class process occurring together with it.

Other examples of nonclass income include receipts of gifts. One person gives another a gift. The recipient thereby obtains income, but clearly the gifting process is neither a fundamental nor a subsumed class process. It is an income-generating, nonclass process of considerable importance in many societies. Another noteworthy nonclass income arises from realizing capital gains on the sale of shares of stocks or bonds. Neither class process occurs in this buying and selling of assets. Stealing is another example. Indeed we have already touched upon other nonclass, income-generating processes in our discussion of laborers who sell labor power to one another, merchants who buy from persons other than industrial capitalists, landlords who grant access to land to persons other than industrial capitalists, and so on. Such persons obtain their inflows of value by engaging in income-generating, nonclass processes exclusively.

Marxian theory divides incomes into fundamental, subsumed, and nonclass kinds according to which processes generate such incomes to any individual or group of individuals. It highlights the relationship between the receipt of income and participation in fundamental, subsumed, and/or nonclass (income-generating) processes, respectively. By defining class and income distribution as completely different phenomena, Marxian theory can pose and answer questions about how class and income influence one another. In sharp contrast, neoclassical and Keynesian theories typically ignore class or else conflate class and income such that one's class position is literally defined in terms of one's quantitative income (as in rich, poor, and middle classes).

Let us summarize the Marxian class theory of income distribution symbolically as follows:

$$Y = Y_{fc} + Y_{sc} + Y_{nc}.$$

Here Y stands for the total income received by an individual. However, to specify the Marxian analysis of that income, we introduce the subscripts fc, *sc*, and *nc* to indicate its fundamental class, subsumed class, and nonclass sources respectively. Thus Y_{fc} represents income obtained from appropriating surplus value in the capitalist fundamental class process. Y_{sc} is the income from participation in the capitalist subsumed class process: receiving a distributed share of surplus value from its appropriators. Finally, Y_{nc} represents income from participation in a nonclass process that itself generates an inflow of value.

Every individual's income over any period of time can be disaggregated and analyzed in these class and nonclass terms. Some of the terms might be zero. An old grandparent's income might be dependent exclusively on gifts from children and grandchildren; hence that person's income equation would set $Y_{fc} = 0 = Y_{sc}$. The board of directors of a bank that lends money might divide its interest income into two kinds, Y_{sc} and Y_{nc}, if some of the interest it earned on loans came from industrial capitalists and the rest came from borrowers who were not industrial capitalists. A productive laborer whose income flowed exclusively from selling his or her labor power would show an equation in which $Y_{fc} = 0 = Y_{sc}$, since his or her income would flow solely from participation in the nonclass process of commodity exchange: labor power for money.

Such an equation can be used to construct a class analysis of any individual's income and likewise for groups of individuals who share a specific class/ nonclass distribution of income. Thus we can and will later write equations for the income of industrial capitalists grouped into, say, the board of directors of a modern corporation. We can also write equations for state officials such as members of Congress, who receive state income, or for clerics who receive the income of a religious institution, and so on. Equipped with such equations, Marxian theory explores the interrelations between class processes, on the one hand, and the incomes of corporations, states, religious establishments, and so on, on the other. Such explorations comprise one part of specifically Marxian social analysis.

4.8.2   Occupying Multiple Class and Nonclass Positions

Any individual or group can occupy more than one class position and thereby receive multiple kinds of class incomes. The same is true for the different nonclass positions and the various kinds of income they may generate. Consider, for example, a woman who sells her labor power to an industrial capitalist and obtains a money wage income in exchange. This woman's income equation would contain a term for this nonclass (exchange process) income:

$$Y = Y_{nc}.$$

However, this woman might also have loaned money to (e.g., by purchasing the bonds of) some industrial capitalist firm. She would then receive interest: a subsumed class payment since it is a distribution by the industrial capitalist of a share of appropriated surplus value meant to secure continued access to such loans. Thus we must extend this woman's income equation to include her subsumed class position:

$$Y = Y_{nc} + Y_{sc}.$$

Finally, let us suppose that she also keeps a passbook account at her local savings bank, which provides her with interest income. This must be included in her income equation as a second kind of nonclass income. This is because the savings bank is purely a borrowing and lending institution. It produces no capitalist commodities, employs no productive laborers, and appropriates no surplus value. Thus it cannot distribute any appropriated surplus value either. The savings bank's interest payment to this woman is a nonclass income to her resulting from her participation in the nonclass process of lending money to someone other than an industrial capitalist.

Her summary income equation must contain two different terms for her two different nonclass sources of income: Y_{nc1} for participating in a commodity exchange process (selling her labor power), and Y_{nc2} for participating in a process of lending to someone other than an industrial capitalist:

$$Y = Y_{nc1} + Y_{nc2} + Y_{sc}.$$

Consider a second example, a man who inherits land from his relatives and then leases part of that land to an industrial capitalist for locating a commodity-producing factory there. The rental payments received constitute a subsumed class income, Y_{sc}, to this man:

$$Y = Y_{sc}.$$

However, suppose that this man also hires two people to work on another portion of his land producing crops for sale. Upon their sale, the man realizes a fundamental class income—namely the surplus value he appropriates from these workers. To take account of this, we must amend his total income equation to include the surplus value he appropriates, Y_{fc}:

$$Y = Y_{sc} + Y_{fc}.$$

If, finally, this man also takes a full-time job—that is, sells his labor power too—he will obtain nonclass income: wages received in exchange for his labor power, Y_{nc}. His complete income equation would then be

$$Y = Y_{sc} + Y_{fc} + Y_{nc}.$$

As these examples suggest, Marxian theory presumes that individuals and groups often occupy multiple class and nonclass positions that generate their incomes. Moreover individuals will likely change their mixes of class and nonclass income flows across their lifetimes. To know the amount of any individual's or group's income is far from sufficient for a Marxian class analysis of that income, individual, or group. That class analysis requires that we pinpoint the class and nonclass components of anyone's income.

The reason why class is so important here is that it returns us to the general purposes of Marxian theory. Marxists want to know how individuals, groups, and incomes relate to the class structure because of their interest in changing that class structure. Hence studying the size of a person's or group's income, or knowing merely one component of it, is inadequate from the Marxian point of view. Such knowledge abstracts from and ignores the class complexities of anyone's income, while those complexities are precisely what Marxian analysis aims to understand.

Analyzing income distribution in terms of class (fundamental and subsumed) and nonclass processes helps focus attention on how class structures influence social life. Marxian analysis explores how most individuals participate in multiple different income-generating processes. Thus political strategists seeking to enlist people in movements to change a society's class structure need to understand the multiple, different class involvements that individuals' incomes reflect. They need as well to project how class changes will likely impact on the incomes of various social groups. Marxian theory responds to such needs.

This Marxian theory therefore opposes theories that divide people into "classes" according to the sizes of their incomes. That use and meaning of the term "class" is radically opposed to what we have found in Marxian theory. As we understand Marxian theory, it distinguishes clearly between income, on the one hand, and class processes, on the other. As the examples above indicate, we cannot deduce an individual's class positions from the size of his or her income, nor can we deduce an individual's income from his or her class participations. In Marxian theory the relationship between income and class is more complex than that.

4.9   The Complex Class Structure of Capitalist Firms

A central part of modern economic theories concerns the causes and consequences of the behavior of capitalist firms. Of course, different theories generate different analyses of these firms. In neoclassical theory the behavior of capitalist firms is reduced ultimately to the desires of their resource suppliers, their technological possibilities, and the preferences of their customers. Keynesian theory emphasizes the uncertainty, behavioral rules, and "animal spirits" that shape enterprises' actions. We can show the different consequences and implications of Marxian theory by elaborating its unique way of approaching firms. Building on our introduction to the Marxian theory of the firm in section 4.5.5 of this chapter, the following section presents a further class analysis of modern capitalist firms.

4.9.1 Class Analysis of Capitalist Firms

By "capitalist firm" we mean an enterprise in which some initial sum of money is expanded quantitatively. Because its value is enhanced, that sum of money functions as capital. This self-expansion of value defines the firm as a "capitalist enterprise." As noted earlier, there are different kinds of capitalist enterprises. Industrial capitalist enterprises expand value by appropriating surplus value generated by productive laborers who produce commodities for sale. Merchant capitalist enterprises expand value by buying and then reselling commodities for more than their purchase prices. Moneylending capitalist enterprises expand their capital by earning interest on the money they lend.

For each capitalist enterprise, Marxian theory specifies its inflow and outflow of values in specifically class analytical terms as follows:

$$Y_{fc} + Y_{sc} + Y_{nc} = E_{sc} + E_{nc}.$$

The Y terms in this equation have already been discussed in this chapter. The E terms require a brief explanation. E_{sc} refers to expenditures made by this enterprise from the surplus value it appropriates. These are subsumed class distributions expended by the firm to secure various conditions of existence for its appropriation of surplus value (Y_{fc}). E_{nc} refers to those expenditures by the firm that are not subsumed class payments (not distributions of appropriated surplus to secure its conditions of existence). The expenditures under E_{nc} aim rather to secure the conditions of existence for the firm's continued receipt of Y_{sc}, and Y_{nc}. In this way they parallel the role of E_{sc}, aiming to secure continued surplus value appropriation.

Every capitalist firm can have such a Marxian class analytical equation written for it. Firms will differ from one another according to the differing values taken by the five terms in their respective equations. For example, an industrial capitalist firm exclusively engaged in commodity production can be represented simply as follows:

$$Y_{fc} = E_{sc}.$$

Its capitalists appropriate surplus value, Y_{fc}, which they then distribute to subsumed classes, E_{sc}, in hopes of securing their conditions of existence.

By contrast, a purely merchant capitalist firm would be represented simply as follows:

$$Y_{sc} = E_{nc}.$$

This merchant capitalist firm's income, Y_{sc}, is derived exclusively from its participation in the capitalist subsumed class process—that is, buying commodity outputs *at a discount from their value* from an industrial capitalist. The merchant capitalist firm then spends E_{nc} to secure the conditions of existence of its participation in the subsumed class process that generates the Y_{sc}. These merchant expenditures might include payments for the unproductive labor power of clerks and bookkeepers, rent for warehouses, and other expenses associated with buying and reselling of the industrial capitalist's commodity output.

Finally, consider how Marxian theory approaches a capitalist enterprise engaged exclusively in consumer lending. This firm expands its capital by lending to individuals for consumption purposes and obtaining interest payments on as well as repayment of such loans. Its Marxian class analytical equation would be

$$Y_{nc} = E_{nc}.$$

This firm draws purely nonclass income. It earns no fundamental class income, because its performance of the nonclass process of lending money does not involve the appropriation of surplus value (no commodity is produced and no productive laborers are hired by the lending capitalist). It likewise earns no subsumed class income, because the consumer-borrowers it lends to are not themselves industrial capitalists. Therefore they do not appropriate surplus labor and so cannot pay interest out of appropriated surplus value.

None of the three kinds of capitalist firms described above needs to stay forever tied to its particular source of income. Capitalist firms can and do change historically. They variously add, change, and drop income-generating processes as they react to the opportunities they perceive in their environments. Industrial capitalists may find it advantageous to use revenues to make loans to employees, thereby adding a Y_{nc} to their Y_{fc}. Merchant capitalists may decide to stop depending solely on their suppliers for commodities and begin to hire productive laborers to produce the commodities they will then sell, thereby adding Y_{fc} to their Y_{sc}.

In general, the Y_{fc}, Y_{sc}, and Y_{nc} terms variously equal or exceed zero as the specific history of each firm unfolds. At various times a particular enterprise can earn Y_{fc} and/or Y_{sc} and/or Y_{nc}. General Motors Corporation, for example, can make cars (earn Y_{fc}), charge interest for loans to other industrial capitalists (earn Y_{sc}), and charge interest for loans to car-buying consumers (earn Y_{nc} via its former subsidiary, General Motors Acceptance Corporation). In any given year, Y_{fc} may be greater or smaller than either Y_{sc} or Y_{nc}, according to the development of the economy and the corporate strategies of GM's board of directors.

In recent decades corporations often have purchased shares of another corporation and then have decided to merge the companies into one operating corporation. For example, an industrial corporation may earn Y_{fc} producing only steel products. Its corporate board decides whether for competitive, speculative, or other reasons to purchase the common stock of an energy company. New revenues Y_{sc} arise when the purchasing board receives dividends distributed to it by the corporate board of the newly owned energy company. At some point the steel company's board makes use of its power of ownership of the energy corporation to merge the two independent companies into one legally unified corporation with one board of directors. The newly merged corporation would produce two distinct commodities (called product lines), one of steel and the other energy. At that point the previous $Y_{sc} = 0$ (the subsumed class ownership position disappears) and Y_{fc} expands: the new surplus value of the fully integrated company is the sum of the surplus in the energy commodity and the surplus in the steel commodity. The newly merged company could even take on a completely different name reflecting its changed and expanded business operation. US Steel corporation became US X reflecting its merged steel and energy businesses.

4.9.2 Capitalists and Corporate Boards of Directors

A capitalist can be an individual, or a group of individuals can occupy the social position of a capitalist. In modern capitalist enterprises, called "corporations" for historical reasons, the capitalist is a group numbering typically between 9 and 20 individuals: the board of directors. That group appropriates surplus value and/or receives subsumed class distributions and/or obtains nonclass incomes. The corporation's participation in one or more of these income-generating processes will determine the kinds and sizes of the incomes received by its board of directors.

In the early history of many capitalist enterprises, one person occupied the position of capitalist. A colorful and often mythical literature of tycoons, rugged and risk-taking individual entrepreneurs, and cutthroat competitors often surrounds this early history. However, as capitalist enterprises survived competition and grew, they tended to evolve into corporations whose capitalists were no longer single individuals but rather boards of directors.

Everything Marxian theory says about capitalists holds whether they are single persons or groups. However, an important conclusion of Marxian theory emerges from examining the transition from individual capitalist to board of directors. Contrary to the literature, both popular and academic, "pure" capitalists are more likely to be found among boards of directors than among individual capitalist entrepreneurs.

In the early years of an industrial capitalist enterprise, its single capitalist will likely perform many different functions inside the firm. Beyond appropriating surplus value from productive laborers, the early individual capitalist will likely also engage in managing productive workers, marketing the output, perhaps doing some productive labor alongside hired laborers, lending money or capital to the enterprise, and owning the means of production. In other words, the early individual industrial capitalist also participates in the subsumed class process, not only as a distributor but also as a recipient of shares of surplus value. He or she performs a variety of nonclass processes that constitute the conditions of existence of the capitalist fundamental class process (in our example, managing, merchanting, moneylending, and proving access to means of production), and may well also sell his or her own labor power and so produce as well as appropriate surplus value.

The individual industrial capitalist occupies many different class and nonclass positions within one enterprise. Such an individual is not "purely" an industrial capitalist, not only an appropriator of surplus value within the enterprise. By contrast, members of a modern industrial corporation's board of directors are more nearly "pure" capitalists. Many members of corporate boards of directors have no other function within the corporation beyond appropriating surplus value and distributing it to subsumed classes. Such directors gather periodically at the corporation's headquarters for meetings. They literally personify the corporation and as such are politically, economically, and culturally designated to receive collectively the surplus value appropriated from the corporation's hired productive laborers and then collectively distribute portions of the appropriated surplus to various subsumed classes.

Such board members actually display the classic outlines of the Marxian theory of industrial capitalists. They appropriate surplus value and distribute what they have appropriated. Many corporations do include on their boards of directors individuals who are also top managers within the firm and also at times those who are its major shareholders. Such "impure" capitalists do then occupy two or even three class positions: the fundamental class position of a surplus value appropriator plus one and/or two subsumed class positions, one as a hired manager and the other as a corporate owner. Still this is a far less impure kind of capitalist than the early individual capitalist who typically occupied many different class positions within the firm.

An individual who occupies multiple class positions within an enterprise—say, those of appropriator and manager—will then often function at both ends of a value flow. The top corporate manager (CEO), who also sits on the board of directors, will not only distribute appropriated surplus value as a board member but will also receive a distributed portion of that surplus as a paid manager. Similarly the early individual capitalist entrepreneur often functioned both as lender and borrower in the process of loaning personal capital to the enterprise in which he or she appropriated surplus labor and also a receiver of interest on the loan. The early surplus-appropriating entrepreneur also might have been the sole business owner or one of only a few owners. He or she would then function both as distributor and recipient of paid dividends.

Marxian theory focuses on the multiple class positions occupied by individual capitalists at various points in an enterprise's history. The goal of this analysis is to produce a history and current assessment of the enterprise that stresses its changing relationship to the class structure of the society in which it exists. From this standpoint, capitalists appear frequently to pass sums of value to themselves via the multiple class and nonclass positions they occupy. Indeed it would be more precise to say, for example, that individuals as industrial capitalists pass sums of value to themselves as subsumed class managers, moneylenders and owners. Moreover a Marxian theoretical accounting system for enterprises would measure and compare class and nonclass value flows to yield consistent arithmetic formulations and applications of the theory.

This means that arithmetic measures in Marxian theory will likely differ from arithmetic measures in non-Marxian theory since the objects of those different theories are defined and understood differently. We can illustrate this by presenting a Marxian analysis of the widespread term "profit," which figures prominently in nearly every kind of economic theory. Our class analysis and the resulting arithmetic measures and relations it suggests produce a new and distinctly Marxian interpretation of what industrial profit is and what meaning it can have for Marxian analysis.

4.9.3 A Marxian Theory of Industrial Profit

A capitalist enterprise's general income and expenditure equation can be investigated to understand, in Marxian class analytical terms, the meanings of "profit." We will begin by considering a firm that is engaged only in commodity production and whose sole source of income is appropriated surplus value:

$$Y_{fc} = E_{sc}.$$

We will extend this equation by disaggregating this firm's expenditures as follows:

$$Y_{fc} = E_{sc1} + E_{sc2} + E_{sc3} + E_{sc4} + E_{sc5} + E_{sc6} + E_{sc7},$$

where

E_{sc1} = subsumed class payments to landlords,

E_{sc2} = subsumed class payments to moneylenders (bankers),

E_{sc3} = subsumed class payments to managers' salaries,

E_{sc4} = subsumed class payments to managers for capital accumulation (buying more C and V),

E_{sc5} = subsumed class payments to merchants,

E_{sc6} = subsumed class payments to the state (taxes),

E_{sc7} = subsumed class payments to shareholders (dividends).

Typically modern US corporations define their "profits" (sometimes labeled "net income") as the residual when "costs" of production are subtracted from "revenues" received when output commodities are sold. To produce a class analysis of profit we must determine the class meaning of such "costs" and "revenues." The meaning of "revenue" is relatively straightforward. Revenue amounts to what we have earlier called $W (= C + V + S)$. However, the concept of costs poses more problems.

Modern corporations do not accept, know, or use class terms. Nor do the government statistical services that define, gather, organize, and publish the economic data relied upon by most analysts of capitalist economies. Thus they do not see or measure costs in terms of, for example, $C + V$. If they did, their concept of costs would equal the Marxian concept of constant capital plus variable capital $(C + V)$. Then their concept of profit might, at least initially, be the equivalent of the Marxian concept of surplus value. However, that is not the case.

The usual corporate concept of costs includes more than $C + V$. For example, their costs typically include also rents, interest payments, managerial salaries, and discounts to merchants. In Marxian theory these payments by a capitalist are portions of the appropriated surplus value, portions distributed to subsumed classes. They are thus crucially different from C and V, which are commodities purchased prior to and consumed in the production of a surplus.

From the Marxian theoretical standpoint, then, what such a corporation calls its "profit" would be understood in Marxian terms as follows:

$$\text{Profit} = W - [C + V + E_{sc1} + E_{sc2} + E_{sc3} + E_{sc5}],$$

or since $W - [C + V] = S$,

$$\text{Profit} = S - [E_{sc1} + E_{sc2} + E_{sc3} + E_{sc5}],$$

where

E_{sc1} = subsumed class payment to landlords,

E_{sc2} = subsumed class payment to moneylenders,

E_{sc3} = subsumed class payment to managers,

E_{sc5} = subsumed class payment to merchants.

Thus, in class analytical terms, what capitalist corporations and most govern-ment statistics in capitalist societies report as profits is definitely not the same as what Marxists mean by surplus value. Quite the contrary, these profits are merely one part of surplus value—namely the sum of the subsumed class pay-ments to managers for accumulating capital (E_{sc4}), plus the subsumed class payments to shareholders (E_{sc7}), plus the subsumed class payments to the state (E_{sc6}). The popular term of American corporations, "after-tax profits," would then be the sum of E_{sc4} plus E_{sc7}.

Marxian theory's basic distinction between surplus value and profit is pos-sible only because of its class analytical foundation. It is the focus on class processes that leads Marxian theory to that distinction. Moreover some central conclusions of Marxian economics depend on this distinction between surplus value and profit.

For example, Marxian theory draws no necessary conclusion about the fun-damental class process from falling corporate profits. This is because, as our equations above demonstrate, falling profits could result from *either* a reduced surplus appropriation in the fundamental class process (a smaller S) *or* increased subsumed class payments from the surplus (a larger E_{sc1}, E_{sc2}, E_{sc3}, or E_{sc5}). Industrial capitalists' profits could fall not because less surplus value was appro-priated from productive laborers but rather because various subsumed classes were able to extract larger distributions of surplus. Both kinds of change could occur at once to produce falling profits. Indeed profits would fall if industrial capitalists appropriated additional surplus at the same time as the extra demands of subsumed classes siphoned off more than that addition.

Marxian theory likewise draws no logical inference about "efficiency" from relocations by capitalist enterprises from one region to another. Often such moves are explained or justified on the ground that the industrial capitalists were simply responding to differences in profit rates, moving from regions of lower rates to those of higher rates of profit. According to this argument, such moves are considered efficient because profits necessarily reflect the efficiency with which capitalist enterprises transform inputs and labor power into com-modity outputs. In non-Marxian theories efficiency is directly connected to profitability. Thus inferring efficiency gains from relocations to regions of higher profits makes sense. But this argument does not make sense from the standpoint of Marxian theory.

In Marxian theory, an industrial corporation that changes its geographic location to achieve greater profits does not thereby necessarily achieve any greater "efficiency." Consider, for example, a Marxian measure of efficiency defined in terms of the total amount of labor input ($EL + LL$) required per unit of commodity produced. The above industrial corporation's move might then be explained by the possibility that land rent, merchants' fees, and/or managers' salaries are lower in the Sun Belt than in the Northeast. Firms that relocated might actually suffer losses in efficiency in the Marxian sense. That is, they might produce fewer commodity outputs per unit of total labor input ($EL + LL$). However, that reduced efficiency, which would diminish the amount of surplus value appropriated from productive laborers, would be more than offset by the reduced subsumed class payments to landlords, managers, and merchants. The results would be higher calculated profits, continued movement of capitalist enterprises from the US Northeast to its Southwest, *and a trend toward lower efficiency in Marxian terms.*

Similar reasoning leads Marxian theorists to recognize that rising industrial capitalists' profits can mask a deteriorating rate of surplus value. Class struggles between industrial capitalists and productive laborers over the rate of exploitation could diminish the quanta of surplus value appropriated by capitalists (falling S). However, this decline could be hidden statistically if subsumed class payments were falling even more rapidly, for example, as when interest rates drop quickly because of central bank policies. In the absence of direct attention to the complex changes taking place in both the fundamental and the subsumed class process, Marxian theory rejects inferences about class structures and changes drawn from statistical movements in published corporate profits.

Marxian theorists do not deny, of course, that industrial capitalists can and often do make their decisions with the objective of maximizing their profits or profit rates. What Marxian theorists want to stress is that such decisions aimed at that objective are peculiar effects, in part, of a non-Marxian theory lodged in the capitalists' minds. To accept that objective and make decisions accordingly may well maximize profits. Non-Marxian theories may well draw a necessary equivalence between maximized profits and what they conceptualize as productive efficiency. However, from the Marxian standpoint, maximization of profit (as understood in class terms through the equations above) has no necessary relation to the appropriation of surplus value or its distribution to subsumed classes or the ratio of commodity outputs to commodity and labor inputs.

In Marxian theory, maximizing profits is perfectly consistent with both rising and falling rates of surplus value, rising or falling distributions of subsumed class payments, rising or falling efficiency ratios of outputs to total labor inputs in production. Marxian theory criticizes non-Marxian theories for seeking to justify capitalism by equating what is nothing but its peculiar rule for capitalist decision-making with some absolute standard of efficiency. The profit-maximizing rule of capitalist enterprises (making prices equal marginal costs in the neoclassical theory of the firm), hallowed in the texts of non-Marxian theorists, is then no magic path to the optimum efficiency of all possible worlds. Marxian theory shows that rule to be perfectly consistent with all kinds of inefficiency in class processes as well as the physical transformation of inputs into outputs.

One conclusion about corporate strategies which Marxian theory reaches is that the rule of profit maximizing, which does not make for efficiency, does serve another purpose. It does maximize those particular subsumed class payments which are *not* subtracted from S in the profit equations above—chiefly E_{sc4} and E_{sc7}.

In terms of those equations, profit maximization becomes a means by which to deliver the maximum possible flow of value to shareholders (dividends) and the maximum possible flow of value to the discretionary control of boards of directors (retained earnings). Pursuing the rule of profit maximization has little to do with efficiency and much to do with favoring dividends, the retained earnings of corporations, and what boards of directors decide to do with those retained earnings (e.g., accumulate capital). *Profit maximization turns out to be a rule for the maximization of a subset of subsumed class distributions of the surplus value, no more and no less.*

Across the history of capitalist societies, the specific subset of subsumed class distributions defined as "profit" has varied. Sometimes the distribution of surplus value for the personal consumption of the enterprise's capitalist(s) has been included. Modern commentators on large industrial corporations have debated whether dividends should be excluded from the profit subset because corporations aim to maximize after-dividend profits. Even at one historical moment, different capitalist enterprises may include different subsumed class distributions within what they maximize as profit. For example, private utility companies, which are subject to state regulations on their allowed profit rates, may maximize subsumed class distributions other than dividends and retained earnings, and so on.

Profit, then, as reported by corporations, used by most contemporary analysts, and formalized in neoclassical and Keynesian theories, is a category that does not belong to Marxian theory. Marxian class analysis completely alters the concept by transforming it into a variable subset of subsumed class distributions. It goes even further by stressing that profit-maximizing rules (rules that maximize whatever happens to be the currently fashionable subset of subsumed class distributions) bear no necessary relation to what concerns Marxists: class processes and their interconnections with nonclass processes, including the technical efficiency of transforming inputs into outputs in commodity production. As in most other areas of economic analysis, here we can see again how Marxian and non-Marxian theories make very different sense of the performance and achievements of capitalist economies.

4.10 The Complex Class Structure of Other Social Sites

The unique Marxian class analysis of industrial capitalist firms may also be applied to other social institutions. We will here substitute another term—social site—for "institution" because we don't need the connotation of permanence often attached to "institution." "Site" connotes merely a place in a society, a point where certain social processes and relationships occur and may or may not last long. "Site" is more consistent with the Marxian theoretical view that all processes and relationships are overdetermined, contradictory, and hence constantly changing. Below we examine Marxian theory's approach to and unique understanding of three sites in modern society: households, states, and international economic relations.

4.10.1 Class Analysis and Households

Like enterprises, households are sites in society at which many social processes occur. In enterprises and households, for example, many of the same processes can occur: people speak, dream, eat, breathe, give orders, do labor, pay taxes, and so on. Other processes occur chiefly at one site but not the other. Sleeping and child care occur in households but are probably largely prevented in enterprises, while commodity manufacture and sale are more likely to occur in enterprises than in households.

However, as even these few examples suggest, there is no hard-and-fast separation of sites in any society according to which particular processes occur in each. For example, households have sometimes in history been important or even the main sites where commodities—especially farm products and home crafts—were produced for sale. In such times, few people distinguished households from enterprises. At other times, sites have been rigidly separated: certain processes were proscribed at one site and strictly reserved for another. For example, sexual processes have often been strictly and/or legally constrained to the household and nowhere else. Child-rearing was often treated similarly. While distinctions among sites are never fixed permanently, we can define them as specific subsets of social processes at particular times and in particular societies. Thus in much of the world today enterprises differ from households according to the different subset of social processes each comprises.

Households are where child-rearing, eating, sexual activity, and so on, usually (if not always) occur in modern capitalist societies. We can contrast what is specifically different about enterprises by stressing that the processes of producing commodities (in the case of industrial capitalists), accumulating capital, buying labor power, and distributing dividends occur predominantly there and not in households.

Marxian theory asks two broad questions about sites in society that other theories do not ask: Do class processes occur at any particular site chosen for theoretical scrutiny? If they do, which class processes occur there, and how do they interact with other social processes? Here we propose to ask and briefly answer these questions in regard to present-day households. The results represent a remarkable analysis of the household and its relation to modern capitalism that is radically different from neoclassical or Keynesian theorizations of households.

Fundamental and subsumed class processes can and typically do occur inside households. That conclusion of Marxian theory is reached through the following sort of analysis. Labor inside the household produces goods and services: raw food materials are transformed into finished meals, cleaning equipment is utilized to transform disorderly, dirty rooms into clean, neat ones, and torn clothing is repaired, to cite but a few examples. These production processes rarely result in commodities (products that are sold); households in the United States do not typically sell prepared meals, cleaning services, or clothing repair services. However, the absence of commodity production is not equivalent to the absence of class processes (production, appropriation, and distribution of surpluses).

The production of these meals, cleaning services, and repair services involves not only the natural transformation of physical substances through labor but also the fundamental and subsumed class processes. To identify whether and how class processes occur in households, we must distinguish between necessary and surplus labor. Can we identify inside households some people who are direct laborers, who produce not only the goods and services they consume in the household but also do some surplus labor yielding a household surplus? Marxian theory replies affirmatively.

Many housewives have traditionally performed the necessary labor required to make the meals they eat, clean the rooms they occupy, and repair clothing they wear. Such women traditionally also perform surplus labor—that is, they produce a quantity of meals, cleaned rooms, and repaired clothing that exceeds their own consumption of these products. Their husbands, and/or others living with them inside households, often appropriate (and often consume) the surplus labor embodied in these surplus products.

We have identified the existence of a fundamental class process inside such households as well as a particularly gendered organization of who produces versus who appropriates the household surplus. Of course, this gender organization need not and has not historically always been the same. Husbands and wives could reverse class positions. Communes, tribal societies, cooperatives, and other household arrangements have displayed various distributions of men and women among class positions across history. However, most traditional households of recent history conform to the Marxian class analysis that identifies women as performers and men as appropriators of household surplus labor.

Given Marxian theory's affirmation of the existence of class processes inside modern households, which kinds of class processes occur there? Clearly, those are not capitalist fundamental class processes. Husbands do not buy their wives' labor power or sell, as commodities, the products of their wives' household work. No values, surplus value, or prices typically attach to such products. The class processes inside these households must therefore be noncapitalist.

Next, to identify which noncapitalist form(s) of the fundamental class process occur in households, Marxists consider the other basic forms so far identified in their theoretical tradition. That quickly leads them to conclude that traditional households today displays class processes most nearly like the feudal (as exemplified in medieval Europe from the twelfth to the sixteenth centuries). Marxian theory points to the typical husband's "duty" to protect wife and household, while the wife's duties concern "serving" and "obeying" the husband. The latter relationship closely resembles the medieval serf's dependence on the feudal lord for protection and payment of rents to that same lord. The wife is tied by many traditional, religious, and legal constraints to perform surplus labor for her husband quite like serfs labored for their lords. Traditional wives have believed it was the natural, moral, or religious order of the world to deliver household surplus labor to her husband (typically embodied in physical goods and services rather than in money forms).

Traditional households in recent history have thus been sites of feudal class processes, in the Marxian view, while firms have chiefly been sites of capitalist class processes. Marxian theory thus constructs a complex class analysis of modern society; it is understood to encompass two very different class structures at two different sites: homes and enterprises. Indeed this Marxian analysis challenges the label "capitalist" for many modern nations as an unacceptable oversimplification. Such a single label risks missing the specific differences between feudal households and capitalist enterprises and the problems people encounter in moving between these different and often clashing class structures. Marxian theory avoids such risks by directly confronting the different class structures of these two sites and posing questions about how they interact with one another and with the nonclass processes of the society.

The existence of the feudal fundamental class process in households implies the existence of the feudal subsumed class process. Husbands distribute portions of their appropriated household feudal surplus product to secure their conditions of existence as feudal appropriators. Since the household of our example has only two people in it, one or the other must play the role of the subsumed class receiving distributed shares of the surplus. Thus, for example, suppose that one of the rooms cleaned by the wife were set aside for paperwork connected with household management. If the wife does this management work, her cleaning of that management room would be a surplus that she produces, that her husband appropriates, and that he then allocates to her performance of household management. That management provides a condition of existence for the husband's position as feudal surplus appropriator. If, alternatively, the husband performs household management in that designated room, he would distribute the wife's surplus product (cleaning that room) to himself as the subsumed class (the manager). The husband would then occupy both the feudal fundamental class position inside the household and also the feudal subsumed class position of household manager.

Marxian theory's next step poses questions about the interactions between the two different class structures of household and enterprise. Consider husbands who move daily between the household class position of feudal appropriator to the enterprise class position of wage-earning productive laborer in a capitalist factory. How will navigating between these two different class positions affect an individual's emotions, physical productivity, ideological persuasion, and political loyalties? How will such an individual's participation in social movements be influenced by the multiplicity of his/her class affiliations? In Marxian theory, understanding husbands includes the specific and multiple class positions they occupy within households and at other sites. Understanding relationships between spouses and between men and women generally likewise requires attention to their multiple class positions and the influences of those class positions upon them and their relationships. Theories that abstract from class cannot pose or answer such questions nor explore the impacts of class (in its surplus definition) on human relationships.

Similarly consider wives who occupy household feudal class positions as serfs. How might they change if they added a second class position—say, as productive laborers in a capitalist enterprise—to their household feudal class position(s)? Or consider how Marxian theory would approach the social role of religious institutions. Marxian theory would ask whether and how religious preaching and rituals provided conditions of existence not only for the capitalist fundamental class process in enterprises but also for the feudal fundamental class process in households. Such a Marxian line of inquiry would produce a particular understanding of the persistently different attitudes of men and women toward religion. Marxian theory similarly raises distinctive questions about children, given its conception of feudal households and capitalist enterprises. For example, do male and female children develop different attitudes toward class (conscious or unconscious) because of the divergent class positions occupied by their mothers, fathers, or other role models? Similarly, how would a Marxian theory account for the value flows from parents to sustain their children, and how do those flows affect the entire household's class structure?

We cannot here even summarize, let alone discuss, the distinctive, new insights into family and household relationships opened up by Marxian class analysis (Cassano 2009). This subsection only introduces the lines of inquiry fostered by applying Marxian theory to households. The remainder of section 4.10 further elaborates the basic Marxian theory of class by considering next the role of the state in modern societies.

4.10.2   Class Analysis and the State

The state, another site in most modern societies, differs from both capitalist enterprises and feudal household because of the precise subset of social processes that occur together in (and thereby constitute) the state. The processes that generally distinguish the modern state from other social sites include the following:

- maintaining a standing military force,
- designing and passing laws for society as a whole,
- adjudicating disputes over those laws,
- enforcing compliance with those laws,
- operating an educational system,
- collecting taxes.

Past and present states have not been the exclusive sites of these processes. In some societies the state does not maintain the only standing military force. That occurs also at other sites (as in enterprises that maintain security forces or even households that employ guards). Similarly in some societies other sites beside the state design laws, enforce them and adjudicate disputes over them: for example, religious institutions may do that alongside the state.

However, the history of modern societies suggests that the list above fairly typifies processes that occur predominantly in the state. Note that the state comprises natural processes (e.g., wilderness preservation), cultural processes (e.g., education), economic processes (e.g., collecting taxes and buying commodities), and political processes (e.g., controlling group behavior via military and legal actions). While many analysts focus chiefly on the political processes in the state (the state is usually treated as an especially political institution), Marxian theorists identify all of the processes of which any state is composed, the nonpolitical as well as the political.

Marxian theory asks specific questions about the state, reflecting the theory's interests and orientation. Do class processes occur in the state? If so, which ones do, and how do they interact with the class and nonclass processes that occur at other sites in the society, such as enterprises and households? A Marxian theory of the state focuses especially (not exclusively) on the relationship, including its contradictions, between that state and the class structure of that society. Our brief introduction here concerns the state that currently exists in the United States.

Marxists inquire whether the capitalist fundamental class process occurs in the state. Does the state hire productive laborers to produce commodities and thereby appropriate surplus value? Does the United States government operate capitalist enterprises alongside those of private corporations? Occasionally it does. The Tennessee Valley Authority, producer and seller of electricity as a capitalist commodity, is a frequently cited example. West European states operate such enterprises on a much greater scale than the United States does. In any case, the answer is yes, capitalist enterprises can be run by the state. In that event another source of revenue to the state (in addition to the taxes and fees it imposes and any borrowing it may undertake) is the surplus value it appropriates by participating directly in the capitalist fundamental class process. We will refer to such a state revenue as

$SY_{fc}.$

The modern state is also typically involved in the capitalist subsumed class process. If the state itself appropriates surplus, it must distribute that surplus to secure the conditions for the continuation of the state's capitalist fundamental class process. The state industrial capitalist distributes surplus value just as private industrial capitalists do. We can represent the state's participation in that subsumed class process as follows:

$SY_{fc} = SE_{SC},$

where SE_{SC} is the distribution of SY_{fc} to secure the conditions for the state's continued appropriation of surplus value.

The modern state also usually participates in another subsumed class process as the recipient of taxes paid by private industrial capitalists. Those taxes are portions of the surplus value appropriated in private industrial capitalist enterprises. The state performs various nonclass processes that secure conditions of existence for private industrial capitalists. These include guaranteeing private property, limiting trade union challenges to private profitability, providing public health services that sustain productive laborers' productivity, providing public education, and so on. Part of the state's costs in performing such processes (e.g., the wages of court clerks, officials, soldiers, and other government workers, plus equipment and buildings used by them) are defrayed by subsumed class payments to the state in the form of taxes imposed on industrial capitalists.

We can incorporate this second source of state revenues as follows:

$SY_{fc} + SY_{sc} = SE_{sc} + SE_{nc},$

where SY_{sc} = state subsumed class revenues, and a necessary additional term SE_{nc} = the nonclass state expenditures needed to secure the state's receipt of those subsumed class revenues. SE_{nc} is added because the state must make these nonclass expenditures to secure the tax payments from private industrial capitalists. These expenditures are nonclass expenditures because they are *not* distributions of surplus value appropriated by the state (those distributions are contained in the SE_{sc} term).

To complete a Marxian class analysis of the state's budget, account must be taken of the state's nonclass revenues (in addition to the fundamental and subsumed class revenues discussed above). The state obtains nonclass revenues whenever value flows into the state that is neither (1) surplus value appropriated from productive laborers hired by the state nor (2) a subsumed class distribution to the state from private-capitalists. Examples include individual income taxes, sales taxes, property taxes paid by productive and unproductive workers out of their wage and salary income and corporate income taxes paid by nonindustrial capitalists (e.g., merchants and bankers) who do not appropriate surplus value from their employees. Such taxpayers also expect the state to provide them with goods and services. States therefore hire people and buy equipment to, for example, build public swimming pools, stage elaborate pageants, subsidize medical care for elderly, indigent, or all people, and provide military security and public education.

States do not typically provide these goods and services as capitalist commodities sold in markets. If they did, the resulting government net revenues would be appropriated surplus value (SY_{fc}). Rather, taxes in the form of nonclass revenues pay for producing such services and delivering them to the general population according to citizenship, age, need, location, or other non–market-price criteria.

The state's complete budget equation in class-value terms can thus be represented as follows:

$$SY_{fc} + SY_{sc} + SY_{nc} = SE_{sc} + SE_{nc1} + SE_{nc2},$$

where SY_{nc} refers to nonclass state revenues, SE_{nc1} refers to nonclass state expenditures made to secure the state's subsumed class revenues, and SE_{nc2} refers to nonclass state expenditures made to secure the state's nonclass revenues. This Marxian class analysis of the state in a modern society suggests a number of distinctive conclusions unavailable to alternative theories of the state. First, the state is a complex social site at which multiple class as well as nonclass processes occur. Second, the state has many different relationships with class and nonclass processes at other sites in society. Third, the state, as a social site, is complexly interdependent with such other sites as enterprises and households. The state is therefore neither "above society" in the sense of existing beyond the rough-and-tumble processes of everyday social life nor is it some external or extraneous institution relative to enterprises and households.

Marxian theory stresses the multiplicity of the state's social roles. The state is not merely the tool of capitalists, providing them with the conditions they need to go on exploiting productive laborers. Nor is the state simply an institution of, by, and for all citizens, taxing them and using those revenues to provide public services for everyone's benefit. The former analysis is inadequate; it sees only the SY_{sc} and SE_{nc1} portions of the state equation. The latter analysis is similarly inadequate; it sees only the SY_{nc} and SE_{nc2} portions. Marxian theory rather combines all four of those terms plus the SY_{fc} and SE_{sc} terms into a properly complex class and nonclass conceptualization of the state.

A conclusion suggested by the Marxian approach concerns precisely the SY_{fc} and SE_{sc} components of the state equation. These represent the state's participation in the capitalist fundamental class process and then in the subsumed class process too as the distributor of surplus value. State-capitalist enterprises do just that; they appropriate surplus value from productive laborers hired in the markets for labor power and they distribute subsumed class payments. It follows from the Marxian theory presented in this book that *the existence or growth of such state-capitalist enterprises is not a transition to socialism or communism understood as non- or postcapitalist economic systems.*

For Marxian theory, socialism and communism refer to societies in which noncapitalist forms of the fundamental class process prevail. Such societies are altogether different from those in which state industrial capitalist enterprises appropriate surplus value from the productive laborers they hire and exploit. The existence of state industrial capitalist enterprises alongside or instead of private industrial capitalists signals neither a transition to nor a realization of communism or socialism. In contrast, most neoclassical and Keynesian treatments of socialism define it as or associate it with a major economic role for the state. Neoclassical economists therefore sometimes conflate Keynesians and socialists, whereas Keynesians usually stress how the role they advocate for the state is significantly less than what socialists seek. For Marxists the relative magnitude/quantity of the state's economic role is not what defines socialism; it is rather the qualities—the specific class dimensions—of state and private enterprises that are most relevant for a social movement beyond capitalism.

For Marxian theory, "communist" is the name for one form of the fundamental class process, a specifically noncapitalist form that displays the following general characteristics:

- productive labor is designed and performed collectively,
- surplus labor is appropriated collectively,

- collective appropriators of the productive laborers' surplus are identical to the productive laborers.

To participate in the communist fundamental class means to be both a collective performer and collective appropriator of surplus labor. Unlike the capitalist fundamental class process that separates the producers of the surplus from its appropriators *as different groups of people, the communist fundamental class process unifies the producers and appropriators of the surplus in one and the same group of people.* Despite its brief and summary character, this sketch of the communist fundamental class process suffices to show why, from the standpoint of Marxian class analytics, the decision of a state to operate capitalist industrial enterprises has no necessary relation to socialism or communism as alternative class systems.

Historical evidence suggests different explanations for why modern societies have often established state industrial capitalist enterprises alongside private industrial capitalists. Sometimes private-capitalists want commodities priced too low to allow any surplus value to be realized by any private industrial capitalist that produced them. Examples include telephone, telegraph, and postal services, rail and air transportation, electricity, gas, and steel—all inputs to most capitalist enterprises. One solution would be for the government to establish capitalist industrial enterprises that could charge the low prices desired by private-capitalists by relying on subsidies drawn from other government revenues. Such state-capitalist enterprises exist to strengthen rather than threaten private capitalists. There is also historical evidence that occasionally citizens' movements press for state industrial capitalist enterprises to produce goods and services for mass consumption when private-capitalists refuse to do so or would charge unacceptably high prices. The Tennessee Valley Authority that provides inexpensive electric power across several states was partly a response to this sort of pressure.

Marxian theory also offers a unique class perspective on social struggles over state budgets. The Marxian class equation for the state projects the logic of such struggles in terms of shifts among its six terms:

$$SY_{fc} + SY_{sc} + SY_{nc} = SE_{sc} + SE_{nc1} + SE_{nc2}.$$

The Marxian analysis begins by noting that private-capitalist industrial enterprises have an interest in expanding SE_{nc1} and reducing SY_{sc}. They want increased state provision of the conditions of existence for private exploitation while they demand lower taxes on the surpluses they appropriate. To the extent that these private industrial capitalists succeed in realizing these interests, they will either (1) transfer the costs of the state onto others (SY_{sc} and/or SY_{fc}) or (2) shift state expenditures away from serving others ($SE_{sc} + SE_{nc2}$) to instead serve their own needs (SE_{nc1}), or both.

Such transfers of the costs of the state can be accomplished by political and cultural processes: by politicians altering tax rates and by public relations campaigns depicting tax reductions on industrial capitalists as means to increase jobs. Such shifting of state expenditures can be accomplished as well by cultural programs aimed at changing popular perceptions of expenditures serving corporations (SE_{nc1}) so that they are seen instead as serving the mass of people (SE_{nc2}). For example, the state's military expenditures secure capitalists' abilities to continue exploiting productive laborers in multiple ways (protecting against foreign and domestic enemies of capitalism, buying industrial capitalists' outputs, providing private industrial capitalists with technical innovations discovered in military laboratories, etc.). A concerted media campaign might redefine the state's military expenditures as urgent outlays to protect "the general public" perhaps from "terrorists." If successful, that campaign could increase military expenditures and decrease other state expenditures on the general public (raising SE_{nc1} and lowering SE_{nc2}).

Finally, a fully developed Marxian theory of the state in modern societies would have to take account of the noncapitalist class structures interacting with capitalist class structures in those societies. To illustrate one step in that direction, we can extend our state equation to specify the state's relationship with both capitalist enterprises and feudal households:

$$SY_{fc} + SY_{sc1} + SY_{sc2} + SY_{nc} = SE_{sc} + SE_{nc1} + SE_{nc2} + SE_{nc3}.$$

Here we introduce a new distinction between SY_{sc1} taxes levied on industrial capitalists—and SY_{sc2} taxes on feudal households. The state is thus shown to be subsumed to feudal surplus appropriators in households as well as to capitalist appropriators in enterprises. The state correspondingly performs some nonclass processes that provide the conditions of existence for the feudal fundamental class process in households. Examples include public education curricula that endorse feudal household class structures; passing and enforcing laws of property, inheritance, marriage, abortion, and divorce that support such structures; and subsidizing such structures through marriage and household tax exemptions and credits. At the same time the state performs, as noted, various nonclass processes that secure the conditions of existence for industrial capitalists. SY_{sc1} remains our term for the subsumed class tax payments made by industrial capitalists while SY_{sc2} designates subsumed class tax payments by feudal households.

By the same logic, SE_{nc3} must be added to our state equation to show state spending on processes that provide the conditions of existence for feudal households' fundamental class processes. Such spending includes parts of outlays on public education, legislation, judicial administration, and tax collection. Those outlays aim to secure the conditions of existence for household feudalism and thereby to secure the tax revenues derived from those feudal surpluses.

This extended state equation analyzes value flows to and from the state in terms of their interacting multiple class and nonclass components. Such Marxian categories differ sharply from those used in non-Marxian theories of the state. However, non-Marxian theories and their categories govern the definition, collection, and organization of published data on states in modern societies. Those data, for example, typically distinguish between business taxes and individual taxes. These are not Marxian class analytical distinctions. "Business taxes" lump together what Marxian analysis needs to keep separate. "Business taxes" abstracts from (disregards) the difference between taxes on surplus appropriators (industrial capitalists) and taxes on subsumed classes (bankers and merchants). SY_{sc1} and SY_{nc} are taxes with importantly different relationships to a society's class structure.

The same critique applies to state expenditures. Consider, for example, those lumped together in the non-Marxian category "legislative activities." Those expenditures would be treated differently by Marxian theory. They would be disaggregated into SE_{sc}, SE_{sc1}, SE_{nc2}, and SE_{nc3}. The specifics of that disaggregation would depend on whether the legislation provided conditions of existence for the state's own appropriation of surplus value or for the state's other sources of class and nonclass revenues.

Marxian analysis of the state in modern capitalist societies asks different questions, organizes its accounts of value flows by means of different categories, and generates different answers from those of non-Marxian theories. The Marxian theory of the state focuses attention on the variety of its class and nonclass component processes. It explores especially the complex linkages between those processes and the class and nonclass processes that occur at other sites in the society. Marxian theory strives to understand especially the relationship between the state and society's class structure. That is neither a goal for nor an achievement of neoclassical or Keynesian economics.

4.10.3   Class Analysis and International Relations

As a theoretical and practical political tradition, Marxism has long been committed to what it calls "internationalism." In the Marxian view, capitalism has expanded from its west European base to colonize and transform the entire world economy. Therefore today the transition to a new and better society necessarily involves an international movement. Such a better society, in the Marxian view, depends on an international transition to postcapitalist class structures, whose egalitarian, democratic and collective forms of producing, appropriating, and distributing surplus labor warrant the label "socialist" or "communist."

Their concern with internationalism has led Marxists to pose questions about international relations. How did capitalism generate a world economy? How do class processes link nations together or keep them apart? How do class processes interact internationally with nonclass processes? What connections exist between international class processes and domestic class structures? To answer such questions, Marxian theory adopts a general approach to international relations that focuses on their class components and how these interact with domestic class structures. Sketching such an approach is our task here.

Over the last few centuries, an expanding Europe was a major force in shaping and reshaping the complex set of processes linking the different nations of the world. At various times and in varying degrees many different processes composed such linkages. Pillage, theft, crusading, wars and colonization sometimes connected different nations, as did religious missions, commodity exchange (trade), foreign investment, distribution of motion pictures, and labor migrations. These are a few of the major international linking processes that have comprised our planet's evolving international relations.

What Marxian theory adds to the understanding of international relations is an exploration of their class dimensions. Both fundamental and subsumed class processes can exist between and thereby link two different nations. To take the example of a capitalist fundamental class process, we might consider a corporation in one country whose board of directors hired and appropriated the surplus labor of productive workers in a different country. The appropriation of such surplus labor would then occur across national boundaries. The same applies to the capitalist subsumed class process. For example, industrial capitalists in one country who appropriated surplus labor from productive workers there might then pay interest or dividends to moneylenders or shareholders in another country. Such subsumed class payments across national boundaries are components of international relations. Thus, lending in one direction between nations is a nonclass process comprising international relations, while a subsumed class interest payment in the reverse direction would be a class process comprising international relations. Of course, noncapitalist as well as capitalist class processes can and do occur across national boundaries.

Some examples will suggest the implications of such a Marxian class analysis of international relations. An investment bank on Wall Street lends money to an industrial capitalist in Brazil. The latter uses that money to hire Brazilian productive laborers to produce computer components which are sold in Europe. These complex relationships include and connect:

- the capitalist fundamental class process inside Brazil;
- the nonclass lending process between New York and Brazil;
- the capitalist subsumed class process: Brazilian interest to New York;
- the nonclass process of commodity exchange: Brazil's exports.

Of course, this list is partial. It does not include all of the processes involved in this example of international relations. Letters and telephone calls between New York and Brazil are international cultural processes; diplomatic maneuvers associated with the loan are international political processes; and climatic conditions affecting air travel between New York and Brazil are component international natural processes.

The specific processes chosen for the list above reflect the focus of Marxian theory. They also permit some distinctively Marxian conclusions about international relations. First, the three particular international flows of funds in our example are not exploitative; that is, they are not appropriations of surplus value. Exploitation only occurs inside Brazil, as exploitation of Brazilians by Brazilians. Other parts of the world provide key conditions for the existence and continuation of Brazilian exploitation.

By contrast, consider a situation in which a multinational industrial corporation based in Texas closes factories producing automobile components inside the United States and establishes a subsidiary in Liberia. That subsidiary hires Liberian productive laborers to produce the same automobile components to be shipped to the multinational corporation in Texas for sales throughout the United States. In this case the multinational corporation appropriates in Texas surplus value produced in Liberia; value flows internationally from the latter to the former. This capitalist fundamental class process is thus international, part of the international relations between the two countries. Likewise the foreign investment from the multinational corporation to establish the subsidiary in Liberia was another value flow comprising international relations.

What Marxian theory highlights here are differences that exist among the class and nonclass processes that constitute international flows of value. The flow of value from Brazil to the New York bank was a subsumed class process, while the flow of value from Liberia to the United States was a fundamental class process. The international relationships in the two cases differ because the social consequences of the two different kinds of class processes differ.

We can illustrate the differing social consequences by further elaborating our two examples. In the New York–Brazil case, international relations entail the support of Brazilian industrial capitalism and the sharing of its fruits between industrial capitalists in Brazil and moneylenders in the United States. In the Texas–Liberia case, international relations entail the contraction of industrial capitalism inside the United States and its expansion in Liberia. Inside all three countries—the United States, Brazil, and Liberia—there will be complex class and nonclass consequences of these particular international relations with one another. Moreover those consequences differ from those that would flow from international relations connected with labor migration, remittances sent home by emigrants, changing commodity imports and exports, and so on.

Non-Marxian analyses that ignore or abstract from class miss the important class implications of international relations. For example, if the flows of value from Brazil to the United States rise over some decades, non-Marxian observers might conclude that this is a negative sign for the development of capitalism in Brazil. They might then describe the international relationship between the two countries with adjectives such as imperialist or exploitative. For a Marxian analysis, the key question concerns the class and nonclass nature of the value flows within the relationship between the United States and Brazil. If those flows reflect rising monopoly prices obtained for US exports to Brazil, the negative conclusion might be warranted. However, if those flows reflect instead rising subsumed class payments from expanding Brazilian industrial capitalists to US banks, one might conclude the opposite, namely that the value flows within the international relationship between the United States and Brazil are major supports for capitalist development inside Brazil.

Non-Marxian approaches typically treat such flows very differently. Interest flows from Brazil to New York would be called payments for a service (access to loaned money). Surplus appropriated in Texas and produced in Liberia would likewise be called payments for another kind of service: return on invested capital. Such approaches remove class distinctions and indeed block out notions of class altogether. Hence they do not ask or answer questions about the class implications of the value flows within international relations.

Consider a long-standing critique of the modern world's system of international relations. It explains widening gaps of wealth and income between rich, industrialized nations at the center and the peripheral, economically deprived hinterland nations. Critics denounce the unjust and one-sided pattern of net value flows from periphery to center, proposing new and different international relations that would reverse the net flows. Only then, they argue, could the poor nations of Asia, Africa, and Latin America finally emerge from their desperate and deteriorating social conditions.

The Marxian theory developed in this book disagrees with such reasoning, while sympathizing, of course, with the goal of transforming poor nations. Redirecting international value flows might not significantly change the central issue for social progress in Asia, Africa, and Latin America: the transformation of their national class structures. Even if Brazilian capitalists no longer paid interest to New York banks, that might be because Brazilian capitalists had found ways to more intensely exploit their workers and to rely on their own expanded surpluses instead of foreign loans from New York. Rising rates of Brazilian exploitation could and likely would exacerbate income and wealth inequalities inside Brazil and exercise all sorts of other negative influences on social development there in the present and future.

Similarly some non-Marxian theories of international relations take inspiration from neoclassical economists' celebration of private property and markets.

They conclude that poor nations around the world should immediately remove all legal, cultural, and political barriers to the maximum expansion of commodity trade as the solution to poverty. Drawing poor nations into a world commodity market, they argue, would bring them the benefits of prosperity and growth enjoyed by the world's rich center countries.

Marxian theory recoils from such a prescription because it is class blind. It fails to see the capitalist class structures in the center and the periphery. It therefore fails to appreciate how their interactions are major supports for social problems in both parts of the world economy and for the massive inequalities between them. Hence extending capitalist class structures via expanding world trade would only deepen the problem. The policies needed instead, Marxian theorists argue, should aim for transformations from capitalist to noncapitalist class structures.

Appendix A: Why Does Marxian Theory Make Class Its Entry Point?

In this appendix we consider a question often put to Marxists: Why do you make class your entry point rather than individual preferences and productive capabilities, macroeconomic structures and their associated rules or laws of behavior, political power, race, gender or many other possible aspects of society? While we touched on this issue earlier in this book, a fuller statement may be useful here.

The answer now (as also in Marx's day) follows from what Marxists believe to be the social role of a theory. A theory invented and spread will have an impact on every other process in society. Part of that impact stems from the theory's entry point. The entry point of a theory affects society by drawing attention to it. To produce a new theory is, among other things, to focus interest on its entry point.

Marxian theory has always self-consciously drawn attention and interest to the class process. Marx himself believed that his fellow-revolutionists did not adequately understand class as defined and understood in relation to the social organization of the surplus. They likewise missed the importance of class processes—producing, appropriating, and distributing surpluses—both in the societies they sought to change and in those they dreamed of establishing. His theory aimed to rectify this situation: to focus attention on class and its relations to all the other, nonclass aspects of society and social change.

The point was not to claim that class was any more important a part of society than power, individual preferences, institutions, language, race, or gender. Rather, Marx's purpose in making class his entry point into social analyses was to remedy the ignorance and underestimation of class which, in his view, undercut the revolutionary projects he supported. In this way he added the issue of class to the agendas and strategies for change of many of his contemporaries.

However, after Marx, the class issue in terms of the organization of surpluses faded among the many issues that inspired movements for social change over the decades. More recently activists have stressed instead issues of the democratic distribution of power and of racial and gender inequalities. Movements for broad social democracy and racial and gender equality developed social theories whose entry points were power, race, and gender. Those theories focused attention on those particular aspects of society. While some of those theories were influenced by Marxian theory, they tended to substitute nonclass processes for the class process as their entry points.

This situation has now provoked a pendulum swing back toward a concern with class in its surplus definition and usage, lest Marx's insights be lost to the movements for social change. People have become increasingly interested in Marxian theory for reasons quite similar to Marx's original motivation in producing his theory. Yet again, another severe capitalist economic crisis that erupted in 2008 reminded millions of the risks, dangers, and problems of capitalism. Broad public interest revived in reading Marx and the Marxist tradition.

One result of renewed attention to the Marxian tradition is greater interest in the Marxian theory presented here. It addresses the question of why class is Marxian theory's entry point by stressing the current need for those interested in social change to confront the issue of class and to incorporate it into their strategies. One set of social conditions produced Marx and the revolutionary movements of his time. Current conditions have produced a revival of interest and work in Marxian theory, and for similar basic reasons. That is why class remains Marxian theory's entry point.

Appendix B: The "Transformation Problem"

As much or more than any other topic in Marxian economics, the relationship between "values" and "prices" of commodities has engaged debates among Marxist, neoclassical, and Keynesian economists. As this book makes clear, values are central to Marxist arguments about exploitation, competition, business cycles, and most other aspects of capitalist economies. Yet neoclassical and Keynesian economics—and thus most of the last century's discussions of economic issues—use prices, not values, in their arguments. So the question arose: Are value and price theories/analyses simply different, alternative ways to understand capitalism, or is one correct and the other false?

The major classical economists such as Adam Smith and David Ricardo used values in their work. Sometimes they equated values to prices and sometimes they viewed values as the average or long-term price around which daily prices fluctuated. In general, classical economists did not think the value–price relationship all that important. They focused on other topics such as how economic growth occurred, how the total output of society was divided among capitalists, workers, and landlords, why economic crises kept recurring, and so on. Marx, as a close student of Smith and Ricardo, followed them in this regard. He too relegated the value–price relationship to a secondary status (discussed in a small number of chapters in Vols. 2 and 3 of his major work, *Capital*).

What made the relationship between value and prices important was a sharp critical attack on Marxian economics by one of its opponents, the Austrian economist Eugen von Bohm-Bawerk (1851–1914). In 1896 Bohm-Bawerk published a book attacking Marx's economics as fundamentally flawed *because of its value theory*. He insisted that for Marx's economics to be valid, he had to show that commodities' values stood in a clear, consistent, and fixed relationship with their prices. Values—and hence value analysis—had to be precisely and consistently transformable into prices and price analysis. Bohm-Bawerk aimed to show that Marx's own effort to "transform" (Marx's own term in *Capital*, vol. 3) values into prices was logically inconsistent and flawed, thereby invalidating the totality of Marxian economics.

Marxists disagreed: most defended Marx's "transformation" as logical and defensible; many debated alternative interpretations of Marx's transformation; and some argued that the bulk of Marx's critique of capitalism did not depend on the nuances of the mathematical relation between values and prices.

Across the twentieth century Marxists and anti-Marxists debated what came to be known as "the transformation problem." A vast literature developed (although interest has waned over the last decade). Since neoclassical and Keynesian economists focused so much on markets and market prices and since they disliked Marx and Marxism, they mostly embraced the idea that Marx's notion of commodity values introduced something metaphysical, unrealistic, and unnecessary (and perhaps politically motivated) into economics. So Marxists mostly defended while neoclassical and Keynesian economists mostly attacked Marxian value theory.

One position that emerged in the last generation of debates over the transformation of values into prices achieved a kind of resolution (Wolff, Callari, and Roberts 1984). In this view, which we present below, Marxian value theory and the price theory endorsed by neoclassical and Keynesian economists are recognized as different ways of understanding how capitalist economies work. There is no need to debate which is correct any more than there is a need to debate whether Christianity or Buddhism is correct. The better approach is to explore and learn from their differences, what each teaches and prioritizes, what each illuminates and obscures.

Marx specifies the relationship between values and prices in several sections of *Capital,* Vol. 2 and especially in the first section of *Capital*, Vol. 3. There he introduces qualifications to the value analysis used initially to introduce many of his basic ideas in Vol. 1. In that first volume, Marx presents his labor theory of value; it builds upon but also differs in important ways from the labor theories of value in Smith and Ricardo. In Marx's formulation, as we have observed in this chapter, the value of each commodity is defined as the amount of "socially necessary abstract labor time" (SNALT) needed to produce it. In our text example, 14 hours of labor is socially necessary to produce a chair. Marx's Vol. 1 analysis entailed a simplification in order to develop the theory of surplus value central to what Marx contributed that was new and different to economics. It is a simplification because it abstracts from all the other constituent causes/determinants of a commodity's market price. It simplifies by assuming that the SNALT needed to produce the commodity is the *only* determinant of (and thus equal to) its price in the market.

In Vols. 2 and 3, Marx can and does go beyond the initial simplifying assumption. He there shows how additional, typical aspects of capitalist economies—beyond the SNALT needed to produce commodities—also influence the market prices of commodities. In this way Marx differentiates the earlier SNALT-defined values of commodities from their later elaboration into prices. Prices are overdetermined by many different aspects of a capitalist economy; they are not essentialistically determined by (nor are they equal to) commodity values. Consider two of many possible examples.

In Vol. 2, Marx shows explicitly how the differing times it takes for two different commodities to be produced and circulated ("turnover times") make their prices diverge from their values. This happens when and because the two capitalist industries producing the two commodities compete. Marx shows how their competition entails changing the quantities that each industry supplies to the market until the profit rates for both industries equalize. The competition that yields equal profit rates changes commodity supplies in relation to market demands for them which makes their prices diverge from their SNALT-defined values since the latter abstracted from (ignored) the constitutent influence of different turnover times and interindustry competition on prices. In Vol. 3, Marx likewise shows how the different compositions of capital (ratios of constant capital to the sum of constant and variable capital) in different industries interact with competition and equalizing profit rates to further differentiate commodity prices from their values.

Marx's labor theory of value is not, in our reading, conceptualized as an alternative to a price theory. Rather, it is one particular way to understand the workings of capitalist economies including the commodity prices generated in market exchanges. His labor theory of value explains and explores markets and prices in terms of their nonreductive connections to the exploitation inside capitalist enterprises that his writings stress. In Marx's view (especially in the "circuits of capital" discussion at the beginning of Vol. 2), analyses of capitalist economies that do not connect markets and prices to surplus labor and production are theoretical alternatives that effectively deny the existence and relevance of exploitation. In other words, Marxian theory explains prices by a value analysis that is complex and considers many causes but prioritizes the relation of prices to exploitation. In contrast, neoclassical and Keynesian theories explain prices as also complex but exclude exploitation and SNALT altogether from any explanatory role. Given such profoundly different theories of price, it is little wonder that Marxian theory reaches such different conclusions from those reached by neoclassical and Keynesian theories.

A final but important technical note: many twentieth century discussions of the relation of Marx's values to prices turned on the mathematics of that relation. Various problems arose because analysts within and without the Marxian tradition (1) interpreted SNALT to be defined in purely and exclusively physical/technical labor terms, and (2) presumed that market prices (P) were determined by values (V) in the unidirectional relationship of $V \rightarrow P$. In other words, these discussions assumed that values were determined only by the physical and technical requirements to produce commodities. Using the language of traditional Marxism, values became an effect rooted in the forces of production as their essential cause.

In proceeding in this essentialist way—forces of production as the ultimate cause of price—problems arose concerning the consistency of mathematical solutions (with basic propositions) in Marx's general analysis of value and surplus value. In other words, Marx's value theory became suspect, if not rejected, because of logical inconsistencies attributed to it—a serious criticism of any theory.

However, starting in the mid-1980s several Marxist researchers showed that all those consistency problems could and would be resolved if analysts proceeded differently in their initial presumptions. This new approach first appeared in Bruce Roberts's seminal work (Roberts 1981). Most important, first Roberts and then others showed that logical inconsistencies would disappear if analysts rejected essentialist reasoning and embraced instead the causal logic of overdetermination. The outline of their alternative argument follows. Commodity values, defined as before in terms of SNALT, should be understood with emphasis on SN, namely the phrase "socially necessary." That meant, to them, that the quantum of value every capitalist paid for purchased commodity inputs into production (the means of production) equaled the prices that capitalist had to pay for those inputs. Those input commodity prices defined what was "socially necessary," what capitalist had to pay in the market to acquire those inputs. *The value of the capitalist's outputs was thus partly determined by the prices paid for the produced commodity inputs.* Returning to our example, the value of a chair was the sum of 8 hours of living labor plus the *prices of these inputs*. Because of well-known assumptions

Marx made in Vol. 3 of *Capital* (about capitalists located in different industries deploying differing compositions of capital and competitively seeking the highest profit rate on their capital across the economy), the prices of capitalists' purchased commodity inputs turn out to be different from their values. For example, the labor attached to the inputs no longer will be the 6 hours of other workers' past labor, as we previously specified in the text, but instead a different number. That different number will reflect the different social context considered by Marx, namely his two new assumptions in regard to differing compositions of capital and competition. Hence that new number must be added to the 8 hours of living labor to yield the new value (V) of a chair. Symbolically, the revised Vol. 3 formula for the value of the commodity becomes $P + LL = V$, where P stands for the prices of the purchased inputs. Thus P stands for this new number that must be added to living labor, if capitalists are to purchase the means at what they cost in the market so as to combine them with living labor to produce outputs.

Instead of the traditional one-way mathematical determination of prices by values, the new approach proceeded with a two-way mutual determination of prices by values and values by prices within the framework of prices and values as both over-determined in this book's sense and use of that term. Technically, two related and simultaneous transformations occurred: values were transformed into prices *and* prices were transformed into values $P \leftrightarrow V$, where the $\leftrightarrow$ stands for the two-directional relationship.

With the basic consistency issue thereby resolved, attention can return to what we think are the basic lessons taught by the transformation problem literature and debate. These lessons include, first, that Marxian theory yields a different understanding of capitalist economies—including prices—than neoclassical and Keynesian theories do. The second lesson is that the relation among these theories is not a matter of which is right and which wrong but rather a matter of how we will all act differently in and on our world depending on which (or which combination) of these theories we find persuasive. The third lesson concerns recognizing that the struggles among proponents of these theories help shape our world and affect us all.

Appendix C: Capitalist Competition

Part 1

Consider the chair industry in which three competitive firms produce identical chairs. We start by assuming they have identical cost structures. To facilitate discussion, we also assume that one hour of labor is equivalent to one dollar. The following table lists the chair-firms vertically as firms number 1, 2, and 3 and lists horizontally their respective value categories read either in $ or labor values. Using the same numbers as presented in the text, capitalists of firm 1 purchase $6 of C, $6 of V, and appropriate $2 of S from workers employed in that firm. The same numbers apply to capitalist firms 2 and 3. We use the letter q to denote the number (1) of chairs each produces. The letter W stands, as before, for the total value of chairs produced, which is $14 for each, and the value per unit is W/q, or in this case $14. We can call this number the amount of labor each private-capitalist requires to produce one chair. Because all capitalists are assumed to be alike, it is also the average or social value per chair in this assumed competitive industry. As we will soon see, competition will produce a difference between this individual firm's—or its private value—and the average of all firms'—or social—value per unit.

Other important ratios are listed horizontally to reflect the firms' respective economic performance: their business success is measured by the value profit rate $r = S/C + V = 1/6$, their index of mechanization k is measured by the quantitative importance of C as a proportion of their total capital $k = C/C + V = \frac{1}{2}$, and their relative efficiency in the industry is measured by their average production cost $AC = C + V/q = 12$. Marx spends a good number of pages in *Capital,* Vol. 1 explaining why mechanization, as measured by k, tends to rise in capitalist development. As we will see, one reason is competition:

Capitalist	C	V	S	W	q	r	k	AC
1	6	6	2	14	1	1/6	1/2	12
2	6	6	2	14	1	1/6	1/2	12
3	6	6	2	14	1	1/6	1/2	12

Suppose that firm 2 raises its productivity. It now produces two chairs in the same labor time that formerly produced one. As explained in the text, we assumed its capitalists hired more supervisors (managers) to gain this efficiency advantage. This one change will change everything in the industry.

Firm 2's capitalists have now become the least cost producer in the industry. We can easily see this by calculating the change in their average costs: divide the same $12 of $(C + V)$ costs by 2 chairs to get the new AC of $6. In our table, then, capitalist 2 sees its average cost (AC) drop from $12 to $6, while its competitors' AC remains unchanged at $12. In addition the value of a chair falls in the industry to $10.50. We calculate this new and lowered per-chair value as a (weighted) average of the three capitalist firms' amounts of private labor times: $10.50 = [14(1) + 7(2) + 14(1)]/4$, where 4 is the new total number of chairs produced across the three producers.

It is worthwhile spending a moment examining exactly what this market unit value represents. It averages together the *private* amounts of labor each capitalist enterprise requires to produce its chairs. Notice that capitalist 2's business strategy has successfully reduced the amount of labor required to produce each chair from 14 to 7, while its competitors still require the same and hence more labor time to produce their chairs. The average of all producers' labor times needed per chair produced is merely the particular way that markets socialize these different private labor times.

Now, when each capitalist firm sells its chairs at this new market price of $10.50, the profits realized by each capitalist enterprise are very different from what they were prior to of capitalist 2's increase in its productivity. Consider first capitalist firms 1 and 3. They come to market expecting to sell their produced chairs at $14 per chair. That selling price would cover fully their respective costs of producing them ($12) and allow each to realize a surplus of $2 embodied in each chair. Unfortunately for them however, their expectations are frustrated. They must sell at the new competitive per-chair value of $10.50.

Their frustration stems from the private action of capitalist 2 in raising its labor productivity. That strategy reduced the market price of a chair from its previous $14 to the new $10.50. Selling their chairs at the new lower market price yields both capitalists a loss of $1.5 that threatens their ability to continue producing chairs. We show this stark result in the following second table:

Capitalist	Total revenue	Total cost	Profits	Average cost
1	10.5	12	−1.5	12
2	21.0	12	9.0	6
3	10.5	12	−1.5	12

Not only have the expected profits of $2 per chair for capitalist 1 and 3 disappeared, but matters are still worse. They no longer can cover their costs of doing business in this industry. While each needs $12 of sales to cover its production costs, each can sell its output only for $10.5. Yet the market loss incurred by capitalists 1 and 3 is equal exactly to capitalist 2's gain in profits. Let us explain. Capitalist 2 comes to market quite happy to sell each of its chairs for $7, for that is the amount of (private) labor it required to produce each. However, to its delight it finds it can sell its chairs at the higher *social* average of $10.50 per chair. As shown in the second of our tables, it sells its two chairs and earns $21 in total sales revenues as against its unchanged $12 of costs. Capitalist 2's profits have soared from $2 to $9. Put differently, it has been able to reduce its average production costs proportionately more than the fall in the market price. Is there any question but that strategies to lower average costs pay off in a competitive market?

Market competition results in a redistribution of value of $3.5 from each of capitalists 1 and 3 to capitalist 2, enabling the latter's profits to expand from $2 to $9. This difference of $7 is what Marx calls a super profit, the extra profits earned by capitalist 2 above and beyond its unchanged surplus value of $2. It gains this $7 of super profits at the direct expense of reduced values received when capitalists 2 and 3 sell their chairs.

Part 2

Following the text, suppose that the board of directors of firm 2 decides to pursue a different strategy from that examined in part 1 above. Rather than distributing surplus to expand supervisors, the board instead distributes surplus to accumulate capital aimed at altering its system of production. Its goal is to become more mechanized—capital intensive. The board accomplishes this by buying additional machines and tools (constant capital) but without purchasing more labor power. In other words, it raises its composition of capital k. This new distributive strategy is illustrated in the following table. There capitalist 2 expands its constant capital from $6 to $12 without employing more workers. It thereby raises its k to 2/3. This accumulation strategy also raises its labor productivity from one to two chairs (the same number of workers as before are now equipped with more machines and tools allowing them to produce more chairs). Average cost of production for capitalist 2 falls to $9.

Capitalist	C	V	S	W	q	k	AC
1	6	6	2	14	1	1/2	12
2	12	6	2	20	2	2/3	9
3	6	6	2	14	1	1/2	12

The new market value of a chair becomes $12. Once again, the average falls to all because capitalist 2 found a different way to innovate and raise its productivity. The following table shows the resulting new profit position for each competing firm:

Capitalist	Total revenue	Total cost	Profits
1	12	12	0
2	24	18	6
3	12	12	0

Capitalist 2 earns a super profit at the direct expense of capitalists 1 and 3. Like the previous case, unless the latter respond, their continued operation is problematic. Suppose then that these capitalists do react to this threat to their continued existence. They decide to replicate the business strategy of capitalist 2. They too accumulate $6 of C, raising their composition of capital to 2/3. They too reduce their costs of production to $9. We show the new result in the following and last of our tables:

Capitalist	C	V	S	W	q	k	AC
1	12	6	2	20	2	2/3	9
2	12	6	2	20	2	2/3	9
3	12	6	2	20	2	2/3	9

Clearly, this strategy for capitalists 1 and 3 has paid off: they appropriate and realize the same $2 of surplus value they had prior to the offensive action of capitalist 2. It is also true that their recovery is at the expense of capitalist 2: it no longer earns a super profit, but at least it too appropriates and realizes $2 of surplus value. However, some major changes also have occurred and they point to one of Marx's most well-known arguments in regard to the contradictions of capitalism.

On the one hand, the exchange value of chairs has fallen to $10 per chair. Competition has forced each and every capitalist to accumulate capital (or risk going out of business) accompanied by an increase in the composition of capital (k). The social result of these competitive actions on the part of all capitalists is to make more wealth available at more affordable prices for the citizens of capitalism: the capitalist economy delivers 6 rather than 3 chairs at $10 rather than $12 per chair. Posed in terms of traditional Marxism, capitalist competition helps develop the forces of production enabling more wealth to be forthcoming. This example reflects the actual history of just about every kind of capitalist commodity from food to housing to shoes to cars to electronics. In each, interacting capitalist competition and accumulation has resulted in historic decreases in average costs of production and values per unit.

On the other hand, a new and serious problem arises. If we look back at the last table for a moment, we can see that the value profit rate also falls for each and every capitalist from its initial rate of 1/6 to its new rate of 1/9. In other words, to receive the same surplus value of $2 as before, each capitalist now requires more capital ($18 rather than $12) to be advanced. This fall in the return on capital can discourage profit-oriented capitalists and lead them to reduce their subsumed class expenditures (actually reduce their rate of expansion) and hence cause a recession or even depression. Reacting to a lower profit rate, they contract new capital accumulation and other distributions (to managers, research and development, borrowings, dividends, etc.). As the effects of reduced business expenditures flow throughout the economy, unemployed labor and unused means of production arise. Besides lost jobs and excess industrial capacity, the loss to society is potential wealth that could have been produced if not for the fall in the profit rate.

Marx concludes that capitalist competition is inherently contradictory: the interaction between capital accumulation and markets leads to more wealth produced (more chairs in the expansion) followed by less wealth (fewer chairs in the contraction). As we see, these are not independent events; rather, they are both integral parts of how capitalism functions.

Appendix D: Rising Exploitation with Rising Real Wages

Recall the earlier equation for the value of labor power:

$V = e \cdot q.$

Let us now calculate what portion of the change in V is accounted for by changes in each of the two factors on the right-hand side of this equation. First, there is the change in the per-unit value of wage commodities multiplied by the initial standard of living: $\Delta e \cdot q$. Second, there is the change in the standard of living multiplied by the initial per-unit value of the wage commodities: $\Delta q \cdot e$. Adding both changes, we derive the change in V:

$\Delta V = (\Delta e \cdot q) + (\Delta q \cdot e).$

We may rewrite this equation in terms of percentage rates of change:

$$\frac{\Delta V}{V} = \frac{\Delta e}{e} + \frac{\Delta q}{q}.$$

It follows that a 10 percent decline in the value of labor power ($\Delta V/V$) and a simultaneous 20 percent decline in unit values of wage goods ($\Delta e/e$) would equal a 10 percent *rise* in real wages ($\Delta q/q$).

5 Late Neoclassical Theory

with Yahya M. Madra

5.1 Introduction: Why This Chapter?

This chapter introduces some interesting recent developments in and extensions of neoclassical theory. We do this for two reasons. First, some economists claim that these changes effectively refute several basic criticisms of standard neoclassical theory, and many of these changes have been sufficiently integrated into that theory to be frequently included in introductory microeconomics textbooks. Second, a smaller number of economists also claim that certain recent extensions and developments represent more: a break from neoclassical economic theory that inaugurates a new and different kind of economic theory. If the second of these claims were persuasive, then we would need to add another, fourth economic theory to the three already considered. We think students should be aware of these theoretical changes and the claims surrounding them. They represent still another dimension to the continuing struggles within economics as a field of inquiry.

Part of any examination of any field of study is to figure out if, when, and how its practitioners break from tradition and launch radically new ways to think about the objects in that field. This is as true in economics as it is in physics or art. Indeed Keynesian economics represents such a break in the 1930s from what was then the hegemonic neoclassical tradition. Similarly Marxian economics broke in the nineteenth century from the classical tradition of Smith and Ricardo. In this chapter we will explain why the recent developments and extensions in neoclassical economics do not mark a similar break or sea change in economic thought. The neoclassical tradition has rather effectively incorporated the recent changes without compromising either its entry point or logic. Thus we title this chapter "late neoclassical theory." In our view, while neoclassical theory keeps evolving, it nonetheless continues its basic approach to the new issues it engages. As this chapter shows, neoclassical theory's evolution has produced interesting, new understandings of some important topics and issues. These include: how and why markets fail and how society should respond; how to incorporate into its analysis interactive, strategic behavior of firms and individuals; how to extend the opportunity cost concept to include costs of market transactions and information; even how to incorporate altruistic alongside self-interested behavior. Nonetheless, these recent developments and extensions remain well within—rather than marking breaks from—the basic neoclassical framework discussed in chapter 2.

However, this chapter's presence does raise another question. Why include and focus on recent developments and extensions of only neoclassical theory and not of the other two economic theories compared in this book? Actually, we did include a parallel, albeit limited, examination of recent developments within the Marxian tradition when we distinguished traditional (determinist/ mode of production) from nontraditional (overdeterminist/class) Marxian theories. And we did consider some interesting changes and extensions in the Keynesian approach such as post-Keynesian economics in chapter 3. Additionally section 5.3.3 below takes up again a key point of post-Keynesian economics, namely how the social environment shapes human behavior.

Our reason for including this chapter is much influenced by two events. First, given the dominance of neoclassical economic theory in academe, the media, and political discourse over the last generation, we believe our readers should be aware of the theory's evolution and the claims of some to have broken from it. Second, the global economic crisis that erupted in 2007 reopened the protracted struggles among neoclassical, Keynesian, and Marxian approaches and policies. Those struggles include claims by some participants to have conceived altogether new ways to understand and resolve the crisis. We think they overstate their arguments. No such radical breaks have so far occurred. The basic contest among the three major paradigms continues. It shapes our world and our future, and thus provides a major motivation for writing this book.

5.1.1   Criticisms and Their Consequences

As with any theory, economic or otherwise, neoclassical theory has received criticism over the many years of its development. Some alleged its inadequate representation of key events and major changes in the real world. It mirrored the real world inadequately and thus explained it improperly. Neoclassical theory just does not correspond to what really occurs, such critics argue, since production and consumption have complex and unaccounted for extra-market effects (called "externalities"), giant corporations typically wield power in all kinds of markets, individuals behave in ways that cannot be explained by the axioms of choice, the actions of the state and its agents have complex effects on the workings of supply and demand, recessionary and inflationary cycles impact capitalist economies, and the class stucture of society interacts with everything else in the economy. These kinds of criticisms stem from views that may well accept the analytical sophistication of neoclassical theory but question whether it truly reflects or adequately captures what occurs in the real world. From this perspective, the theory suffers from a lack of "realism."

Other critics focus more on the structure and logic of neoclassical theory. For example, some claim to have found serious internal inconsistencies. For them, the neoclassical explanation of value and distribution presented in chapter 2 is flawed. One of the most famous of these criticisms argues that neoclassical theory cannot explain the distribution of income in society because of its inherent difficulty in measuring the value of capital. In that argument, there may not be any unit by which this resource input can be measured independently of the equilibrium prices that neoclassical theory claims to explain partly on the basis of specific quantities of that input. Consequently one of the entry-point concepts of neoclassical theory, the initial capital endowment, can no longer be considered an essence.[1]

A different but related criticism questions the neoclassical notion of exogenous preferences of individuals. Our preferences for goods and services, leisure versus labor, and present versus future incomes are not given but always vary in response to social change including economic processes. Thus, these critics say, neoclassical theory errs in explaining market prices and other economic outcomes as based on (essentially caused by) "given" preferences. This is because preferences are not given. They are shaped by the entire social context in which they arise and that context includes economic events and changes. Hence market prices, incomes, and savings for future consumption are not merely effects of our preferences but likewise and simultaneously causes of them. In mathematical terms, prices and incomes must be variables included in the individual utility functions discussed in chapter 2. In addition, as psychology teaches, we are only conscious of a few of all the societal and natural factors affecting our choices. Our preferences for friends and lovers are partly functions of our unconscious as are our preferences for economic objects. And our unconscious is continually shaped and altered by our economic as well as cultural and political activities. For this criticism of neoclassical theory, our preferences—and the axioms of choice from which that theory derives those preferences—cannot be essential, ultimate causes of economic phenomena since they are caused and changed by those same phenomena they seek to explain. Those critics find it illogical to treat preferences as exogenous in the face of mutual causation between preferences and prices and incomes.

No easy, clear-cut demarcation line separates criticisms directed at the lack of realism of neoclassical theory and criticisms of its internal inconsistency. The two kinds of criticism often converge in the works of one writer or even with one argument. Moreover these criticisms have emerged from both neoclassical theorists and analysts committed to Keynesian and Marxian theories.

Keynes, for example, began his major contribution by criticizing the notions of marginal productivity of labor and marginal utility that underlay the neoclassical theory of labor markets. Marx often ridiculed certain assumptions of classical economics that passed intact into neoclassical theory. For example, he thought it absurd to define capitalists' profits as rewards to something called capital, an object, when for him profits emerged from a particular relationship between laborers and capitalists. Keynes and Marx confronted the neoclassical entry-point concepts with their very different entry points (prescribed structural rules for Keynes and class for Marx). Their criticisms were less attacks on neoclassical theory's logical consistency or lack of realism (although they included such attacks) than they were affirmations of different theories of how economic realities are organized and how they function.

Criticisms of neoclassical theory have always had different results. Theorists who find merits in the criticisms seek to develop alternative ways of explaining economic events that overcome neoclassical theory's lack of realism and/or logical inconsistencies. Among them, some ultimately introduce a different new entry point and/or different logic and thereby become "nonneoclassical." Keynes did that in the twentieth century in one way while Marx broke from classical economic theory in another way in the nineteenth. Other critics modify some of the theory's entry-point concepts and logic yet remain within the basic framework of the neoclassical way of thinking. Such theorists aim to develop the existing body of neoclassical theory to respond to its critics by enhancing its logical consistency and empirical realism. Over recent years they developed new ideas and arguments about pervasive market imperfections, observed human behavior that deviates from the assumptions of the neoclassical tradition, and strategic actions that take account of the expected behavior of others. Neoclassical theory changed over the years partly as a result of the criticisms leveled against it. The change and development of the theory is the subject of this chapter.

Criticisms are among the conditions that produce changes in all theories. Criticisms have pushed and continue to push neoclassicists to ask new kinds of questions of their theory, questions not previously asked. Criticisms provoke efforts to correct discovered "errors" or contradictions within the theory. Creative individuals may be stimulated to invent new concepts to deal with the criticisms. Paradoxically, the richness, power, and uniqueness of neoclassical theory derive in part from the attacks of its harshest critics.

Our discussion will be organized around three distinct yet connected neoclassical responses to criticisms. The first set of responses concern neoclassical theory's concept of markets and critics' claims of ubiquitous market imperfections. The second set of responses deals with human behavior that critics argue does not conform to neoclassical theory's standard rationality assumptions. Last, the third set of responses treats critics' insistence that in the real world firms and individuals must and do take into account expected responses of others while traditional neoclassical theory assumed they do not.

5.1.2   The Responses: An Overview

Neoclassical economists have developed new approaches to market analysis when those markets exhibit imperfections rather than the competitive perfection assumed in the traditional theory. The market imperfections considered include, for example, the deployment of power by one or a few buyer(s) or seller(s) to determine price, the lack of perfect information among buyers and sellers, the impossibility to write completely specified and enforceable contracts among market participants, the external effects of market transactions on noncontracting third parties, and technologies that yield continually declining average costs as output increases. One interesting result of the theoretical efforts to accommodate and understand these imperfections within neoclassical theory has been new explanations for why nonmarket institutions (firms, governments, judicial systems, etc.) arise as societal solutions to various forms of market failures resulting from market imperfections.

The responses to critics and resulting new approaches considered here fall under the heading of *late neoclassical theory* because they continue to refer to a Pareto optimal allocation of resources (through perfectly competitive market economies) as their goal, reference point, and standard of optimality. Recall that Pareto optimality referred to a competitive market equilibrium in which anyone who increases their well-being makes someone else worse off. Late neoclassical theory retains that standard but in the modified form of *minimizing the deviation from Pareto optimality* to measure the success/efficiency of any "solution" to market imperfections yielded by a firm, government, or court system. In other words, the central goal of economic analysis becomes how to move the economy closer to the traditional standard of Pareto optimality. That standard remains entrenched in late neoclassical theory and, as discussed in our chapter on neoclassical theory, that standard derives from and depends on the traditional entry points and essentialist logic of neoclassical theory. In that sense late neoclassical theory represents developments and changes that remain committed to the neoclassical tradition.

But responding to critiques of markets as imperfect is only one part of late neoclassical theory. Given the humanism informing neoclassical theory, it is no surprise that its assumptions about human behavior have also come under scrutiny and criticism. Critics have provoked neoclassical practitioners to modify those assumptions, especially the notions of individuals making their decisions independently of one another and in sole pursuit of their individual self-interest. New notions of human behavior have arisen that take into account nonselfish (non–self-interested) motivations and cognitive limitations to the human mind. Nonetheless, the basic humanism informing late neoclassical theory remains what it was in the neoclassical tradition; it is only that the human nature driving the economy is presented in a "more realistic" construction.

Late neoclassical theory's new specification of human behavior has also involved certain important modifications and extensions of the traditional assumptions of rationality and preferences. Recall that traditionally neoclassical theory views tastes for goods and services, leisure, and future income as derived from axioms of choice (as summarized in chapter 2) that are part of human nature. These natural axioms of choice define what human rationality is: the individual aim to maximize individual well-being in the face of given constraints. For neoclassical theory, human beings behave rationally if and when they acquire the most of what they want while taking into account their limitations.

The result is the traditional neoclassical notion of choice-making individuals who forgo no available opportunity to better satisfy their consistently defined, complete preferences. A rational human being is always an opportunist and purely self-regarding (i.e., one who only thinks and looks inwardly). Just as evolutionary theorists coined labels—*Homo habilis* to *Homo erectus* to *Homo sapiens*—to mark human evolution, economists coined *Homo economicus* to signify the emergence of this kind of opportunist, self-regarding, "rational" human being. This was understood to be "modern human," thereby equating modernity with the particular neoclassical definition of rationality.

Criticisms directed against this notion of an individual as always opportunist and only self-regarding prompted some neoclassicists to modify their definitions of rationality to include non–self-serving goals and aspirations. A Keynesian criticism (discussed in chapter 3) of neoclassical theory attacked it for not adequately acknowledging the role of uncertainty in all human decisions. Thus some neoclassicists also transformed traditional ideas about human rationality by questioning individuals' cognitive capacity to process the vast amount of information about commodities needed to be able make the "rational" decisions that best satisfied their preferences.

While such criticisms of traditional neoclassical notions of rationality yielded some interesting developments (especially in the emerging field of "behavioral economics" discussed below), the newer notions of how individuals behave still are defined in relation to the standard figure of *Homo economicus*. That traditional idea of the rational human being continues to serve as a normative (if not descriptive) standard. Newer notions of rationality maintain the tradition of seeing a redefined human rationality as determining the economy as a whole (humanism). Hence our decision to locate the recent responses to critiques of neoclassical rationality within late neoclassical theory.

New theories of equilibrium were responses to critiques of traditional neoclassical theory's notions of market behavior among individuals and institutions. Recall that in the standard neoclassical theory of equilibrium, individuals are assumed to be price-takers. In making decisions, they need consider only the information provided in the given prices of commodities they face along with their given endowments and available technology. Put differently, in the standard neoclassical economic model of a fully competitive society, rational individuals do not need to know what other individuals think in order to decide what to buy, sell, save, and invest.

Some neoclassical economists call this type of decision-making "parametric" to sharply distinguish it from "strategic" decision-making where individuals or institutions do make decisions that depend on the expected decisions and actions of others. Critics claim that the parametric environment does not adequately mirror the real world of decision-making. Real decision-making in imperfectly competitive markets must take into account all the possible actions and reactions by other market participants. Basically, decision-makers incorporate others' reasoning process into their own reasoning process. Their survival and success require the formulation of a strategy to deal with such interdependence.

Consider a business environment with imperfect competition: firms no longer are price-takers but instead price-makers. Each firm must then make its output and pricing decisions strategically, taking into account the expected actions of other firms. In analyzing this (and many other) strategic decision-making situations, neoclassical economics increasingly adopted a new notion of equilibrium named after the mathematician John Nash.

The traditional neoclassical market equilibrium is one in which demand and supply intersect. A Nash equilibrium is different: it occurs if and when no interacting agent benefits from unilaterally changing his or her chosen strategy. In recent years a still different notion of equilibrium has emerged. Some economists prefer to formulate the problem of equilibrium at the aggregate level of a population distribution of behavioral traits rather than at the micro level of interactions among rational individuals. These economists have come up with a notion of evolutionary stability. It specifies a stable distribution of patterns of behavior within a given population. They claim that such a notion is far more useful than the strictly individualistic premises of the Nash equilibrium idea.

While the developments of the Nash and evolutionary notions of equilibrium have rendered neoclassical theory more versatile and mathematically sophisticated, they did not break from the theory's traditional normative project. They continued the long-standing neoclassical desire to articulate a logically consistent and universally applicable theory of societal reconciliation that harmonized divergent economic interests. The search for an equilibrium solution—whatever its form—is a quest for a way to deal with economic differences and consequent conflicts within society generally and within capitalist economies in particular. The search for social harmony has a long intellectual history in economic theorizing, starting with Smith, followed by Pareto, and continuing today with these developments in late neoclassical theory.

Before we examine these major extensions of the neoclassical approach in more detail, let us emphasize again the shared qualities that lead us to situate them as late expressions of neoclassical theory. First, they all continue to refer (implicitly or explicitly) to the traditional neoclassical approach as their basic benchmark. For example, they may newly conceptualize human behavior but only through its deviations from or violations of the standard axioms of choice. Second, they construct their approaches to the economy with the aim of determining the conditions under which the diverse interests of individuals are or can be harmoniously reconciled. To the extent that some late neoclassical theorists move away from these two theoretical practices, they may yet begin a move beyond neoclassical theory. That remains a possibility for some who may even produce a new way of theorizing the economy much like Marxian and Keynesian theories did.

5.2   Theories of Market Imperfections

From its inception, neoclassical theory was criticized for adhering to an idealized model of perfectly competitive markets. Critics rejected the neoclassical assumptions that all economic actors (both firms and households) were price-takers, that contracts were fully specified and had no unaccounted (external) effects on third parties, that all individual actors had full and complete information, and that no missing markets exist. For such critics, traditional neoclassical economic theory was unrealistic in depicting a world composed of atom-like rational individuals who interacted with one another only in and through smoothly functioning competitive markets. And from its inception, neoclassical theorists tried to incorporate analyses of some possible deviations from the ideal world of perfect competition. Over the course of twentieth century, the types of deviations studied and the ways of handling imperfections through economic policy have changed in response to ongoing and changing criticisms.

A common charge in most of the criticisms is the failure of markets to work properly. The charge is serious, for market imperfections would preclude capitalism from achieving the efficiency of production or consumption that was always a major part of its self-justification. The sources of market imperfections specified by critics vary. They include the unaccounted for externalities or spillover effects stemming from production and consumption, market power wielded by giant corporations, state interference in the operation of markets, and the inability of human beings to foresee the future. They all interfere with the ability of human beings to make the rational market choices that result in a Pareto-type optimality of production and consumption. Market imperfections result in a societal mess: citizens enjoy less wealth than they should, they suffer the deleterious effects of unemployed resources, and they face increasing political tensions among their citizens over distribution of less wealth than they could have. Very little is optimal about this kind of world.

Broadly speaking, there have been two major kinds of criticism targeting the neoclassical notion of perfect competition in markets. They arose in different historical contexts. The first wave of market imperfection theories focused on two sets of problems that critics saw in capitalist economies: (1) unaccounted social effects on society arising from private economic activities and (2) social effects when firms or other institutions (e.g., unions or governmental bodies) used concentrated power to control a commodity's price. More recent critics of market perfection arose after 1950 and attributed market failures to "transaction costs" and "information failures." While the newer theories did not supplant the earlier ones, they did change one important aspect of the discussions. In the first generation of theories, the state was usually seen to offer the only solution for market imperfections. In the more recent theories, a variety of other kinds of institutions are favored as dealing more effectively with market failures.

5.2.1 Externalities and Ways of Managing Them

Recall that standard neoclassical theory assumes that individuals interact with one another only through and in markets. This means they only exchange what is stipulated in the contract that governs their private exchange. Hence they affect one another only via those markets. Suppose, however, that an observed market transaction causes an externality, namely an effect—external to the market transaction—that impacts third parties or nature. Traditional neoclassical theory does not recognize or account for this externality even though it surely belongs in a listing of the market transaction's costs and benefits and hence its efficiency.

For example, suppose that one individual's consumption of cigarettes produces an adverse effect on the utility of another with whom the smoker has no market relation. Consumption of this or, by extension, just about any commodity may yield such externalities, for one individual's consumption will often impact the welfare of others. Externalities may be positive as well: individuals who choose and pay for vaccinations against disease thereby benefit others—third parties—who neither paid for nor obtained vaccinations. Consider a production example in which oil drilling for offshore wells releases toxins into the water that kill fish and thus adversely affect the fishing industry. Hence economic transactions in oil markets can harm third parties who do not participate in the oil markets. In these cases private decisions of consumers or producers have impacts on others, but the social costs and benefits of those impacts remain unaccounted for by or in any market. Thus the deals reached in markets, efficient for the deal-makers, may well be inefficient once we consider the real, socially consequential costs and benefits the deal-makers and their markets ignore.

Public goods provide another important example of externalities. Consider the government providing national defense or clean air and water. In these instances of state-provided collective consumption, there cannot be private markets of the sort theorized in traditional neoclassical theory. Each citizen in the society consumes, as it were, the same amount of the public good irrespective of whether that citizen wants it or not. No one can be excluded from the benefit of national defense, a more healthy physical environment, or public education. The inability to exclude others from receiving these benefits is what marks public goods. The example of public goods also underscores the usefulness of distinguishing between positive and negative externalities, although there will likely be disagreement in judging what is negative and what is positive. For instance, while many citizens may well consider national defense to be a benefit to society, others may fear the social risks of a "military-industrial complex" and thus consider national defense to be a cost (meaning a negative externality).

Around the 1920s a British neoclassical economist Arthur Cecil Pigou (1877–1958) offered a new way to theorize negative externalities by distinguishing between "private" and "social" costs of a commodity. While the private costs of a commodity (the marginal cost of its production) are reflected in its price, its social costs (imposed on third parties and nature by its consumption, production, or both) are not. To return to our offshore oil production example, consider an oil drilling company in a competitive market that maximizes its profit by equating its marginal cost of drilling to the market-determined price of oil. In other words, $P_{oil} = MC_{private}$ where the subscript "private" stands for the oil company's private marginal costs of production. If oil drilling also causes environmental damage of one kind or another, that represents a cost to society. That social cost is not usually taken into account by the firm's focus on its private costs alone. This social cost is outside of—external to—the private supply of oil by this and other private firms that cause similar externalities in their different lines of business. Put differently, the (private) marginal cost curve of firms previously discussed did not include this social cost.

The result is stark: this market fails to yield the optimum, socially efficient output of oil. By extension, the same critique applies to other markets if they exhibit similar negative externalities. The market price for oil should be higher than what it is in the private market; it fails to count properly all the real costs (including environmental) incurred in its production:

$$P_{oil} < MC_{private} + MC_{social}.$$

The new added term, MC_{social}, represents the social cost of private drilling's environmental impact. Since the market price of oil fails to reflect its real (private and social) costs, more of the commodity will be produced and consumed than would be efficient and optimal in the neoclassical sense. Such externalities thus reduce overall social welfare. Notice here that the Pareto criterion or standard of efficiency remains: the externality produces a deviation from the traditional optimal standard of $P = MC$ because of an unpriced environmental cost. The externality discussion inaugurated by Pigou does not question the Pareto criterion itself. Thus, if the government levied an appropriate tax (known as a Pigouvian tax) on oil, the market price of oil could be raised to ensure that $P_{new} = MC_{private} + MC_{social}$, where P_{new} stands for the tax-adjusted price of oil.

In supply–demand terms, Pigou's extension of neoclassical theory creates a new and higher supply curve (it shifts up and to the left) to include the added social costs. The new neoclassical argument follows directly: goverment intervention via a tax equilibrates the assumedly unchanged demand for oil to this newly upward-shifted supply of oil. The resulting new higher price represents a market outcome returned to social efficiency in the definition provided by traditional neoclassical theory. The latter remains the benchmark for this late neoclassical theory.

State officials who levy such a Pigovian tax would have to estimate the social costs involved: never a straightforward business. The same applies to positive externalities. For example, state intervention to reduce cigarette consumption produces documented health benefits to society but also costs from (1) diminished opportunities for tobacco farmers, their families, and communities and (2) more demands on social security because reduced smoking enables people to live longer. And the list of externalities is very long as well as contested.

In fact, what economists, politicians, and others do is to count only some of the many costs and benefits that they think are important at that moment or at least those that they are aware of. Before Pigou, what were counted were private costs and private benefits. After Pigou, at least some social costs and benefits were added. Of course, the underlying question of which of the many social benefits and costs will be counted is hardly just a theoretical issue in economics. Rather, we struggle over the recognition and inclusion of social costs and benefits and the outcome of those struggles is what gets placed onto the social agenda. Clearly, today we recognize both private industry's and private consumption's impact on the natural environment. That impact and the counting of its costs result from many social forces. These include new theoretical work (e.g., the 1962 publication of Rachel Carson's pathbreaking book *Silent Spring*) to an organized environmental social movement to a general public awareness that our private lives impact nature and hence our continued ability to enjoy life. Similarly the negative externalities on our private lives arising from the capitalist business cycles are more or less recognized. Reducing or eliminating them motivated Keynesian economics and its policies. However, the costs to our lives arising from capitalist class exploitation are not now well recognized; hence little is done to deal with them. Unlike environmental or business-cycle externalities, they still remain mostly unacknowledged and unpriced.

A number of neoclassical economists (in particular, the more conservative) are very wary about government interventions into and constraints placed on the freedom of firms and individuals to make private decisions in their self-interest. They argue that a capitalist society should not allow the government to attempt nearly impossible cost and benefit calculations and then create taxes and subsidies based on them. Such neoclassical theorists argue that the externality-driven taxes and subsidies have their own consequences on markets (including their externalities) that could move the economy away from a Pareto position. A far better way to proceed, they argue, would be to recognize externalities but then allow affected parties privately to negotiate the compensations for those externalities. These economists base their solution on the Coase theorem named after the neoclassical economist who originated this argument (Coase 1960).

According to this theorem, if solid property rights exist and are fully delineated, and if transaction costs (e.g., arising from hiring a lawyer) are negligible, the problem of social cost can be fully and efficiently resolved through mutually beneficial trades among affected parties. To return to our offshore oil drilling example, those who benefit from it may well be different from those who are adversely affected by it. Viewed from the perspective of Pareto efficiency, offshore oil drilling makes some worse off (e.g., the fishing industry, tainted fish consumers, and those who prefer less polluted environments), but not drilling makes others worse off (e.g., businesses with losses from reduced drilling, workers with such losses, their local communities, and automobile drivers required to pay higher gasoline prices if oil drilling were reduced). From this perspective, prohibition or taxation of drilling will entail an injustice toward the latter groups and they will need to be compensated for their losses.

If the property rights to the sea basin where drilling is planned were well delineated, then either those who wish to keep it free from pollution will have to compensate the losses of those who wish to drill, or vice versa. If the oil company holds these property rights, the fishing community has to be willing to compensate the oil company for forgoing this business opportunity. If the fishing community holds the rights, then the oil company has to compensate the fishing community for its losses incurred by drilling. If a third party holds the rights, then both the fishing community and the oil company will have to bid for the property. But since neither would bid beyond their respective expected returns, the drilling will only happen if its benefits outweigh its costs. Notice here that according to the Coase theorem, it doesn't matter who owns the property rights but only that the rights are fully specified.

The Coase theorem says that under these assumed conditions—property rights exist and are specified, transaction costs are low, and not too many parties are involved—then private market transactions are efficient. In other words, all externalities have been fully accounted for; they have been internalized into market transactions. This remarkable result shows the power of neoclassical theory to confront a major criticism (ubiquitous market failures due to externalities), adjust its concepts in reaction, and then reaffirm the basic tradition in the form of a late neoclassical theory. No wonder that its originator, Ronald Coase, won the Nobel Prize in economics in 1991.

Of course, both neoclassical economists and their critics have analyzed the conditions that Coase specified as necessary for his "solution" to the externalities problem to apply. Critics stress that property rights are hardly ever completely specified and transactions can be very costly, especially when many parties are affected by externalities. For example, when information (e.g., pertaining to long-term consequences of externalities) is less than perfectly available, it would be misleading to assume that those adversely affected by an economic activity's externalities will be able to assess fully and costlessly those adverse effects. Even if markets exist for such information, not everyone has equal access to or can afford the information. This problem alone tilts the level of the negotiation field.

For example, in a world of income and wealth inequalities, to assume that a fishing community has monetary power equal to that of a multinational oil company will also be misleading. Consider this situation: given incomplete information (discussed in more detail below), financial institutions cannot transparently assess the default risk of prospective borrowers. Borrowers who don't have enough collateral to cover the risk of default will be discriminated against and their credit rationed. This may disadvantage fishing communities who want to carry on costly negotiations with the oil company, negotiations needed to arrive at a Coase solution to the externalities of offshore oil drilling. Unlike the oil company, the fishing community needs credit to carry forward these negotiations if they lack sufficient collateral. Without access to credit, the community cannot afford to carry on negotiations with the oil company. In short, in a world with positive transaction costs, underspecified property rights, information asymmetries, and in this example, wealth and income inequalities, critics might well argue that Coasean market-based solutions do not manage externality problems better than Pigovian government-based solutions.

Such criticism typically provokes some neoclassical economists to find other ways to reaffirm the traditional canon. The more conservative among them might insist on a restructuring of the economic order through institutional and legal reforms. Their goals would be to broaden property rights (through privatization, copyright laws, patents to new forms of knowledge, etc.) and reduce transaction costs (through market deregulation, digitalization, or fostering new forms of privatization and decentralization). Needless to say, this is an endless process: it is possible neither to establish fully delineated property rights nor to eliminate all transaction costs. In addition new market imperfections may arise from broadening property rights: while patents do turn intellectual discoveries into private property, they can also enable the owners to wield monopoly powers in markets. However, more liberal neoclassical economists take a different approach. They argue that because it is impossible to establish in every case the superiority of market solutions over government solutions, and vice versa, the respective costs and benefits of each solution should be compared before choosing between them. Rather than advocating only market-based solutions, these liberal economists argue for a mix of solutions involving markets and governments and still other institutions of civil society.

In the liberal, mix and match approach the question of gathering and distributing pertinent information does not automatically favor private markets alone. Hence public questioning and debate can occur in regard to which externalities' costs and benefits will be included or even how affected communities will undertake cost–benefit analyses. The mix and match approach allows for considering various scientific positions and even principled, ethical positions over economic growth, and unrestrained use of energy sources. It even allows for directly questioning the market's ability to gather and disseminate information about social costs.

The more conservative, pro-market approach criticizes and rejects such public questioning and debate of social costs and market capabilities. Instead, the size and scope of social costs are correctly found in the information that is transmitted through markets and the prices determined there. Of course, such a reliance on the efficiency of markets to convey appropriate information via prices is perfectly consistent with the traditional neoclassical approach to this and indeed most economic issues. Not surprisingly, criticisms arise in response.

First, in the conservative approach, only those who have received or have access to economic resources—profits, wages, returns to owned capital—can signal their preferences as to social costs. The signaling individuals' effective preferences will also depend on the size of their income or wealth or lack thereof. Individuals without incomes of any sort will not have their preferences included in the market place. Some individuals' market votes will count more than others because they receive higher incomes than do others and hence are able to have relatively more influence over market outcomes pertaining to social costs. In this sense, a market-based system of displaying preferences compromises the one-person, one-vote criterion of modern democracies. The conservative approach thus provokes opposition from all who argue that decisions pertaining to social costs (especially those that affect life in the most general sense) should be determined democratically by each person's vote counting as much as does the next regardless of their individual incomes or wealth.

Second, when considering global problems such as climate change, substantial international cooperation and a long-run horizon are required. International cooperation can be difficult, and reliance on market outcomes alone can be myopically shortsighted. For example, in order to calculate the present value of an estimated cost of an economic activity in the future, a society has to decide on a discount rate. (We already encountered this discount rate of interest in chapter 2, note 9, when discussing what the present worth of future consumption is to an individual.) Neoclassical theorists typically argue that the relevant discount rate equals the long-run interest rate in the economy and the latter, in turn, equals the long-run real growth rate of the economy. From this perspective, negotiation over the discount rate is simultaneously negotiation over the long-run growth rate for the economy. Some problems can emerge.

Relatively poor countries may well have a very different discount rate than relatively wealthy countries. In the latter, because the long-run rate of economic growth and interest are lower, the present discounted value of social costs is that much higher than in faster growing, higher interest rate, and relatively poorer countries. How will a market-based approach deal with this difference among countries? Additionally markets provide societies with mostly short-run time horizons when sometimes long-run time horizons are more relevant to the decisions that must be made. Recognizing these limitations of markets enables alternative institutions to be considered. Economists who favor those alternatives to markets disagree and debate with those who view markets as always the best solution.

Today, in most advanced capitalist economies, public policies on externalities incorporate, to different degrees, both Pigovian taxation (e.g., excise tax on cigarettes; extra charges for water use aimed at reducing water pollution) and Coasean marketization (e.g., externalities handled through the court system). Cap-and-trade mechanisms are designed and instituted by governments as a hybrid that combines the two approaches. While limiting the maximum level of toxic emissions within an economy according to scientific criteria and political concerns, cap-and-trade mechanisms also leave the distribution of resulting costs of pollution (and of rewards to nonpolluters) to market negotiations among enterprises that buy and sell pollution permits. The traditional neoclassical market mechanism and Pareto optimality have been reaffirmed as applicable to externalities.

5.2.2   Forms of Imperfect Competition

Across the twentieth century and even before, many observers noticed that the capitalist economy was increasingly marked by firms wielding enormous market power. In industry after industry competition among firms resulted in only a few successful survivors. For example, in the US automobile industry, a few industrial giants emerged to dominate that industry (until the advent of major foreign competition). Economists also noted that advertising had become more important for the few large firms that survived competition. However, a few huge firms with market power and massive advertising are a phenomenon not easily incorporated in the traditional neoclassical approach to markets and price determination.

Recall two basic points of that tradition: all firms are price-takers and they can sell as much as they want at the market determined price. The quantities that firms produce and sell depend only on their marginal costs. No firm would spend on advertising because to do so would be irrational, as a competitive firm—by definition, one of many in a perfectly competitive market—can always sell all it can produce at the going price. In other words, the operating constraint on its profits is not sales but rather costs. Why then would a firm ever incur the expense of advertising? The answer is that competition is not as perfect as assumed in neoclassical theory. In a world of imperfect competition advertising makes sense. Neoclassical theory had to—and did—adjust its ideas to this new world of jumbo corporations, advertising, and imperfect competition.

Our discussion will focus on the case of monopoly and then on competition that is imperfect because of the existence and effects of monopolies. A monopolist firm supplies and controls all of the market; it is the sole seller of a commodity, the only firm in the industry producing that commodity. A monopoly firm's selling price is the market price for every buyer. Numerous reasons are offered for why monopolies can arise in different industries; we will explain only two, but they are important.

One possible cause of monopoly is technology. Suppose that one particular firm in a competitive industry characterized by many firms institutes a new technology different from what every other firm uses. As this firm succeeds and expands its output, it enjoys what other firms do not: the average production cost per unit of output declines (that is what economies of scale means). At the given market price such a firm makes ever more profit as its costs per unit of output keep falling further below that market price. So it can grow all the faster. Eventually its expanding output grows so large that it accounts for the major portion of the industry's supply. At that point its expanding output alone begins to impact the market price driving that price down. Other firms producing this same commodity then face a major problem: their average costs have not fallen since they do not have the technology that yields economies of scale. A falling price drives them out of business. The only survivor is the firm with economies of scale. A monopoly has been generated.

The monopolist firm can earn more money by advertising if doing so yields enough additional demand to yield more additional revenue than the cost of the advertising. The monopolist, unlike the competitive firm, can only sell more output if either the price per unit of output falls or else advertising secures extra buyers even without a fall in price. The monopolist chooses between these strategies according to which generates more net revenue. Nothing like this is done in a competitive economy of the sort assumed by neoclassical theory.

Notice in this discussion that one of neoclassical economic theory's entry-point ideas has been altered. We have introduced the possibility of a technology that yields economies of scale as a firm expands. One response that rescues the neoclassical assumption of competition is the argument that in the real world all technologies eventually lose any economies of scale they might have enjoyed when some input is limited in its availability and thus costs rise ever more as production expands beyond that limit. In other words, all firms eventually run up against a limited input and thus experience diseconomies of scale. By means of this argument, neoclassical economists have sought to rescue the legitimacy of assuming competitive economies where, at least in the long-run, temporary monopolies do not survive.

Another possible reason for the emergence of monopolies can be traced back to the very neoclassical assumption of opportunism—human beings forever seek opportunities to better satisfy their desires (in the case of firms, to gain more profits). Such human beings exist not only in firms but also in government and elsewhere too. An entrepreneur may achieve monopoly status in an industry by securing an exclusive patent from a government (by persuasion, lobbying, bribes, etc.). Self-interested bureaucrats can solicit bribes in exchange for providing privileged market positions—monopoly positions—to firms. A monopoly can arise as a result of payoffs given to and received by opportunists who operate both in the private and public spheres. Not only technology but human nature too can cause monopoly.

Let us turn to an examination of how neoclassical theory treats monopoly and so responds to its critics' arguments that monopolies undermine their theory's relevance and applicability. Neoclassical economists introduced the idea of marginal revenue and have developed it into a sustained argument about imperfect competition. To explain their argument, consider a profit equation for a firm having monopoly power:

$$\Pi = p \times q - c(q),$$

where Π stands for the firm's profits, p for the price of the commodity being produced and sold, q for the quantity of the commodity produced and sold, and $c(q)$ for its total cost of production, specified as an increasing function of the quantity it produces. Note two changes in what we discussed previously in chapter 2: there we used the variable pbar (as in $\bar{p}$) to stand for the market-determined price and c for total costs, the sum of wage $(w \cdot h \cdot L_i)$ and capital $(r \cdot K_i)$ costs. Here p no longer is barred (as in $\bar{p}$) because the firm is a price-maker, not a price-taker. Also c once again stands for total costs, but now it is defined as a function of the number of units produced. We made these changes in the profit equation to better understand what happens when the monopolist, unlike the price-taking perfectly competitive firm, can manipulate both p and q variables.

Assuming its goal is as always to maximize its profits, the monopoly firm's strategy is to set the level of output and accordingly the price in a way that would maximize the difference between its costs and revenues. However, a new problem arises: gaining power over price means that the firm also shapes the quantity it can sell. For example, raising its price to gain more profits will also reduce the demand for its product, reducing the quantity it can sell and perhaps eroding its profits. What should it do? Here is where the concept of marginal revenue comes into play. It refers to the extra revenues gained by a firm per unit of extra output produced and sold:

$$MR = \frac{\Delta TR}{\Delta q},$$

where Δ indicates, as before, a change in the appropriate variable. A perfectly competitive firm's marginal revenue equals the market determined price, for its decision to change its quantity has no impact on that price (since it is one of a huge number of competitive firms supplying the market). Hence the competitive firm's total revenue changes according to the quantity it produces and sells at that unchanged market price. Matters are very different for a firm having monopoly power. Its total revenue changes not only according to what quantity it produces and sells but also because the price it gets varies with that quantity (since it is the only seller in the market). We can write these two related impacts on the monopoly firm's revenues as follows:

$$\Delta TR = \Delta q \cdot p + \Delta p \cdot q,$$

where the first term $(\Delta q \cdot p)$ stands for the changed revenues accounted for by changing the firm's production and the second $(\Delta p \cdot q)$ for its changed revenues due to a price change. Unlike perfect competition both variables are under the control of the monopoly firm.

Dividing both sides of the equation by Δq, we get the firm's marginal revenue:

$$MR = \left[\frac{p \cdot \Delta q}{\Delta q} + \frac{\Delta p \cdot q}{\Delta q} \right] = \left[p + \frac{\Delta p}{\Delta q} q \right].$$

Consider more closely the second term ($\Delta p/\Delta q \cdot q$) in the equation. It has a negative sign, for it reflects the so-called law of demand: an inverse relationship between price charged and quantity sold. For a monopolist to produce and sell more of its good, it must lower the price.[2] Paradoxically, a monopolist's power over price always creates a sales problem for itself—that's the importance of this second term. That implicit sales problem for any firm having monopoly power is what the concept of marginal revenue captures.

To maximize its profit, the monopolist must find the optimum combination of price to charge and quantity to produce given the market demand conditions and the cost of production for what it sells. Returning to our profit equation, we can ask how a monopolist's profits will change when it varies its output: $\Delta \Pi = \Delta TR - \Delta c$. Divide both sides of this equation by Δq. Use the above concept of marginal revenue (MR) for $\Delta TR/\Delta q$ and our previously discussed marginal cost (MC) in chapter 2 for $\Delta c/\Delta q$:

$$\frac{\Delta \Pi}{\Delta q} = \left[p + \frac{\Delta p}{\Delta q} q \right] - \frac{\Delta c}{\Delta q}$$

where the first bracketed term on the right-hand side of the equation represents the marginal revenue and the second unbracketed term represents the marginal cost. If $\Delta \Pi/\Delta q$ is positive, then clearly an increase in the output level will add to profits; put differently, for $\Delta \Pi/\Delta q$ to be positive, $MR > MC$ and an incentive exists to the firm to expand its profits by producing more. If $\Delta \Pi/\Delta q$ is negative, then producing more will reduce its profits, for $MR < MC$. In this case the firm's incentive is to reduce production. The profit-maximizing condition is when the monopolist sets its marginal revenue equal to its marginal cost. At that point profits are at a maximum. At that point the monopolist no longer has an incentive to raise its price (and sell less) or lower its price (and sell more); neither action will gain any more profits.

The relationship between the demand line and the marginal revenue line is depicted in figure 5.1. Because the marginal revenue gained will always be less than the price charged, the marginal revenue line is drawn always to fall below the demand or price line.

The firm produces where the MR line intersects the MC line at point B on the graph. That is its optimal position, where it maximizes profits. We then locate on the graph its corresponding profit-maximizing level of output (Q^*)

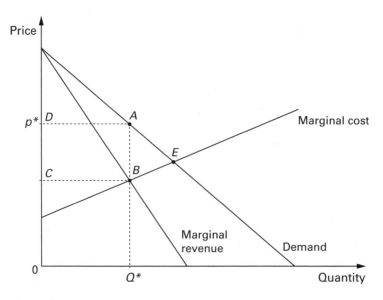

Figure 5.1
Profit-maximizing point for a monopolist.

and price level (P^*). Clearly, the price must be located on the price line for that line depicts what buyers are willing to pay for the determined level of output. Because (and *unlike* perfect competition) price is above marginal cost, the monopolist firm will earn positive profits, an "economic rent." The rectangular area between points $ABCD$ is the total economic rent going to the monopolist. Unlike perfect competition, in imperfect competition it is not competed away.

Let us compare the situation of the monopolist with the perfectly competitive market outcome. To facilitate the comparison, we will interpret the marginal cost curve in figure 5.1 to stand for both the supply of the monopolist and the aggregate market supply under conditions of perfect competition. Similarly the demand line in the same figure will be assumed to depict the demand facing the monopolist and the aggregate market demand in competition (i.e., not the same as the demand facing each competitive firm, which is still perfectly elastic). Once these assumptions are made, it is possible to identify point E in figure 5.1 where the MC line (now representing the market supply curve) crosses the market demand line as the market equilibrium for the perfectly competitive case. Compare points E and A: in monopoly $P > MC$, whereas in competition $P = MC$. This is a straightforward way of comparing the two different market situations: the equilibrium price in competition is lower than the monopolist price and the competitive equilibrium level of output is higher than that in monopoly. Consumers are worse off in markets dominated by monopolies: they pay a higher price for a lower level of output. More broadly speaking, under monopoly, society will be using its scarce resources less efficiently; there will be unemployment (as the output levels are below what they could be under perfect competition) and there will be under-utilization of capital (the monopolist could produce more but is prevented from doing so by the impact of more output sold on prices). In thus comparing competition and monopoly, note the use again of Pareto efficiency ($P = MC$) as the standard for measuring the costs to society of monopoly power.

By adding the concept of marginal revenue, neoclassical theory has revised its entry point to include the issue of market power. The theory still deploys its other entry-point concepts and essentialist logic, and it still searches for and finds an adjusted equilibrium position (now where $MC = MR$). Moreover, because that new equilibrium is usually analyzed in relation to the "optimal" Pareto equilibrium, the latter retains its position as the standard benchmark of economic well-being in this late neoclassical theory. Monopoly is thus understood in neoclassical theory as a deviation from Pareto optimality. Neoclassical economists help design and endorse legislation aimed at eliminating or constraining monopolies to return the economy closer to perfect competition. The latter remains, as always, the neoclassical goal.

The discussion of monopoly power in neoclassical economics has also influenced Keynesian economics. Some Keynesian approaches use monopoly power to write a new price equation for the macro economy: $P = (1 + m) \cdot MC$, where P stands for the aggregate price level, m for what is called the "markup" coefficient, and MC for marginal cost. In competition, $m = 0$ and $P = MC$. Some Keynesian approaches introduce a new structural rule—that of the markup (m) – and apply it to many macro topics (wage bargaining, inflation, unemployment, etc.) and much else too.

A continuum of possible forms of imperfect competition lies between the extremes of monopoly and perfect competition. Most actual cases of imperfect competition fall within that continuum. For example, consumers may switch their purchases (of soap, toothpaste, or sneakers, etc.) from a monopoly firm to a different firm that offers a good substitute product. The market power of a monopoly is thus inversely related to the availability of substitutes. That is why monopolies try to earn their customers' loyalty, to convince them that no true substitutes to their products are available. They seek to differentiate their product from all others so that their monopoly prices do not drive their customers away. They do this by means of advertisements, marketing, labeling, packaging, product development, and customer loyalty programs tied with financing.

The more successful a firm's product differentiation, the more market power it will wield. Of course, unless some technology or legal restriction blocks others from entering into an industry, the presence of monopoly and its profits will attract new firms to enter and compete. This suggests that at any given moment industries will likely vary across an economy, ranging from more to less competitive. Over time any industry can move from competitive to monopolistic and then quite possibly back again.

Neoclassical economists became interested in other forms of imperfect competition as well. Oligopolistic competition refers to a market situation in which a small number of firms operate such that each is large enough to have a nonnegligible impact on price. Using our previously defined terms, they compete with each other *strategically* (as opposed to *parametrically*). In other words, the key and new assumption is one of interdependent decisions in regard to what each firm decides to be its output decision. Each takes into acccount in its private decision what it expects other firms to do. These deciding and competing firms may not all be of the same size.

For example, in the Stackleberg model (named after the German economist Heinrich Freiherr von Stackelberg, 1905–1946), a bigger sized leader competes with a smaller sized follower. Because only two firms compete in such an industry, its market structure is called duopoly. The leader begins first by considering how the follower will respond to its output decision. Based on the predicted best response of the follower, the leader makes its profit maximizing output decision. In response to the leader, the follower firm makes the predicted output decision. This economic behavior is very different from how neoclassical theory describes economic decisions made by perfectly competitive firms. The latter take others' decisions as given, whereas in leader–follower models, the leader needs to take into account predictions of responsive behavior by the follower (in the form of a functional relation) in reaching its own profit-making decision.

For those interested in the formal mathematics of this approach, we briefly outline profit equations for the follower and the leader:

$$\Pi_f = p(q_l + q_f) \times q_f - c_f(q_f),$$

$$\Pi_l = p[q_l + q_f(q_l)] \times q_l - c_l(q_l),$$

where the subscripts f and l refer to the follower and the leader, respectively. Notice that price is here specified as a function of the aggregate quantity decisions of the two firms: $p = p(q_l + q_f)$.[3] This means that the first two terms in the two equations are price functions. Now the strategic dimension of the model is reflected by the leader treating the quantity that the follower (q_f) supplies as a function of what the leader decides to do (q_l). That strategic reasoning works as follows. The follower is assumed to calculate first a function for the profit maximizing level of q_f for any given q_l; in other words, the follower decides on what to produce to maximize its profits by taking its competitor's output decison as a given to it. Then the leader is assumed to know and use this function to decide on the profit maximizing level of output (q_l). Finally, once q_l is set, the follower calculates its own output level ($q_f(q_l)$).

The leading firm captures the larger and the follower the smaller part of the market. When compared to the case of perfect competition, oligopolistic market structures tend to produce less market output at a higher price. When compared to the case of monopoly, oligopolistic structures tend to perform better from the perspective of consumers, that is, produce more ouput at lower prices. Once again the benchmark standard for the analysis remains the price and quantities appropriate to the neoclassical notion of perfect competition.

The neoclassical tradition tends to treat cases of duopoly with competing firms of equal size through the Bertrand model (after the French matematician Jean Louis François Bertrand, 1822–1900). In this model no product differentiation is assumed. Consumers buy the commodity with the lower price, and this creates an incentive for each firm to bid down the price. Firms continue to compete over price until it equals the marginal cost. As a result, even though there are only two firms in the market, the output and the price levels end up being equal to what would have happened under perfect competition. This conclusion of the Bertrand model holds only under the assumption that the competing firms do not engage in collusive behavior. We will return to this problem of collusion below when we discuss the basic contours of late neoclassical developments in game theory under theories of equilibrium.

Neoclassical theory engendered a range of government policies against imperfect competition. On the one hand, a traditional anti-monopoly position argues that the government should pass and enforce laws against business wielding monopoly power. Antitrust laws arose at the end of the nineteenth century with the deepening worry in the United States about the emergence of monopolies and colluding or merged firms ("trusts") that act to constrain production and trade and thereby fix higher prices. The Sherman Antitrust Act (1890), the Clayton Act (1914), and the Robinson–Patman Act (1936) were three major pieces of legislation aimed to restore competition in the United States. In several major court cases monopolies such as Standard Oil Company and American Tobacco Company were targeted for disaggregation into smaller independently owned, competing firms. A related policy had the government moving against collusive (e.g., price-fixing) behavior as in the case of oligopolistic competition. Still another policy was government regulation of a monopoly firm's economic behavior when it was allowed to continue to operate as a monopoly. The best example of that policy was the regulation of American Telephone and Telegraph Company's monopoly for years prior to its being broken up into independent companies. Many neoclassical economists also tend to argue that another way to deal with a national monopoly is to deregulate its market by eliminating trade protection (tariffs and quotas) that favor the national producer. They advocate opening markets and keeping them open to international competition. Consumer electronics and automobiles are two US industries whose market structures were dramatically changed by the impact of international competition.

However, a number of neoclassicists tend to be more cautious and skeptical about government intervention or even regulation. Some argue that if a company achieves a monopoly status, that should be conceived as its prize for winning the competitive struggle. The firm whose managers deploy a new technology enabling it to become the low-cost producer and beat its rivals "deserves" the rewards provided thereby by its achieving a monopolistic position in its market. Such economists have insisted on the social benefits of the gains in productive efficiency that firms used to move from competitive to monopolistic. They have likewise stressed the greater expenditures on research and development (for new technologies and new products) made by monopolistic as opposed to competitive firms. Late neoclassical theory contains a range of arguments and debates about imperfect competition—unlike the traditional neoclassical focus on perfect competition. However, that range remains tied to the basic entry points, essentialist logic, and Pareto optimal "success" criterion characteristic of the tradition.

5.2.3 Transaction Costs and Economic Organization

In 1937 Ronald Coase posed another important, basic question to traditional neoclassical economic theory: "Why do firms exist?" That theory offers little in the way of an answer. It simply assumes that firms automatically transform inputs into outputs in a manner that maximizes profit (given technology and all prices). Critics of this neoclassical approach to the firm came to dismiss it as equating the firm to a mysterious "black box." What they meant was that in the neoclassical view, firms simply solve a minor technical arithmetic problem: how much to produce given technology and prices. The solution to that problem, for neoclassical economics, is to produce where marginal cost equals price. That is a trivial matter, leaving the firm's complex structure, functions and purposes unexplained and untheorized. Neoclassical theory, critics have argued, seems to pay no attention to the organization of power and the myriad other cultural and economic processes that shape what firms are and do.

It would seem that the nature of a firm, like any other important social institution, is a far more complex entity than what is assumed in traditional neoclassical theory. The models of imperfect competition discussed above certainly suggest a more sophisticated and institutionally detailed analysis of firm behavior. Finally, another and perhaps more basic problem confronts the traditional neoclassical approach to firms. That tradition has always affirmed that market transactions among independent individuals and firms are economically superior to the sorts of dependent relationships within hierarchically commanded institutions. After all, Adam Smith had claimed that private, independent market transactions would yield, as if led by an unseen hand, an unintended but nonetheless social optimum. The singular route to achieve that utopia was found in private property and markets. It was *not* found in the power wielded by a despot or a hierarchical bureaucracy of corporations or government planners. How then should neoclassical theory explain the continued existence and growth of firms and corporations as "islands of conscious power in this ocean of unconscious cooperation" (Coase 1937)?

The central thrust of Coase's answer was to recognize that the exchange process itself is not without costs. It is costly to write and enforce market contracts. It is costly to maintain the market as an institution (like all other institutions). Based on the recognition of those costs, Coase argues that firms exist because, as an organizational form, they can do some things more cheaply than markets can do them. In other words, for some undertakings necessary to the production and exchange of commodities, firms offer the least cost alternative to markets. Notice once more that this answer rests on the use of the traditional neoclassical standard of efficiency (narrowly defined cost minimization).

Transaction costs provide the quintessential example. Such costs arise because they are intrinsic to the acts of buying and selling. For example, two ways exist to search for a home to buy. One way is to carry out and coordinate all the tasks by yourself: you search for the desired sized home in various locations, get information about the quality of education in these different locations, compare home prices there, organize the gathered information into a coherent totality, and so forth. Some of these tasks can be accomplished or facilitated with purchases. For examples, newspapers offer real estate pages with home prices, notebooks can hold gathered information, and computer programs organize and print gathered information. Other tasks require your time and that suggests including the opportunity cost of your time spent searching, recording, and managing the whole undertaking of buying a house (the potential income and/or utility forgone by not spending your time otherwise).

The other way to buy a home is to hire a brokerage firm that performs all the tasks listed above and more. The hiring of a brokerage firm incurs a single transaction cost compared to the many transaction costs incurred if you carried out all the required tasks yourself with the accompanying purchases. If the brokerage firm can provide its service at a cheaper cost to you (including the opportunity cost of your time), we have an answer to why such a firm exist. Firms may arise because they can perform sets of tasks at lower costs (perhaps by realizing economies of scale) than if markets alone were relied upon to accomplish each of the tasks separately.

Consider all that firms actually do. In addition to production, they carry out all kinds of other complementary processes: search for cheap production inputs, find good managers, discover new production technologies and product lines, maintain and extend their customer base, handle contract negotiations and legal services, manage risk, and so forth. Any firm may prefer to internalize these processes, if they can be carried out at a lower cost than by making many market exchanges. Influenced by Coase's work on the firm, some neoclassical economists have argued that costs may be lower to a firm when it internalizes these processes—within its own hierarchical bureaucuracy—instead of relying on many market transactions to secure them. It not only spreads its total costs over many different products; it may thereby realize economies of scale. Connected to the latter is what economists call "team production": when employed individuals specialize in various tasks including production, searching for cheap inputs, marketing, lawyering, and so forth. Managers plan, organize, and direct the many diverse but related tasks with the aim of raising the firm's (team's) productivity and lowering its average costs (winning the game). When they succeed, the firm realizes economies of scale. Firms will normally internalize some and rely on markets for other of their activities, depending on which option better serves profitability.

Coase's transaction-cost idea, followed by other neoclassical economists' similar work, developed a more general theory of nonmarket institutions. That theory is consistent with traditional neoclassical ideas pertaining to individuals' rational self-interested behavior and the implied optimality of competitive market outcomes. For such late neoclassical theories, nonmarket institutions such as firms arise when they can secure processes more cheaply than market transactions. Such institutions may also undertake processes because of market failures. Markets may fail because rational agents tend to behave opportunistically (by not delivering on contracts if they have the opportunity to do so, by minimizing their work effort once hired, by free-riding if and when opportunities arise to do so, etc.). Consequently costs involved in performance measurement and contract enforcement arise. A firm often deals with such problems of markets failing by incurring internal costs of supervision and enforcement.

In striking contrast to the traditional neoclassical "black-box" theory of the firm (e.g., in which the marginal productivity of labor is costlessly monitored, measured, and renumerated), late neoclassical theories of the firm problematize the productivity of labor. For them, labor productivity is not given; it rather presents employers with a crucial and possibly costly problem after employees are hired. Simply put, such employees may seek and find ways to avoid effective work. The firm is an organizational structure aimed at addressing this productivity problem. In fact some neoclassical economists have extended this framework to explain the evolution of institutions throughout human history

(North 2005). According to them, institutions arise not only to economize on transaction costs but also to solve incentive problems stemming from ubiquitous opportunism.

5.2.4 Information Failures and Missing Markets

The attention of some neoclassical economists was drawn to critics' challenges against the traditional neoclassical assumption that everyone in a market has the same complete information about all available commodities. The critics had claimed that relevant market information was asymmetrically (i.e., unevenly, unequally) distributed and strategically used in many markets. Neoclassical economists responded by exploring what happens when contracting agents have asymmetric information pertaining to the quality of the commodity (good or service) being exchanged. The new approach distinguished between two kinds of information problems: those that emanate from hidden information (the problem of *adverse selection*) and those that flow from hidden action (the problem of *moral hazard*) (Arrow 1974). We consider each in turn.

The problem of adverse selection results from the asymmetries of information among market-contracting agents (prior to the moment of exchange). For example, when insurance companies cannot discriminate between high- and low-risk groups (relevant information is hidden from them), they are forced to raise insurance rates across the board. This has the undesirable effect of driving low-risk groups out of the market (they cannot afford the too high premiums), leaving the insurance companies with only high-risk groups (for some of whom the premiums may even be too low). This is why the problem facing the firm is called one of adverse selection.

The problem of moral hazard results from the difficulty of monitoring the behavior of an (already) contracted agent. For instance, when one party (principal) hires another (agent) to act on its behalf, the interests and motivations of the latter do not necessarily line up with the interests and motivations of the former. An agent may have incentives to take actions that are undesirable from the perspective of the principal. For example, an assumedly opportunistic and rational individual who buys an insurance policy from an insurance firm will have an incentive to take more risky actions, precisely because the possibly negative consequences of doing so will be borne not by her/him but rather by the insurance firm.

One important application for such theories is found in analyses of input markets. Consider, for example, the labor market. Suppose that firms cannot distinguish adequately between high- and low-quality workers. They are confronted with an adverse selection problem. In addition the asymmetries of information on the part of the firm's managers and its workers mean that workers, once hired, will have opportunities and incentives to take actions that do not necessarily line up with the interests of the managers. The firm also faces a moral hazard problem.

To solve these two problems, firms pay a wage rate above the market-clearing (full employment) wage rate. This new higher wage rate (also known as the "efficiency wage") and the accompanying unemployment in the labor market are thought to solve both cost problems in a single stroke. An efficiency wage higher than the market-clearing equilibrium wage provides the appropriate signal to attract adequately qualified workers and ameliorates the firm's adverse selection problem. The persistence of unemployment (caused by the prevalence of the efficiency wage rate) provides increased incentives to those already employed to properly perform the job that managers hired them to do. If they don't, they could lose their current job. In that eventuality, they lose not only the difference between the efficiency wage rate and the market-clearing wage rate but also incur significant costs of a job loss (periods of unemployment between jobs, lower probability of re-employment, etc.). This "information approach" produces an explanation for a persistent nonclearing labor market. For that reason alone, it is claimed to be "more realistic" than the traditional neoclassical model of full employment equilibrium. The information approach belongs to the set of late neoclassical theories because it extends the tradition yet also continues to use and adhere to traditional neoclassical assumptions of opportunistic, self-interested behavior on the part of all economic agents. Here too *Homo economicus* inhabits the theoretical terrain. And here too individuals' private choices are shown to yield a social optimum (efficiency).

The information approach has also been extended to credit markets. There the lender's problem is one of risk: the borrower may not repay the loan. If the lender charges the same interest rate to all borrowers, the lender faces an adverse selection problem: too few borrowers who present a low risk of default and too many whose risk of nonrepayment is high. At a singular rate charged to all debtors, more risky debtors borrow more than they would if they faced a higher rate reflecting their higher risk and less risky debtors borrow less than they would if they faced a lower rate reflecting their lower risk of default. The information approach shows then why an equilibrium interest rate in a market that combines these different borrowers is inefficient because of adverse selection.

Lenders can deal with this problem by charging different interest rates to borrowers of differing risk: higher for more risky and lower for less risky debtors. Differentiating debtors according to risk moves the credit market from a relatively inefficient to a more efficient allocation of credit. Of course, lenders would have to assess differential risk on the part of their customers. Lenders typically ask potential borrowers about their financial status. However, given traditional neoclassical theory's assumption of opportunistic, self-interested behavior by all individuals, an incentive exists for more risky borrowers to withhold or distort relevant information gathered by lenders (thereby possibly securing loans at lower interest rates). To deal with this information problem, lenders require collateral to help guarantee repayment in case of default. Such extensions (comprising late neoclassical theory) enabled neoclassical economists to make sense of a range of economic phenomena that did not fit the traditional perfectly competitive model of credit markets while retaining the drive to find optimal equilibria in markets.

5.3 New Theories of Human Behavior

Late neoclassical theory understands the firm as a far more complex and interesting entity than the narrowly technocratic optimizing calculator proposed in and by traditional neoclassical theory. Late neoclassical theory does something similar with the traditional view of human behavior. It responds to critics who questioned the relevancy of reducing individuals' choices to exogenously given preferences governed by given axioms of rank ordering, nonsatiation, and so forth. Traditional neoclassical theory conceives a choice-making person as a computer: perfectly logical and wonderfully consistent but also devoid of emotion, conflicting desires, and contradictory preferences, and strangely immune from societal influences. That conception also yields someone in severe need of psychological counseling. Late neoclassical theory has begun to move away from this mechanistic view of economic behavior to a more nuanced, uncertain, and psychologically enriched view of why individuals act as they do. This emergent view is the subject of this section.

Neoclassical economists introduced new concepts and connections that questioned, if not undermined, the idea of exogenously given preferences. Their criticisms of traditional neoclassical theory's image of individuals as mechanistic self-interest optimizers went furthest in the late neoclassical theories grouped under the heading "behavioral economics." Interestingly this group of late neoclassical theories can be usefully approached by a brief return to a concept explored in our earlier chapter on Marxian economics: overdetermination.

From the perspective of overdetermination, any individual's economic behavior (or indeed any behavior) is understood as the product of different and multiple determinations emanating from all the natural, cultural, political, and economic processes comprising the total context in which that individual exists. You, your desires, and your behavior are the combined effect of a whole host of natural processes of body and mind inherited from a long line of mostly unknown ancestors and of emotional processes stemming from both conscious and unconscious feelings of love, hate, hope, fear, jealousy, serenity, anger, empathy, and so on. In addition you, your desires, and your behavior are influenced by political processes: the legislation, administration, and adjudication of the rules and customs created within your family, clan, tribe, community, and state. Further you, your tastes, and actions are also partly effects of cultural processes: the production and disseminations/communications of meanings about life through language, religion, literature, music, art, education, and mass media. Finally, our actions and ourselves are also in part effects of economic processes: the set of ways we produce and distribute goods and services, labor and wealth. All of the diverse processes that comprise the totality into which we are all born and where our lives combine to make us what we are at each moment. Individual behavior, economic or otherwise, is in that sense overdetermined by all those processes; it is not reducible to the effect of any one or a subset of them. That is what overdetermination means.

Conceived in this overdeterminist way, every behavior from who you date to eating anchovies to sacrificing leisure time to gain income to not running red lights is socially, emotionally, and naturally contrived. Causal complexity including many diverse influences explains our behavior. Economic causes—income, prices, class, and so forth—must be included in what the term social means here. One implication of this alternative way of thinking about choice is crucial: if you believe that choices help shape the economy—a core argument of neoclassical theory—then from an overdeterminist perspective you will also believe that the economy helps cause those same choices. Individual choices are both a cause and an effect of economics. This mutual causation between the two differs markedly from traditional neoclassical theory's notion that preferences are only a cause and never an effect.

Overdetermination implies that each of us is a singular being precisely because of the different array of determinations combining to constitute each. We thus evaluate uniquely whatever alternatives we confront. No uniform measuring rod exists that transcends each of us. Whenever common rankings emerge, they represent no more than agreements forged among us at that moment. Your singularity as a person and evaluator of alternatives reflect partly the impacts of others—ancestors, parents, relatives, teachers, friends, ministers, legislators, sports figures, corporate directors, and managers. But you are hardly a passive decision-making entity, a mere bearer of influences. Rather, and precisely because of these constituting influences, you make decisions that impact others who impact you, and so on. Putting it all together, you are at one and the same time both a cause and an effect of the behavior of others.

In other words, and to contrast this view with that of neoclassical theory, no one can be conceived to be a decision-making island, an isolated entity. Rather, we are all interconnected. Therefore quite parallel to late neoclassical theory's view of firms' strategic behavior, individuals too can and should be understood to engage in similarly interdependent ways. They make choices that are influenced by and influence other individuals' choices. In this regard and as we will explain below, the interdependence of preferences helps explain why, for example, stock markets rise and fall. Purchasing stocks may have little to do with carefully and logically scrutinizing the value of companies. Instead, it may more reflect buyers' guesses as to what other buyers and sellers—the "crowd"—will do. Our guesses about the crowd shape what we do and thereby what the crowd does. Similarly our consumption decisions are affected by others' consumption decisions. Indeed the utility we derive from consuming a commodity and the intensity of our preferences reflect the utilities and preferences of others. If not for such interdependence, we wonder what the term fashion could mean. Current styles of dress, cars, homes, and electronics help determine which products figure in our utility functions, how we rank those products, and what we count as life's necessities.

Finally, interesting recent contributions of social theory underscore the conflicting desires within individuals and why individuals' preferences are hardly the stable, consistent decision-making machines implied by neoclassical theory. In the disciplines of political theory, sociology, feminist theory, cultural studies, psychology, and psychoanalysis, individuals are theorized to be composed of multiple, ceaselessly shifting, and potentially conflictual "subjectivities." Our different subjectivities yield the conflicts and compromises that we observe in our and others' individual behaviors. Late neoclassical theory's exploration of human behavior engages some comparable ideas.

Individuals participate in multiple processes during any day and across a lifetime. A person may participate in a market exchange process selling the capacity to work for a wage: that person then occupies (creates) a wage-laboring position (subjectivity). This same person takes on a different position and added subjectivity when he or she participates in a religious process. Similarly other subjectivities arise when he or she participates in still additional economic, cultural, and political ones too. An individual becomes a consuming being when participating in the process of consumption, a political being when participating in the process of voting, and so on. These and other participations create the varying subjectivities of a person. We all are a complex bundle of potentially conflicting and conflicted subjectivities interacting and vying with one another and overdetermining our social behavior.

Such an approach helps explain conflicts in voting. A wage worker might not be inclined to vote for a political candidate who advocates a cut in workers' health insurance or reduced taxes on the rich. From the perspective of the worker as an economic being, those actions may not appear to serve his or her economic interests. Suppose, however, that the same political candidate favors restricting rights to abortion and reducing "big government." Those positions might well conform to the worker's religious and political beings. Hence the worker is conflicted: at one and the same time he or she feels a preference for and against the candidate. If the conflicted worker eventually votes for that candidate, that does not necessarily imply irrationality, stupidity, or gullibility on the workers' part (ascriptions sometime made because the worker's vote appears to be against his or her economic interests). Rather, the worker, just like the rest of us, likely struggles with and tries to reconcile multiple and differing subjectivities and their corresponding interest calculations. Voting is uncertain and continually variable as voters struggle over different and conflicting beings. We would guess that many a successful politician already has learned this lesson.

Recent theorizations of multiple and contesting subjectivities clash with the traditional neoclassical idea of a well-ordered and always stable choice-making person. For a final example, consider a married woman and mother who occupies two positions: in one she is pushed by a whole host of social processes (associated with marriage, religion, and traditional gendering notions) to stay home and provide household goods and services for her spouse and children; at the same time other social processes (arising from women's liberation movements, severe economic times, new gendering notions) push her out of the home to take a wage-laboring position. She is conflicted: at one and the same time she prefers to stay and not to stay at home. Once again, this does not illustrate irrationality on her part. It illustrates instead a part of the modern dilemma faced by many women. Indeed, for many, the conflicted preference for opposites cannot be resolved, so they do both. The resulting "double-shift" of women working hard outside and inside households only produces new conflicts and struggles. The latter even can lead to the disappearance of one of the competing positions—divorce eliminates the obligation to work for the husband.

If our preferences are interdependent, determined and determining, and conflictual and inconsistent, that yields a notion of human nature very different from the *Homo economicus* figure offered by traditional neoclassical economics. We are comparing two very different underlying psychological theories of human behavior. The neoclassical view arose and is still firmly rooted in nineteenth-century utilitarian psychology. The more current view owes much to late twentieth-century psychological and psychoanalytical thought.

In the following section we will survey some recent departures from the traditional neoclassical approach to human behavior generally and to economic rationality in particular. We begin by distinguishing between two distinct aspects of the neoclassical concept of rationality: (1) the preferences that inform the decision-making and (2) the decision-making act itself. On both aspects there is theoretical movement away from the neoclassical tradition. Regarding preferences, the new literature affirms motivational heterogeneity. For example, individuals' preferences do not express only self-interest but rather also reflect our interest in others. Our motives are diverse and conflicting, egotistic but also altruistic. Society and its multiple, diverse institutions shape both sets of motives inside each of us in endlessly varying combinations, balances, and tensions.

Regarding decision-making, new literature stresses the cognitive limitations of the human mind and their consequences for decision-making. We make decisions based on a very limited, vaguely understood, and biased understanding of the available alternatives. We are not the mechanistic, utility-maximizing calculators of traditional neoclassical theory. After surveying these two movements, we will turn attention to the emerging field of behavioral economics. It weaves together various insights culled from debates on rationality and behavior in a pragmatic, problem-solving way. At that point we will examine whether it breaks completely from the neoclassical tradition's view of *Homo economicus.*

5.3.1 Theories of Motivational Diversity

Traditional neoclassical economic theory assumes that individuals behave calculatively (i.e., their behavior conforms to the axioms of choice). Thus they seek to take advantage of all available opportunities to advance their self-interest. In the last quarter of the twentieth century, some neoclassical economists began to relax this assumption of "opportunism." There was an increasing interest in motivational diversity (altruism and reciprocity) beyond straightforward opportunism. As a result research and debates on motivational diversity have concentrated on two specific questions: Does motivational diversity exist? And, if so, why?

The first question continues to be relevant because a significant number of neoclassical economists still insist that *Homo economicus* accurately represents human nature, even when motivational diversity appears to exist. Such neoclassical economists claim that behavioral traits that appear to be other-regarding are actually self-regarding: these qualities either reflect an enlightened, long-term but nonetheless still selfish perspective, or else they arise because of externally imposed constraints (norms, rules of behavior, or moral laws) on our otherwise selfish behavior.

Late neoclassical theory's introduction of externally imposed constraints exposes yet again the tendency for neoclassical theory's primary humanism to occasionally lean on a structuralism for support. In this case a late neoclassical theory imports an unacknowledged form of structuralism into its otherwise humanist approach. The behavior of *Homo economicus* now conforms not only to some innate human nature but also to moral laws and rules of behavior imposed by the social structure into which *Homo economicus* is born and matures.

One interesting application of motivational diversity appears in a variant of the "efficiency wage" model discussed earlier. Akerlof (1982) theorized the labor contract between employers and employees as a "partial gift exchange." Employers pay wages greater than the market-clearing wage in return for workers' extra effort. Again the idea is that a market-clearing wage leaves employers and employees making strategic decisions with asymmetric information that end up with inefficient outcomes. By giving workers the gift of a wage higher than what a simple market mechanism would produce, they obtain in return employees who do not shirk or otherwise maneuver around employers at the latters' expense. In a sense, workers' opportunistic behavior is modified and redirected by means of a partial gift of higher wages. Even though both employers and workers modify their behavior in this mutually beneficial "gift exchange," they remain opportunistic agents, for otherwise no need for a partial gift exchange would arise. They behave calculatively and opportunistically because, given that the markets can fail because of strategic decision-making and asymmetric information, departing from the norms of traditional neoclassical theory improves the well-being for both parties.

In contrast, some economists argue for a genuine motivational diversity in a clear break from the neoclassical tradition. Drawing upon evidence from the emerging field of experimental economics, they note that individuals behave in nonselfish ways "systematically"; they do so even in the absence of social constraints (norms, morals, etc.). One typical example from this field is "the game of ultimatum." Two subjects are observed. The first divides up the proverbial pie as he or she wishes and offers a slice to the second subject; the second subject either declines or accepts the offer. The rule covering this game is this: if the second declines the offer, neither party gets any pie. Traditional neoclassical theory predicts that the second subject—being self-interested and independent of anyone else and their preferences—should always prefer the thinnest of slices to no slice at all and would thus accept whatever size piece the first subject offers. Nevertheless, experiments have shown that, unless the first subject makes a "fair" (50–50) offer, the second subject tends to reject the offer (Güth, Schmittberger, and Schwarz 1982). This result violates traditional neoclassical theory's nonsatiation axiom. The experimental results compelled many to ask whether concerns for "fairness" should be incorporated into the theory of economic choice in a more systematic manner, at the level of behavior motivation.

Some experimental economists want to introduce *Homo reciprocans* as a completely new personality type. Such a "reciprocating" individual has a human nature that seeks to cooperate with those willing to cooperate and to punish those who do not. What differentiates *Homo reciprocans* from *Homo economicus* is the former's commitment to cooperate and punish, even when doing so is personally costly (Fehr and Gächter 2000). For example, when a

Homo reciprocans observes a fellow citizen evading a tax obligation, he or she would confront the tax avoider or report the individual to authorities, even if such acts were personally costly. *Homo economicus*, in contrast, would not take action unless calculation showed its cash benefit outweighing its cost.

Proponents of *Homo reciprocans* argue that merely the presence of a critical number of *Homo reciprocans* in a population of mixed personality types can explain why societies implement and sustain egalitarian mechanisms of economic redistribution and democratic institutions of political participation (Bowles and Gintis 1998). Critics, however, argue that *Homo reciprocans* is not a new personality type. Instead, *Homo economicus* selfishly maximizes preferences that include punishing rule breakers or noncooperators. In such arguments, human action (including action harmful to the self) is always presumed to be motivated by self-interest, and the researcher always searches for, and invariably finds, some interest that the acting individual is served by his or her action. The individual who lost money by reporting a fellow citizen was still acting to maximize self-interest, gaining more utility from the pleasure of reporting misdeeds than the utility forgone because of the lost money.

For those who do claim that individuals display systematic deviations from opportunism, the central question concerns what determines how one becomes an opportunist, an altruist, or a reciprocan or any particular combination of them. Is it evolutionary dynamics or reasoned choice? While the evolutionary perspective formulates the question of motivational diversity as a matter of the population distribution of preference types (self-regarding, other-regarding, reciprocity, etc.), the reasoned choice perspective formulates the question as a matter of the autonomy of a person to entertain different preference rankings.

Some late neoclassical economists have imported methodologies from evolutionary biology to explain the persistence and survival of nonselfish behavioral traits (altruism and reciprocity) within populations (Smith 1982). Individuals were found by economists to display both self- and other-regarding preferences in various combinations (Becker 1981). Using biological "group selection" models, those economists argued that, while nonselfish individuals could be abused by selfish individuals, if the nonselfish formed communities and minimized interactions with the selfish, they could thereby increase their fitness and survive in a mixed population. Other late neoclassical economists explored the conditions under which different behavioral traits are replicated, learned, and mimicked by individuals. What these approaches share are explanations of diverse behavioral traits not as matters of reasoned choice but rather as outcomes of "selection" processes where the comparative "fitness" of particular traits determines their survival. Note that this selection process implies an underlying natural/social structure that determines the diversity of behavioral traits: a structuralism rather than a humanism.

Another Nobel Prize winning economist, Amartya Sen, treats individual preference diversity differently. Sen initially defines rationality quite broadly as "reasoned scrutiny" on the part of individuals. Most important, he argues, that for rationality to mean anything at all, it must involve a deeper kind of individual freedom than merely the freedom to choose among commodity bundles. A rational individual should be understood to have the capacity to choose among alternative criteria used to form preference orderings. Sen thus breaks from traditional neoclassical theory's reduction of rationality to particular, predetermined axioms of choice within one particular process of maximizing self-interest subject to constraints. Sen opens a door to individuals' motivational diversity by adding a new (meta-)layer of preferences over preferences. Motivational diversity is deepened into individuals' freedom to reconsider, alter, modify, or replace preferences. In this formulation individuals are conceived to be capable of self-reflexively switching among different preference patterns.

While indeed a novel idea for neoclassical economics, much in Sen's argument depends on how this meta-choice over how to choose is made. One possibility might pursue another optimization model: each individual optimizes something in choosing which set of preferences to use. A very different possibility might affirm that different individuals' preference sets are socially overdetermined. Moving toward an overdeterminist position carries the cost, not of analytical rigor, but rather of losing mathematical tractability (McCloskey 2006).

Choosing between the evolutionary and the reasoned choice perspectives sketched above is indeed a critical choice for neoclassical economists. If they select evolutionary selection as the cause of motivational diversity—a structural mechanism—they violate the methodological individualist commitments of traditional neoclassical theory. If neoclassical economists instead choose rational deliberation—a process of individuals' optimizing choice among alternative choice criteria—they retain the methodological individualist commitments of the neoclassical tradition.

Whatever further evolution awaits these debates among traditional and late neoclassical theorists, what remains common to them all—even those drawn by the structuralism of natural selection idea or the overdetermination lurking in Sen's formulations—is a basic humanism. Human beings—with their natures either given by some intrinsic rationality or else more or less shaped by nature and history—remain the entry point. What such human beings believe and do is what causes or determines the pattern and flow of economic events. Late, as well as traditional, neoclassical economics would thus still differ from and clash with Marxian economics whose entry point is class. However, some among the neoclassicals—those more or less interested in theorizing human rationality as naturally and socially overdetermined—would have worked their way to positions closer to the overdetermination logic increasingly favored among Marxists.

5.3.2 Theories of Bounded Rationality

Another late departure from traditional neoclassical notions of rationality and the optimization process (maximizing one's utility subject to constraints) has focused on human beings' cognitive limitations and the practical limits on information available to them when making decisions. These limitations led the economist Herbert Simon to develop a notion of "bounded" rationality (1978).

Consider a comparison between how a human and a computer play the game of chess. The example is a typical one used to help explain Simon's notion of bounded rationality. A computer can easily map all possible paths involved in a chess game; a human chess player can envision only a limited number of rounds of the game. The human chess player may well be rational, but in contrast to a computer, he or she faces cognitive limitations. The decision-making of the individual is bounded.

This human limitation is particularly important because the standard neoclassical economists' notion of rationality assumes a considerable, if not impossible, amount of cognitive competence on the part of the human subject. For example, the typical competitive general equilibrium model assumes that a rational individual needs to access and process private information (about his or her endowments, technologies, and preferences) and public information (about the quality and market prices of all commodities and all the possible states of the economic environment). How does one expect individuals to make optimal decisions if it is impossible for them to process cognitively or gain access to all of this required information? The neoclassical assumption of optimality is based on a cognitive impossibility.

The models of imperfect competition discussed earlier in this chapter only add to the information and processing demands faced by the individual. In leader–follower models, individuals and firms are assumed able to process, in addition to all the information listed above, the private information for all the other individuals and firms in the economy. Moreover they are assumed able to instantaneously reason through interdependent decision-making. Interdependent decision-making refers to strategic decision contexts where the decision of any one individual or firm is contingent upon the decision of another individual or firm. No human being could possibly possess the cognitive ability to gather and process all this required information.

Simon offered a different way to think about how individuals make their decisions. They do not deploy a strategy of optimization as per traditional neoclassical theory. Rather, they use a "satisficing" process. Unlike an optimizing individual, a boundedly rational, satisficing individual makes the best decision that he or she can based always on limited information. Individuals are not computers. People always need to bring the reasoning process to an arbitrary end (based on cognitive limitations) so as to make a decision. This satisficing conception of rationality understands individuals to rely on institutions and to invoke rules of thumb, habits, and other social devices (intuition) to make these decisions.

One late neoclassical reaction to Simon's theory of bounded rationality and satisficing behavior is to reintegrate it back into the optimization paradigm. Optimization is then theorized as something that entails a cost. Given human cognitive limits, to optimize costs money: a transaction cost entailed to overcome those cognitive limits. By incorporating a cost of optimization into the optimization problem itself, some late neoclassical economists could formally model bounded rationality within the optimization framework of traditional neoclassical economics. While such treatments of bounded rationality are mathematically elegant, we think they miss Simon's valuable insights into the process of limits on individual (and firm) decision-making. Simon's work fundamentally challenges the apparatus and basis of neoclassical theory's aim to specify how and why capitalist market economies can reach socially optimal equilibrium points.

5.3.3 Behavioral Economics

The theories of motivational diversity and bounded rationality examined so far proved unable to dislodge the key position of *Homo economicus* in neoclassical economics. Its essentialized entry point—the individual with his or her preferences and human nature—remains in place. However, as discussed above, those alternative approaches raised basic and critical questions about the status of that essentialized entry point. They challenged key parts of the neoclassical tradition. Nonetheless, those theories and their challenges remain more or less on the margins of mainstream neoclassical economics, even though they increasingly appear as added chapters in microeconomics texts, rather as they do in this book. While important enough to be recognized and taught, those challenges have hardly reached the status of inaugurating a new entry point to economic theorizing, a genuine break from and beyond neoclassical economics.

Yet, partly in response to those theoretical challenges, still newer developments have arisen that may well go beyond posing critical questions in regard to *Homo economicus*. They may evolve into a completely new vision of how to specify the economic behavior of individuals. Were such an evolution to occur, then the heading of "late neoclassical theory" might no longer fit. A new, non-neoclassical and post-neoclassical theoretical break might then be achieved. We will briefly examine this new development, for much may be at stake for neoclassical theory.

A number of economists have delved into the fields of evolutionary biology, cognitive psychology, sociology, and related disciplines focusing on the complexity of human behavior. One result is the emergence of a new and highly variegated research field called behavioral economics. While difficult to define, this new field displays some distinctive characteristics. Beyond already discussed motivational issues and cognitive limitations of human subjects that pertain to behavioral economics, we will concentrate here only on the psychological insights of behavioral economics. In doing so, we can examine the potential of this work to achieve a break from the neoclassical framework.

One important strain of behavioral economics demonstrates (via experiments) how the traditional neoclassical explanation fails to represent adequately the complex reality of human behavior. For example, according to neoclassical theory, rational agents are assumed always to make their choices in a consistent manner regardless of the way the problem is framed. Experimental results do not support that core hypothesis. Rather, experiments show that human beings are affected by the way choice problems are presented (Tversky and Kahneman 1990). Different ways of framing choice problems yield different conclusions (choices). Hence social context affects the choice. To the degree that choices are in fact socially contrived (dependent), neoclassical economists can no longer postulate a predetermined set of axioms leading to choices that are independent of social context.

Consider the following experiment illustrating how social context matters. Suppose that society faces a flu epidemic resulting in the expected death of 900 people. The government devises and presents two scientific plans of action to combat the flu:

Plan A: this action results in 300 people saved.

Plan B: this action allows everyone to be saved with a one third probability and no one to be saved with a two thirds probability.

Now consider the following alternative scientific presentation (framing) by the government:

Plan C: this action results in 600 people who die.

Plan D: this action allows no one to die with one-third probability and everyone to die with two-thirds probability.

A moment's notice shows that plan A and plan C are identical, as are plan B and plan D. They differ from one another only in the way the government presents them to society. In standard neoclassical theory, a rational economic agent should not be affected at all by the manner in which the problem is presented. The agent makes the same choice in both presentations. Yet, repeated experiments conducted with randomly selected individuals with similar distributions of characteristics show that when presented a choice between A and B, the majority chooses A and when presented between C and D, the majority chooses D. Experiments such as these demonstrate that contextuality and textuality (literally how something is worded) do matter in human decision-making. This and other like experiments suggest that human behavior is socially manipulable. Experiments such as these go beyond merely questioning a sovereign and rational consumer (who knows what he or she wants, whose actions reflect his true interests alone, and who always acts opportunistically). These experiments indicate the need for a radically new way to theorize individuals' economic behavior, very differently from the neoclassical tradition.

Given this critical stance toward neoclassical theory, some behavioral economists look to its critics for support. In doing so, they encounter the two major critical and alternative theories contrasted in this book: Keynesian and Marxian economics. For most, Keynesian economics has been the attraction because, unlike Marxian economics, it is not anticapitalist in its vision. Behavioral economists responded to Keynes's use of "animal spirits," "herd behavior," and "money illusion" to explain inconsistencies in the behavior of investors, consumers, and laborers that arise from the way social context frames and influences their decisions. According to Keynes, when humans are deciding to do something—for example, a corporate board of directors deciding whether to invest in new plant and equipment—they cannot weigh all the expected costs and benefits of their proposed action. The word "expected" denotes the future and that is unknown. Keynes's famous line is: "We simply do not know." Hence as we already explained in chapter 3, uncertainty is an integral part of the human condition. That is why we gain entertainment from fortune-tellers and fortune cookies alike. Some handle this knowledge problem by assigning (objectively or subjectively determined) probabilities to different possible outcomes. However, as we explained earlier in this book, to assume that individuals can assign probabilities to different outcomes is to assume a prior condition: they already know the future, albeit probabilistically. In other words, in this kind of assignment, they become certain about uncertainty. But gaining that, or indeed any certain knowledge, is precisely the problem.

Given the fundamental uncertainty haunting human behavior, it is impossible for economic actors to predict the outcomes of their actions, let alone make cost–benefit analyses of all the diverse consequences of various possible strategies. Instead, Keynes argues that economic agents (i.e., our hypothetical corporate board of directors) act according to their animal spirits, following "a spontaneous urge to action rather than inaction." Sometimes this spontaneous urge to action enables actors to navigate through the fog of uncertainty; at other times, it does not. For example, when the mood is sour, animal spirits can work to motivate the corporate board to recoil and prefer inaction over action—noninvesting over investing—even when inaction may not be warranted by economic events of the day.

Hyman Minsky (1914–1996), a well-known post-Keynesian economist, argued that the economic behavior of investors changes as the economy moves through cycles of boom and bust. During booms, economic actors become too optimistic and overly eager to take action, while they tend to become too pessimistic and prone to inaction during recessions. These Keynesian and Minksian theories of the psychologically erratic and fundamentally unstable nature of economic actors contradict the traditional neoclassical theory of modern economic human. The latter forms rational expectations by correctly reading and understanding changing circumstances in the present and future and responds by continuously adjusting his behavior (e.g., see our appendix to chapter 3). The traditional neoclassical notion is very much at odds with the Keynesian and post-Keynesian idea of economic human caught up in a web of unavoidable societal influences that complexly shape his behavior often resulting in wild swings and surprises.

Behavioral economists and Keynesian and post-Keynesian economists share a common causal idea: contextuality matters. For the behavioral economists, experiments organized to study decision-making individuals provide conclusive evidence for that idea. For Keynesians and post-Keynesians, supporting evidence comes from observing how financial and corporate investors act across the macro business cycle. Despite this similarity, a number of behavioral economists avoid Keynesian economics because of its structuralism. Like the neoclassical economists, they prefer a humanist approach to theorizing economic behavior, even though they would replace the traditional neoclassical notion of the individual with an individual far more socially conditioned.

Other theories such as those of "herd behavior" and "money illusion" can also be understood as offering versions of contextuality. Keynes explained that herd-like behavior prevails in the stock market not simply because people have an inherent tendency to follow others but rather because of how the market is structured. The price of a traded security may have some connection to the underlying value of the company issuing that security. But its price also, and mainly, reflects guesses of market participants—buyers and sellers—about the future price of the traded security. Hence the price reflects the anticipated average public opinion about the value of the traded security. If what shapes individuals' market decision-making is their guesses about what the average market participant will guess, the result will be "herd behavior."

The explanation regarding "money illusion" builds on individuals' cognitive limitations. Money illusion refers to confusing the nominal value of a currency with its real value (i.e., its nominal value adjusted for the rate of inflation). In other words, if one is holding money in a savings account earning 3 percent interest per year but prices are increasing by 3 percent per year, then the real return on savings is effectively zero. The illusion would be to think that one is earning a real return of 3 percent on savings. According to Keynes, workers resist reductions in their money or nominal wages, even when prices are falling. They think in terms of money (nominal) wages rather than understanding that it is real wages that matter. When firms resist cuts in nominal prices of what they sell even when their costs of production fall, that too may follow from money illusion: thinking in terms of nominal rather than real terms. Here too some behavioral economists avoid invoking Keynes because they reject Keynesian structuralism. Instead, they ascribe money illusion to some inherent limitation of the human mind.

Behavioral economics has begun to develop a rich and nuanced anthropology of the economic behavior of human beings in modern societies. Based on experiments, behavioral economists have cataloged the multitude of ways in which human behavior diverges from the presumptions and predictions of the neoclassical tradition. Based on its psychological explorations, behavioral economics confronts a choice: will it remain a research field that merely catalogs various shortcomings of the traditional neoclassical model and account of human behavior or will it break from neoclassical theory to formulate a new theory of human behavior?

5.4   New Theories of Equilibrium

The notion of equilibrium, like the notion of rationality, is central to the neoclassical tradition. Achieving equilibrium in the economy is understood as achieving a reconciliation of, a kind of harmony among, the potentially conflicting interests of different economic agents: buyers and sellers, employers and employees, lenders and borrowers, and so forth. When combined with the assumption that each individual is economically rational (i.e., makes decisions that best satisfy his or her preferences), equilibrium signifies that every individual was able to completely satisfy his or her wants (choosing among commodities to consume, whether to consume now or later, and how to choose between leisure time and real income) given the individual's initial distribution of endowments and technology. In this sense, neoclassical economists' notions of rationality and equilibrium construct and represent a kind of utopian dream: realizable on earth via establishing the market and property institutions of capitalism. Its utopian dimension has helped neoclassical economics become an important and powerful image in multiple other disciplines and in politics as well as within the discipline of economics.

It is also true that throughout its history, neoclassical economics has conceptualized the notion of equilibrium in multiple, and not always complementary, ways. One primary aim of its practitioners has always been to prove that equilibrium can be defined and achieved in a capitalist economy. This has meant demonstrating mathematically the "existence" of an equilibrium point that can and will emerge out of market interactions among buyers and sellers given the traditional neoclassical assumptions regarding human behavior, technology, and a given initial distribution of endowments. On the basis of proving that an equilibrium point exists, neoclassical economists undertook to prove further that such an equilibrium is also "unique" (there are not multiple and hence alternative equilibrium points raising thorny problems of choice among them), "stable" (any departure from an equilibrium sets in motion mechanisms that restore that equilibrium), and "efficient" (in Pareto's sense that it maximizes the welfare possible for each and all without diminishing any one's welfare).

We begin this section by reviewing the different notions of equilibrium already contained within traditional neoclassical theory. Next we consider two new concepts of equilibrium, increasingly embraced by neoclassical economists, that fall under our heading of late neoclassical theory. The first refers to Nash equilibrium and more generally to the field of classical game theory. The second refers to evolutionary stability and more generally to evolutionary game theory.

Classical game theory defines Nash equilibrium as a stable point where no interacting agent benefits from unilaterally changing his or her chosen strategy. The proponents of Nash equilibrium argue that their notion of equilibrium, precisely because it takes into account the strategic (interactive) aspects of decision-making, supersedes because it is superior to the traditional neoclassical approach to decision-making that does not accommodate those strategic aspects.

Evolutionary game theory conceives of equilibrium as a strategy, not a point, and does so in terms of a population distribution. It defines an "evolutionary stable" strategy as a pattern of behavior such that, if generally followed in the population, those who deviate from it in small numbers will survive less well than others. Proponents of evolutionary game theory argue that their modeling of the problem of equilibrium at the level of the population distribution of behavioral patterns breaks from what they see as classical game theory's narrowly individualistic framework and unrealistic assumptions about human rationality. Breaking from classical game theory's thesis of rational individuals choosing the best strategy, they argue instead that individuals, through learning, adapt their behavior through repeated plays of a game. This general process of learning, rather than rational contemplation and instantaneous calculation, yields the set of strategies that have the highest capacity to establish and enforce an evolutionary stable equilibrium.

In what follows we will investigate whether or to what degree the concepts of Nash equilibrium and/or evolutionary game theory represent breaks from traditional neoclassical theory or fall under our heading of late neoclassical theory.

5.4.1 Different Notions of Equilibrium in the Neoclassical Tradition

An early variant of the idea of equilibrium figures implicitly in Adam Smith's notion of the "invisible hand." If every individual agent freely pursues his or her economic self-interest, the competitive market guides and eventually harmonizes their conflicting interests, yielding the maximum feasible wealth for all. The uncoordinated and self-interested behaviors of rational economic actors are tamed by the key institutions of private property and competitive markets. As noted throughout this book, the political corollary is to reduce the role of the state to securing those two institutions. As noted earlier in this chapter, the neoclassical tradition has broadened to include the state's provision as well of public goods that cannot be provided by private markets.

In traditional neoclassical economics, equilibrium has a very strong normative thrust. It was seen as the antidote to the chaos that Hobbes foresaw if individuals were allowed to act in their own self-economic interest without other constraints. Where Hobbes predicted a powerful state apparatus necessitated by such chaos, traditional neoclassical economics represented the counterargument that no such state apparatus would be necessary. In the eighteenth and the early nineteenth centuries, classical liberal theories aimed, above all, to establish and protect the rights of individuals and civil society against encroachment by king, church, or other powerful social groups. They sought to counter Hobbes's arguments by establishing that self-interested individuals' behaviors—in the institutional context of private property and markets—could avoid chaos and reach a harmonious equilibrium point without needing any state intervention. Traditional neoclassical theory's equilibrium represented a harmonious and spontaneous reconciliation of conflicting economic self-interests; it required no interventions of any "visible hands" (state, church, etc.). Smith's "invisible hand" thus had great normative value and political significance for classical liberals.

Its normative and political importance explains why the concept of equilibrium occupied the attention of so many economists in the over two hundred years since Adam Smith. The earliest neoclassical conceptualizations of equilibrium were those of four great nineteenth-century economists. William Stanley Jevons (1835–1882) and later Francis Ysidro Edgeworth's (1845–1926) conceptualized equilibrium in terms of reaching a mutually beneficial exchange between two self-interested, economically rational traders. Significantly different was the vision of equilibrium articulated by Leon Walras (1834–1910) who went well beyond an equilibrium limited to two trading agents. Walras envisioned a state of generalized equilibrium across a system of markets where each market (populated with multiple buyers and sellers) simultaneously reaches equilibrium. Unlike Jevons's and Edgeworth's representation of markets as processes of negotiation and bargaining between two economic agents, Walras's general equilibrium was envisioned as a singular auction in which equilibrium prices are reached through iterative adjustments by buyers and sellers to prices announced by an imaginary auctioneer. The prices successively announced by such an auctioneer will continue until a general equilibrium is obtained that equates all supplies and demands across all markets. Walras's work allowed neoclassical theorists to claim that equilibrium is possible for any complex modern economy with many interrelated markets.

Paradoxically, this important neoclassical notion of general equilibrium—premised on that theory's profoundly individualist humanism—required and rested on a structuralist assumption. Reaching equilibrium required specification of the structural rules governing the imaginary auctioneer's functions. Neoclassical theory thereby imposed a structure to which the human subjects have to conform if equilibrium were to be found and achieved. Humanism can and, in the case of general equilibrium theory, did need to rely on a structuralist moment to reach its goals. Something parallel happens when a Keynesian structuralist economics needs to introduce a humanist moment: an individual investor with animal spirits determining investments.

A third notion of equilibrium emerges in the writings of Alfred Marshall (1842–1924), famous for producing the first textbook version of neoclassical economics in his canonical work *Principles of Economics* (1920). Marshallian equilibrium analysis examines a change in a single market while assuming everything else is being held constant. Thereafter economists became famous (in some eyes infamous) for using the Latin phrase *ceteris paribus* when analyzing markets. The models used were called partial equilibrium models because they focused only on changes in a particular industry and market. They ignored changes in all other industries and markets that were occurring or would occur because of induced changes in the observed industry and market. No interactive effects were allowed to occur between the investigated industry and the rest of the economy. In contrast, general equilibrium models allow economists to trace how a change in, say, a price can impact not only a particular market but in fact all markets. For example, a price change that occurs in a single market ripples throughout the economy: it may lead households to make adjustments not only in the demand for the good whose price has changed but also in demands for all the other commodities that they desire. Those changes will impact firms in different industries producing those respective goods, and those effects will lead to still other changes, and so forth.

Not surprisingly, those neoclassical economists who work with Walrasian general equilibrium analyses tend to find Marshallian models of partial equilibrium limited and wanting. In contrast, those who work with partial equilibrium models find general equilibrium models to be too abstract and unmanageably complex with correspondingly limited practical use when analyzing a particular industry.

Traditional neoclassical theory contains three different notions and uses of equilibrium: exchange, general, and partial equilibrium. While they occasion arguments and debates among neoclassical theorists, all three concepts of equilibrium share at least two very important attributes. First, they all affirm traditional neoclassical assumptions regarding economic rationality: all economic agents are self-interested maximizers of individual utility or profit. *Homo economicus* is their common presumption. Second, despite differences, all three approaches focus on the mathematically tractable conditions under which an equilibrium state can be reached. They share a drive to demonstrate how and why competitive markets enable uncoordinated and self-interested actions of economically rational agents to yield equilibrium.

However, in the final quarter of the twentieth century, criticisms arose directed against traditional neoclassical theory's concepts of equilibrium. They led to new and different ways of formulating the idea of equilibrium. Both the exchange and partial equilibrium concepts were understood to be too limited in their empirical applicability. Too often the ceteris paribus way of reasoning invited ridicule: too much had to be held constant in order to say something that then had too little real significance. The general equilibrium system did not fare much better. Research demonstrated that the set of assumptions necessary to mathematically prove the efficiency, the stability, and the uniqueness of a general equilibrium system was so complex and restrictive that it turned the analysis into a "special case scenario," thereby rendering the qualifier "general" meaningless. In addition to all of this, and perhaps even more important causally, the final quarter of the twentieth century saw neoclassical economists increasingly interested in addressing problems outside of competitive market-adjustment mechanisms.

As neoclassical economists responded to claims that real markets were imperfect and systematically failed to perform as perfect markets had implied, they needed concepts of equilibrium that did not rely on the "invisible hand" of competitive markets. Earlier in this chapter, we showed how late neoclassical theory extended analyses of imperfect markets to firms, households, bureaucracies, and so forth. As economists then interacted increasingly with scholars and decision-makers from other disciplines, economics proliferated new or "applied" fields and subfields, including public economics, environmental economics, economics of industrial organization, economics of the household, economic geography, sports economics, health economics, and economics of gender. Indeed what is now called applied micro theory has become almost a distinct approach to human behavior. For these reasons neoclassical economists needed more versatile concepts of equilibrium that did not rely solely on "market mechanisms" and that applied to a wider range of social contexts. For many, game theoretic approaches provided precisely this desired versatility.

5.4.2   Nash Equilibrium and Classical Game Theory

Those introducing game theory into economics include Augustin Cournot (1801–1877), Emil Borel (1871–1956), John von Neumann (1903–1957), and Oskar Morgenstern (1902–1977). What today is known as classical game theory began in the 1950s with John Nash at Princeton University (1951). The proliferation of game theoretic research within economics, however, started in the 1980s when the discipline grew increasingly more dissatisfied with the standard neoclassical concepts of partial and general equilibrium for the aforementioned reasons.

Game theory became relevant to and important in economics when it was recognized that economic agents needed to make guesses about others' reactions to their own actions in deciding how to act in markets. The dilemma facing economic agents struck increasing numbers of economists as very much like the dilemmas people encounter in playing certain sorts of games. For example, in a draw poker game, each player must make a strategic choice regarding the cards initially dealt to that player: how many and which cards to hold and how many cards to draw from the deck. Winning or losing depends on the strategic choices of the players.

Each of the two or more players knows the rules of the game and assumes that about the other players. Each player chooses an action, taking into account the actions of the other players. Each player is assumed to be rational (desiring to win and not lose) and will play in a correspondingly rational manner. This is called common knowledge rationality (CKR). Investigating the conditions for and operations of strategies to win games of various sorts turns out to offer many insights into parallel choices and actions imposed on individuals and firms in actual markets. Some of those insights bring with them new conceptions of equilibrium. The question guiding our discussion is whether the impact of game theoretic research on neoclassical economics has yet produced a breakaway to a new and different kind of economics or whether we have here again something less different and thus better labeled as late neoclassical theory.

Consider, for instance, the following game with two players, A and B. Both players can choose between the same two strategies available to them, either "follow self-interest" or else "be altruistic." The strategies available to players

Table 5.1
Invisible hand game

| | | Player B | |
		Follow self-interest	Be altruistic
Player A	Follow self-interest	4, 4	2, 0
	Be altruistic	0, 2	0, 0

are called their "action set." We call this the Adam Smith game of "invisible hand" because it demonstrates the classical claim that the best economic and social outcome is achieved if and when every individual pursues his or her self-interest. Within these two players' identical action sets, self-interested behavior is superior to altruism. This Adam Smith game is represented in table 5.1 in normal (or matrix) form.

To explain briefly, the first value in each "cell" of the matrix refers to the assumed numerical payoff to player A and the second value refers to the assumed numerical payoff to player B. Thus, if player A follows a self-interested strategy, we can read horizontally to see A's assumed payoff results: either 4 or 2, depending on player B's strategic choice. If player B is also self-interested, player A receives 4, whereas if player B is altruistic, player A only receives 2. If player A pursues the alternative strategy of altruism, reading horizontally across the table shows that player A receives no payoff regardless of player B's strategy. For player A, then, self-interest dominates altruism; it achieves the best outcome in the game as it does in economic and social life. Examining the possible outcomes for player B yields the same result: the strategy of pursuing self-interest dominates (is superior to) an altruistic strategy.

The conclusion of the game is this: self-interested behavior for both players is the dominant strategy equilibrium.

The dominant strategy equilibrium in this game also happens to be a Pareto efficient, unique, and stable equilibrium. It is Pareto efficient because there is no other strategy combination that would make any player better off (without making someone worse off). It is unique because there are no other strategy combinations that result in equilibrium. It is stable because the instrumentally rational players have no incentives to move away from this equilibrium state. This game's results thus match the perfectly competitive model stressed by traditional neoclassical economics.

However, games—like markets—need not always have a unique dominant strategy equilibrium. Neoclassical economists have looked to games without one unique strategy equilibrium to see what lessons they might offer concerning markets that likewise lack unique equilibrium points. The Nash equilibrium concept proved useful in just this way. As noted earlier, Nash equilibrium was defined as a stable state where no interacting agent benefits from unilaterally changing his or her chosen strategy. Now we can further develop this definition.

A Nash equilibrium outcome is a combination of strategies that are best responses to one another under the assumption of common knowledge rationality. A strategy is deemed to be a best response if it produces the best possible outcome, given the opponent's action set. To return to the invisible hand game, the best response of player B to player A's selfish behavior is to be selfish, and vice versa. Since playing selfish is a mutual best response, the upper left cell in table 5.1 is a Nash equilibrium outcome. As we will now see, all dominant strategy equilibria are also Nash equilibria, but not all Nash equilibria are dominant strategy equilibria.

Consider, for instance, the "assurance game" in table 5.2. The dilemma faced by workers in an "open shop" workplace is whether to join a strike. If the players can coordinate their actions and participate together in a strike, they will get a raise, indicated by positive numbers in the cells of the matrix. If instead they cannot coordinate their actions and one of them strikes, while the other continues to work, the one that strikes loses the job indicated by a zero in the cell. This assurance game is a version of a larger class of coordination games in which the social problem is to coordinate the actions of agents for the mutual benefit of them all.

In this game of "assurance," there are no dominant strategies, but two Nash equilibria: either no one should strike or all should strike simultaneously. To explain: if worker A strikes, worker B's best response is to strike, and if worker B strikes, worker A's best response is also to strike. In both cases, 4 is greater than 2. Similarly, if worker A does not strike, worker B's best response is also not to strike, and vice versa. In both cases, 2 is greater than 0. Therefore both the upper left and the lower right cells are Nash equilibrium outcomes. But which one is preferable? Do the players have enough information to make the appropriate and coordinated choice? Given its assumed payoff structure, the strike–strike outcome Pareto-dominates the not-strike–not-strike outcome: workers would be better off if they could coordinate their actions and strike.

Table 5.2
Assurance game

		Worker B	
		Not strike	Strike
Worker A	Not strike	2, 2	2, 0
	Strike	0, 2	4, 4

Table 5.3
Driving game

		Driver B	
		Left	Right
Driver A	Left	1, 1	0, 0
	Right	0, 0	1, 1

Hence this game does not pose a serious problem. The players have a clear incentive to choose the strike–strike outcome.

Suppose yet that another sort of game—called a "simple pure coordination game"—where the outcomes are identical: neither Nash equilibrium is superior. In such a situation the problem arises of coordinating the choices of the players or agents. Consider, for example, the "driving game" in table 5.3 as a pure coordination game.

In this game the problem is to coordinate the actions of the drivers such that both drive on the left or on the right side of the road. Individual agents with instrumental rationality—who pursue narrow self-interest independently of one another—will not coordinate and so may not finally arrive at Nash equilibria (upper left or lower right cells). For instrumentally rational players, there is nothing evident in the payoffs that will ensure that each acts to achieve the better outcome for both.

To generate a unique and stable equilibrium in such a game, some game theorists introduce the idea that the players must reject instrumental rationality (pursuing narrowly defined self-interest) to explicitly coordinate their actions. Only then might they secure one of the two Nash equilibria in the assurance game above. Thomas Schelling (1960) developed the concept of "salience" (or "focal points") to describe the role played by institutions that would coordinate agents' decisions in such games, nonrepeated, one-shot games, where there is no form of communication. Schelling's example is the case of two strangers intending to meet in New York City on a certain day but without having decided in advance on where and what time to do so. They cannot communicate (he writes in 1960 long before cell phones). What should the strangers do to meet? When asked, Schelling's students proposed "at 12 o'clock mid-day" (a "focal point" during the day) and "in front of the information booth at Grand Central Station" (a "salient" place well-known and accessible in a main railway station). The concept of "focal points" or "salience" can be extended to include conventions, social norms, and institutional arrangements to which players can refer to coordinate their actions. By invoking these various assumed structures, they can settle on one of the equally attractive or identical Nash equilibria.

Let us now consider the famous, widely invoked, and often applied "prisoner's dilemma" game (table 5.4). In its traditional version it begins with two

Table 5.4
Prisoner's dilemma game

		Suspect 2	
		Defect	Cooperate
Suspect 1	Defect	3, 3	0, 5
	Cooperate	5, 0	0.5, 0.5

suspects under interrogation for committing a crime. Questioned separately, they have no opportunity to communicate with one another. Yet they need to cooperate—coordinate their actions—such that neither confesses to the crime (call this "cooperate" or "deny" the crime). However, the interrogators are clever: they establish a payoff structure that provides an incentive for each suspect to admit to the crime ("defect" or "confess" to the crime).

Each suspect or prisoner faces a dilemma. If one suspect chooses to defect (confess to the crime) and the other cooperates (denies the crime), then the one who defects walks away (in exchange for testifying against the other) and the one who cooperates goes to jail for the full sentence. If both cooperate (deny the crime), the frustrated interrogators pin a minor charge on the suspects that leads them to receive a smaller jail time. But since the incentive structure compels these instrumentally rational suspects to defect (confess), they both do so and receive fewer years in jail than the maximum sentence, but more than the minor punishment they would have received if they had cooperated (both denied the crime). Hence it is in the suspects' interest to coordinate their decisions such that both deny the crime, but because they can't cooperate, they are left with the only reasonable alternative, which is to confess. It is the only alternative because each knows that if he or she denies the crime, then his or her partner in crime can walk away if that partner confesses.

In table 5.4 read the payoffs as years of imprisonment. In this particular symmetrically set up game, both suspects have a dominant strategy: defecting (confessing to the crime) dominates cooperating (denying the crime) when compared pairwise ($3 < 5$ and $0 < 0.5$). In this game the dominant strategy (and Nash) equilibrium (Defect, Defect) happens to be Pareto suboptimal in comparison to the outcome that would result if both suspects were to cooperate. The problem in this case is that without the presence of communication, trust, or credible threat between the players, instrumental rationality will not work to produce cooperation and thus minor jail time (the Pareto superior outcome). That is why the game is called the prisoner's dilemma. Because the Nash equilibrium is not the best outcome for the players, this game undermines Adam Smith's vision that acting in one's self-interest (e.g., both prisoners confess to the crime) yields a social utopia.

The prisoner's dilemma game is particularly interesting because while the equilibrium outcome is unique and stable, it is also Pareto suboptimal. And just like pure coordination games discussed above, instrumental rationality is not enough to reach the Pareto superior outcome of cooperation. In order to achieve this Pareto superior outcome, the players have to communicate and coordinate their actions. This is possible if the game can be repeated indefinitely and players see incentives for cooperating. For example, consider the possibility that players are part of a criminal organization that does not forgive defectors. This transforms the game into a repeated game (as there is "more" to the game after the defector walks away) and erects a credible threat against a suspect's deviation from the cooperative strategy (the criminal organization would retaliate against the suspect).

Neoclassical economists have made use of the "prisoner's dilemma" game in a variety of contexts. We may consider two examples here. Consider first a household shared by a number of students. While each student has a private bedroom, all share a common kitchen, bathroom, and other living areas. If the common areas are maintained and regularly cleaned, everyone benefits. Cleanliness is a "public good": no housemate can be excluded from it and any student's enjoyment of cleanliness does not diminish others' enjoyment. Cleaning the common spaces requires effort. If individual housemates view cleaning, as traditional neoclassical theory assumes, as a disutility (forgoing leisure time without any offsetting income for doing so), then that theory predicts that each individual housemate will try to minimize cleaning effort and "free-ride" on their housemates' cleaning efforts.

If every housemate reasons in this manner, then the equilibrium outcome, while unique and stable, will be a Pareto suboptimal level of cleanliness in common spaces. Tensions over mounting grime and debris may then lead to household dissolution. Yet many such households do survive. They do so by having housemates meet and communicate, collectively recognizing their participation in an arrangement that requires committed and coordinated behavior by all. Such households solve their public good problem by transforming a noncooperative into a cooperative game.

When the public good in question rises from the level of household or neighborhood (where face-to-face interactions, meetings, and communication are feasible and effective) to the levels of town, state, or nation, other kinds of collective mechanisms would be devised. For example, such public goods could be decided and produced by governments and financed by taxation. The principle remains: some kind of coordinated and organized social or government effort is required to achieve a better result for all.

In our second example of applying the prisoner's dilemma game, we return to the case of oligopoly (the Bertrand model discussed earlier in section 5.2.2) and assume firms of equal size competing for market share. We may dispense with the now familiar details to focus on the possible results of the game. If the firms do not collude, competition among them will bid down the price until it equals marginal cost. If they cooperate, they could collectively set marginal revenue equal to marginal cost and at the resulting price earn more profits than had they competed with one another. However, if one firm defects from the collusive agreement, it can earn even more profits than it would under the agreement, but at the cost of reduced profits for the other firms. If all firms defect from the agreement, they will expand outputs until all profits are competed away and the market returns to the competitive result where price equals marginal cost. The question is: will the firms collude or defect from the agreement?

Given that this is an ongoing, repeated game, they may manage to collude, secure agreement to keep colluding, and thereby achieve a market price above marginal cost that wins higher profits for colluding firms (at consumers' expense). In the three decades following World War II, seven major international oil companies (known as the "Seven Sisters") may well have cooperated to keep oil production under control so that competition among them would not depress prices or threaten the companies' exceptionally high profits. Note that in this case—unlike our previous example of public goods—the cooperative outcome that improved corporate profits also damaged consumers' interests.

Most neoclassical textbooks now devote at least a chapter to game theory and its applications. In recent years applications in economics of coordination and prisoner's dilemma types of games have proliferated. Both types of games demonstrate the limits of traditional neoclassical economic theory in its exclusive reliance on instrumental rationality without considering institutional context and contingency. The game theoretical models help justify the intervention of nonmarket institutions (e.g., governments, collusive arrangements) to arrive at preferable equilibrium outcomes. Nonetheless, game theory retains the neoclassical notion of *Homo economicus* (perhaps with even stronger assumptions) as one of its entry points and retains the centrality of the problem of equilibrium selection. This retention means that while these models affirm the importance of social context and convey interventionist policy implications, they do so from within the individualist and equilibrium focused framework of the neoclassical tradition. For some proponents, this is precisely their strength: game theory provides theoretical justification for a "visible hand" to aid the "invisible hand" while retaining the methodological framework of the neoclassical tradition. For others, this is its limitation: classical game theoretic research may well extend and modify the neoclassical tradition, but it does so while remaining firmly within its theoretical boundaries.

5.4.3 Evolutionary Stability and Evolutionary Game Theory

Unlike classical game theory where agents behave according to instrumental rationality without ever changing that behavior, even as they engage in strategic interactions, evolutionary game theory proceeds differently. Its approach allows games to be construed as dynamic processes in which agents learn and adapt their behavior over the course of repeated plays. Practitioners of this approach import ideas from evolutionary biology into economics: game theorists replace fitness with utility and natural selection (adoption) with learning (adaptation). Displacing instrumental rationality in favor of a learning and adapting agent becomes a key distinction that sets evolutionary game theory apart from the neoclassical tradition. In evolutionary game theory the iconic figure of *Homo economicus* becomes a special case, merely one possible behavioral pattern among many others that may be adopted, adapted, or abandoned.

Despite this important difference, the evolutionary approach is similar to classical game theory in focusing on the problem of equilibrium. However, its concern with dynamic processes of adaptation requires a notion of equilibrium different from that central to both traditional neoclassical economics and classical game theory. Its equilibrium concept is referred to as evolutionary stability. The latter describes a self-enforcing (stable) equilibrium facilitated by social conventions. The latter enable agents to coordinate their strategies in a stable manner over the course of multiple plays of a game. An evolutionary stable strategy is a pattern of behavior such that, if adopted by a sufficient number of agents within a population, those who deviate from it in small numbers will do less well than the rest.

To illustrate evolutionary game theory, we present the payoff matrix of the "hawk and dove game" a game that is a famous example for evolutionary game theory (table 5.5). In this game, agents must make a strategic choice between playing the Hawk or the Dove. If both choose to be Hawks, they spoil the proverbial pie (zeros for both in the upper left cell); if both choose to be Doves, they share the pie (each receives 2 in the lower right cell).

Again, there are no dominant strategies, but there are three different Nash equilibria. Two fall under what can be called pure strategies: those

Table 5.5
Hawk and dove game

		Agent 2	
		Hawk	Dove
Agent 1	Hawk	0, 0	3, 1
	Dove	1, 3	2, 2

located in the two cells where the agents play differently (one Hawk, and the other Dove). *A pure-strategy equilibrium is one in which agents have to play one of the two strategies exclusively.* The third Nash equilibrium is achieved when agents play a mixed strategy. *A mixed strategy equilibrium is one in which the agents can play a combination of two strategies with certain probabilities.*

Let us first concentrate on the two pure-strategy equilibria and the choice between them. Each agent does not know what the other will do but the payoffs to choices are interdependent. If agent 1 plays Hawk, agent 2 should play Dove. If agent 2 plays Dove, agent 1 should play Hawk. The same kind of reasoning applies to the other equilibrium position: if agent 1 chooses Dove, then agent 2 should choose Hawk; if agent 2 plays Hawk, agent 1 should play Dove. In a one-shot (nonrepeated) game without communication between the two players, which of these two pure-strategy Nash equilibria will be the outcome of the game? This is a particularly interesting equilibrium selection problem because the choice between two equilibrium outcomes entails a conflict between the two players: the one who plays Hawk will get three-quarters of the pie and the one who plays Dove will receive the smaller one-quarter portion.

One way to arrive at an equilibrium outcome is through "conventions" (Sugden 1989). This rationale for the equilibrium selection problem resembles but is somewhat more nuanced than Schelling's concept of "salience" discussed earlier. Among the different examples of conventions, we can list "first come, first serve," "finders keepers," "last in, first out," "seniority," "reverse seniority." In some cases even a lottery can be established as a convention. Conventions are societal rules or norms that allow a particular equilibrium result to be established. In that sense they closely resemble structural rules invoked by a game theorist to achieve its result. We have yet another example of how humanism can slide into structuralism.

Let us now turn to examine the mixed-strategy Nash equilibrium. In fact in the conventional, "biological," version of the hawk and dove game, the mixed-strategy equilibrium, interpreted as a "population distribution," is the only solution. The value of the expected payoff of agent 1 when playing Hawk can be stated in the following manner:

$$EV(\text{H}) = p(0) + (1 - p)(3),$$

where $EV(\text{H})$ stands for agent 1's expected value when playing Hawk, p stands for the probability of agent 2 playing Hawk, and 0 and 3 represent the table payoffs to agent 1 (when playing Hawk). The equation calculates the agent 1's expected payoff playing Hawk by weighing the possible matrix payoffs using their respective probabilities. Similarly the value of the expected payoff of agent 1 when playing Dove is

$EV(D) = p(1) + (1 - p)(2),$

where p is again the probability of agent 2 playing Hawk. In mixed-strategy solutions, expected payoffs should be equal to one another because otherwise there would be no incentive to play. Therefore setting $EV(H) = EV(D)$ and solving for p obtains

$$p = \frac{1}{2}.$$

Since the agents are identical and given the payoff structure, each agent will play Hawk half the time.

An alternative way of thinking about this game and result is a lottery in which each agent has a 50 percent probability of winning the right to play Hawk. When translated into a population interpretation, it means that in equilibrium, half of the population will play Hawk and the other half Dove. Given this kind of framework, an evolutionary stable strategy would be to play Hawk half the time; evolutionary stability is achieved when half the population plays Hawk. This outcome changes when the payoff structure changes.

There are a number of different and largely complementary explanations for the growing prominence within the neoclassical tradition of evolutionary game theory and its associated concept of evolutionary stability. We will highlight only three of them. First and foremost, there is the broader tendency toward cross-disciplinary engagements, sometimes taking the form of extending the economic modes of analysis to other disciplines (e.g., use of game theory in political science) and other times taking the form of borrowing methodologies from other disciplines (e.g., borrowing experimental methodologies from cognitive psychology). In the latter vein, as we have already discussed above (see section 5.3.1), neoclassical economists who wanted to study motivational diversity have borrowed modeling methods from evolutionary biology. Sometimes when concepts (or a method) enter into the tradition as legitimate tools of economic analysis, they tend to spread quickly and take a life of their own—especially if there are other factors that make it desirable for economists to deploy them.

Second, once introduced into the discipline, the use of evolutionary models became favored among game theorists as they realized that evolutionary biology's equilibrium concept had the desirable quality of narrowing the set of plausible Nash equilibria. That was a very useful result for a tradition in which the idea of equilibrium played such a central role. Nonetheless, in formulating the problem at the level of a population distribution and in allowing individual actors to learn (adapt) certain behavioral traits, evolutionary models do represent a break from the standard neoclassical assumptions in regard to human rationality.

A third, and perhaps more profound, reason pertains to the broader political and economic policy implications of framing the equilibrium problem in evolutionary terms. Once Nash equilibrium replaced the earlier neoclassical concepts of equilibrium, the notion of equilibrium gained a broader applicability to a range of social issues. This allowed discussion of the conditions of equilibrium (in its broadest sense) to become a discussion of the conditions of social order. In particular, commentators noted that the hawk and dove game and similar types of evolutionary models provide a particular antidote to the interventionist perspectives arising from the prisoner's dilemma type of games. In other words, within game theory we find yet another manifestation of the difference between liberal and conservative neoclassical economists encountered and discussed earlier.

Recall the three attributes of a good equilibrium: efficiency, stability, and uniqueness. Politically we can restate these three attributes as the conditions for a "good society": a stable and efficient social order without an alternative. Put in these terms, it is no wonder that theorists spend enormous amounts of time and intellectual effort on questions of equilibrium. With this in mind, let us reconsider some of the games we already have discussed. To facilitate comparison among them, we present a summary of these three attributes for each approach in table 5.6.

The first game of "invisible hand" combines all three attributes together: it has a unique and efficient Nash equilibrium (and all Nash equilibria are stable). Table 5.6 reports this with the three checks in the first column. This game and its check marks should appeal to conservative neoclassicists. Nevertheless, it is only one of many possible games. Many economists believe that a large number of possible social situations can be better described/modeled by other types of games, for example, those that require solving the coordination problems in the "assurance" and "driving" types of games. Such games interest economists sympathetic to using social institutions to improve on social outcomes that would be reached by individual self-interested behavior alone. Similarly the prisoner's dilemma game is powerful because it provides a rationale for extra-market (governmental, social commitment, and group action) intervention over markets alone. The conclusion of the prisoner's dilemma

Table 5.6
Comparing different types of games

	Game of invisible hand	Game of assurance	Game of prisoner's dilemma	Game of hawk and dove
Efficiency	✓	✓		
Stability	✓	✓	✓	✓
Uniqueness	✓		✓	

game was stark in its implications: the unique and stable equilibrium is Pareto-dominated by another (nonequilibrium) outcome that only can be reached by some extra-market mechanism. This game lends support to neoclassical economists critical of the purely invisible hand type of explanation.

The game of hawk and dove differs from the other three in significant ways. For comparative simplicity we limit our discussion here to the pure-strategy version of the game. First of all, unlike the invisible hand game, no uniquely efficient equilibrium exists. Second, it differs from the assurance game because the two pure-strategy Nash equilibria present a conflict: the choice between the two equilibria results in one of the agents being worse off. Third, it is different from the prisoner's dilemma game in the sense that there is no *unique* Pareto superior outcome.

In other words, the game of hawk and dove does not pose the problem of equilibrium selection in terms of choosing the Pareto efficient outcome, but rather one of choosing an equilibrium outcome in a situation where instrumental rationality fails and the choice involves a conflictual problem of division (of the proverbial pie). In this sense and unlike the prisoner's dilemma story (where extra-market institutions intervene to improve everyone's well-being), the game of hawk and dove's equilibrium is a product of spontaneously evolving conventions. To make the contrast even starker, while the game of prisoner's dilemma provides a rationale for government (and other forms of extra-market) intervention to improve Pareto efficiency, the game of hawk and dove tells a story in which equilibrium can be reached through spontaneously evolving conventions without any need for government intervention. While this result, in and of itself, constitutes an important moment of difference within the field of game theoretic research, the hawk and dove game shares with the others a normatively driven search for finding the appropriate conditions under which a societal equilibrium can be reached. That search defines in part what neoclassical theory has always been.

5.5   Conclusion

Since the 1970s the neoclassical tradition has undergone an interesting transformation. Responding to its internal and external critics and ongoing cross-disciplinary interpenetration, it has extended its analytical reach to entirely new areas. One result has been what some call *specialization* and others *fragmentation*. This chapter has concentrated on three key developments of neoclassical theory's recent extensions: those involving market imperfections, human behavior, and equilibrium. These developments exhibit the influence of research programs imported from other disciplines that have enriched the methodological foundations of the theory as well as the range and depth of its specializations. It is thus understandable that for some commentators, neoclassical economics seems to be fragmenting, its core propositions modified beyond recognition or solidity.

Yet our investigations and survey suggest otherwise. We find that the deeper and common tendency among late neoclassical economic research programs has been to retain neoclassical theory's traditional humanist entry point and its overriding societal aim. What is assumed to drive and determine the economy are preference-maximizing rational actors and their goal, like that of economic science, is to achieve social reconciliation expressed in the form of equilibrium. The theory's new specializations deployed its entry point to new areas of study well beyond the tradition's earlier domains of economic research. New neoclassical interpretations of all kinds of societal institutions were produced using the concepts of transaction costs, bounded rationality, information asymmetries, Nash equilibrium, evolutionary stability, and so forth. Late neoclassical economics began to concern itself with and offer analyses of the entirety of society: what some saw as economics colonizing other disciplines.

We have taken note when some of these developments, such as those in behavioral economics and evolutionary game theory, have undermined if not openly challenged the traditional neoclassical entry point. We would not be very surprised if eventually a real break within neoclassical theory occurs and a new, different entry point is adopted by a significant subset of the then no-longer neoclassical economists. After all, such breaks do occur in any theory and across all disciplines. This book's subject matter is the contested set of differences within economics among neoclassical, Keynesian, and Marxian theories constructed on and by means of their alternative entry points. Those differences arose out of breaks in the history of economics as a discipline.

However, this chapter's examination of various leading neoclassical developments over recent decades suggests to us only a slightly modified neoclassical entry point. That theory—its initial organizing ideas and logic—remains true to its tradition. That is why we use the term *late neoclassical theory* to title this chapter. In embracing all sorts of interesting contingencies—from market imperfections to different human behaviors to game theoretic concepts of equilibrium—neoclassical economists have made the traditional neoclassical project more versatile as well as responding to changing social and intellectual conditions. In this sense neoclassical economics is hardly dead as some Marxists, Keynesians, and even some game theorists and other like-minded critics have suggested. Indeed criticisms have helped neoclassical economics survive and prosper.

6 Oscillations in Capitalism and among Economic Theories

6.1 Capitalism Has Always Been Changing

Capitalism has always varied from economies with more to those with less competitive markets, from economies with relatively more private- than state-operated enterprises to those with the reverse balance, and from economies with more democratic to those with more autocratic politics. Mixtures of these different characteristics have defined different kinds or forms of capitalism throughout its history. Because of these variations, we might more accurately use the plural term "capitalisms" when referring to this kind of changeable economy. Of course, that is not how many, if not most, economists and others understand capitalism. In their view, capitalism is a society with mostly or only private property (and private enterprises) and competitive markets. Some would add the presence of political democracy to those two. For these thinkers, the more the society moves away from the private-property/market/democratic definition of capitalism, the closer it moves to (undemocratic) socialism and communism. We will argue something different in this chapter. We will show how and why capitalism has oscillated from one kind of capitalism to another depending on variations in structures of markets, ownership, and power while its basic organization of the surplus remained the same. We also will pay special attention to the particular similarities and differences between two polar variations whose conflicts shaped so much of the twentieth century: private-capitalism versus state-capitalism.

Over the last one hundred and forty years or so, capitalism not only oscillated among its different forms, but economic theory focused on understanding capitalism also oscillated among alternative kinds of reasoning. Moreover these two different kinds of oscillations are interconnected. The movement from one form of economic reasoning to another has influenced and been influenced by shifts among different forms of capitalism. This complex interaction between economies and economic theories will also be a focus of this chapter. We start with a discussion of the instabilities, contradictions, and sometimes major crises of capitalism as a contributing cause both to its variations and to alternative economic theorizations that understand capitalism differently and correspondingly offer different solutions to capitalism's problems and crises.

6.1.1 Instabilities and Capitalism

Capitalism has been an unstable economic system since its emergence in eighteenth-century Europe as the successor to a millennium of feudalism there. Its instabilities have always been multiple. One, located in the heart of its production system, emerges from the internal contradictions of the relationship between workers and employers. The two sides are mutually dependent but also mutually suspicious, distrustful, and often hostile. The employer–employee relationship periodically explodes (disruptive job actions, strikes, lockouts, protests, unionization drives, etc.) in ways that destabilize and change capitalism. Sometimes these changes yield a kind of capitalism in which labor is relatively powerful compared to capital, and sometimes they yield a different kind of capitalism in which capitalists have the upper hand.

Another instability emerges from competition among capitalist employers. This often drives them to press workers to produce more output per hour, accept lower hourly wages, or give up benefits (medical insurance, holidays, etc.). Such pressures heighten the contradictions already simmering in production. Sometimes employers cooperate or merge to evade the risks or costs of competition. Sometimes competition ruthlessly eliminates all but one or a very few competitors. In these ways competition undermines itself and yields cartels, oligopolies, or monopolies. When the latter use their market power to raise prices, they draw the opposition of those who have to pay such prices. Those opponents can and often do fight back by getting governments to break up the monopolies ("bust the trusts") into smaller and once again competitive enterprises. The high profits of cartels and monopolies can attract new entrants who re-introduce competition. The pendulum thus oscillates between competition and monopoly within most industries and hence between more and less competitive capitalisms. Struggles between advocates of competition and defenders of cartels, oligopolies, and monopoly have repeatedly agitated and shaped politics in ways that destabilize capitalism as well as shape its variations.

Competition likewise drives workers to undercut one another in dealings with employers. Cooperation among workers, as among employers, sometimes enables them to avoid the risks and costs of competition by confronting employers collectively (often via labor unions). When successful, the workers' collective bargaining can obtain better wages, shorter work weeks, and improved working conditions from employers than with individual bargaining. In response, employers may cooperate to undermine unions to re-establish competition among laborers and thus lower wages. Both employers and employees pressure the state for legislation favoring each and working against the interests of the other. Labor markets, like product markets, have oscillated between more and less competitive organizations there and hence between more and less regulated capitalism. Such oscillations have sometimes raised resentments and hostilities to produce conflicts—strikes, lockouts, violence—that shook capitalist societies and helped move them from one variant form to another.

Another source of instability has emerged from capitalism's contradictory tendencies both to reduce and to enlarge social differences. For example, in some ways capitalism's technical dynamism, global growth, and market sensitivities have provided opportunities for individuals of modest backgrounds to gain high incomes and political power. Capitalism developed public education systems that likewise provide far broader avenues for advancement than existed earlier. Capitalism's expansive tendency to produce a world market has provoked and enabled mass migrations that brought together and at least partly integrated people of diverse backgrounds. However, these mechanisms for reducing social differences coexisted with others inside capitalism that pushed in the opposite direction.

Those who accumulate wealth in capitalist economies may use it to block others from doing so (as when monopolized industries create "barriers to entry," e.g., costly brand names and licensing laws that prevent new enterprises from being able to compete). Capitalist development often creates two sectors of industry, big monopoly business versus small competitive business, that foster long-standing animosities between them. Employers pursuing higher profits may deepen divisions within capitalist societies by recruiting low-wage immigrants to replace higher paid native-born, women or children to replace higher paid men, ethnic minorities to replace higher paid majorities, and so forth. Unions may seek to protect their members by discriminations of their own. As with the conflicts among employers and between them and employees, economic inequalities among workers can also sometimes accumulate to provoke social conflicts. Those too can and often do destabilize and radically alter capitalist societies. Any of these inequalities and resulting conflicts may bring about more government interventions into the economy, including regulations of markets, tax impositions, and welfare programs that may coalesce into a state-managed form of capitalism. In reaction to that, social pressures may build to reduce if not eliminate many of these state interventions to produce a much more privately run kind of capitalism.

The struggles between employers and employees, between competitive and monopolistic enterprises, and among unequal and divided social groups have all played important roles in capitalism's changeability and movement among its different forms. Another oscillation—between different views of the state's role in society—also shapes movement among capitalism's alternative forms. In one view, the state is understood and expected to provide a social safety net to all citizens; in another view, the state's role is viewed as much more limited as a protector of private property and competitive markets. When the former role prevails, it may accumulate frustration over "big government" and "state intrusion into private lives" and opposition to taxes, welfare and entitlement spending, and regulations. When the far more limited role for the state prevails, concerns may arise over the conditions of the poor, abusive behaviors of business, and anger at corporations and the rich who benefit from lower tax rates and fewer regulations. Oscillations in the social prevalence of these alternative views of the government's proper role in society add to capitalism's instability just as the latter in turn provokes oscillations among those views.

6.1.2 Capitalism and Economic Theories

The struggles within and the instability and changeability of capitalism also provoked and influenced economic theories. Many major contributors to economics across capitalism's history have been drawn to explain the economic causes and consequences of those struggles and that instability. Neoclassical economics, for example, aimed to celebrate competition and denounce monopoly. It always championed the independence and freedom of individual choice to determine income, wealth, unemployment, and much else. It worried incessantly that a too concentrated industry and a too powerful state would undermine individual competitive capitalism and the optimum economic well-being it promised. In contrast, Keynesian economics looked more to the state and what actions it might take to avoid the costly consequences of capitalist business cycles and to regulate the economy in the interests of a "good and fair society" for all citizens. Against the neoclassical economists, the Keynesians argued that a strong state was needed to support the survival of capitalism and its promised optimum results. And in contrast to both, Marxian economics focused on the worker–employer conflict inside capitalism and its costly social impacts. For it alone, a revolutionary change in that relationship—a transition beyond all forms of capitalism—was required to overcome capitalism's flaws and costs, to realize the potential of modern technology, and thereby to enable generalized economic well-being.

However, there was yet another capitalist instability that, perhaps more than all others, shaped key differences among the three great schools of economic theory. This instability has many names in the history of capitalism. Crisis, glut, boom, bust, underconsumption, overproduction, panic, bubble, business cycle, upturn, downturn, recession, and depression are among them. They all refer to a recurring pattern that afflicted capitalism every few years wherever it took root. It usually begins with a fairly sudden drop in trade, production, and employment accompanied by rising business bankruptcies, withdrawals of bank deposits, creditors demanding repayment and restricting new loans, and so on. Business and personal incomes fall quickly and poverty spreads. As these economic conditions persist, workers accept lower wages than before. Failed businesses sell their machines, equipment, and raw materials at low prices. Rents for factory, store, and office spaces drop. Eventually these declining costs of doing business induce some employers to resume or begin production. The downturn ends when sufficient employers decide to hire and produce thereby creating the demand for other employers to do likewise. The bust thereby turns into an economic recovery that perhaps even booms until the next bust resumes the cycle.

These recurring downturns can sometimes cut deeply, hurt many, and last a long time, depending on the broader economic and social conditions in which they occur. Then the consequent poverty, deprivation, and pessimism about the future may produce angers and resentments especially among the jobless and those facing job and income insecurities. They may direct their animosities toward (1) the employers whose decisions directly caused their job-related problems, (2) fellow workers who still have jobs, (3) those whose wealth was little disturbed by the downturn, (4) the government for contributing or inadequately responding to the downturn, or (5) some traditional social scapegoat. Those suffering through a bad downturn may eventually become critical of capitalism itself. They may then demand fundamental social change including transition to a different economic system that might avoid such cycles, guarantee jobs and incomes, and so on.

6.1.3   How Economic Crises Influenced Economic Theories

Because its boom and bust cycles have persisted and resisted every effort to prevent their recurrence, they have provoked the interests and passions of economic theorists trying to understand capitalism. The classical and neoclassical economists responded partly because cycles generated theoretical and political oppositions to capitalism. Neoclassical explanations usually deny that cycles are intrinsic to capitalism and argue instead that "outside forces" cause them. Such outside forces have included agricultural cycles in soil fertility, natural cycles in climate, and astronomical cycles of sun spots and the moon's gravitational influence on the earth's oceanic tides. Another causal force can be the concentration and use of power. Businesses and/or labor unions, separately or together, can make the overall economy vulnerable to the decisions of a powerful few. For example, a monopoly-caused wage–price spiral can create the conditions for inflation eventually collapsing into recession; a cartel-caused rise in energy prices can push an expanding economy into contraction; the power of business to determine market prices can dampen output and employment and stifle innovation and hence growth. However, the most frequently theorized external cause of capitalism's cycles, for neoclassical economists, has been the intrusion of government into the workings of mostly private enterprises and free markets (i.e., what neoclassicists strictly define as capitalism).

Blaming government policies for capitalism's crises followed logically from the laissez faire orientation born with modern capitalism in Europe during the seventeenth and eighteenth centuries. An emerging capitalism had to struggle against a feudal system defended then by absolute monarchies. The English, French, and American revolutions violently overthrew *both* a feudal economic system and absolute, nonrepresentative, undemocratic political power. The result was transition from absolute central power to decentralized systems of parliamentary checks and balances intertwined with a simultaneous transition from feudalism to capitalism. The latter therefore became deeply associated with anti–strong-government sentiments. This tended to happen more in theory and political rhetoric than in the concrete realities of capitalist economies where governments always played centrally important roles.

Neoclassical notions of government as the cause of cycles responded also to the role government often played in capitalist downturns. Mass pressures often won government distributions of food to unemployed and destitute people, government jobs programs, taxes on capitalists (to pay for countercyclical government projects), and regulations of capitalists (to try to prevent future cycles). Such state interventions worried capitalism's laissez faire partisans. They feared that such government intrusions might become permanent and expansive, eroding their freedoms, privileges, profits, wealth, and social positions. From the neoclassical theoretical perspective, governmental economic interventions threatened to hobble capitalism's growth and even lead to its demise.

One position became prevalent over time among most neoclassical economists. Cycles occur chiefly because of unwarranted government intrusions into a system of private property and markets ("private-enterprise" or "private-capitalism"). That system works best without such intrusions. If and when cycles occur in a private-capitalist economy, they are best corrected by its own mechanisms. State intrusion only makes matters worse. A rise in government spending more often than not will crowd out private investment and hence hurt productivity and dampen economic growth; government deficits give rise to inflationary conditions and/or inevitably higher taxes that both distort and undermine private incentives. Government interventions via laws, regulations, taxes, and spending serve in one way or another to constrain or even take away the property rights of private businesses and consumers to act in their private interests and hence move us away from the overall social optimum neoclassicists promise. The conclusion: the capitalist economic system (private property and free markets) is a self-healing mechanism best left to its own devices.

Modern neoclassical economics recycles these traditional arguments in its central propositions about capitalism's inherent tendencies toward an equilibrium in which resources are fully employed to yield the "optimal" wealth for all. Those propositions reflect a long history of crafting a neoclassical response to the challenge of capitalism's boom and bust cycles, to demands for a way to deal with them, and to pressures for transition to a less unstable, postcapitalist economic system. In this sense neoclassical theory becomes a theory of private-capitalism, and why it alone offers the best solution to business instabilities.

Other economists shared many of the neoclassical economists' preferences for this private form of capitalism but disagreed with parts of their analysis and especially with their laissez faire attitudes to government. Those other economists assessed the self-healing processes of capitalism as doing too little too late to reduce mass suffering and/or to speed economic recovery. Their studies focused on how the workings of capitalism generated cycles and how cycles might be reduced, muted, and shortened. Some reached conclusions that favored such changes as higher wages, greater technical progress, enhanced credit, the opening of foreign trade opportunities, higher domestic tariffs, and other more or less practically feasible economic adjustments. Some advocated government interventions targeted to achieve such changes. Hence they advocated a form of capitalism with a more interventionist role for the state.

However, until the Great Depression of the 1930s—the worst economic downturn to date in capitalism's history—no general theory of how and why its crises occurred had emerged. Likewise no comprehensive set of government policies had been developed to prevent, reverse, or at least minimize capitalist crises and their social costs. The Great Depression entailed vast suffering, huge wastes of resources, and a greatly reduced output of wealth. As a result criticism and protests from fast-growing labor unions and socialist and communist parties as well as from politicians and journalists became major social forces in all capitalist countries. Meanwhile the world's only socialist economy at the time, the USSR, had avoided the global capitalist downturn. Those circumstances provoked breakthroughs to a new general theory of capitalist crises. Keynes's *The General Theory of Employment, Interest and Money*, quickly became the best known breakthrough after its 1936 London publication. From those beginnings Keynesian economics evolved into a major kind of economic theory contesting with neoclassical and Marxian economics for the hearts and minds of politicians, employers, unions, academics, journalists, and the general public.

Keynesian economic theory directly challenges neoclassical theory's argument that capitalist economies either avoid cycles or else adequately self-heal from them. In the Keynesian view, capitalist economies repeatedly settle into equilibria in which workers are involuntarily unemployed, productive resources sit idle, and outputs that society needs go unproduced. Business investment in an uncertain world is very risky; it requires committing resources now to produce outputs for sale in an unknowable future. Businesses (and indeed all market participants) therefore make decisions based on risk minimization, social conventions, rules of thumb, and emotions that together can yield poor economic results. No "invisible hand" guarantees efficient and optimal results in economies where private enterprises, workers, savers, and other consumers interact in free markets. Keynesian analyses show how and why those economies experience periodic crises that can be severe and lasting.

Keynesian economists therefore advocated a non-neoclassical form of capitalism in which selective government interventions would reduce, offset, or reverse crises. Government monetary policies were rethought to use its controls over the money supply and thus interest rates for countercyclical ends. Likewise the government's historic provision of certain public services (military security, a judicial system, a legislative system, social security, etc.) and corresponding powers to tax, borrow, and spend were remade into countercyclical interventions. Keynesian fiscal policy refers to the use of the government's powers to tax, borrow, and spend to prevent, offset, and reverse crises. To secure the benefits of capitalism—economic well-being and growth flowing from private property, private enterprises, and markets—Keynesians believe that governments must intervene systematically with appropriate monetary and fiscal policies. In extreme economic crises, the state may need to intervene and literally take over private property to rescue capitalism from its instability. Keynesian theory became the ideological basis of a state-managed capitalism and its claims to offer the best solution to capitalism's instabilities. In the aftermath of the Great Depression of the 1930s, Keynesian theory was increasingly taught in schools and relied on as the basis for journalists' and politicians' accounts of economic issues.

In the years of Keynesian economic theory's dominance and of state-managed capitalism nearly everywhere from1945 to around 1975, that minority of economists who remained neoclassical in their views saw dire threats to capitalism in the relation of private to public sectors advocated by Keynesians. They reiterated the view that Keynesian economics and the government interventions it rationalized were more causes of than solutions for economic cycles. They reformulated the classic arguments that small, weak states are better than big, powerful ones, that private-capitalism will best heal itself, and so on. Proponents of the two alternative theories viewed each other with suspicion. Each side insisted that the other threatened capitalism's survival. Some neoclassical economists denounced Keynesians as socialists because of their advocacy of state controls and generally "big government." Since Keynes's

General Theory, neoclassical and Keynesian theories have been locked into an ongoing dispute over the causes of capitalist crises and their alternative solutions: a private- versus a state-managed capitalism.

Capitalism's cycles also provoked a different reaction among other economic theorists who were neither neoclassical nor Keynesian. Those economists believed that the social costs of its recurring crises undermined capitalism's claims to be the best possible economic system. The evident sufferings, waste of resources, and injustices associated with economic downturns reinforced and encouraged their other critiques of capitalism. Unlike both the neoclassical and the Keynesian economists, these economic theorists concluded that capitalism's flaws required nothing less than transition to a different economic system, socialism.

The most socially influential group among them, the Marxists, argued that the instabilities of capitalism emerged from the same inner structure that prevented the equality, liberty, and fraternity promised since capitalism's beginnings. Because private-capitalist enterprises interacting in free markets repeatedly generated economic crises, and because Keynesian interventions had not prevented their recurrence, most Marxian economists concluded that enterprises and markets should be socialized. This understanding, first put forward systematically by Engels in his *Socialism: Utopian and Scientific*, became the traditional Marxian view.

Private enterprises should instead be owned by society as a whole; government should operate them to benefit society as a whole rather than shareholders and boards of directors. To these ends, government should plan the flows of resources and products among and between producers and consumers rather than rely on private markets. Public ownership and rational planning could and would match resources to social needs, utilizing all resources to meet those needs. The "anarchy of markets"—everyone dealing for individual advantage—would thereby be overcome. That anarchy regularly produced unemployed workers side by side with unutilized raw materials and means of production. It thereby denied society outputs needed to satisfy citizens and solve problems. Engels argued and most Marxists agreed that the best response to capitalism and its crises was a transition to socialism that substituted socialized property for private property and central planning for private market transactions.

Socialization of property and planning was how classical Marxian theory defined socialism. It was seen as instituting transition toward and thus the first stage of communism. Socialism would finally end capitalism's crises and the massive suffering and losses they imposed. The full potential of the technologies and methods of production and distribution developed under capitalism could finally be realized, once private profit and market gambles no longer ruled economic decision making. The use of reason in a rationally managed, socially oriented economic system would trump the irrational capitalist struggle of every individual against every other and its consequent instabilities, wastes, and injustices.

The three different theories' alternative ways of understanding and responding to capitalist cycles influenced how many adherents each attracted. During economic downturns, neoclassical economics usually weakened, while Keynesian and Marxian economics surged. During economic upturns, the reverse was more likely. The contesting theories and their relative social strengths were shaped by capitalism's oscillations. Likewise the theories in turn influenced those oscillations especially by shaping how governments responded to them. Economic and theoretical oscillations continually shaped and transformed one another.

6.2   Oscillations of Economy and Oscillations of Theory

6.2.1   Classical Political Economy and Marxism

The birth of modern economics is widely associated with the works of Adam Smith and David Ricardo at the end of the eighteenth and beginning of the nineteenth century. They were written under the impact of England's position as the country where feudalism had been overthrown by capitalism early and where capitalism had then developed furthest. Smith and Ricardo celebrated capitalism as a major step forward for civilization. For them, it represented economic growth and technical dynamism, the accumulation of wealth, individual freedom from the narrow limits and constraints of feudal society, and economic opportunity: virtues attributed to capitalism by its enthusiasts ever since. Classical political economy celebrated the progressivity of the capitalism for which it provided the first systematic analysis.

The transition from feudal economies (based on manors where serfs produced surpluses for lords) to capitalist economies (based on private enterprises where employees produced profits for employers) was partly celebrated in economic terms. Capitalism would unleash productivity that had been constrained and held back under feudalism. It would enlarge "the wealth of nations" (Adam Smith's most famous title) far better and faster than feudalism ever had. However, the European transition from feudalism to capitalism across the seventeenth, eighteenth, and nineteenth centuries was much more often defined and emphatically welcomed in *political* terms. Serfs were "freed" from their subordination to feudal lords. Tradition, religion, and the lords' armed force compelled them to deliver large portions of their output to the lords as rents. Serfs were likewise freed from their positions as powerless "subjects" of those peaks of the feudal hierarchies—the royal families—that ruled Europe. In place of absolute monarchy and feudal aristocracies, Europe in those centuries struggled to substitute individual liberty and freedom. Government would henceforth be dependent on the will of the people expressed by voting, representative democracy, and universal suffrage institutionalized in regularly elected parliaments.

The enthusiasts of capitalism as a new economic system allied with those of representative democracy as a new political system. Capitalism and representative democracy were believed to support, encourage, and depend on one another. In the English and later in the American and French revolutions, and eventually elsewhere, capitalism and representative democracy replaced feudalism and absolutist monarchies. The classical political economy begun by Smith and Ricardo was the theoretical expression and celebration of the first century of that historic process, roughly from 1770 to 1870.

However, the spread of capitalism also generated critics and discontents. Capitalism, it turned out, delivered costs and not only benefits, and it did not distribute either evenly across populations. Where economic growth was accelerated by capitalism it often did not mean an end to the poverty suffered under feudalism. Capitalism's tendencies toward urban industrialism created the horrific slums as well as the glittering centers of London and Paris. Capitalism's spread has repeated that process elsewhere into the present. The French Revolution of 1789 had raised the slogan, "liberty, equality, fraternity," to express its goals and purpose. But as the nineteenth century unfolded and capitalism and output grew, the wealth of some exploded impressively, resulting in the objectives of liberty, equality, and fraternity *for all* not being achieved.

Among workers hired by private-capitalist employers and among intellectuals inspired by the democratic enthusiasms of the French and American revolutions, critical voices argued that capitalism had established new forms of exploitation and oppression, different in kind from feudalism but not much different in degree. Slowly but steadily, workers and intellectuals began organizing associations, unions, and political parties to win concessions from capitalists. The latter fought back, attempting to maintain their privileges, wealth and power in often bitter, violent clashes across the nineteenth century. Even when (and partly because) workers won improved conditions in some older parts of capitalism, capitalism spread to produce exploitation and parallel class conflicts in the colonies of Europe, across the western hemisphere, and later in the postcolonial and other parts of Asia and Africa. Wherever capitalism arrived, its operations provoked critics and opponents alongside advocates and celebrants.

Among intellectuals, critical reactions to capitalism took many different paths. One led to Karl Marx's basic critique of the political economy of Smith and Ricardo and his articulation of an alternative systematic economics. Marx's work inspired a tradition that became the mostly widely influential source of critical theory aimed at capitalism. Marx performed for critics of capitalism what Smith and Ricardo had done for its celebrants.

As we have discussed, Marx began from and focused on the class process as his entry point into theorizing how capitalism works. Smith's and Ricardo's very different entry points were markets and prices, economic growth, and the division of incomes among capitalists, landlords, and workers. In Marx's view, Smith and Ricardo had developed theories that were only secondarily interested in labor and production. So Marx took their labor theory of value (especially Smith's notion that commodities' values reflect the toil and trouble of producing them), reinterpreted and applied it to capitalism's system of production, and thereby reached radically different conclusions.

Chapter 4 explored his conclusion that capitalists hire workers to produce commodities only if they can exploit those workers (appropriate the surpluses they produce). In Marx's evocative language, capitalism reproduces itself on the basis of appropriating those surpluses and distributing them to sustain that exploitation. Consciously or unconsciously, workers variously try to escape, change, or end their exploitation. Consciously or unconsciously capitalists try to justify their social positions and their economic returns by theorizing them in non-Marxian ways. Chapter 2 showed how capitalists' profits can be theorized and justified as rewards for capitalists' "savings" (not consuming all their income) and for the risks they take by investing those savings. Capitalists' profits have also been explained as a kind of wage they pay to themselves for their managerial activities or their "entrepreneurship" (conceiving and undertaking business). Classical political economy flattered capitalists by conceptualizing the capitalist-worker organization of the economy as more efficient and able to generate more growth of output than any other economic organization in the past (feudal lord-serf, master-slave, etc.) or any imaginable in the future.

Marx's theory argued against classical economics—and later neoclassical economics—point by point. It also suggested an alternative, socialist organization of production as the basis for an alternative, better society. Against the classical economists' claims that earnings were necessary rewards to capitalists' risk-taking, Marx asked ironically about workers' risks from employers who could fire them when they wished. Against claims that capitalists performed management "work," Marx noted the rise, already in his time, of corporate forms of capitalism in which profits flowed to a board of directors who did no management but rather hired and paid others to do that. As to capitalists getting surpluses for entrepreneurship, Marx responded that the success of any business depended on the energy and creativity of the workers— who got no surplus—as much as the capitalists—who took it all. Most important, Marx argued that the payments that rewarded managers, entrepreneurs, and others who did not directly participate in producing goods and services (clerks, secretaries, etc.) were only possible because the productive laborers produced the surplus from which those payments came. That initial capitalist appropriation of a surplus produced by productive workers always anchored (was the entry point into) Marx's theory and criticism of capitalism.

He also criticized many claims about capitalism's efficiency and its performance as an "engine of growth." Marx stressed capitalism's instability, its recurring cycles of unemployment and bankruptcy that produced the following: (1) workers willing but unable to work alongside (2) idled raw materials, tools and equipment gathering dust and rust with the result that (3) society had far less wealth than it was capable of generating. Capitalism, he showed, was as regularly successful in producing unnecessary losses, poverty and waste as it was in generating prosperity and growth. It was a contradictory system and far less "efficient" than its advocates claimed. Moreover, during its periodic downturns (later called recessions and depressions), Marx showed how the burdensome costs of downturns were unjustly heaped on the unemployed, driving them often into more or less permanent marginality in ghettoized poverty. Such "underclasses" were also products of capitalism and sustained by capitalism's instability, constant markers of its inefficiency and injustice.

For Marxists, capitalism's exploitation and instability necessitated a better system that replaced capitalist with workers' appropriation of surpluses, displaced private property in favor of socialized property, and supplanted markets with social planning. Workers appropriating their own surpluses would end class exploitation and its unwanted consequences: alienation from work and even civic life, consequently impaired worker productivity, strife between employer and employee, and displaced frustration, resentment, and anger onto oneself, family members and government. Socially owned land, machines, tools, and the like, would be used for the benefit of society as a whole rather than for the minority of capitalist owners. Government planning rather than markets as mechanisms to distribute resources and products would end business cycles and their costly consequences.

Marx called this system "associated workers" where, following his class as surplus approach, the new and innovative idea stressed was that the workers who produce the surpluses would also collectively appropriate and distribute them. Workers would then have become their own board of directors inside each enterprise. This was Marx's idea about a transition beyond capitalism at the microeconomic level of the individual enterprise. At the macroeconomic level Marx envisioned a transition beyond capitalism that entailed (1) substituting socialized for private property in means of production (land, factories, offices, capital, etc.) and (2) substituting democratic planning for the market as the main means for distributing resources and products throughout the society. Property ownership and planning could be accomplished centrally by the state or it could be decentralized to regional and/or local levels (or combinations of central and decentralized ownership and planning could become the preferred choice of citizens).

Marx never spelled out his images of socialism and communism in any detail. His comments were sketches, not blueprints for the future (which he derided as idle speculation). He thought that real social change—when capitalism's contradictions and failures generated powerful movements of protest and criticism—would determine the concrete forms of socialism and communism. His analyses of capitalism aimed chiefly to show those movements that to overcome capitalism's injustices, inefficiencies, and wastes required more than the mere *reform* of this or that institution. Genuine social progress required a *revolutionary transition* beyond capitalism to a new social system based on the three distinct features we have outlined. These included (1) transformed organizations of production in which workers collectively produced, appropriated, and distributed surpluses; (2) a socialized rather than a private ownership of the means of production; and (3) the replacement of private market exchange by democratically planned distributions of resources and products. Traditional or orthodox Marxism after Marx tended either to ignore transforming the organization of production inside enterprises or assume it would follow automatically from achieving the other two. We will explain below why transformation of production never happened and how that eventually undermined the economies of "actually existing socialist countries" such as the USSR and in eastern Europe.

Traditional or orthodox Marxism quickly became the chief theoretical alternative to the classical political economy begun by Smith and Ricardo. It also quickly became the theoretical inspiration and framework for major portions of the socialist movements that grew and spread during the second half of the nineteenth century and the first half of the twentieth. They in turn brought awareness of Marxian theory into ever more diverse historical, cultural, and national settings. The results were multiple, different interpretations of Marx's thinking.

These diverse contributions to Marxian theory accumulated a rich, complex tradition of thought. Different interpretations of Marx's writings also sometimes hardened into competing kinds of socialists, especially when they disagreed about major historic events. In World War I, for example, some socialist leaders—like V. I. Lenin in Russia and E. V. Debs in the United States—urged workers not to fight other workers in that "imperialist war" aimed at gains for capitalists. Other socialist leaders supported their respective governments in the war and urged their countrymen to fight. The first nationally successful anticapitalist revolution achieved by socialists in Russia in 1917 provoked a further split among socialists around the world. Those who rallied around the revolutionary government in Russia as deserving the prioritized support of socialists everywhere took the name *communists*—and established new communist parties—to distinguish themselves from those socialists and socialist parties who remained uncomfortable with the new government in the newly named USSR. The latter retained the old name *socialists*. Despite such differences, most socialists and communists shared a commitment to Marxism broadly defined. Later in the twentieth century, many socialists rejected Marxism. It then became more identified with communism and communists.

Over the last half-century those parts of the socialist movements that moved away from Marxism also offered much more limited criticisms of capitalism. For example, many socialist parties in western Europe basically endorse private-capitalist enterprises, markets, and other basic attributes of capitalism but insist that government programs offset certain consequences of capitalism. They advocate the "welfare state"—a system in which government taxation and state services are used to moderate and offset business cycles and to redistribute some income and wealth from the richer to the middle and poorer segments of the population. Socialists focus more on supporting and collaborating with trade unions to secure better wages, job benefits, and working conditions. Countries like Sweden, Germany, France, and Italy—all frequently governed by elected socialist or sometimes labor parties—couple high taxes with national health care, free public education through university, and heavily subsidized housing and mass transportation. Their laws mandate several weeks of paid vacation for all workers, and so on. As we observed in chapter 2, "market socialism" can describe their general approach. This included the advocacy of state enterprises (alongside or instead of private-capitalist enterprises) in what they deemed to be key industries such as energy, communications, transport, automobile manufacturing, and banking.

Communist movements and parties over the last half-century have mostly tended to disagree with socialists and put forward different programs to response to capitalism's cyclical instability and unequal distributions of wealth, income and political power. Communists stress the need to abolish private-capitalism by (1) replacing most private with state-owned and state-operated enterprises and (2) subordinating most markets to central state planning. Socialists and communists disagree over whose program would better realize social values like liberty, equality, fraternity, and democracy. In general, socialists have been more respectful of the framework of parliamentary democracy developed in advanced capitalist societies, whereas communists have preferred to establish workers or "people's" democracies that preclude parties advocating capitalism.

The focus of most communists and socialists on defining their goals in terms of state-owned and state-run enterprises and state economic planning introduced a major problem. They rarely concerned themselves with transforming the relationship inside enterprises between the producers and the appropriators of surpluses. They tended to see that relationship less as requiring a socialist transformation and more as a secondary matter dictated by the technologies of producing goods and services. Or they imagined that the socialist and communist ideal—workers collectively appropriating and distributing their produced surpluses—would automatically follow once state-run and state-owned enterprises and comprehensive planning were in place. In terms of chapter 1, they believed a change in the surplus organization within enterprises was a necessary effect of socializing property ownership and subordinating markets to central economic planning. However, that belief was unwarranted. In fact the result was often the opposite. Socialists and communists who won state power then substituted state officials for the former boards of directors who had been selected by major shareholders to run enterprises. Those officials then appropriated the surpluses produced in the state enterprises and distributed them according to state plans. The notion of workers collectively appropriating and distributing their own surpluses faded.

However, despite collective ownership, planning, and the workers' state's commitment to seek the interests of society as a whole, the state officials running state enterprises resembled the exploiting private-capitalists they had displaced. No doubt, socialists and communists accomplished radical changes in ownership of the means of production (from private to socialized) and distribution of produced wealth (from market to planning). But they had not radically altered the class structure (in surplus terms) inside the enterprises of their societies. In fact, when examining the organization of the surplus in the actually existing socialist and communist societies, it was still basically capitalist in its core division between producers and appropriators of the surplus. But it was now state capitalist versus private-capitalist: a major change but one that left the basic class issue untransformed.

State-capitalism is more than a state-run or state-managed capitalism. The latter marks an economy in which the state and state officials have a major role administering it, even to the point of allocating resources and outputs and perhaps even owning means of production. However, even though the state intervenes in these ways, private-capitalists still appropriate surpluses produced by workers. For example, the United States has had periods—the depression of 1930s, the war years in the early 1940s, and then in and after the 2008–2009 crisis—when government took on major roles in managing the business cycle, as allocator of many inputs and outputs, and even owner of certain inputs. However, save for a very few cases (e.g., the Tennessee Valley Authority), state officials only rarely and temporarily appropriated surpluses produced by workers. Instead, private-capitalists did that within a more or less state-controlled market and even state-regulated property environment. In contrast, in a state-capitalism, surplus appropriators have a necessary connection to the state: they are state officials, whatever the property and market arrangements are.

Marx's revolutionary idea—that going beyond capitalism meant that the workers who produce the surplus would also collectively appropriate and distribute it—rarely obtained sustained attention or programmatic priority from either socialists or communists. Neither seriously proposed transforming enterprises to make the workers themselves their own collective board of directors. That notion of Marx's was discarded by many socialists as they distanced themselves from all of Marxism. Likewise most communists adopted interpretations of Marxism that had little use for notions of going beyond capitalism that required transforming the organization of the surplus inside enterprises. Those few who did worry about going beyond capitalism inside enterprises hoped that somehow state-run enterprises and planning would eventually get there. When they never did, the whole issue tended to fade from view, neglected or ignored by the very Marxists who otherwise embraced his theory. Ironically, their struggles for socialism and communism over much of the twentieth century in the USSR, east European countries, China, and elsewhere became instead unintended and unacknowledged struggles for state-capitalism (Resnick and Wolff 2002).

6.2.2   Neoclassical Economics

After the 1850s Marxian economics increasingly challenged the dominant position of the classical political economy associated with Smith and Ricardo. A growing capitalism experienced many bitter struggles between capitalists and workers interwoven with serious economic downturns. Critical attitudes toward capitalism spread and found their way increasingly to the ideas of Marx and Marxism. Marxism's political challenges to capitalism and its theoretical challenge to classical economics forced their defenders to respond. Those defenders went to work—in politics, economics, and culture—to try to blunt, moderate, defeat, and reverse anticapitalism and socialism. In economics they attacked Marxian theory and built a new theoretical defense and celebration of capitalism. As Marxian economics represented an oscillation of theory away from classical political economy, so the reaction to Marxism's rise was another oscillation back toward a new version of classical political economy that came to be known as neoclassical economics.

During the 1870s the theoretical economics of William Stanley Jevons (1835–1882), Leon Walras (1834–1910), and Carl Menger (1840–1921)—in their English, French, and German-speaking domains, respectively—attempted to revive, update, and renew classical political economy in ways different from and alternative to how socialists and especially Marx had developed it. Another major economic theorist of the time, Eugen von Bohm-Bawerk (1851–1914), built on their foundations explicitly to refute Marx's economics, particularly its theory of price. This group's theoretical debts to—yet also departures from—Smith and Ricardo produced its name: neoclassical economics. Its position as a systematic alternative to the rising influence especially of

Marxian economics recommended it to those who defended and celebrated capitalism.

Neoclassical economics quickly became and has remained the mainstream economic theory favored by most politicians, business leaders, journalists, and academic teachers. It is the "common sense" most people use, consciously or unconsciously, to understand capitalism or "economics" per se. Many proceed as if no alternative economic theory existed or challenged neoclassical economics. The growth and spread of capitalism over the last century did much to disseminate and embed neoclassical economic theory as equally global.

From the 1870s to 1914 neoclassical economics effectively kept Marxian economics socially marginalized, important chiefly among trade unions and socialist parties. However, between 1914 and 1945 historical events—including major oscillations in economies—boosted the social position and appeal of Marxian economics and also created Keynesian economics as another alternative to neoclassical economics. Two devastating world wars (1914–1918 and 1939–1945) drove millions to see capitalism itself as contributing to such catastrophes. The Russian Revolution of 1917 brought to power a government that officially endorsed Marxian economics and denounced capitalism. The new Union of Soviet Socialist Republics (USSR) not only survived wars and revolution but also accomplished a rapid industrialization that converted it from an impoverished backwater of Europe to a global superpower. It credited Marxism for much of its economic success, drawing global attention to Marxian economics. The final important historical event was the Great Depression of the 1930s, the massive global collapse of capitalist economies. Keynesian economics arose as an alternative to both neoclassical and Marxian economics. It has contested with them ever since. Indeed, from the 1940s to the 1970s, Keynesian economics temporarily displaced neoclassical economics from its social dominance.

Once again, during the 1930s, an economic oscillation—when capitalism with relatively little government intervention crashed and transitioned to a heavily state-interventionist capitalism—provoked parallel theoretical oscillations. From neoclassical economics, people changed their ways of thinking to Marxian economics in some areas and to Keynesian economics as the socially dominant paradigm. In the 1970s yet another economic oscillation moved economic theories back in the reverse directions. State-capitalist economies in the USSR and eastern Europe and likewise the "welfare state-capitalisms" or state-managed capitalisms elsewhere all encountered serious problems that provoked returns to less government intervention. President Ronald Reagan in the United States and Prime Minister Margaret Thatcher in the United Kingdom led the reversion back to a "deregulated" capitalism. In addition eastern European state-capitalisms collapsed into replications of those deregulated capitalisms. What occurred there was not a transition from communism to capitalism but instead from state to private-capitalism: state gave way to private surplus appropriators and distributors.

In summary, the 1980s and 1990s marked the movement of economies around the world from the state having more to less of a role in the continuing capitalism. Those economic reversions returned neoclassical economics to dominance and pushed Keynesian economics into a very secondary place alongside Marxian economics. In the final part of this chapter we will return to these more recent oscillations to examine the contested terrain of economics in the early decades of the twenty-first century.

6.2.3   Neoclassical versus Marxian

From its beginnings to the present, neoclassical economic theory's goal was to break totally from all remnants of the various labor theories of value articulated by Smith, Ricardo, and especially Marx. Our chapter on Marxian economics presented Marx's argument that the prices of commodities that emerged from capitalist enterprises contained surplus—the fruit of unpaid work by exploited laborers. Theft was thus located in the heart of capitalism: workers were its victims and capitalists its perpetrators. The business cycle, unequal distributions of income, wealth, power, and culture were connected to capitalism's systematic theft. In response to such theorizing, neoclassical theory criticized and rejected all labor theories of value to reach very different conclusions about capitalism.

For neoclassical theory, (marginal) utility rather than labor was the key to understanding commodity values. Given individuals' production capacities, their desires (preferences) about goods, leisure, and future consumption determined what would be supplied to and demanded in markets and hence prices. Those prices would then interact with technology to determine what every worker's owned labor was worth (wages received) and what every capitalist's owned capital was worth (profits received). In short, given this technology, the distributions of income and wealth depended on and reflected what people wanted (the objects and activities they preferred) and the productivity of whatever they contributed to production. Neoclassical economists celebrated capitalism as a just economic system that generated incomes according to what people wanted and contributed.

Neoclassical theory rejected totally a Marxian notion of class exploitation. Rather, production entailed a partnership between capital and labor. The laborer contributed work and received a share of the resulting output (wages) proportional to what the work contributed. The capitalist contributed means of production and received a share of the resulting output proportional to what that capital contributed. The resulting distribution of income and wealth rewarded workers and capitalists according to what each contributed. Contrary to Marxism, capitalism entailed no theft, no exploitation, and no injustice. No exploitation meant that workers' alienation, struggles with employers, constrained labor productivity, and dysfunctional family life had no connection to class exploitation, for the latter did not exist. In fact and contrary to Marxism, capitalism harmoniously balanced those seeking to maximize their profits and those seeking to maximize their consumption.

For neoclassical theory, economic growth reflected the individual decisions of income earners to save rather than spend their incomes. Savers chose not to consume their income and instead to save and invest it to gain more in the future. Each individual's investment decision provided the funds capitalists could use to produce more. The growth that occurred reflected and rewarded individual choices. Economic growth resulted as Adam Smith's "invisible hand" produced that social "optimum" out of the self-interested decisions of each individual.

Neoclassical economic theory's re-grounding of economics on individual utility rather than social labor aimed not only to displace Marxian economics from contemporary thinking. It also sought to revive classical political economy's celebration of capitalism as the best possible framework for prosperity, social justice, growth, and progress. Its proponents insisted that neoclassical economics was the genuine heir of classical political economy. Marxian economics was, in contrast, an ill-intentioned and politically motivated misreading of Smith and Ricardo. From that perspective, neoclassical economists had little interest in Marxian economics and no use for Marxian economists. Not surprisingly, the latter found few academic positions. A few were at best tolerated, while many never obtained the academic positions that provided neoclassical economists with the time, salaries, and research support to build their theoretical tradition and enlarge the literature of their paradigm. In comparison, Marxists produced fewer students, articles, books, and so forth, with which to persuade the public. From 1870 to 1914 neoclassical economics grew and spread faster than Marxian economics to become the socially dominant school of economic thought in many sectors of modern societies.

World War I changed economies and economics once again. The devastations and costs of that war among contesting capitalist economies drove many Europeans to associate war and capitalism in ways that made the Marxian alternative much more attractive. The successful revolution in Russia in 1917, led by Marxists, reinforced that attraction. Their declared intention was to construct a socialist economy in the newly named Union of Soviet Socialist Republics. The revolutionary leadership took the capitalist factories and enterprises away from their private owners and made them instead the collective property of the whole society operated by the new revolutionary "workers' state." That leadership also organized a state agency to plan the distribution of basic industrial resources and major products rather than relying on markets alone as means of their distribution. When the new USSR survived, rebuilt its economy, and grew into an industrial power, its leadership under Stalin declared it to be a socialist economy, the world's only real alternative ("socialism in one country") to the capitalism dominant everywhere else.

Marxian economics before 1917 had been chiefly a critical analysis of capitalism coupled with a few generalizations about a possible socialist alternative. The economic growth and industrialization of the USSR added an altogether different Marxian economics. The latter was focused on how the economic system of the USSR operated as an example of what socialism meant. The two kinds of Marxian economics coexisted but also changed one another in an often uneasy balance. Marxists outside the USSR, for example, often valued the tradition's critiques of capitalism but were far less well disposed to its affirmations of actual practices in the USSR as what Marxism meant or implied. In any case, the USSR published its version of Marxian economics in virtually all languages and distributed it globally. The years after 1917 saw a major resurgence of Marxian economics, although it had become richer and more diverse than before as the Soviet version often contested with alternative interpretations.

After the 1917 revolution was consolidated inside the USSR, neoclassical economists redoubled their emphases on refuting, attacking, and displacing especially the Soviet interpretation of Marxian economics (often proceeding as if it were the only interpretation). Neoclassical economics intensified its celebration of capitalism by showing how private property in means of production and market competition achieved a "general equilibrium" characterized by the most efficient use of productive resources and the socially optimum distribution of output. Neoclassical economists not only articulated a mathematically elaborated—and therefore, they insisted, supremely "scientific"— theory of capitalism's general equilibrium. They also used it to attack, theoretically and practically, the Soviet system of state enterprises and central planning as inefficient by comparison.

However, the Great Depression that convulsed capitalist countries in 1929 and the decade that followed profoundly altered the two-way debate of the previous half-century between neoclassical and Marxian economics. It became instead a three-way debate among neoclassical, Marxian, and a new arrival: Keynesian economics. Elaborations and extensions of these three theories and debates among them have constituted most of the discipline of economics for the last seventy-five years.

6.2.4 Keynesian Economics

Earlier in this chapter and elsewhere in this book we have referred to the arrival of Keynes and Keynesian economics in response to the Great Depression. As unemployment rates soared alongside bankruptcies and reduced output, politicians fell in the wake of mass poverty and resentment. Marxist criticisms of capitalism viewed the Great Depression as an example of the inefficiency, waste, and injustices of capitalism as a system against which most socialists and communists still defined their politics and goals. However, the Great Depression also generated or reinforced different criticisms of contemporary capitalism from people who wanted state intervention to correct, shape, or partner with private-capitalism to yield better economic results than private-capitalism seemed able to provide on its own.

On the political right, fascist movements surged, demanding an end to capitalist free enterprises and markets on the grounds that they tended to produce catastrophic crashes, to divisively separate workers from employers, and to alienate both from the nation as an entity. In Italy, Spain, and Germany these movements achieved state power under the leaderships of Mussolini, Franco, and Hitler. In the name of national (and often racialized) unity, fascists demanded a reorganization of society. Workers and employers would become parts of one national economic body, their antagonisms eliminated or at least controlled and managed by a powerful national state apparatus. Unlike socialists and communists, the fascist critics of capitalism did not seek a reorganization of production such that state enterprises replaced private enterprises and central plans replaced markets. Instead, fascists proposed a close, mutually supportive partnership between the state apparatus and private capitalists. The latter retained their ownership of most enterprises while the fascist state combined national economic plans focused especially on military expansion with continued heavy reliance on markets. In the fascist view, that partnership would incorporate and subordinate workers into the project of national rejuvenation and growth. Fascism would eliminate the need for unions and socialist and communist parties whose internationalism repelled most fascists. Indeed most fascist governments did not tolerate their existence, often killing or exiling many of them. Fascism then was unlike the state-capitalism of the USSR—private surplus appropriating capitalists in Germany were not displaced in favor of state surplus appropriating officials as in the USSR. The German state under Hitler—more or less like its fascist counterparts in other countries—played a major role in enforcing a tightly controlled partnership between private-capitalists and the state.

There were other major differences between the socialist/communist critics of capitalism and the fascists. Where fascism sought and received alliances with established religion, socialist and communist critics were mostly anti-clerical. Where workers were the celebrated social group for socialists and communists, fascists instead celebrated ethnically "pure" and/or nationalist/patriotic "citizens." For socialists and communists, the class war between workers and capitalists had to be fought to a definitive conclusion in the defeat of the capitalists and transition to a socialist society. In contrast, for fascists the workers *and* capitalists would be required to resolve their differences within the body (corpus) of the unified and purified nation led by the close partnership between the fascist state and the capitalists. Fascism explicitly denounced and rejected democracy in favor of an organic, authoritarian state run—in the manner of a tightly hierarchical family—by a dominant leader like Mussolini, Franco, or Hitler. Socialism and communism explicitly endorsed and supported democracy and sought to extend it from politics to also include economics (which capitalism did not do); however, in their practice when in power, communists frequently ruled undemocratically.

Yet there were also some similarities between socialists and communists on the left and fascists on the right. Both attacked capitalism for its inequities and instabilities and their social costs. Both advocated increased power for the state to intervene in economic life to secure full employment. Both built up mass constituencies in most countries. Perhaps the most important shared quality was both sides' intense antipathy to the capitalist system that had been in place in Europe during the many decades leading up to 1929. Yet despite this shared antipathy, the neglect by communists, socialists, and fascists of the class question—in terms of the organization of the surplus inside enterprises—enabled capitalist class exploitation and its consequences to continue both in communist and fascist regimes.

Others around the world wanted to avoid communism and fascism, even though the state's intervention into the economy enabled growing employment in both regimes. They recoiled from the totalitarian form of government that seemed inescapably tied to all alternatives to capitalism. They sought a new economics that might salvage the inherited capitalism from the consequences of its own instability. They wanted a way to fix a broken capitalism without any need for the major changes advocated by either the socialists and communists or the fascists.

Keynes's work filled the need. In criticizing the neoclassical economics that he had formerly embraced, Keynes directly confronted the economic depression. His explanation for the crash pinpointed causes that aggressive state action could control or offset. That state action required only limited growth in the power of the state and few if any changes in the internal organizations of private-capitalist enterprises. The socialist, communist, and fascist alternatives were all avoided (although in some of his formulations, Keynes approached a moderate socialist notion of state controls over private enterprises' investment decisions). That avoidance made it a reasonable and feasible alternative to the revolutionary messages from left and right.

Keynes's structural analysis of how capitalism worked—different from neoclassical theory's individualist analysis—explained why and how capitalism's basic structures could cause economic behavior that produced an unacceptable economic equilibrium. It was an equilibrium that left many workers unemployed, much productive capacity unutilized, and thus yielded far less output than what the available resources and technology made possible. Keynes and his followers showed how the state could correct or offset the effects of those structures to yield a better equilibrium with less unemployment and more output. Recurring capitalist cycles could be avoided, moderated, or offset by using Keynesian structural economics and applying its policy prescriptions. As importantly, this economic policy could be accomplished without sacrificing the parliamentary democracy to which advanced capitalist economies had adapted by then.

From the 1930s through the 1970s, Keynesian economics first struggled against and then largely replaced neoclassical economics as the socially dominant theory. It was taught in most colleges and universities and informed the new generation of journalists and elected politicians. Its enthusiasts boasted, especially in the 1950s and 1960s, that Keynesian economics had overcome capitalism's cycles or at the least rendered them relatively shallow and short-lived. In their view, Keynesian economics had overcome or fixed capitalism's major flaw and it had done so with relatively little social upheaval.

Neoclassical economics fell into a subordinate relation to Keynesian economics from the 1930s until its return to supremacy in the 1970s. In those years most economics departments taught what was called a "synthesis" of microeconomics and macroeconomics: they emphasized macroeconomics while teaching a version of neoclassical economics in microeconomics courses. That version minimized the latter's laissez faire dimensions. Where individual consumers, workers, and enterprises were concerned, the old neoclassical economics was taught as the microeconomics prerequisite for the more interesting and exciting macroeconomic topics chosen by most students and emphasized by most faculty. Those topics included economic development, international finance, public finance, economic history, and so on. Class work on these topics usually emphasized the structural analysis of economic events and the monetary and fiscal policies developed chiefly by Keynesian economists.

Within this synthesis of neoclassical and Keynesian economics, those in the United States who emphasized the Keynesian part mostly associated with the Democratic Party. Those who emphasized the neoclassical part associated more with the Republican Party. However, such was the dominance of Keynesian economics that even a conservative Republican President Richard M. Nixon once said, "We are all Keynesians now." Until the end of the 1970s, purely or predominantly neoclassical economists remained a small minority within the discipline.

The defeat of all major fascisms in World War II and the immediately following cold war with the USSR, eastern Europe, and China fostered this synthesis of Keynesian economics as the major theory and neoclassical economics as the minor partner. Together they could sustain a kind of "vital center" against the defeated fascism and the newly enlarged communism. A strong government could protect and advance a private-capitalism in both economic and political terms. A strong government could foster development efforts aiding and complementing private enterprise in third world nations to counter revolutionary or communist movements there. Strong international authorities—United Nations, World Bank, and International Monetary Fund—could provide the political and economic supports and, when and if necessary, management of growing international linkages connecting one capitalist country to another.

Of course, all economists did not fit neatly into the camp of these synthesizers, or into that of Marxists. For example, some neoclassical economists rejected any alliance with Keynesian economists. They steadfastly affirmed and developed laissez faire notions that state intervention was the source of capitalism's problems and that removing or strictly limiting state intervention was the best policy for whatever ailed capitalism. One of the most visible and successful of these economists was Milton Friedman (1912–2006), an economics professor at the University of Chicago and an eventual Nobel Prize winner. Under his supervision a cadre of strict neoclassical economists emerged first to challenge Keynesian economics and then to displace it from theoretical hegemony in the 1970s. Another Chicago economist and Nobel Prize winner was Friedrich Hayek (1899–1992) who relentlessly defended free markets against any form of Keynesian macro management.

Among Marxist economists, some responded to the strengthening of the USSR and its growing allies by further reorienting Marxist theory so it became still less a critical theory of capitalism and ever more a theory of the actually existing economies in the USSR, eastern Europe, China, and so on. They stressed how Marxian theory and its policy implications represented the best way for poor nations to exit poverty quickly. Other Marxist economists instead argued in favor of certain overlaps between Keynes's and Marx's arguments—especially their critical stances toward private, laissez faire capitalism. They sought a Keynes–Marx alliance/synthesis to oppose the Keynes/neoclassical synthesis. Still other Marxist economists took a stronger oppositional position attacking both neoclassical and Keynesian economics as merely alternative apologies for capitalism.

From the 1930s to the 1970s proponents of the three major contesting economic theories—Keynesian, neoclassical, and Marxian—engaged in debates and struggles. The Keynesians prevailed over the neoclassicists while the Marxists, who criticized both, reserved their sharpest attacks for the neoclassicists. All three economic theories experienced internal conflicts alongside their debates with one another, and all three changed. The theoretical developments helped to shape how the United States, the USSR, and many other countries managed their different experiences with economies in which government intervention ranged from significant to dominant. When, in the 1970s and 1980s crises beset those economies, their governments dramatically altered their interventions. The consequent economic, political, and cultural changes reacted back upon economic theories to further transform them: another phase in the interaction between and interdependence of economic theories and social reality.

6.3   Two Modern Oscillations: The 1970s and the Crisis That Began in 2007

It was likely more than coincidence that the 1970s marked yet another set of intertwined oscillations: in economic systems and among economic theories. State-interventionist capitalisms of various sorts and degrees gave way to a renewal of private (often called "neoliberal") forms of capitalism. Keynesian economics and the classical or orthodox tradition of Marxian economics gave way to a resurgence of traditional neoclassical economics. Then, as had happened before—and why this book devotes a whole chapter to these oscillations in economies and economics—the economic crisis of global capitalism that erupted in 2007 was a blow to the dominance of neoclassical economics and gave a boost to a renewed Keynesianism and to new formulations of Marxian economics. Likewise this latest capitalist crisis brought the state back into economic intervention on a massive scale with huge fiscal stimuli, record-breaking increases in the money supply, and all sorts of new state actions aimed at overcoming the crisis. Of course, this general overview of these latest oscillations masks the many particulars of time and place. It is to some of these that the remaining sections of this chapter are devoted.

6.3.1   Three Collapses: State Intervention, Keynesianism, and Orthodox Marxism

The 1970s brought the welfare state economies of the United States, western Europe, Japan, and many other industrial capitalist countries to a critical impasse. Increasing numbers of capitalists were opposed to paying taxes to fund the costs of welfare states; those taxes hurt their competitiveness in a global economy, they argued, and thus also their broader national economies. At the same time popular support for welfare states was decreasing partly because of disappointment that state services were not better in a period when real wages stopped rising in many countries and partly because the state's tax burden was increasingly shifted onto individuals from corporations. In the aftermath of the 1930s Great Depression, the private sector had been viewed as the problem and government intervention as the solution. In the 1970s this perception was widely reversed.

A remarkably parallel movement engulfed the USSR and eastern European countries in the 1980s. Their "actually existing socialisms" (or state-capitalisms as we have described them) likewise arrived at a critical impasse. After decades of sacrifice undertaken to "build socialism," the masses of people were dissatisfied with the wide gaps that still separated their standards of living from those in the capitalist West, in the absence of civil liberties, and the excessive powers of state and communist party bureaucracies. At the same time the chief power among them, the USSR, could not cover all the costs of its new post–World War II status as the only other super power beside the United States engaged in a cold war and hugely expensive arms race with the United States. Military spending and huge outlays for industrialization (to catch up with the West) left relatively little for raising the standards of living of people who had long sacrificed for and been promised exactly that. It also left unaddressed the rising tensions between the producers of surplus inside state enterprises and the state officials who appropriated the surplus. With restive workers and citizens, state repressions tightened there with the predictable result of further disaffection from their systems. The actually existing socialisms of the USSR and eastern Europe imploded relatively peacefully but quickly at the end of the 1980s. In the cold war world that defined the global contest as between "the only two alternatives: capitalism or socialism/communism," the movement to end actually existing socialism/communism saw no alternative but a return to capitalism. This meant dismantling much of what the state's role in the economy had been and substituting private enterprises and markets.

In the United States and other advanced capitalist countries, the mid-1970s saw the worst economic downturn since the Great Depression, just what Keynesian economics was supposed to prevent. The combination of inflation and stagnant economic output—called "stagflation"—undermined the confidence of many in the Keynesian system of systemic government intervention. With the elections of Reagan and Thatcher to the top political posts in the United States and the United Kingdom, a major shift back from more to less state intervention became official policy. An era of deregulation, privatization (selling or turning state activities back to private-capitalist enterprises), and significant tax reductions began that lasted until the onset of the Great Recession of 2008. Advocates of this major shift insisted (or at least hoped) that less government would free up private business to produce lasting economic growth and thereby solve capitalism's problems. The social welfare aspects of the Keynesian era were more or less reduced depending on the political and cultural conditions of each country: quicker and larger reductions occurred in the United States and the United Kingdom, for example, than in continental Europe.

From these economic shifts followed corresponding shifts in the relative social positions of neoclassical and Keynesian economics and economists in most countries. They switched roles. The neoclassical economists returned to dominance and the Keynesians became very much secondary partners as they lost power, influence and positions in politics, media and the academy. Careers and careerists had to reinvent themselves or falter. Students observing the shift in theoretical winds adjusted their curricular choices, aspirations, and career paths. The ascent of neoclassical economics, given its close alliance with conservative business forces, also participated in a more concerted opposition to socialism and Marxism (e.g., as expressed in Reagan's demonization of an "evil empire"). Part of that opposition was an accelerated arms race—far more affordable for the NATO alliance than for the USSR—that drained the Soviet economic system's resources hastening its demise.

6.3.2   From State- to Private-Capitalism: The Starkest Case

However historic the transitions from state-interventionist to more private-capitalisms in the United States and the United Kingdom and however dramatic the political breaks marked by the ascendancy of Reagan and Thatcher as the new leaders, their transitions were not the kind of basic social discontinuities represented by the collapse of Soviet and eastern European socialism. A brief discussion of the primary stark case of economic and social change—the USSR—can shed light on the whole global process of such oscillations. For a full discussion, see Resnick and Wolff (2002).

Orthodox Marxists in the former USSR and elsewhere understood its collapse as that of socialism. They reasoned that socialism existed in the USSR because the state had socialized property ownership and subordinated markets to central state planning. This conception of socialism neglected the organization of surplus within Soviet enterprises. It missed completely that the surplus appropriators inside state enterprises were Soviet state officials, the famous Council of Ministers, who acted similarly to private-capitalism's board of directors selected by major shareholders. The Soviet workers themselves did not collectively appropriate the surpluses they produced inside the enterprises or industries where they worked. That is why we have applied the term state-capitalism to this system. The Council of Ministers distributed the surpluses they appropriated from workers and did so according to the priorities established by the Communist Party and the leaders of the Soviet state.

For more than fifty years, this Council put relentless pressure on Soviet workers to produce ever more surpluses to build and especially to industrialize their state-capitalism. The Council, like the Party and the Soviet state, referred to this as building socialism, since their orthodox definition made socialism a matter of state property ownership and planning. Distributions went to expand heavy industry including military hardware, provide for a state bureaucracy and a state security apparatus, support a powerful communist party, and fund a vast array of public goods. Allocating more resources to enterprises producing capital rather than consumer goods conformed to orthodox Marxian theory of what had to occur in the first stage of communism, namely develop the "forces of production." Distributions to expand military hardware were necessitated not only by the arms race with the United States but also to support Soviet foreign policy elsewhere in the world. A growing state bureaucracy was required to plan, organize, and control growing state industry.

Because tensions and struggles typical in capitalism arose inside Soviet state-enterprises, surplus distributions went to support more communist party officials and secret police to manage them. The ubiquitous stresses and strains of Soviet life stemmed directly and indirectly from the pressures for ever more surpluses Soviet officials placed upon workers coupled with the inability of the workers to appropriate and distribute their own surpluses. The Soviet state did provide workers with a significant flow of public goods including subsidized education, housing, and transportation, affordable and often free health services, and free sports and art programs. Yet these benefits of Soviet society did not suffice to overcome deepening alienation after the 1970s.

Workers producing ever more surpluses to meet ever rising state demands meant in Marxian terms a rising rate of exploitation. In other words, workers' exploitation worsened in what was defined as a workers' society. Those hard-pressed workers eventually reacted with growing resentment, lowered work efforts, and deepening alienation from the socialism and communism that Soviet leaders claimed was in place. While state pressures on workers to produce more surpluses had a long history, its context changed in the late 1970s.

From the late 1920s to the 1970s, state officials successfully appropriated rising surpluses and distributed them to transform a very poor Tsarist Russia into a major industrial Soviet power. It withstood and defeated the invading Germans in World War II. Immediately after that war, it engaged in a cold war with the United States even as it continued to develop its industry, generated a military establishment more or less adequate to its defense, and increased the delivery of state services to its people. Soviet workers supplied ever more surpluses to fund these successful developments. Their wages were stagnant for much of this half-century while their productivity constantly rose because of the machinery pouring out of the USSR's prioritized capital-goods industries. From the perspective of Marxian economics, this is another way of saying that Soviet workers' rate of exploitation rose: the success of Soviet state capitalism was built on a rising rate of class exploitation.

Given this book's comparative approach, it is worth noting a difference between Soviet and US development. Before the 1970s, in the United States, rising worker productivity was partly used to pay rising real wages. The latter was a kind of compensation for the stresses of the former. In the USSR, that was not the case. Rising productivity went almost completely toward industrial development, state, and party needs. This difference is reflected in the level of opposition Soviet workers felt for their system in the 1980s compared to the very different level in the United States then. Ironically, the 1970s is also the time when US real wages stopped rising (never yet to resume) while productivity kept rising. The effects of this on consumption were temporarily postponed by having more US family members doing paid labor and by undertaking large household debts, but the end of those options for over-indebted US working families helped cause the crisis that began in 2007 and the subsequently rising political tensions inside the United States.

Soviet state and party officials worked out an effective strategy to offset the rising exploitation of their workers and the possible threat that posed. It largely succeeded until the 1980s. The strategy was to proclaim Soviet workers as the vanguard of a new socialist civilization that would bring peace, harmony, and plenty to the world. The major obstacles to achieving that civilization were the underdeveloped economy inherited by the Soviets in 1917 and capitalist countries' efforts to undermine and destroy post-1917 socialist successes. State and party aimed to persuade Soviet workers that their sacrificed consumption growth was necessary to free the resources to overcome both obstacles. Another part of official strategy was political. Distributing surplus to the police apparatus enabled the state to monitor and control workers' resentments. For decades this dual strategy of sacrifice and control worked to contain tensions between workers and Ministers and between citizens and the state.

By the 1970s, pent-up desire of the Soviet population to enjoy US and European standards of living could no longer be postponed after generations of sacrifice. Yet the Soviet economy could not produce enough surpluses to meet the growing demands upon it: ever costlier arms race, a disastrous war in Afghanistan, rising costs of new technologies necessary for continued industrial growth, growing state and party bureaucracies needed to control increasingly restive populations, and so on. Raising real wages would constrain the surpluses needed to meet those demands. Various reform efforts failed largely because they could not grapple with the fundamental issue of sufficient surplus. Workers' frustrations boiled over onto state-retail stores where they angrily confronted equally upset retail clerks who lacked consumer goods to sell, onto interpersonal tensions of families and households, onto enterprises where ever less work was accomplished, and onto communist party officials for their complicity with an increasingly disliked system. Not surprisingly, workers and others increasingly came to believe socialism and communism were the problem rather than an exhausted and no longer effective state-capitalism.

When the USSR and its eastern European allies imploded, the newly emerging states organized the logical next step for the state-capitalist economies that they conceived to be socialism/communism. They formally reverted to private-capitalism by returning state-enterprises to private ownership and dismantling planning institutions in favor of markets. Parallel crises and similar less-extensive changes occurred also in the Peoples Republic of China, which entered an era of rapid development of private-capitalist enterprises, although the political dominance of the Chinese Communist Party was not changed as had happened in the USSR and eastern Europe. As always, the pace and other particularities of the reversion toward private-capitalism from state-capitalism varied in each country.

Despite particular differences, these oscillations inside the Russian, eastern European, and Chinese economies shared numerous qualities with those inside the US, European, and other similar economies. In the former, state-owned and state-operated industrial enterprises gave way, to greater or lesser degrees depending on each country's specific conditions, to private-capitalist enterprises. In them, private- replaced former state-capitalists. More regulation by the state gave way to less. Market mechanisms of distribution advanced relative to planning mechanisms. In the Western, private-capitalist countries much the same direction of change occurred (although they had, of course, much less state intervention to begin with and less history of state-capitalist appropriation).

Thus the opposite oscillations earlier in the twentieth century (to *more* state intervention in Russia in 1917 and likewise in other countries' responses to the Great Depression of the 1930s) were now reversed everywhere during the 1970s and 1980s. In the private-capitalist countries, these latter oscillations back from more to less state intervention provoked the relative decline of Keynesian and Marxian economics and the renewed ascendancy of neoclassical economics. In the countries that more or less abandoned their Soviet-style economies, a rapid decline followed in the influence of the formerly dominant, officially endorsed, orthodox Marxist economic theory. Its place was taken by the usual three alternative, contesting economic theories: neoclassical, Keynesian, and various versions of Marxian economics including the old orthodox Marxism trying to survive and also altogether new interpretations of Marxian economics.

6.3.3   Back to State Intervention

We turn finally to the latest oscillations affecting both economies and economic theories. They were occasioned by global capitalism's 2007–2008 meltdown into what came to be called the Great Recession, the worst capitalist crisis since the Great Depression of the 1930s. A sharp decline in the US housing market quickly spread to credit markets and from there, via world markets, into general economic collapse everywhere else. Millions lost jobs and homes, world trade and production shrank, and governments everywhere were panicked by an imminent collapse of economic activity. Washington, London, Berlin, Beijing, Tokyo, and governments in many other capitals intervened massively in their economies in ways very like what had been done in the Great Depression. Governments pumped the equivalent of trillions of dollars into their monetary systems to coax a resumption of lending. Governments purchased assets of little value from banks to recapitalize them, took over insurance and other financial companies, and bailed out all sorts of enterprises with loans and via direct equity investments.

Many of the banks and other enterprises that benefited from this government largesse were deemed "too big to fail" (their demise would ramify and collapse other enterprises in uncontrollable chain reactions). They got massive state assistance on the presumption that the assistance would "trickle down" to benefit small businesses and the mass of workers and consumers. Parallel "trickle down" economics had been the object of much social criticism in the 1930s.

Governments incurred huge deficits borrowing money for their economic interventions (from businesses and the rich who would not invest or otherwise spend it in a fast declining world economy). They dared not raise taxes to obtain this money since increased taxes risked further depressing a tottering economy and also risked alienating the corporations and the rich whose contributions increasingly sustained political parties and careers. Governments poured the borrowed funds into their economies to offset their private sectors' collapses. In addition they used their central banks (The Federal Reserve System in the United States) to massively intervene in their credit markets to boost the money supply and lower interest rates to historic lows.

After thirty years of deregulation and privatization, celebrated and furthered by the return to social dominance of neoclassical economics, global capitalism crashed. Huge state intervention programs around the world returned to become the orders of the day everywhere. The claims of neoclassical economics that deregulation and privatization would guarantee economic growth and prevent or overcome cyclical instability seemed dramatically disproved. Indeed the heads of private-capitalist banks often took the lead in bringing government in to rescue them from their failed investments and loans. Fearing economic catastrophe, nearly everyone supported massive government intervention using public money to salvage failed private enterprises. Presidents George W. Bush and Barak Obama both did exactly that as did most other governments regardless of their political complexions.

This latest economic oscillation back to state-interventionist capitalism is again provoking changes in the alternative economic theories and their relative social positions. The self-confident dominance of neoclassical economics has been badly shaken. Many neoclassical economists have switched their allegiances to become Keynesians. Yet, because the neoclassical dominance was so great, it still retains considerable influence. A much less lopsided struggle now pits a defensive neoclassical economics against a renewed Keynesian economics informing political campaigns, media presentations and academic activities.

The global capitalist crash that began in 2007 also had complex effects on Marxian economics. On the one hand, it seemed to validate the Marxian criticism of capitalist cycles: that they are intrinsic to the system, that their causes have never been overcome, and that the resulting suffering, wasted resources, and lost output demonstrate the inefficiency and injustice of capitalism. There are many signs of a renewed interest around the world in Marxian criticisms of capitalism. On the other hand, the lasting disrepute of the USSR and of Soviet-style economies counteracts the appeal of Marxian critiques of capitalism. To build on the renewed interest in Marxian economics, its practitioners would likely need to project an image or model of an alternative to capitalism quite different from Soviet-style economies.

One independent group of Marxist economists collaborating from different countries has begun to do just that. It offers a critique of Soviet-style economies. It argues that their definition of socialism was overly focused on the macro-level of economics: on private versus social ownership of enterprises and on planning versus markets. It argues further that their definition of socialism badly neglected the micro-level of individual enterprises. They replaced private boards of directors with state officials who received and distributed the surpluses/profits generated across enterprises. This meant much too little micro-level change for most workers: as before, they came to work, delivered the products and the surpluses embodied in them *to other people*, and returned home. Such Marxists argued therefore that Soviet-style socialism might better be described as a state-capitalism, since the internal organization of state-enterprises remained capitalist. Class exploitation had been preserved for the few: no longer private citizens (elected by shareholders) they were instead state officials.

Such Marxist economists also argue that for a differently defined socialist alternative to replace such state-capitalism there would have to be fundamental change in the organization of surplus inside enterprises. Following Marx's suggestions, enterprises would have to be internally reorganized such that surplus-producing workers become also their own collective boards of directors. Instead of small, elite boards of directors elected by major shareholders, this reorganization of the surplus would yield workers' self-directed enterprises, giving all workers both a specific and a general job description. For example, each worker might do a particular task from Monday to Thursday, but on Friday all workers meet to decide democratically what, how, and where to produce and what to do with the surplus/profits they produce. These Marxist economists describe their proposal as economic democracy; only when such a democracy is instituted inside enterprises has a society created the micro-level constituent of a genuine socialism (Wolff 2012).

This and other kinds of new Marxian economics are now growing, developing, and debating in a framework of renewal. Because older capitalisms are managing their current major crises by massive state debts, they face socially costly and divisive debt management problems. In many cases those problems threaten long-term declines in jobs, wages, and working conditions for public and private employees (something widely referred to as "austerity policies"). Marxian criticisms of capitalism are finding growing audiences there. In the new and more robust capitalisms in Asia and elsewhere, the extremes of wealth and poverty and horrendous working conditions likewise provoke criticism that leads critics yet again toward Marxian economics.

The future will show us how the latest economic oscillation back from a crashed private-capitalism toward state-interventionist or state-capitalisms will affect the three contesting economic theories. What history has already shown is that each theory changes and adjusts in its own way to such oscillations and that the relative strengths and support for each theory continually change as well. It contradicts history to imagine that today's dominant theory will remain so.

Capitalism arrived on the world stage as a new economic system that soon provoked intellectuals to provide theories of how it worked. Because it arrived early in Great Britain, it was British thinkers who provided those key early theorizations that we now refer to as "economics." A naturally expansive system, capitalism spread from region to region and from industry to industry thereby provoking an ever wider range of thoughtful reactions which matured into formal theorizations. Because capitalism often displaced older ways of production rudely or violently, it provoked critical theorizations alongside those that celebrated capitalism's arrival. Because capitalist employers often generated great wealth yet also often treated their employees badly, and because labor–capital conflicts proved endemic, critics and admirers of capitalism theorized the system differently. When serious problems beset capitalism—as they always have—the theorists who celebrated capitalism could and did split about how the system worked and how best it could be supported and sustained. When capitalism enjoyed periods of growth and relative labor peace, the criticism often subsided and the critics found smaller audiences.

Thus the discipline known as economics came to include the classical and neoclassical schools, the Keynesian school and the Marxian critical schools as the major contending and enduring traditions of theorizing capitalism. Capitalism was the mother and father of them all. It remains their object of analysis even as they struggle over their very different reactions to their parents and their system. To understand capitalism requires attention to them all, engaging their different perspectives to find and fashion our own. To solve capitalism's problems likewise requires learning what each theory has to teach. That means refusing any theory's or theorist's claims that one theory captures the whole truth and so you need not listen to or learn from the others. No sooner have supporters of one kind of economic system proclaimed its permanence than yet another oscillation has proved them wrong. No sooner has one economic theory become dominant and proclaimed its absolute truth than conditions change and an alternative theory becomes dominant.

The bottom line here is that economic theories matter. They all contain insights and ideas formulated by people seeking to understand a system they loved or hated (and sometimes both together). It also matters which theory is dominant in the sense of being believed by social leaders or effective majorities of people. A dominant theory shapes how most people think about and act in an economy and that determines how that economy evolves and works. The dominance of neoclassical or Keynesian theories tends to support capitalism, but it is no guarantee that capitalism's internal contradictions and problems will not outweigh those theories' goals. Likewise, the dominance of Marxian economics would tend to support a socialist economic system alternative to capitalism, but that too is no guarantee that socialism's internal dynamics will not outweigh the theory's goals. Honest and open debate among all the alternative major economic theories offers the best hope that we can use the fullest sets of insights to move society forward whether that be to a capitalist or a socialist future.

7 The Importance of Theoretical Differences

7.1 Marxian versus Keynesian versus Neoclassical Theory

This book has examined the three most important economic theories contesting in the world today. Earlier chapters described each theory and suggested some of the different consequences that flow from each. In this concluding chapter we have two purposes. The first is to summarize how these theories differ systematically. The second is to explain and compare their different impacts upon our lives. We aim to show how alternative ways of thinking in general, and these three economic theories in particular, shape societies in very different ways.

Let us recall that each theory has a unique structure. Each theory uses different concepts or sentences to make its sense of the world, to construct its particular knowledge of social life in general and of the economy in particular. We can assess each theory's uniqueness by posing and answering two questions. First, where does each theory begin? In other words, what are the entry points of each theory? Second, what is the method or logic used by each theory to produce its other concepts and connect all its concepts? That is, how does each theory move from its entry points to a developed understanding or knowledge of the economy? Marxian, Keynesian, and neoclassical theories differ radically in their answers to these questions.

7.1.1 Different Points of Entry

Marxian theory begins with the concept of class. This is the initial concept or entry-point idea with which it organizes its understanding of all the other objects in or aspects of the world that it seeks to grasp. It thus always connects prices, wages, and profits—among its particular objects of interest—to its organizing concept of class. Marxian theory produces a class knowledge of those objects. We can say therefore that it is a class theory of the meaning of these objects.

Neoclassical theory, by contrast, begins with the following concepts: (1) individuals who are self-interested and utility maximizing, (2) individual endowments of productive resources, and (3) individuals' inherent technical ability to transform nature by means of productive resources. From and with these three entry-point concepts, neoclassical theory produces the meaning of all the other objects that it seeks to understand. It thus always connects prices, wages, and profits to its organizing concepts of individuals' preferences, resource endowments, and technology. We say therefore that neoclassical theory is an individualist theory: the nature of human individuals determines the structure and specific qualities of the economy.

Keynesian theory introduces entry-point concepts of (1) mass psychology (populations' "propensities" to save out of their incomes) and conventions for making economic decisions, (2) the power of institutions (e.g., labor unions and government) to shape individual behaviors in markets, and (3) the "animal spirits" that govern individual investors' decisions about when and where to invest how much. Neither the concepts of class, as in Marxian theory, nor those of individuals' preferences or utility maximization, as in neoclassical theory, function as entry points in Keynesian theory. Rather, certain structural features of a society—its social psychology and key institutions—are Keynesian theory's entry points in constructing its understanding of the economy.

Comparing Marxian, neoclassical, and Keynesian economic theories' respective entry points, it is clear that they differ sharply in how each begins to build its distinctive understanding or knowledge. As the earlier chapters on each theory showed, different points of entry contribute to different explanations for economic relationships and events. People persuaded by neoclassical theory see and participate in social life differently from those persuaded by Marxian or Keynesian theory. This is partly because their theories have different entry-point concepts.

It follows that individuals will likely act differently depending on which theory they use in thinking about the economic aspects of their lives and social surroundings. As with theories people use to understand other objects of interest to them (love, nature, politics, etc.), economic theories have conscious and unconscious effects on how people think and act. To underscore the importance and power of entry points, we will provide several concrete examples later in this chapter.

7.1.2 Different Logics

Each of the three economic theories not only has distinctive entry-point concepts but they also connect those entry points to the other concepts within their theories in different ways. Each theory's sentences link its entry points to other concepts to construct its propositions and arguments about how economies work and evolve. Just as important as the entry points in each theory is its way—its system—of linking concepts to one another. We refer to that linking system as the logic of the theory. Theories differ not only in their entry points but also in their logics.

Neoclassical economic theory employs a logic known in philosophy as "deduction." All concepts introduced *after* its entry-point concepts are carefully deduced or derived from those entry points. For example, neoclassical economics connects its entry points of human preferences, technology, and resource endowments *in a deductive way* to such subsequent concepts as the supplies of and demands for all commodities and resources. In other words, supplies, demands, and prices are caused by—derived from—preferences, resource endowments, and technology.

We could just as well read this last sentence in reverse. Then "derived" would be replaced by its opposite, "reduced." In neoclassical theory, price is first reduced to its causes, supply and demand, and then they are further reduced to what ultimately causes them: preferences, resource endowments, and technology. These latter three aspects or dimensions of individual human natures are the final causes of everything else in an economy. They are the *essential determinants* of everything else. Everything else in an economy is logically reduced by neoclassical economic theory to being an effect determined by its entry points. The logical system of neoclassical economics, its deductive or reductive or deterministic way of connecting its concepts, is an example of what philosophers call essentialism.

While Keynesian theory differs from neoclassical economic theory in its entry-point concepts, it does not differ in its logic. Keynesian theory too is essentialist. Its propositions and arguments self-consciously show economic events and conditions (especially the periodic cycles or crises of capitalist economies) to be caused or determined essentially by the theory's entry points (mass psychological propensities and conventions, institutions, and "animal spirits"). To summarize: neoclassical economic theory privileges the individual as the essential cause of everything else—an "individualism"—while Keynesian theory instead privileges social conventions and institutions as such an essential cause—a "structuralism." Both theories divide the components of an economy into essential causes or their effects.

The Marxian economic theory articulated in this book deploys a different logic that is anti-essentialist. Called "overdetermination," this logic links each concept within the theory, including its entry point of class, as both cause and effect of every other concept within the theory. For Marxian theory, nothing is *either* a cause *or* an effect of other things; everything is caused by everything else and participates in causing everything else. Thus no concept within the theory is reducible to being an effect of one or a subset of the other concepts in the theory. No concept is the cause of another, since each concept is both caused (overdetermined) by all other concepts and participates in causing (overdetermining) each of them. Everything in the theory—every object conceptualized in and by the theory—is both cause and effect of everything else.

Thus Marxian theory does *not* posit or understand class as an essence. Class is *not* the ultimate cause of the events and conditions in the larger economy and society; they are not merely the effects of class. Rather, Marxian economic theory proceeds from class to other aspects of the economy and society (e.g., commodity prices, enterprise profits, and state economic policies) by demonstrating how they are simultaneously causes and effects of class. Those other aspects are not presumed to be ultimately caused by or reducible to class. Class is not their essential cause any more than any of them are the essential causes of class in society.

Marxian theory is thus an open-ended process in which class—the entry-point and central focus of Marxists for specific historical reasons—is linked to an ever-growing range of other concepts, other aspects of social life that strike Marxists as important to understand. The link is one of overdetermination. Class and nonclass aspects of life are woven together as mutually interactive, interdependent causes and effects of one another. The goal is to explain how each aspect is simultaneously the cause and the effect of all others. Marxian theory aims to specify the overdetermined relationship between the class and nonclass processes comprising societies. Of course, as with all theories, its proponents—Marxists—can and do disagree in their particular analyses of these overdeterminations. Then too, as noted earlier in the book, some Marxists operating within traditional Marxism reject overdetermination and seek instead to construct deterministic arguments in which class does function as the essence that determines the other aspects of economy and society.

Neoclassical theory is also an open-ended process albeit in a different way. Its proponents can and do disagree about the particulars of its individualistic entry points and deterministic/essentialist logic. Some of this disagreement was discussed in our late neoclassical theory chapter. Likewise Keynesians have their internal disagreements over their theory's particulars as they go about extending and revising their theory in an open-ended way. We saw a bit of this too when discussing post-Keynesian economics. However, what divides neoclassical from Keynesian economists are their different entry-point concepts; what unites them is a shared essentialist logic. What separate both of them from Marxian economic theory are different entry points and different logics of analysis.

Different understandings of how economies work and change will be produced from the three different theories because of their different entry points and logics. Indeed these different understandings raise an important question. Can we really say that the different economic theories are analyzing the same things when they use the same words? When basic concepts denoted by words such as "labor," "value," "profit," and "capital" appear in the statements of all three theories, do they have the same meanings? Or do the three theories display not only different entry points and logics but also different objects of their analyses?

7.1.3   Different Objects of Analysis

Proceeding from their different entry points, the three theories utilize their logics to construct explanations of whatever their practitioners take as interesting objects to analyze. We might refer to any theory's explanation of some topic as an exit point of that theory: the place at which it arrives in moving from its entry point by way of its logic. Starting from different entry points and proceeding by way of different logics, theories reach different exit points.

This means that we are typically confronted in the world with written or spoken objects of analysis that, despite carrying the same label, have different meanings. For example, Marxists and non-Marxists differently define and use the concept of "capitalism." The same applies to many other basic economic concepts. Although both groups of theorists often use the same words, these words take on their unique meanings according to the particular theories that use and thereby define them. Much the same happens in other realms of life; for example, different people who use words like love or happiness can bring very different meanings to those words.

At times, economic theorists produce new words, nonexistent in contending theories, in order to distinguish their particular meanings and make them more persuasive. Marx, for example, invented and defined "surplus value" as something different from "profit" to distinguish his notion of class from other theories' notions of that term. Neoclassical theorists invented "marginal utility" to differentiate their concept of human choice from those of others. Keynesian theorists developed "marginal propensities" to save and consume to help separate their notion of how markets work from those of the neoclassical economists.

If the same term represents different meanings in different theories, is one correct or more correct than the others, and are those others then false? Is Marxian theory's or neoclassical theory's or Keynesian theory's meaning of "capitalism" the true meaning? An old tradition in human thought argues that one of any alternative conceptualizations of any object (e.g., capitalism) must be the truest, the closest to what actually exists in the real world. We will return to this key issue at the end of this chapter. Here we need only note that this old tradition of thought itself depends on very particular (and not universally shared) theories about what reality, knowledge, and truth are. It turns out that different theories of reality and knowledge give very different definitions of what the "correctness" of any theory means.

Table 7.1
Theories of value

Theory	Entry point	Logic	Object
Marxian	Class (*S/V*)	↔	Prices and incomes
Neoclassical	Wants (*U*) and scarcity (*technology and endowments*)	→	Prices and incomes
Keynesian	Social structures (*mass psychology, social conventions and institutions*)	→	Prices and incomes

7.1.4 Different Theories of Value

Table 7.1 summarizes the three theories of value presented in earlier chapters. It displays concisely the indexes of difference among the theories. Reading the entry-point column of the table, we find the theories' different organizing, focal concepts. Under the object column, we observe their differently produced explanations of the objects "prices" and "incomes." Alternative logics are represented by either a unidirectional arrow (essentialism/determinism) or a bidirectional arrow (overdetermination). In the neoclassical and Keynesian rows, we see that their entry points determine their objects. In the Marxian row, the overdeterminist logic makes entry point and objects mutually determinant in a context in which all social processes combine to overdetermine each one.

The meanings of "price" and "income" as objects of analysis depend upon and vary with the particular concepts and logics each theory uses to define or make sense of them. This also applies to other concepts. For example, the entry-point concepts of "need" and "scarcity"—essential causes in neoclassical theory—take on very different meanings in Marxian theory. There they are conceived to be overdetermined by nonclass and class processes. In neoclassical theory, "need" and "scarcity" have specific, fixed meanings, while in Marxian theory, "overdetermination" means that individuals constantly change what they understand those terms to be and therefore how they act in relation to their changing understandings of "need" and "scarcity."

We have now come full circle to the beginning of this chapter. We have answered our two questions by showing how the entry points and the logics of the neoclassical, Keynesian, and Marxian theories differ. That has permitted us to see that these theories' objects of analysis necessarily differ as well. We may now confront the other major issue of this chapter: How and why do these theoretical differences matter in our lives?

7.2 Analytical Consequences of Contending Theories

Neoclassical, Keynesian, and Marxian theories coexist in modern societies. Individuals and groups use one or varying mixtures of them in making sense of the world. People's thoughts about the world—the differing senses they make—shape how they understand problems they face and the solutions they devise and pursue. The economic theories people use influence how they understand those who use different economic theories and whether they agree, disagree, ignore, ally with, or oppose the ideas and projects of those who use different theories. Different theories contribute to different actions and so change the world in different ways.

In this section we explore some different social consequences of the three theories. We will demonstrate that the three theories' different analyses of economic objects influence people persuaded by them to take different kinds of action. The behaviors of individuals and groups are partly shaped, consciously and unconsciously, by the theory or theories they use and by their reactions to others' actions and theories. Since our lives are impacted by the actions of those around us, studying different theories can help us understand and cope with those actions.

7.2.1 Income Distribution: The Neoclassical View

Keynesian, Marxian, and neoclassical economists have long debated one of the most important questions ever to confront economics: Why are some people relatively poor and others relatively rich? In other words, what explains income and its distribution in societies? Different answers to this question—based in part on the different economic theories—help shape citizens' conscious and unconscious attitudes toward poverty and affluence. These attitudes in turn influence where and how we want to live, work, and attend schools. Differing and clashing attitudes toward the rich and poor are displayed in books, plays, films, and radio and television programs.

Different theories and their explanations for the distribution of income also influence politics: the parties and candidates, the laws enacted, how judges and juries interpret those laws, and whether and how laws are actually enforced. The different theories and explanations influence our daily lives as well as the politics around us whether or not we are explicitly aware or conscious of them. Indeed one purpose of this book is precisely to increase your awareness of the influences of different economic theories on your life and your society.

Let us now compare directly the different theories' explanations of income distribution and see where their different explanations lead. Neoclassical theory argues that different incomes are caused and therefore explained by the choices that individuals make (their preferences), combined with the technology and productive resources they each bring to produce goods and services. Wealth and poverty are thus understood to be essentially the results of individuals' choices, endowments, and technologies.

Neoclassical explanations proceed by examining what choices are made given the endowments individuals have and the available technology. To take a prominent example, individuals *choose* to save parts of their incomes and devote the resources thereby saved from consumption to invest in the increased production of goods and services. In economic jargon, individuals decide to save and then provide their savings as capital for the production process. To take another example, individuals also *choose* to supply a certain number of labor hours to an economy's enterprises rather than consume that time in leisure. The first kind of choice determines the amount of capital available for investment in an economy while the second kind of choice determines how much labor is available for production in an economy. Notice how economic growth and productive output are each shown to result essentially from individual choices based on individual preferences.

In neoclassical theory, individuals are thought to exercise free will in choosing to sacrifice present consumption of their income and/or to sacrifice their leisure time. The incentive for making such sacrifices is the future reward they expect and deserve for doing so—as in the sports adage: "No pain, no gain." Neoclassical theory concludes that everyone's income is ultimately determined by the free choices each has made. To put it bluntly, you get the income your voluntary choices deserve.

Of course, the rewards to saving out of income and to performing labor also depend on the choices of others in neoclassical theory, especially those who own (are "endowed with") productive resources (land, machines, equipment, etc.). They can choose to provide those resources to enterprises for use in production. If they provide them, they obtain in return shares of the output (rents for land, profits for machines and equipment, etc.) as their incomes. The output made possible by resources depends, of course, on technology. Thus neoclassical economic theory reaches the conclusion that the distribution of income among wage-earners, rent-earners, and profit-earners depends on and reflects the choices individuals make, their endowments, and technology.

Neoclassical theory reduces each individual's income to its conceptual entry points. We all receive income in direct relation to how we choose to use our time and our endowments of productive resources. The more we sacrifice, the more we can contribute to production, the more we can and should obtain of the fruits of that production. We should therefore look to our individual choices, our self-interested behavior, to explain our high or low incomes.

It follows in neoclassical theory that the relatively affluent do not earn their income at the expense of the poor. The choices of the former to work long and hard and to be thrifty are independent of the latter's opposite choices. Each individual gets rewarded—his or her income—according to his or her choices about contributing to production. No one's wealth is the result of another's poverty. The distribution of income in a capitalist economy therefore displays a basic kind of justice. If the poor are dissatisfied with their poverty, they must change their ways and sacrifice more; in short, they must make choices like the rich did. For neoclassical theory, there is no other way.

7.2.2 Capitalism: The Neoclassical View

Neoclassical economic theory elaborates this powerful conclusion into one of the most influential claims found anywhere in social theory. A society that establishes capitalism will achieve the maximum possible wealth consistent with the free choices of its citizens. By establishing capitalism, neoclassical theory means establishing two social institutions. The first is a free and fully competitive market for all resources and produced goods, a market in which no individual can control prices and all individuals pursue their economic self-interests. The second is legally enforced private property, including the right of owners of resources and products to dispose of them as they please.

Capitalism conforms best then to what neoclassical theory assumes to be the wealth-accumulating nature of human beings. The theory understands capitalism to be the optimum social system—efficient and just—because it best facilitates what we all want to do: accumulate wealth for ourselves. It prompts and encourages each citizen to make decisions based on individual self-interest—that is, maximum wealth for each consumer and producer. As shown in our earlier chapter on neoclassical theory, the basic institutions of capitalist society guarantee a social equilibrium that maximizes both producer profits and consumer satisfactions.

This conclusion was first broached by Adam Smith, later presented in mathematical terms by Wilfredo Pareto, and still later given formal "proof" by Gerard Debreu (winning him the 1984 Nobel Prize in economics). It implies that capitalism is an intrinsically harmonious economic system. Producers and consumers seeking their own self-interest will thereby promote one another's (and the whole society's) interests automatically and optimally. Everyone ends up in the best possible economic position, and no one can become better off (acquire more wealth) unless someone else becomes worse off.

This neoclassical argument implies that the institutions of capitalism should be established everywhere as soon as possible since they best enable and facilitate what every rational individual and nation wants. Where capitalism exists, it must be protected from irrational forces that would replace it with inferior economic and social institutions such as collectivized (not private) property and centralized economic planning (not markets). Such noncapitalist institutions would impose all manner of production inefficiencies and consumption dissatisfactions. Where capitalism does not exist, rational self-interest drives people to establish it. In particular, poor nations must recognize that unfettered capitalism is *the* best way to become rich.

A second implication of this neoclassical conclusion is that capitalism rewards hard work and thrift. Since individual incomes flow from the contributions individuals make to production, the more labor individuals contribute, the higher their wage income will be. The greater the portion of their income they save and contribute to (as capital invested in) production, the more their profit income will be. Hard work and frugality are the twin virtues that, if practiced by poor persons in a capitalist system, enable them to escape poverty.

A third implication is that, given individual wants and capitalist institutions, wealth can be gained by raising the productivity of resources. Technological changes can and do increase the incomes of those who supply the resources whose productivity is raised by those changes. Capitalism is thus a technically dynamic system, since every citizen of a capitalist society has an interest in gaining more income by enhancing the productivity of whatever resources he or she contributes to production. Notice again the universally harmonious, mutually reinforcing interaction of capitalist institutions, technical changes, and rising incomes.

7.2.3   Poverty: The Neoclassical View

It follows directly from the neoclassical theorization of income distribution in capitalist economies that poverty (both individual and national) occurs for one or more of three basic reasons. First, social barriers may block individuals' rational pursuit of self-interest by interfering with the workings of free markets. Neoclassical literature recognizes and discusses three kinds of such barriers. The first kind derives from human weaknesses—for example, the desire of individuals to gain market control, monopolize resources or goods, and thereby manipulate prices. The second kind involves certain natural limits on human capabilities—for example, the inability of human beings to predict the future. Uncertainty can distort market choices. The third kind of barrier concerns the properties of some production technologies—for example, economies of scale—that can facilitate monopolies displacing competition in markets and hence the monopoly pricing that distorts market outcomes. All three kinds of barrier can cause the wealth of individuals and nations to fall below what it could be without them. All three can thus create poverty.

The second neoclassical explanation for poverty in capitalist societies follows logically from the basic theory: some individuals choose it. They express their preference for leisure by choosing it over wage labor. Likewise they prefer to consume now rather than save and invest their savings as capital earning future income (profit, rents, interest, etc.). Consequently they are poor. Not barriers to rational choices, but rather the preferences and resulting choices of individuals, groups, and whole nations explain their poverty.

The third neoclassical reason for poverty concerns neither barriers to free markets and private property nor preferences and choices. It concerns productivity. If the resources an individual contributes to production are of little use, then that individual will in turn obtain little reward. Individuals who contribute low-productivity resources (unskilled labor, low-fertility land, etc.) will be rewarded with correspondingly small portions of output. Their incomes will be low in proportion to the low productivity of the labor and other resources they bring to production.

To counter these causes of poverty, neoclassical economists propose the following sorts of policies. A rational government should identify and eliminate barriers to free markets. The goal must be to create perfect capitalist market institutions in which each citizen has an equal chance to be rich or poor depending on individual personal preferences and choices and the technological productivity of individually owned resources. Neoclassical economists thus call for removing market "imperfections," although they can and do disagree among themselves on how best to achieve this shared objective. For neoclassical economists, poverty freely chosen by individuals does not constitute a problem requiring or meriting any government action.

7.2.4 Income Distribution: The Marxian View

Marxian theory rejects the neoclassical arguments that (1) the distribution of income in capitalist economies is essentially caused by human nature (preferences, technical capacities, etc.) and (2) income distribution and wealth production achieve some "optimum" when humans pursue their self-interest in free markets. Instead, Marxian theory approaches the issue of income distribution by inquiring about individuals' participation in certain class and nonclass processes. In particular, it focuses on those class and nonclass processes that involve individuals receiving flows of value (in the form of money or commodities). These flows are what Marxian theory calls "incomes."

To obtain income requires participation in class and/or nonclass processes that generate income. In contrast, neoclassical theory disregards the Marxian concept of class altogether. Class thus plays no role in the neoclassical theory of income distribution.

To briefly summarize the Marxian theory of income distribution, we will consider examples of class and nonclass processes that generate incomes to individuals. The nonclass process of commodity exchange (*nonclass* because it is a different economic process from the production, appropriation, or distribution of a surplus) generates income. John sells his shirt to Mary, who pays for it with money. John obtains money income for participating in this nonclass process of commodity exchange. Mary also receives an income, although hers is an inflow of value in the form of a shirt, while John's inflow takes the form of money.

However, what is far more important for the Marxian theory of income distribution is an altogether different commodity exchange process. Mary sells her labor power to an employer in exchange for a money wage payment. Mary obtains this wage income because she participates in this particular commodity exchange process.

Seeking to understand income distribution in capitalist economies, Marxian theory asks how the size of wage income is determined. It begins by proposing the following two-part basis for wages: (1) Mary must purchase and consume commodities (food, clothing, shelter, etc.) in order to produce her capacity to work each day, her labor power, and (2) in exchange for selling her labor power to her employer, she must obtain a value flow in money sufficient to purchase those commodities. The value of labor power (the wage income gained from selling it) is approached in Marxian theory by first examining two of its determinants: (1) the bundle of specific commodities that wage-earners consume in order to reproduce the labor power they sell and (2) the value of each commodity in that bundle.

Marxian theory proceeds to explain the many diverse social forces that overdetermine both of those wage components. The specific commodities that sellers of labor power consume at any time and place are influenced by culture, nature, politics, and economics; they vary with history and geography. Moreover, since these influences are constantly changing, the composition of wage-earners' consumption bundles likewise changes. At the same time the value of each commodity in the bundle—the amount of socially necessary labor needed to produce it—is also changing. That value is overdetermined by all the other processes of society (technology, labor relations, organizations of production, climate, etc.). They all influence the amount of labor necessary to produce each commodity.

For Marxian theory, wage income is thus overdetermined by all of the processes of society. It is not reducible to any one or a subset of social processes and thus not reducible to an intrinsic human nature. Marxian theory does not explain wage income, as neoclassical theory does, by looking at only two of its determinants: the choice between real income and leisure and the marginal productivity of labor. Marxian theory recognizes that individual choice and marginal productivity participate in determining wage income, but it does not ignore all the other determinants. The Marxian approach emphasizes the overdetermination of wages, with special attention to the role of class processes. This special attention follows from Marxism's critique of exploitative class processes structures and its concern to move society toward non-exploitative economic systems. Neoclassical and Keynesian theories share neither that critique nor that concern.

To illustrate the breadth of the Marxian theory of income distribution, we consider next the capitalist fundamental class process. As shown in our earlier chapter on Marxian economics, this process involves the production and appropriation of surplus value. This appropriation by industrial capitalists constitutes a flow of value to them. It is realized as an income for them when they sell the commodities produced by the productive laborers they employ. The difference between the value of those sold commodities and the value of the hired labor power and purchased means of production used up in producing those commodities, what Marx called surplus value, is the capitalist's income. It is a one-way flow of value for which the capitalist makes no return flow. It is that "something for nothing" that outraged Marx and led him to call its occurrence "exploitation."

By including (and focusing upon) this fundamental class process in its analysis of the distribution of income, Marxian theory differentiates itself from neoclassical and Keynesian theories. Moreover Marxian theory recognizes that still other class and nonclass processes can also generate incomes and therefore shape an economy's income distribution. For example, the capitalist appropriators of surplus value distribute portions of it (the *subsumed class process* analyzed in our earlier chapter on Marxian economics) to a variety of recipients. Those distributions are incomes for them (managers, owners, bankers, wholesale and retail merchants, landlords, state officials, etc.). They obtain those incomes by virtue of their participation in the capitalist subsumed class process. For a last example, Marxian theory considers individuals who participate in such nonclass processes as enrolling in various government programs that provide them with cash benefits (transfer payments) or engaging with family members who provide regular gifts. These benefits and gifts constitute incomes for their recipients.

Thus the distribution of income among the citizens of a society depends on the sets of class and nonclass income-generating processes in which they each participate. Which of those processes exist in any society at any time and how citizens may or may not participate in them are conditions overdetermined by that society's entire culture, politics, economics, and natural environment. There is no way, for Marxist theory, to reduce this complexity to the neoclassical proposition that income distribution depends only on choices, techniques, and resource endowments.

7.2.5   Income Distribution: The Keynesian View

The key difference between the neoclassical and Keynesian theories in analyzing income distribution emerges from the Keynesian explanation of the relation between savings and investment. For Keynesians, savings and investments are not essentially caused by individual choices about savings based on preferences for present and future consumption. Instead, savings reflect social psychology (e.g., the marginal propensity to save) and social conventions of behavior given uncertainty about the future. Investments are the result of "animal spirits"—a summary term for the many different influences upon enterprises' and individuals' decisions as to when, where, and how to invest. When the total of what enterprises and individuals plan to save exceeds their plans to invest, a recurring situation, unemployment rises and incomes fall. An economic equilibrium may then be reached in which total wealth produced is far less than the maximum of which a society is capable. Consequently the division between wages and profits is shaped by the specifics of that unemployment equilibrium.

Keynesian theory likewise largely insists that institutions such as labor unions shape the supply of labor relative to demand for it and thus the resulting level of wages. This differentiates Keynesians from neoclassical theorists who prefer to see wages resulting from each individual worker's choices between real income and leisure. In general, Keynesian theorists see the distribution of income as essentially determined by aspects of the macro-level structure of the economy—savings rules, social conventions, institutions, and mass psychology. Once again, the structuralism of Keynesian economics distances it from the individualism of neoclassical economics.

Finally, Keynesian theory ignores the influence of class in the Marxian sense of the production, appropriation and distribution of surpluses. Like neoclassical theory, Keynesian theory explains the distribution of income without reference to surpluses. Keynesian theory does share with Marxian theory a rejection of the neoclassical notion that a capitalist economy tends to generate any optimum or just distribution of income or output of wealth. However, given the different entry points and logics of Keynesian and Marxian economic theories, they contextualize and develop their shared rejections of neoclassic theory very differently.

7.2.6 Different Explanations of the Returns to Capitalists

Table 7.2 summarizes the neoclassical, Keynesian, and Marxian explanations of the source of the value returns to capitalists in a society. In the table $MP(K)$

Table 7.2
Returns to capitalists

Theory	Entry point	Logic	Object
Neoclassical	*MRS and MP(K), MP(L)*	$\rightarrow$	Returns to capitalists
Marxian	*FCP*	$\leftrightarrow$	Returns to capitalists
Keynesian	*Social structures and MP(K) and MP(L)*	$\rightarrow$	Returns to capitalists

represents the marginal product of the capital resource and $MP(L)$ the marginal product of labor. MRS refers to the marginal rate of substitution between present and future consumption: individuals' preferences for present consumption relative to future consumption (and hence their willingness to save and provide their savings as capital supplied to the production process). According to neoclassical theory, then, the origin of the returns to capitalists is explained in terms of two essences: (1) the inherent productivity of means of production ("capital" in the form of machines, tools, etc.) and of labor as measured by $MP(K)$ and $MP(L)$ and (2) the choices of individuals to sacrifice gratification now for more later as measured by MRS. In short, the value return to capitalists is a just reward for their personal sacrifices and the productivities of the resources they contribute to production.

In contrast, Keynesian theory dispenses with the individual choices (MRS) stressed by neoclassical theory. Instead, it focuses on the structural conditions that shape the supply of labor, the savings out of incomes, and investment behavior. Those factors—together with the productivities of capital and labor—determine returns in the Keynesian view.

According to a Marxian theory that differs markedly from both the neoclassical and the Keynesian, the origin of what capitalists receive (surplus value) is the surplus labor produced by hired productive laborers and appropriated by their employers, industrial capitalists. The value return to capitalists is thus a fruit of the exploitation that takes place in the capitalist fundamental class process (FCP).

The marginal productivity of "things" and labor and the individual choices about real income and leisure and consumption today and tomorrow are not the essential causes or explanations of anything in Marxian theory. Individual choice and productivity matter in Marxian theory, but not as essences that determine everything about the economy. Rather, they are merely two of the many factors that overdetermine all the aspects of any economy, such as income and its distribution among individuals. In Marxian theory, the labor power supplied by an individual may be very productive, but the wages received need bear little relationship to that high productivity.

Marxian theory stresses that industrial capitalists appropriate the surpluses produced by others. Those capitalists—today chiefly members of corporate boards of directors—do not themselves participate in producing the outputs that their corporations sell. In that sense their marginal productivity is zero. Nor are their profit returns the results of or rewards for producing the tools, equipment, buildings, or raw materials used up in production. Those used-up means of production were all purchased earlier from other capitalist enterprises. Inside those enterprises, similarly exploited workers produced those means of production. Profit-receivers in Marxian theory obtain a portion of the income of society because of the social position—position in a fundamental class process—that they occupy, not because of anything productive that they do.

Of course, managers inside those industrial enterprises and their owners, as well as others located outside enterprises such as state officials, merchants, providers of technology, and bankers, do receive incomes because of the labor they perform, risks they take, or capital they provide to the corporate board. Their respective incomes represent distributed portions of the already appropriated surplus value by that same corporate board. These individuals (occupants of subsumed class positions) receive those incomes because they provide certain conditions that enable the productive laborers to produce the commodities that capitalists sell and that contain the surplus values that capitalists appropriate.

Additionally any corporate board member may receive more than one flow of value: beyond appropriating surplus value as a collective exploiter of productive labor, an individual board member may also receive dividends for being an owner of the enterprise and perhaps also a salary if he or she also functions as a paid corporate manager. In the latter two (subsumed class) functions or positions, the individual *as owner* provides the capitalist enterprise with access to property (thereby incurring a risk of losing a portion or all, if the enterprise is unsuccessful), while the individual *as manager* provides various conditions (supervision, purchasing, sales, etc) necessary for the firm's productive laborers to generate the surpluses that its capitalists appropriate. Marx went to some lengths to distinguish between individuals who received income from class exploitation, namely from receiving unpaid labor that yields surpluses, and those who received incomes from other activities. Those other activities included, for example, owning and lending or other kinds of labor that did not generate surpluses (what he therefore called unproductive labor) and rather provided conditions of existence for productive labor. Marx focused his criticisms on the waste and injustice of capitalist exploitation, the exploitative relation between capitalist employers and hired productive laborers, and what he saw as its disastrous social consequences.

That is why Marxian theory emphasizes and focuses upon the class process in society: unpaid labor. The class concept thus provides the cutting edge separating Marxian from both neoclassical and Keynesian theories generally and from their approaches to income distribution in particular.

7.3 Political Consequences of Contending Theories

The three different theories compared in this book clash in the modern world. For example, a major point and purpose of neoclassical theory is to deny precisely what Marxian theory affirms: that class exploitation is a determinant of income distribution. A major point and purpose of Keynesian theory is to explain the inefficient, wasteful, and socially disruptive instability and cycles of capitalist economies and to warrant government economic interventions to offset them—arguments that neoclassical theory rejects. In its turn, Marxian theory denies what neoclassical theory affirms: that human choice and technology determine the social distribution of income. Marxian theory also denies what Keynesian theory affirms: that a government-maintained fully employed labor force along with good paying jobs yield a social optimum.

Neoclassical theory informs the political agendas of most conservatives. It underlies their shared concern to remove what they see as market imperfections that prevent individuals from making those decisions which would bring each one the income he or she wants and deserves: an income distribution that conforms to the human nature and preferences of all citizens. Marxian theory informs the political agendas of Marxists. For them, a major political objective is basic change toward a more just society that would end class exploitation much as earlier slavery and serfdom were abolished. Marxists seek the alternative distributions of wealth and income (and also political power and cultural access) that they believe would follow from a nonexploitative class structure.

Social democrats and "liberals" (in the US rather than the UK definition of that term) mostly follow Keynesian theory in favoring regulations, transfer payments, and other government interventions that effectively *redistribute* income. They argue for such redistribution precisely because private, free-market capitalist economies, in their view, function and distribute income in inefficient and wasteful ways that yield lower levels of national income than those economies could produce. Marxists are more interested in making the class changes that will reorganize the allocation of income and wealth so that no subsequent government-mandated redistribution—in the Keynesian mode— would be required.

The theoretical differences carry far-reaching implications. For Marxists, even if market imperfections were somehow removed according to neoclassical prescriptions, class exploitation would not be eliminated. Even if full employment, eradication of monopolies, perfectly disseminated information, and an end to market discrimination on grounds of race or gender were achieved, class exploitation could continue or grow. Likewise, in the Marxian view, even if the Keynesians' fiscal and monetary policies moderated or alleviated capitalist business cycles, that would leave unaddressed the exploitation of labor and all its unwanted economic and social consequences. In other words, the desired Keynesian objective of a fully employed labor force is also from the contending Marxian perspective one that is fully exploited. Meanwhile neoclassical economists oppose the sorts of government economic interventions that Keynesians propose because they think that such interventions distort the optimal production and income distribution that could and would be achieved by laissez-faire capitalism.

Of course, tactical alliances among proponents of the three theories can sometimes occur. For example, Keynesian and Marxian economists have sometimes agreed on government employment programs during recessions. To take another example, neoclassical and Keynesian economists have sometimes agreed that Marxian economists do not deserve positions in university economics departments and prevented their employment. However, the profound theoretical differences among the three theories and their political implications usually make those alliances temporary and limited.

7.3.1 Political Conditions Shape Theories

Marxian economists have a particularly difficult time obtaining a hearing for their theory and its conclusions because of the political and ideological demonization of Marxism in most societies across the twentieth century. With the passing of the cold war, transformation of the Soviet Union and its European allies, and major shifts in the other "actually existing socialisms" of the twentieth century, the re-entry of Marxian theory into the discussion and debates over economic issues is under way. Yet certain legacies of the demonization of Marxism remain in the forms of widespread ignorance about or distorted stereotypes of Marxian theory's arguments. Something similar afflicted Keynesian economic theory since the 1970s. Then the resurgence of deregulated and relatively privatized capitalisms revived and promoted neoclassical theory. Keynesian economics was deposed from the dominant position it had occupied in academe and among policy-makers in the wake of the Great Depression.

Now, in the wake of the Great Recession that began in 2007 and continues across the writing of this text, neoclassical economic theory's position has been weakened. The depth and length of this capitalist downturn have called its promises into question. The political, social, and cultural damage done globally by this crisis has likewise challenged the theory. The failures of the mainstream economics profession—overwhelmingly committed to neoclassical theory—to foresee, anticipate, or successfully cope with the crisis has also undermined its social prestige.

The great debate among the three main alternative economic theories has therefore resumed. The economic crisis since 2007 reminded people across the globe that neither the neoclassical nor the Keynesian approaches proved able to manage capitalism's cycles, let alone prevent them. The collapse of the USSR had already earlier raised fundamental questions likewise about Marxian theories. The defenders of unreconstructed, orthodox versions of all three theories remain busy making their arguments. Yet the renewed and reopened debates among them have produced self-criticisms and soul-searching among many proponents in all three camps. Those are yielding new formulations and new theoretical initiatives. We have integrated several of these into this book's systematic and summary presentations and comparisons of the three theories. For example, changes in neoclassical theory seemed to us to be deserving of distinct discussion in chapter 5 on late neoclassical theory. Likewise we have tried repeatedly to distinguish between traditional and overdeterminist Marxian theory. We also signaled changes in Keynesian theory between its more traditional version and newer developments in post-Keynesian and new-Keynesian economics.

7.3.2 Struggles among Theories and Theorists

Interactions among neoclassical, Keynesian and Marxian theorists have varied from occasional collaborations to polite but friendly disagreements all the way to intensely hostile confrontations. By theorists, we mean all those who think in some systematic way about economic issues, not just the professional theorists. Among political groups (social movements, political parties, labor unions, etc.) influenced by one or the other theory, relations have gone back and forth from alliances to persecution and occasionally to outright physical destruction. What kinds of relations existed among the three groups of theorists depended of course on the complex social conditions of each particular time and place.

One enduring issue, however, has been and remains the issue of class. Marxian objectives include the transformation of class structures, the radical alteration of social relations whereby some people produce, while others appropriate and distribute surplus labor. Neoclassical and Keynesian objectives do not include such a transformation, and that basic difference sooner or later arises in debates among the three theories. Clearly, something socially important is at stake. Another enduring issue has been the role of the government in the economy. The neoclassical economists argue for a minimal role against the Keynesians who argue for a much greater role. The former argue all the more against traditional Marxists who have supported the greatest role (more recent formulations of Marxian theory sharply downgrade emphasis on the authority of the state compared with traditional Marxism).

Marxian economic theory is one thing; the political demands and strategies of its proponents are another. Marxian theorists can and do disagree on how politically to achieve the class changes their theory favors. Likewise neoclassical and Keynesian economists can and do disagree among themselves on how to advance the political agendas associated with their respective theories. It is important to remember this lest the heat of disputes among the three theories lead any of them to suggest or insist that a theoretical commitment must necessarily be associated with one or another political strategy or tactic.

Overwrought—usually in the course of intense political or ideological struggles—Keynesians and Marxists have thus sometimes equated neoclassical economics with condoning or even welcoming recessions and unemployment despite the mass suffering they cause. No doubt some neoclassical economists have done that, but many others have not and have instead supported many kinds of government assistance for the unemployed, for example. Neoclassical economists disagree about how best to advance the political agendas associated with their thinking.

Overheated during tense political and ideological times, neoclassical and Keynesian economists have similarly sometimes equated Marxian economists and Stalinism (a reference to repressive policies in the USSR from the 1930s to the 1950s). Some Marxists were Stalinists; many were not, and few remain so today. Marxian theorists, like all others, disagree among themselves about how best to advance the political agendas associated with their theory.

It is dangerous for any society to forget that everyone gains when alternative theories have the opportunity to present and debate their entry points, logics, conceptualizations, and conclusions. The history of the last century's debates among neoclassical, Keynesian and Marxian theories shows that none of them has always had all the answers. Economic crises and failures have occurred under the prevalence of all of them in one country or another, at one time or another. Societies that shut down their theoretical debates and contestations—whether by government or by private actions—also lost the benefits of the questions, criticisms, and analyses offered by the excluded theories and theorists.

The recent global capitalist crisis reopened the space for economic debate to include Keynesian and Marxian theorists who had been largely excluded since the 1970s. Those theories' challenges to neoclassical theory are multiplying in large part because of the challenge to that theory provided by the crisis itself. The renewed debate is as welcome as it is long overdue. Even neoclassical economists will be stimulated by the renewed theoretical competition to re-examine, re-question, and refine their theory. Important questioning and rethinking within journalism, academe, policy-making, government, labor unions, and so on, may well be revived by the re-opening of genuine debates over economic theories, realities, and strategies.

7.4   Which Theory Do We Choose?

We face three different theories that conceptualize the economy differently, endorse different definitions and standards for what is true, and have different consequences for our lives. While all three agree that the economic system we live in is capitalism, their respective concepts of capitalism have little in common. Neoclassical theory sees a privately owned and privately run economy in which competitive markets link optimizing producers and consumers. Keynesians see an economic structure that, while basically sound and effective, can and repeatedly does produce an inefficient and wasteful equilibrium that requires systematic government intervention to overcome. Marxian theory sees a particular kind of class structure in which exploitation is reproduced, with disastrous social consequences alongside rapid technological change. Choosing between the theories amounts to choosing between alternative conceptualizations of the world we live in.

The contesting economic theories have practical impacts on our societies. Practitioners of the three theories regularly reach different conclusions about how to understand and respond to inflation, recession, war, domestic violence, extreme wealth inequality, and most other urgent social issues. Given the contradictions among the theories, between the divergent analyses they produce, and between the political solutions they support, how are we to choose between them?

We are actually familiar with this dilemma in many other parts of our lives. Different religions present us with alternative concepts of God, morality, and the meaning of our lives. Different medical practitioners offer us different diagnoses of and remedies for illnesses. Different traditions of cuisine, hair style, dress, and sexual relationships likewise show us a range of alternative ways of living our lives.

It is a peculiarity of some cultures that they generally favor tolerance toward or even encourage differences in religion, medical practice, life styles, and artistic judgments, yet also display great intolerance toward differences in economic theories. There they seem to expect differences of opinion to give way—to be resolved—such that one theory is considered absolutely right. Such cultures often believe that alternative concepts of God should coexist and interact with one another and that it is inappropriate to ask about which among them is correct. Yet they ask exactly that of alternative economic theories: Which one is correct? Which one "fits the facts"? Which one is to be embraced while the others are banished to the realm of falsehood?

In our view, intellectually mature societies are characterized by a broad acceptance of the fact that economic theories are and will likely remain irreducibly different. The rejection of intolerance in religious, cultural, medical, and other areas of social life can and should be extended to include rejecting intolerance in the realm of economic theories. The cross-fertilizations, diversities, and general enrichment of societies that result from religious, political, and artistic tolerance would also emerge from tolerance toward all three economic theories. In any case, with or without tolerance, the differences and contestations among neoclassical, Keynesian, and Marxian economics have continued for many decades. So the question remains: How do we choose among these basic theoretical alternatives?

7.4.1 Choosing Theories Because of Their Consequences

We might base our choices on the different effects produced in our lives by each theory. Consider some of these effects. One is the awareness of exploitation in society. Marxian theory literally teaches people to see something in human relationships that is not acknowledged by other theories. Becoming aware of class via Marxian theory often leads individuals to try to alter or eliminate exploitation. Another effect of a Marxian awareness of exploitation as an aspect of class processes would likely be a different way of understanding nonclass processes in society. For example, such nonclass processes as unequal distributions of power between men and women, whites and blacks, capitalists and workers, property owners and the propertyless would be seen as different from class processes and also in a relation of mutual overdetermination with them.

Other effects of embracing the Marxian theory discussed in this book include a commitment to overdetermination rather than essentialism. Such a commitment ends any need to look for final, ultimate, essential causes or truths. Instead, it presumes that different theories or explanations are born from the complex social conditions—natural, political, economic, and cultural—that combine to overdetermine them. Each theory differs not only in its specific propositions but also in the standards of truth, logic, and consistency it erects for its propositions. Such a commitment to anti-essentialist ways of thinking carries the implication that no explanation of anything is ever finished, or true beyond revision, or more than one among several alternative explanations.

The effect of Marxian theory's consistent commitment to overdetermination is that subscribers to such a theory view their own position too as but one of several alternatives. They recognize that Marxian theory is no more a final truth than is any other theory. That admission, in turn, may open up a democracy of difference, a nondogmatic attitude toward social theories that seeks to understand them as richly different reflections of the complex currents shaping any modern society. Such an admission does not contradict taking a partisan position, welcoming some and opposing other theories because of their social consequences.

If this partial list of effects flowing from adherence to Marxian theory strikes you as attractive, you might then adopt and use Marxian rather than neoclassical or Keynesian theory. Yet you might also throw up your hands in frustration at the seeming chaos of accepting that the different theories that swirl around you cannot be ranked according to their truths, that they are just there, all different and all clamoring for your allegiance. You might also fear that if theories are different, without one being essentially right and thus the others finally wrong, might not some horrid, evil theory gain sway over most people's minds and actions? For individuals who are attracted to Marxian theory because they approve of the effects of its use, these are perfectly reasonable worries. But before we discuss these worries, we should consider the different effects of adopting neoclassical or Keynesian economic theories.

One of neoclassical theory's profound effects is its recognition and celebration of something that was repressed by the dominant religious theories prior to capitalism. That "something" is neoclassical theory's entry point, which it makes the essence of economy and society: the individual human being. This key idea is connected historically to what we discussed earlier, namely the rise of "humanism." Humanism attracted many people who had lost their earlier allegiance to religious theories focused on God as the cause, essence, and purpose of life. Humanism focused instead on individual human beings as the creators and centers of the world and on individual happiness as the goal of life.

Humanism is a broad, general theory—perhaps we should call it a philosophy—that explains the nature and development of society as the heroic struggle of each and every human being to discover and develop his or her given potential in the face of societal constraints. This central idea is likewise the entry point and essence for neoclassical economic theory. The latter is a particular form of humanism.

It follows that an individual might choose neoclassical theory because its consequences or effects include steps aimed at maximizing personal liberty, at making social institutions permit and indeed facilitate the essential human struggle to realize individual potentialities. Such an individual might choose neoclassical theory because it applauds and leads logically toward capitalist institutions, which are understood to be optimally appropriate to our human nature. Neoclassical theory leads to a political program of social changes that promises to end market imperfections and minimize government intervention in economic affairs. For all these reasons you might well choose to view the world through the neoclassical rather than the Marxian or Keynesian theoretical lens.

A different individual might welcome and applaud capitalism as a system, yet be troubled by its instability, recurrent cycles, and the mass suffering they entailed (as Keynes himself was). Accepting capitalism as beset by imperfections and flaws, such an individual might find persuasive the theory of Keynes as to why capitalism was unstable and how the government could and should intervene to correct or at least alleviate the results of capitalist instability. Such an individual might embrace Keynesian theory as a welcome midpoint between neoclassical and Marxian theories, a place from which one could reject both neoclassical and Marxian theories as extremes. Liberals in the United States and social democrats in many other countries have often found their ways to variants of Keynesian economic theory for such reasons.

Actually a moment's reflection should confirm that each person's preference for one theory over another is influenced by a long list of personal and social factors. More than just the effects of alternative theories shape an individual's choices among them. Other influences on theoretical preference include family background, schooling, religious beliefs, age, sex, current family situation, employment conditions, political attitudes, and so forth. Moreover, since these influences change across lifetimes, theoretical preferences change too.

For example, at one time a person might prefer neoclassical theory perhaps partly because its political implications seem less dramatic and less threatening than do those of Marxian or even Keynesian theory. This preference might also stem in part from where that person stands in the class structure. If the individual is a receiver of surplus value from productive laborers, he or she might prefer neoclassical theory because it denies the whole idea of surplus and asserts instead that all incomes are rewards to individuals for what each contributes to production. It also might be preferred to Keynesian theory for its laissez-faire policy: no government interference in or barriers to continued receipt of surpluses understood as just rewards. High-income recipients might understandably become deeply committed to neoclassical theory, even to the point of thinking that no other reasonable or logical theory existed. Keynesian theory might appeal to someone whose commitment to neoclassical economics could not survive a major economic crisis in a largely privatized, market capitalist economy. However, a Keynesian might change theoretical allegiance if government economic interventions seemed to make economic conditions—inflation or growth—worse, not better.

Marxian theory often changes people's thinking about what capitalism is and how it works. Thus it can offend or worry those who benefit from capitalist class processes or embrace humanist philosophy or endorse neoclassical economics. Societies where a capitalist class structure prevails often include many people distressed by Marxian theory. Marxian claims that the individual freedoms celebrated by neoclassical theory, schoolbooks, and politicians' speeches are actually conditions for mass exploitation trouble them. Some will react by preferring neoclassical because they don't want the disruptive consequences in their personal lives that would flow from taking Marxian arguments seriously. Needless to say, individuals who have suffered from various kinds of discrimination, injustice, or oppression within capitalist societies might be more welcoming of a theory that fundamentally criticizes capitalism.

Choosing among the three theories in terms of the varied consequences they entail is a complex matter involving all of the varied influences that shape our attitudes and preferences. The choice we make among theories is as complex as most other important choices we make in our lives. We are aware of some of our reasons for choosing as we do, but there are reasons we do not recognize until long after the choice has been made, and there are still other reasons we never become aware of. When we choose among theories because of their consequences, we are actually choosing for many other reasons as well, although we are aware of only some of them.

In the language of this book, all choices are overdetermined and contradictory. Every aspect of our lives plays a different role in shaping our choices and our partial awareness of the reasons for them. Our choices are contradictory because the infinite, varied influences on them and on our awareness push and pull us in different and often conflicting directions. We become acutely sensitive to this when we find choices difficult to make, when we struggle—sometimes over long periods—with the pros and cons we must contend with.

In Marxian theory all preferences are overdetermined by all of the class and nonclass processes of society, whether or not an individual is aware of all the overdetermining influences. Our choices among theories are based only in part on their different social consequences. The logic of overdetermination requires Marxists who find it persuasive to reject the idea that any one basis—such as consequences—can determine theoretical choices. Marxian overdeterminist logic implies that just as class processes themselves are overdetermined, so too are the theories that exist in any society as well as the choices individuals make among them.

7.4.2 Choosing Theories Based on an Absolute Standard

Another basis for choosing among neoclassical, Keynesian, and Marxian theories might be examining which of them is closest to the truth, which of them best captures how the economy really works. The standard of truth is then correspondence with reality: which theory best "fits the facts." That is an absolute standard that does not vary with one's perspective. One chooses among alternative perspectives (theories) by measuring each of them against the single absolute standard of correspondence with reality.

However, it turns out that choosing on this absolute basis is every bit as complex as basing one's choice on the consequences of theories. There are different ways of choosing just as there are different theories to choose among. As economists debate alternative economic theories, so philosophers debate alternative ways of choosing among theories. Indeed such philosophic debates are part of an entire branch of philosophy called epistemology: the study of thinking and truth and the relationship between them.

Just as there are alternative economic theories of what capitalism is, there are also different epistemological theories of what thinking and truth are. To believe that "truth" is something simple and straightforward, something we all define in the same way, is to ignore the different ideas and definitions of truth that have provoked debates and controversy for centuries into the present. To believe that you can decide among alternative economic theories according to which is closest to the truth—an absolute standard—immediately requires you to confront the following problem: How do we decide among alternative theories as to what "the truth" is? This problem confronts those who propose to choose among neoclassical, Keynesian and Marxian theories on the basis of their approximation to "the truth."

7.4.3 Empiricism

One theory of truth (one epistemological theory) defines it as the correspondence of an idea with reality. The argument runs as follows: There is a real world out there which people can know by means of our five senses. Sight, smell, touch, hearing, and taste serve as channels through which the facts of "the real world out there" imprint themselves on our brains. When we think, we concoct ideas about how the world works. To determine which, if any, of these concocted ideas are "true," we compare the ideas to the "facts" of the world that our senses have gathered. The ideas that best "fit the facts," that correspond most closely to what our senses reveal about the real world, are then acclaimed as true.

This epistemological theory is called "empiricism." It is widely influential today; many people prefer it to the alternative theories of what truth is. For individuals who believe in empiricism, the choice among neoclassical, Keynesian, and Marxian economic theories should properly be based on which theory best "corresponds to the facts." Empiricists evaluate the three economic theories (as they do with alternative political, biological, chemical, and other theories) in terms of their correspondence to the facts of the real world. The choice among them is then made according to which theory corresponds most closely.

This standard is absolute because it does not recognize the possibility of multiple alternative truths. It confers the positive title of "true" on one theory while negatively dismissing alternative theories as "less true" or "false." Empiricism insists that we all sense the facts of reality in the same way, that we all see, hear, smell, taste, and touch "reality" in an identical way. Our senses provide an absolutely accurate and reliable means of knowing the real and thereby of assessing theories about the real as to whether or not they are true (correspond to the real).

Most neoclassical economists believe in such an epistemology. They defend their preference for neoclassical theory on the grounds of its greater realism, its closer correspondence to reality as against Keynesian and Marxian theory. Most Keynesian and Marxian economists hold to the same epistemology. They too believe that their theory is true while the alternatives are not, and they too define truth as a theory's correspondence to factual reality. However, when they test neoclassical theory against the facts, they conclude that Keynesian or Marxian theories achieve the better fit, so they each defend their respective theory as true against neoclassical economics, which they find to be less true or simply false. Debates among proponents of the three economic theories often involve confrontations of data and statistical measurements that support each side's claim that it best fits the facts.

The shared empiricist epistemology of such contesting theorists guarantees a great absolutist battle. None can grant an alternative theory any status other than error. Moreover each empiricist theorist eventually asks why opposing theorists persist in beliefs that the theorist's facts show to be false, to be in less correspondence with reality. The answer reached by most empiricist theorists is that alternative theorists have ulterior motives that make them cling to what is "factually" untrue. Many empiricist debates over different economic theories degenerate into mutual accusations of dogmatic adherence to false ideas, bias, distortion, and the lack of scientific method or honesty. They can turn very ugly with theorists charging those who differ with purposely encouraging false ideas in order to further or prevent economic and social changes.

7.4.4 Rationalism

Another theory of truth—rationalism—claims that there is a real world out there that human beings can know by means of thought—that is, by means of logical reasoning. The assumption here is that the world has an underlying logic or order that human rationality can capture. Indeed rationalists believe that reason, either with or without divine revelation, has accumulated a basic store of true knowledge about the world's underlying order. Moreover that knowledge can and should serve as an absolute standard or measure of the truth. Thus the truth of any theory's statements about the world can be ascertained by measuring such statements' correspondence to that accumulated knowledge. In economics, rationalists believe that their basic theory—whether Keynesian, neoclassical, or Marxian—provides the knowledge against which to measure the truth of any statement about the economy.

When used in economics, rationalism insists that true relationships in the economy cannot be discovered via sensory observations because our senses receive an infinite chaos of impressions, an overwhelming mass of data. Our brains cannot process all that information; they therefore focus on only *some* of the infinite impressions gathered by our senses. When, for example, we look at a person, our eyes literally see an infinity of facts but our brains select out a few to register, to "think about." In the rationalist view, people inevitably *select* from among all the data gathered by the senses those which they think to be important or significant. No one can or ever has tested any idea against all the facts as empiricists claim. Rationalists thus reject empiricism as impossible and incoherent as a theory of truth.

Rationalists insist that all people select which facts to register and consider according to some theory about which facts are the ones to select. The "empirical facts" that appear to each individual depend, in the last instance, on the theory that guides that individual's receptivity to (selection among) sense impressions. Rationalists focus then on what they see as the core of any theory—namely the logic or reason governing its selection among the infinity of facts—rather than on the particular "facts" that its proponents selectively gather and present. Rationalists argue over which theory has a logical structure that most exactly matches the presumed logical order of economic reality. Rationalists are confident that the best theory, whose logic mirrors the inherent logic of reality itself, will best select the facts that are relevant to an explanation of actual economic events.

Some neoclassical, Keynesian, and Marxian economists endorse the rationalist approach, sometimes consciously but more often without any awareness that they are taking one among alternative epistemological positions. Neoclassical, Keynesian, and Marxian rationalists claim that theirs is the one theory whose logic matches the truth of economic reality. Each set of rationalist economists claims that its theory is the highest stage achieved by rational thought about economics and is therefore the closest approximation yet to knowing how economic reality works. Each sees its theory as the absolute standard against which to measure any statement made by anyone about economics. Consequently each tends to dismiss alternative theories as simply inadequate understandings of reality. Each attacks all the others as erroneous and false.

Empiricists struggle over which theory best fits "the facts." Rationalists argue over which theory best captures the underlying logic of economic events. Rationalists as well as empiricists in the three camps charge each other with ignorance of "the facts" or ignorance of "correct theory" or of ignorantly clinging to outdated ideas for ulterior and intellectually dishonest purposes. There is rarely room among rationalists or empiricists for the notion of alternative theories' offering different ways to make sense not only of the world but also of truth itself.

7.4.5   Choosing Economic Theories and Choosing Epistemologies

Disagreements over the definition of "truth" affect our choices among alternative economic as well as other theories. The empiricist and rationalist notions of a single absolute truth based on the factual reality and the logic of thought, respectively, are not the only epistemological notions available to us. There are others to consider because choosing among economic theories plunges us into the related choice among alternative epistemologies.

Consider an epistemological theory different from both empiricism and rationalism. It asserts that our senses influence and are influenced by the theories we believe. It also asserts that both thinking and sensing are shaped by all the other aspects and activities of our lives. In other words, our senses and our thoughts are overdetermined and thus not independent of one another. How each works is shaped by everything else in our history and environment. This epistemological theory of truth argues that measuring different theories against "the facts," as in empiricism, or against "one true logic," as in rationalism, produces no absolute truth whatsoever. The reason for this is that "facts," "logics" and theories are not independent entities. They mutually overdetermine one another. Thus neither facts nor reason can serve as an independent or absolute standard of theoretical truth, since alternative theories influence the facts and logics they hold up as truth standards.

For example, pessimists and optimists see very different things when they watch the same evening TV news program. Vegetarians and nonvegetarians experience different taste sensations when they eat the same foods. Religious people feel something quite different from those who are uninterested in religion when they touch a holy relic. Two students with opposing political views hear a teacher's lecture in very different ways. How we each think about the world affects how our senses interact with it, and vice versa. In each of the examples above, it would not be surprising to find one party insisting that he or she never saw, tasted, felt, or heard what the other party insists were his or her sensations. In parallel fashion, individuals reason differently if they occupy different class and nonclass positions in society. For example, sellers and buyers of labor power think about life differently because of the diverse experiences linked to those different positions. Thoughts that occur to some individuals never occur to others. Whether the world has a rational order and what that order is are not agreed matters among all people. Rationalism's claim to offer an absolute universal standard of truth is not sustainable.

From the standpoint of such a nonabsolute epistemology, people can and do disagree over their sensations as well as over their conceptualizations. It follows that a theory that fits the facts for one person—as he or she senses those facts—may not do so for another person. A theory that captures the underlying logic of reality for one person—as she or he produces that theory—may not do so for another person who reasons otherwise. In the spirit of such an epistemological position, then, different theories are true for different people. There is no need to imagine or look for one theory that alone will fit "the" facts, as the empiricists claim, because there is no one set of facts that everyone senses and recognizes as "the" standard of truth. There is likewise no need to look for one theory that alone captures the logical order of reality, as the rationalists claim, because people do not all apprehend the same logical order. There is no theory that captures everyone's differently apprehended realities equally. Instead, there are theories and truths, both plural, that reflect and shape the different ways people sense, think about, and live in the world.

In terms of economic theory there are clear differences among the three epistemologies just described. Empiricists would resolve the debate among neoclassical, Keynesian, and Marxian economics by testing all against what they sensed to be "the" facts. In their view, the facts they perceive must likewise be the facts for everyone and therefore the absolute standard of truth for everyone. Rationalists would resolve the debate among neoclassical, Keynesian and Marxian economics by testing all against what each rationalist considered to be the logical order of reality. In their view, the true theory they discover via testing it against the rational order of reality—their absolute standard—must be the truth for everyone. By contrast, the alternative epistemological approach believes that thinking and sensing are overdetermined by each other and by everything else in society. Therefore different theories will occur and appeal to people who sense, think about, and live in the world differently. People will reach different conclusions about the truths of alternative theories much as they believe in different definitions and standards of truth.

The world clearly is full of people who believe different theories are true because they have different notions of what truth is. There are different standards of truth just as there are different theories of society, economy, nature, and so on. This is a nonabsolutist epistemology; it recognizes no single standard of truth and hence no one true theory standing above false theories. In this view, different ways of thinking about the world stand alongside different ways of sensing it. Theories are differently true; truths are irreducibly plural.

Once again, it is important to add that granting the multiplicity of truths in no way precludes choosing which theories you embrace and which you oppose. It only means that your choice is not based on an absolute standard of truth but rather on other standards such as the beauty or social consequences or complexity you associate with alternative theories.

As we confronted the problem of choosing between two economic theories, we worked our way to the parallel problem of choosing among epistemologies (or theories of truth). Just as it turned out that truth could not be an unambiguous arbiter of our choice between economic theories, so we are now wise enough not to search for yet another absolute standard to solve our problem in confronting alternative epistemologies.

Our world is full of different, contesting theories about everything. While we may not (yet) be aware of them, alternatives exist to the way we think about everything. Nothing is thought about in the same way by everyone. There are also good reasons to believe that we become wiser the more we understand the alternatives, whether we choose them or not. Freedom of choice, as a moral value, presumably extends beyond the array of toothpastes in a drugstore to include the array of economic theories circulating in our world. This book was intended to alert you to some alternatives and choices you might not have been aware of or understood. Our presumption was that with greater choice you would have greater freedom and wisdom too.

The choice you eventually make will depend on all of the influences that overdetermine you. If your choice is empiricism or rationalism, then you will likely join the debate over the truth of neoclassical versus Keynesian versus Marxian theory. If your choice is against empiricism or rationalism and for a nonabsolutist epistemology, then you will likely find yourself basing your choice among economic theories not on a criterion of truth but rather on the alternative consequences and associations of the theories that exist in our world. In either case we hope that you will be aware of how and why different people choose differently. We also hope that you will pursue far more aware- ness, tolerance, and discussion of theoretical differences than has been the tradition within the discipline of economics generally and particularly within that tradition in the United States.

Solutions to long-standing economic problems often require that we try different ways of thinking about those problems, try grappling with different theories. Marxian theory is different from the neoclassical orthodoxy that still prevails in America today and from the resurging Keynesian theory, both of which are far better known than Marxian theory. The latter includes a variety of careful, logical, and elaborated ways of thinking about capitalist economies. Marxian theory's critical and revolutionary thrusts make it different in ways that trouble some. However, just those qualities allow it to produce economic analyses that are not only different but also arrestingly original and eye- opening. Much is lost by continuing to ignore Marxian theorizations of the structure, dynamics, and problems of capitalist economies.

7.4.6 A Final Thought

We do not seek to frustrate you about the choices confronting anyone who takes seriously the workings of the mind. That alternative theories of truth, economics, and indeed everything else exist is a premise of this book. That you therefore confront choices among all of these alternatives is, we believe, a condition of life rather like breathing, eating, and so forth. In our view, there is no way of escaping the freedom of choice even for people who pretend or believe that no choice exists.

Making the choices you actually have available to you, periodically re-examining them to open yourself to the possibility of making different choices—these are important, exciting, and invigorating parts of a full and self-conscious lifetime. We wrote this book to aid you in realizing (becoming conscious of) the existence of choices among available economic theories. We also wrote it to stress the importance of the economic theory choices we all make (consciously or otherwise). They matter enormously in our personal lives as well as in our societies, whose direction and future depend on those choices and their complex consequences.

There is nothing admirable in pretending that choices do not exist. We understand that faced with difficult decisions, people can become frightened. It may be tempting to deal with hard choices by acting as if there really were no choice to make, as if it were a simple, obvious matter. In thinking about economics, all too many people proceed as though there were only one obvious way to ask and answer all questions. They think of economic theory as a single concept, not a theoretical plural. They avoid the hard theoretical choices by ignoring them, falling into line behind whatever happens to be the majority view at the time. They run from their own freedom of choice to the comfort and security of accepting other people's choices without recognizing that they too can choose, that alternatives do exist.

If you become aware that your way of thinking involves a choice from among such alternatives, you will, we hope, want to learn more about those alternatives. You will, we hope, want to struggle honestly with past choices you have made to see if they remain the choices you want to make today. We aim our words above all at those of you who think of yourselves as responsible citizens determined to use your minds to the utmost. Theoretical choices are terrible things to waste.

Notes

Chapter 1

1. Piaget (1971), p. 7.

Chapter 2

1. An individual's money income, y, may be spent on goods and services, $p_1 \cdot q_1 + p_2 \cdot q_2$, where p_1 and p_2 represent, respectively, the prices of the two different commodities, and q_1 and q_2 are the respective quantities of the two goods demanded. The income equation for the straight line AB in figure 2.3 becomes

$$q_2 = \frac{y}{p_2} - \frac{p_1}{p_2} \cdot q_1,$$

where p_1/p_2 represents the slope of this line, or

$$\frac{\Delta q_2}{\Delta q_1} = -\frac{p_1}{p_2}.$$

2. This price ratio is precisely the given slope of the income equation presented in note 1.

3. The notation Δ is a shorthand way of conveying a change in a variable. Thus $-\Delta q_2$ means a decrease in the amount of q_2 consumed and $+\Delta q_1$ indicates an increase in the amount of q_1, consumed.

4. Recall that neoclassical theory considers the relevant measure of utility to be the marginal (the incremental and not the total) utility experienced by an individual when he or she consumes more or less of a commodity.

5. Advanced texts in neoclassical theory show how a change in demand for any commodity can be broken down into two distinct parts: a so-called substitution effect, in which the level of utility is kept constant and a consumer is shown to move along the same preference curve in figure 2.5a, substituting the cheapened commodity (q_1) for the other (q_2), and a so-called income effect, in which initial prices are kept constant and a consumer moves to a higher preference curve because of changed income. Neoclassical theory combines these two effects into what it typically calls the Slutsky equation. Named after the person who first published this result in 1915, the Slutsky equation is considered a fundamental rendering of the neoclassical theory of value, for its purpose is to specifically relate individuals' changed demands for commodities to their underlying preferences for those commodities.

6. This marginal rate of substitution is calculated in the same way we calculated our previous rate. Recall that along any preference curve between real income and leisure we have

$-\Delta y^R \cdot mu_{y^R} = +\Delta l \cdot mu_l$, where we assume that a utility loss in real income is exactly offset by a utility gain in leisure. Solving the equation for $\Delta y^R / \Delta l$ yields

$$\frac{\Delta y^R}{\Delta l} = -\frac{mu_l}{mu_{y^R}},$$

which is our $MRS_{l y^R}$.

7. A similar diagram can be constructed to relate output to a variable amount of capital input with an assumed fixed input of labor.

8. This marginal rate is calculated exactly like the previous rates. Recall that along any preference curve relating present and future consumption, we have.

$$-\Delta c_{t+1} \cdot mu_{c_{t+1}} = +\Delta c_t \cdot mu_{c_t},$$

where, once again, we assume that a utility loss in future consumption is exactly offset by a utility gain in present consumption. Solving this equation for $\Delta c_{t+1} / \Delta c_t$, we have

$$\frac{\Delta c_{t+1}}{\Delta c_t} = -\frac{mu_{c_t}}{mu_{c_{t+1}}},$$

which is our $MRS_{c_t c_{t+1}}$.

9. Any individual is assumed to be able to choose between consuming all of his or her real income now and saving a portion of it in order to make such savings available for future consumption: $y^R = c_t + SAV$, where SAV stands for current savings out of real income. In our previous notation, c_t, represented the individual's current real expenditures on the two commodities, q_1 and q_2. We may write this future consumption in terms of current savings as

$$c_{t+1} = SAV(1 + r^R),$$

where $A'B = c_{t+1}$ and $AA' = SAV$. Any individual's current income may be written then in terms of present *and* future consumption:

$$y^R = c_t + \frac{c_{t+1}}{(1 + r^R)},$$

where $c_{t+1}/(1 + r^R)$ tells the consumer what his or her future consumption is currently worth. Solving this equation for c_{t+1} yields $c_{t+1} = (1 + r^R) \cdot y^R - (1 + r^R) c_t$, and $\Delta c_{t+1} / \Delta c_t = -(1 + r^R)$, which is the slope of line AE in figure 2.14. If the individual decides not to save, then $y^R = c_t$; and if he or she decides to save all current income and thus not to consume anything now, then $y^R = c_{t+1}/(1 + r^R)$. In the latter case we have simply $y^R = SAV$.

10. Capital income is understood here to mean the marginal return to capital and not short-run producer's profits (the difference between revenues and costs), which are competed away in the long run.

11. Following Smith's insight, neoclassical theory adds a powerful story of what may well happen to the price of any commodity, if it rises today because of a shift in demand for it. Suppose that in figure 2.17b the aggregate demand shifts up and to the right (because consumers desire more of it). At that moment, and before any producer has time to react, a higher market price means that producers in the industry face a favorable profit situation. As time passes, they have the opportunity to respond by hiring additional labor to expand their supply. Consequently the initial price rise begins to be eroded as firms, driven by the profit motive, expand production along their supply curve in figure 2.17a. Far more interesting, however, is what happens to price in the long run when existing firms have had sufficient time to augment new labor hires with the hiring of new capital (perhaps embodying new technologies) and sufficient time passes enabling new (domestic and/or foreign) firms to enter this industry (attracted by the profits to be made there). In the long run, the supply curve in the industry in figure 2.17 (b) would have shifted to the right until no profit incentive remains for either existing firms to expand production any more or new firms to enter the industry. The conclusion is dramatic for its societal implications: short-run profits

are competed away, if existing and new firms are allowed to respond to the profit motive. Indeed the very price rise in the very short run stimulates a supply response on the part of private business that ultimately serves to drive down the initial price increase. The new supply curve could in fact have shifted so much to the right (because of introduced technology and new firm entry) that the resulting new equilibrium price is even lower than the old. Smith's insight about market competition in and across markets is that it enables a society to experience continually rightward shifting supply curves and the dramatic benefits they deliver to a population: higher productivity and lower prices.

12. Summing up all of these individual supply curves, we derive the aggregate supply in each industry for commodity 1 and commodity 2:

$S_1 = \Sigma s_1^i$ and $S_2 = \Sigma s_2^i$,

where Σ stands for summation and i signifies n possible producers. The aggregate demand may then be written as

$D_1 = \Sigma d_1^j$ and $D_2 = \Sigma d_2^j$,

where j signifies that the demand has been summed across N possible consumers. The equilibrium condition in each market is $S_1 = D_1$ and $S_2 = D_2$.

Chapter 3

1. *Econometrica* (1937) 147–59.

2. A further discussion of some of these differences between the neoclassical and Keynesian conceptions of the labor market appears in the appendix to this chapter.

3. The typical textbook model of demand, which is based on these assumptions of fixed prices and wages in commodity markets and a liquidity trap in the money market, can be written as

$Y^R = cY^R + I + G,$

where c is the Keynesian marginal propensity to consume, I stands for investment, and G represents government spending. Solving the equation for Y^R yields

$$Y^R = \frac{1}{1-c} \cdot I + \frac{1}{1-c} \cdot G,$$

where $1/(1 - c)$ stands for the multiplier. If I does not change, then $\Delta Y^R = 1/(1 - c) \cdot \Delta G$. The essential determinant of Y^R has become the state.

4. Individuals' uncertainty about the future is often understood in neoclassical theory in terms of risk taking: investors make decisions under probabilistic conditions. Although written at an advanced level, Douglas Vickers provides a critical and very insightful argument explaining why Keynesian uncertainty is different from neoclassical risk and why this key difference matters to a Keynesian approach (Vickers 1994).

5. For the development of their respective post-Keynesian approaches to economics, see Shackle (1972), Davidson (1991) and Minsky (1986).

6. See the appendix to this chapter.

Chapter 5

1. This particular criticism of neoclassical theory has a long history that produced an enormous literature. One of its most important contributors, Piero Sraffa (1898–1983), helped generate an entire school of thought aimed at exposing the logical inconsistency of neoclassical theory. Sraffa's classic book is subtitled *Prelude to a Critique of Economic Theory* (1960).

2. Since $\Delta p/\Delta q$ will always be negative, the second part of the expression in parenthesis that measures the effects of the price change on *all* the units sold will always be a deduction from the unit price. One might think of it as a "correction factor" that adjusts price to the presence of monopoly power. With no monopoly, there is no need for a correction factor and consequently $MR = p$; with it, $MR < p$.

3. This is sometimes called an inverse demand function. Up to now we have made demand a function of prices; here we assume that that demand function has an inverse so that we can write prices as a function of the quantity demanded.

References

Akerlof, George A. 1982. Labor contracts as partial gift exchange. *Quarterly Journal of Economics* 97 (4): 543–69.

Akerlof, George A., and Robert J. Shiller. 2009. *Animal Spirits: How Human Psychology Drives the Economy and Why It Matters for Global Capitalism.* Princeton: Princeton University Press.

Arrow, Kenneth J. 1974. *The Limits of Organization.* New York: Norton.

Becker, Gary S. 1981. Altruism in the family and selfishness in the market place. *Economica* 48 (189): 1–15.

von Boehm-Bawerk, Eugen [1884]. *Capital and Interest.* http://www.econlib.org/library/BohmBawerk/bbCI.html.

Bowles, Samuel, and Herbert Gintis. 1998. How communities govern: The structural basis of prosocial norms. In A. Ben-Ner and L. Putterman, eds., *Economics, Values, and Organization.* Cambridge: Cambridge University Press, 206–30.

Cassano, Graham, ed. 2009. *Class Struggle on the Home Front: Work, Conflict and Exploitation in the Household.* London: Palgrave Macmillan.

Coase, Ronald H. 1937. The nature of the firm. *Economica* 4: 386–405.

Coase, Ronald H. 1960. The problem of social cost. *Journal of Law and Economics* 3 (4): 1–44.

Debreu, Gerard. 1959. *Theory of Value: An Axiomatic Analysis of Economic Equilibrium.* New Haven: Yale University Press.

Engels, Frederick [1892]. *Socialism: Utopian and Scientific.* First English publication http://www.marxists.org/archive/marx/works/1880/soc-utop/index.htm.

Fehr, Ernst, and Simon Gächter. 2000. Fairness and retaliation: The economics of reciprocity. *Journal of Economic Perspectives* 14 (3): 159–81.

Friedman, Milton. 1962. *Capitalism and Freedom.* Chicago: University of Chicago Press.

Gabriel, Satyananda J. 2006. *Chinese Capitalism and the Modernist Vision.* London: Routledge.

Güth, Werner, Rolf Schmittberger, and Bernd Schwarze. 1982. An experimental analysis of ultimatum bargaining. *Journal of Economic Behavior and Organization* 3 (4): 367–88.

Hicks, J. R. 1937. Mr. Keynes and the "Classics." *Econometrica* 5: 147–59.

Hobbes, Thomas [1651]. *Leviathan.* http://oregonstate.edu/instruct/phl302/texts/hobbes/leviathan-contents.html.

Jevons, William Stanley [1871]. *The Theory of Political Economy.* http://www.econlib.org/library/YPDBooks/Jevons/jvnPE.html.

Keynes, John Maynard. 1936. *The General Theory of Employment, Interest and Money.* London: Macmillan.

Lenin, V. I. [1902]. *What Is to Be Done?* http://www.marxists.org/archive/lenin/works/1901/witbd/.

Lenin, V. I. [1916]. *Imperialism: The Highest Stage of Capitalism.* http://www.marxists.org/archive/lenin/works/1916/imp-hsc/.

Lenin, V. I. [1917]. *State and Revolution.* http://www.marxists.org/archive/lenin/works/1917/staterev/index.htm/.

Marshall, Alfred. [1890] 1920. *Principles of Economics,* 8th ed. London: Macmillan.

Marx, Karl [1859]. *A Contribution to the Critique of Political Economy.* http://www.marxists.org/archive/marx/works/1859/critique-pol-economy/preface.htm.

Marx, Karl [1867–1895] 1991. Capital, *Volumes 1, 2, and 3.* London: Penguin.

Marx, Karl [1861].Writings on the Civil War in the United States. http://www.marxists.org/archive/marx/works/1861/us-civil-war/.

Maynard Smith, John. 1982. *Evolution and the Theory of Games.* Cambridge: Cambridge University Press.

McCloskey, Dierdre N. 2006. *The Bourgeois Virtues: Ethics for an Age of Commerce.* Chicago: University of Chicago Press.

Menger, Carl [1871]. *Principles of Economics.* http://mises.org/etexts/menger/principles.asp.

Nash Jr., John F. 1951. Non-cooperative games. *Annals of Mathematics,* 2nd ser., 54 (2): 286–95.

North, Douglass C. 2005. *Understanding the Process of Economic Change.* Princeton: Princeton University Press.

Pareto, Wilfredo. [1927] 1971. *Manual of Political Economy* (transl. from French). New York: Augustus M. Kelley.

Piaget, Jean. 1971. *Structuralism.* New York: Harper and Row.

Resnick, Stephen A., and Richard D. Wolff. 1987. *Knowledge and Class: A Marxian Critique of Political Economy.* Chicago: University of Chicago Press.

Resnick, Stephen A., and Richard D. Wolff. 2002. *Class Theory and History: Capitalism and Communism in the USSR.* London: Routledge.

Resnick, Stephen A., and Richard D. Wolff. 2006. *New Departures in Marxian Theory.* London: Routledge.

Ricardo, David [1817]. *On the Principles of Political Economy and Taxation.* http://www.marxists.org/reference/subject/economics/ricardo/tax/index.htm.

Roberts, Bruce. 1981. Value categories and Marxian method: A different view of value-price transformation. PhD dissertation. Economics Department, University of Massachusetts, Amherst.

Samuelson, Paul. 1939. Interactions between the multiplier analysis and the principle of acceleration. *Review of Economic Statistics* 21 (2): 75–78.

Samuelson, Paul. 1948. *Economics.* New York: McGraw-Hill.

Schelling, Thomas C. 1960. *The Strategy of Conflict.* Cambridge: Cambridge University Press.

Simon, Herbert A. 1978. Rationality as process and product of thought. *American Economic Review* 68 (2): 1–16.

Smith, Adam [1776]. *The Wealth of Nations* www2.hn.psu.edu/faculty/jmanis/adam-smith/ Wealth-Nations.pdf.

Sraffa, Piero. 1960. *Production of Commodities by Means of Commodities.* Cambridge: Cambridge University Press.

Vickers, Douglas. 1994. *Economics and the Antagonism of Time.* Ann Arbor: University of Michigan Press.

Walras, Leon. [1874] 1965. *Elements of Pure Economics* (trans. By William Jaffe). Homewood, IL: Irwin.

Wolff, R. D. 2012. *Democracy at Work: A Cure for Capitalism.* Chicago: Haymarket Books.

Wolff, R. D., A. Callari, and B. Roberts. 1984. A Marxian alternative to the traditional "transformation problem." *Review of Radical Political Economics* 16 (2–3): 115–35.

Index